SOUL COMPANIONS

Conversations With Contemporary Wisdom Keepers – A Collection of Encounters With Spirit

First published by O Books, 2008
O Books is an imprint of John Hunt Publishing Ltd., The Bothy, Deershot Lodge, Park Lane, Ropley, Hants, SO24 0BE, UK
office1@o-books.net
www.o-books.net

Distribution in:

UK and Europe
Orca Book Services
orders@orcabookservices.co.uk
Tel: 01202 665432 Fax: 01202 666219 Int. code (44)

USA and Canada
NBN
custserv@nbnbooks.com
Tel: 1 800 462 6420 Fax: 1 800 338 4550

Australia and New Zealand
Brumby Books
sales@brumbybooks.com.au
Tel: 61 3 9761 5535 Fax: 61 3 9761 7095

Far East (offices in Singapore, Thailand, Hong Kong, Taiwan)
Pansing Distribution Pte Ltd
kemal@pansing.com
Tel: 65 6319 9939 Fax: 65 6462 5761

South Africa
Alternative Books
altbook@peterhyde.co.za
Tel: 021 555 4027 Fax: 021 447 1430

Design: Stuart Davies

ISBN: 978 1 84694 000 0

A CIP catalogue record for this book is available from the British Library.

Printed in the US by Maple Vail

O Books operates a distinctive and ethical publishing philosophy in all areas of its business, from its global network of authors to production and worldwide distribution.
No trees were cut down to print this particular book. The paper is 100% recycled, with 50% of that being post-consumer. It's processed chlorine-free, and has no fibre from ancient or endangered forests. This production method on this print run saved approximately thirteen trees, 4,000 gallons of water, 600 pounds of solid waste, 990 pounds of greenhouse gases and 8 million BTU of energy. On its publication a tree was planted in a new forest that O Books is sponsoring at The Village www.thefourgates.com

SOUL COMPANIONS

Conversations With Contemporary Wisdom Keepers – A Collection of Encounters With Spirit

by Karen Sawyer

Winchester, UK
Washington, USA

Soul Companions

"*Soul Companions* is a stunning book. It assembles an amazing collection of interviews with some of the finest and most unusual people from the worlds of alternative thinking and teaching. For anyone interested in the future of human growth and development this is an absolute 'must read'."

~ **John Matthews**: author of 'Walkers Between Worlds'

"An extraordinarily ambitious project reaching to 'the ends of the Earth' and into the realms beyond. Dip into this compendium of accounts of spirit guides from every Earth culture, and you enter a slipstream of consciousness that leaves 'the real world' looking flat and crumpled as a cardboard cutout. *Soul Companions* is truly a gift and a source of nourishment for the soul."

~ **Carolyn Burdet: Kindred Spirit Magazine**

"*Soul Companions* is an amazing and enlightening anthology of profound experiences shared between some of the world's most revered wisdom keepers and their spirit guides. Inspiring and empowering, it lights a path for all of us to follow."

~ **John Perkins**: New York Times bestselling author of *'Confessions of an Economic Hit Man'* and *'The Secret History of the American Empire'*.

"I would like to express my deep admiration and gratitude to Karen Sawyer for this truly remarkable and satisfying book. That it will, in generations to come, survive as a much loved, battered and dog-eared treasure attests to the fact that it is both timeless and timely no matter which century one happens to be reading it in. This book will flick switches."

~ **Ellis Taylor**: author of *'In These Signs Conquer ~ Revealing the Secret Signs an Age has Obscured'*.

"The world of the spirits is completely normal for many cultures and normal for our culture, if we dare to admit it. *Soul Companions* reinforces this reality, and affirms our own deep connection to the unseen – dare you not accept it?"

~ **Sacred Hoop Magazine**

ACKNOWLEDGEMENTS

The word 'acknowledge' means to accept, admit or recognize the truth or existence of something. It also has the word 'knowledge' in it, which is apt as, first and foremost, I wish to thank all those who so generously shared their knowledge and wisdom within these pages, and who taught me so much during the writing of this book.

Special thanks to: Llyn Roberts, fellow O-Books author and kindred spirit, for her friendship and support. Simon Buxton who has been my mentor throughout – a truly fine fellow. My dear friend Kristina Solbakken Ashdown for her dedicated translation of Sami shaman Ailo Gaup's story from Norwegian into English.

Thanks to 'the invisibles' behind the scenes: First and foremost my publisher John Hunt, and all at O Books. The head of The Foundation for Shamanic Studies in Europe, Paul Uccusic, for his help. Vicki from Malidoma Somé's office for her endeavors (although it wasn't to be, your efforts are sincerely appreciated). Diane Marshall, who arranged my interview with Uncle Angaangaq. Judi Sion who arranged my interview with Tom Kenyon. Sue Morris from the Botkalo office… and to all those who pointed me in the right direction.

Thanks also to: Joel and Debby Kaplan for their mountain magic, Mel (you know what for), the gifted spirit artist Angela George for her insights and inspiration and Pat Reynolds, for her Orgonite and superb editorial skills.

Ultimately, I wish to acknowledge my family. Deep gratitude to: my parents, Hugh and Glenys Sawyer for their consistent love and encouragement. To my sister and brother Bean and Ian Moore for their infectious enthusiasm and for 'holding the vision' every step of the way, and to my niece, Mya Le Moore, with her awesome poetry – respect! To my Auntie Gill at the Forge Wellbeing Centre in Corsham, Wiltshire. To my soul companion, the circle-building Vince – without you, this book would not be what it is. To my children Loren Ash Campbell Sawyer, Pixie Morning Sky Reeve-Pereczes, and Eocha Elen Pereczes – a BIG thank you for reminding me to play.

Finally, I wish to thank the Soul Companions who have inspired and helped me to write. For without you, there would be no book.

CONTENTS

To Loren, Pixie and Eocha.
And to *all* my soul companions.

And I have felt a presence that disturbs me with the joy of elevated thoughts;

a sense sublime of something far more deeply interfused,

whose dwelling is the light of setting suns,

and the round ocean and the living air and the blue sky, and in the mind of man;

A motion and a spirit, that impels all thinking things, all objects of all thought,

And rolls through all things.

~ William Wordsworth (1770 – 1850), from *'Lines Composed A Few Miles Above Tintern Abbey, On Revisiting The Banks Of The Wye During A Tour. July 13, 1798.'*

AUTHOR'S PREFACE

The isolation of life as we perceive it to be is an illusion. Whether we are conscious of it or not, there are *many* dimensions of existence overlapping and permeating the world as we know it. 'It' is part of us and we are part of 'it' – we are never alone because we are *all-one*. Every one of us – whatever nation, race, religion or belief – has spirit helpers that guide us on our journey through life.

Most of us are content to live our whole lives unaware of, or ignoring the presence of, these guides – too ensconced in the routine of earthly life to think much about it. It is undoubtedly more 'comfortable' to go through life ignoring what cannot be proven or explained with the logical mind, rejecting many ideas that may challenge conscious reality and thus change our lives. Stepping outside this 'comfort-zone' is not difficult – it requires only our intent and desire to do so and is well worth the effort. Living a life awake and alert to the gentle nudges from our spirit allies can enrich our lives, enabling us to reach our full potential and stretch our capabilities beyond what we thought were ever possible.

We are alive at a fascinating time in human history. I believe that the 'veil between the worlds' is being drawn aside like curtains. Our perception of the world is expanding to encompass other energies in alternative dimensions. Daily interaction with the no-longer-invisible realms of Spirit will soon become the norm.

When I was about nine years old, I tried to imagine what it would be like to be dead – to be gone, finished… end of story. I lay on my bed, closed my eyes and repeated the words: *'If me is me and me is me…'* As I relaxed, I unwittingly entered a deep meditative state. What I found there was another 'me' – not the Karen I *thought* I was, but the part of me that is infinite consciousness… the spirit within.

Of course, this was at odds with what I was being taught at school, the accepted scientific view being that life ends when the physical body dies. I had also attended 'Sunday School' as a child, so was aware of the religious belief that we are immortal souls with eternal lives, but there seemed to be conditions attached to this that just didn't sit well with me – you can only go to heaven if you're 'good', and if you're not, well... Yet 'good' and 'bad' are relative terms, so the future doesn't bode well for any of us!

Many years later, I was to learn that ancient traditions worldwide have long believed that death is a natural continuum, accepting that death is not 'the end' but is instead a gateway to other dimensions and a new cycle of life. They acknowledge the invisible realms that co-exist with the physical world. This made perfect sense.

'Spirit guides' can be a confusing turn of phrase... one that has become associated mainly with channeling and mediumship. It's an interesting word – 'spirit'. Most of us associate it with ghosts of the dead and yet when we say that someone 'has spirit', we mean that they have a tremendous amount of *life* energy.

I used to naively think that all spirit guides were 'dead people', alive in another dimension 'somewhere up there'. Through my research for this book, I now fully accept that, dead or alive, *every life form has a spirit body* and therefore has the potential to be a spirit guide. Whether physically incarnate on the earth plane or in a world invisible to the untrained eye makes no difference... we just live in different places. Spirit guides are interdimensional beings who are very much alive, often (but not always) living in an alternative dimension to our everyday existence. These realms are not heavenward – they exist all around us.

Guides come in all shapes and sizes, for reasons that will become clear as this book unfolds. As some of these stories reveal, animals and pets can be 'angels in disguise'... they are with you for a reason. Other accounts illustrate that, as multi-dimensional beings, *we can be our own guides* as well as being guides to other people. You may be guided by ancestors or relatives (it may come as a surprise to learn that they are exactly the same as they were before they passed over – no halo or wings!), or by those from the high spiritual realms of Light or angelic spheres. Some people work with beings from other planets. Others, particularly in the shamanic tradition, have spirit animals as allies. Elemental spirits (from the faerie realm that includes gnomes, sylphs, salamanders and undines) can also be guides, as can everything in nature, including Earth itself… this beautiful planet has a spirit, too.

Contact with spirit beings is a natural and accepted daily occurrence in many indigenous tribes throughout the world. Traditionally, those who are 'called by the spirits' to be a bridge between the worlds become a shaman or 'medicine person'. Some shamans enter an altered state of awareness by 'journeying' to contact spirit helpers, or allies, in order to gain information that will heal or be of benefit to the people.

By contrast, in our Western society, the ability to communicate with spirit (or mediumship, for want of a better word) is often treated with skepticism or, at best, is seen as an extraordinary gift blessed to a chosen few. We are suspicious of anything we can't see with the naked eye and want tangible proof that something exists. Yet we readily accept that radios and televisions are picking up invisible messages at different frequencies and are translating that information into sound and pictures… they, too, are 'mediums'.

Other worlds exist that are in the same place as our radio and television signals, but on different frequencies. A human being is a highly sensitive instrument that does more or less the same job as your T.V and radio. We are all able, consciously and subconsciously, to tune into these frequencies.

I was in my teens when I discovered that other forms of life exist within our own… One night as I was drifting off to sleep, I opened my eyes and saw several small silvery-white orbs, dancing and zipping around one another. They suddenly took off, disappearing through the wall!

A few years later, I saw a large red orb bobbing around on the Black Mountain in Wales. It split into two, danced around and merged into one again. Observing it for some time, it occurred to me that it was *intelligent* and knew my mind. Using my thoughts, I urged it to come nearer – and it did, at which point I become nervous and told it to back off – and, again, it did. We played this game for a while until I became anxious about its origin and purpose and mentally told it to go away. It did and, realizing it was benevolent, I yelled, "Come back!" (It didn't… it had probably had quite enough of my silly behavior by then). To this day, these orbs of light continue to appear in my life.

It is my belief that *we are all mediums*, to a greater and lesser degree. Every one of us has the ability to transform our perception of reality to integrate and tune into other dimensions. It just takes a little practice. When this ability is fully developed it can involve conscious communication with Spirit.

Working with Spirit is different for everyone – a personal relationship that reveals itself in a unique way. By writing this book, I have brought people together to collectively share their experiences with and beliefs about Spirit. This book is, to me, a community – a communication in unity. After all, we are individual beings and yet collectively we are one… like pieces of a broken mirror, each an aspect of itself in another reflection.

I divided the stories in this book into chapters purely to enable the book to flow for ease of reading. This was quite a challenge, as most of these stories were impossible to place, and would happily sit in a multiplicity of chapters. It just goes to show that you cannot define an experience with Spirit…

The huge range and diversity of these stories reveal fascinating insights into the evolving connection between other dimensions of existence and the earth plane. Where possible, I have invited the spirit beings themselves to have their say (it is always more interesting to hear both sides of a story!).

Most of these stories I have transcribed and written from my conversations with the contributors. Some stories have been penned by the contributors themselves, while others are a combination of the two. I have given those who authored their own stories the 'by' line.

During the writing of this book, I have met and interviewed some remarkable souls. I give my heartfelt thanks and appreciation to everyone who was willing to participate. My wish is that you will be as inspired as I have by their experiences.

Karen Sawyer, June 2007.

CHAPTER 1

SYNCHRONICITIES, SIGNS & MESSAGES

Coincidences are spiritual puns.
~ G.K. Chesterton (1874 - 1936)

Your guides are always sending you signs and messages. If they *really* want to make a point they will create a 'meaningful co-incidence' in your life to make you sit up and take notice. The Swiss psychologist Carl Jung termed these events '*synchronicity'*.

Often, unexpected and seemingly random events (sometimes seemingly insignificant, sometimes of gargantuan proportions) will give me answers or point me in the right direction. For instance, I initially didn't set out to write *this* book. Oh no. It happened like this… I was walking down the street when, out of the blue, I was inspired with a few lines of prose. I played around with the lines in my head intending to write a song when I got home, but it turned itself into a children's story instead. For years, I approached book publishers with my idea. It was always rejected, but I didn't give up. 15 years later, I was flicking through a newspaper when an advertisement 'jumped out' at me, asking, "Do you want to be a published writer?" (Of course I did). I enrolled on a writing course with aspirations of becoming a children's novelist. My course assignments began in the non-fiction sector and I soon became a published freelance writer, writing a wide variety of features for both national and international magazines. I wrote about the things that I found interesting and inspiring (oddly enough, one of the first articles I wrote for a magazine was about synchronicity!) – each feature leading on to the next in a random yet bizarrely connected way until, one day, it was suggested that I write about a U.K. trance medium. This sparked my interest in spirit guides, which evolved into the book you now hold in your hands.

My story shows that sometimes the things you set out to do in life may elude you. Often the coincidental 'twists and turns' in life appear to take us in completely the opposite direction to where we *think* we want to be going. If this appears to be the case, it may be that you are being directed towards something that you had not consciously already considered, but which would ultimately be more fulfilling and appropriate for you in the long-term scheme of things.

Your spirit allies gift you with synchronicities as an opportunity for you to reconnect with the flow of life, intuitively pointing the way towards your heart's desires. Following a coincidence through can enrich your life, bringing you a better understanding of yourself and how mysterious and magical life really is. So go with the flow and enjoy the ride!

Signs and synchronicity are intrinsically linked. Some signs are obvious – their message is loud and clear. Others are more ambiguous. For instance, while working on this book one afternoon, I suddenly heard the squawking of birds outside. The chimney amplified the noise and I could hear it quite clearly in my living room. Suddenly, a jackdaw 'exploded' from the fireplace, followed a few seconds later by its companion. Now, I have an irrational phobia of 'flapping things' around me, so it was quite a shock… I confess my initial response was to raise my arms above my head, cowering (think Alfred Hitchcock's *'The Birds'*). My heart hammering, I rose to the occasion – swiftly confining my berserk dog to the porch and grabbing my shawl so that I could 'flap', too, should the need arise. Being in such close proximity to these wild birds was a profound experience. I felt it was a definite sign. But what did it *mean?*

The significance of any sign or message is all down to personal interpretation and is relative to your perception in that moment. Oftentimes, your perspective may need some adjustment before you can decode the message. This change is a natural process, which is why sometimes a passage of time elapses – it could be minutes, or it could be years – when, suddenly, out of the blue you have a profound realisation… a moment of illumination. Someone may say something to you or you come across some information that triggers its deeper significance, and, like pieces of a puzzle, it all becomes clear.

Trying to analyze the meaning of a sign prematurely only gets in the way of the message itself (and will also drive you nuts!). Your logical brain will make no sense of a message delivered by Spirit, which is where your intuition comes into play – for the intuitive 'mind' will always discern the true meaning of a sign. Intuition doesn't follow a logical thought process … it simply *knows* what it knows, with no reasons to explain 'why'. It's likely the message will make no immediate sense, or it may make perfect non-sense to you (but don't be at all surprised if everyone else concludes that you *are* nuts, after all).

All will be revealed in time. You can't rush your intuition. We'd all like to have instant answers, but it doesn't work like that – at least, not for me anyway – a little patience is required. Let go of wanting to know and, remaining open, continue on your way. The answers will emerge.

I was driving down a country lane a while ago, completely enjoying the experience of the sunny day and the beauty of my surroundings. At the time, I often expressed the desire to teleport myself anywhere in the world – to be away in an instant, without the inconvenience and time wasted traveling. That day, the truth dawned on me, and I heard a voice within say, "It's the *journey* in life that is beautiful."

Although it's human nature to seek answers and explanations, it's prudent to remember and gracefully accept that some things will always remain a mystery, while others may become clear in time. Often, it's enough to acknowledge that you've been given a sign, and give thanks. If you can learn to sit comfortably in a space of not-knowing, you will find yourself at One with 'The Unknowable' – the essence of Spirit itself. After all, to quote a Chinese Proverb, 'A bird does not sing because it has an answer – it sings because it has a song'.

SOUL FRIENDS

by David Spangler

A spiritual teacher since 1964, David Spangler is probably best known for his work as co-director and spokesperson for the Findhorn Community in northern Scotland. He has lectured widely on spiritual philosophy, personal development, futures studies, and community development. David's books include 'Reimagination of the World: A Critique of the New Age, Science, and Popular Culture' (which he co-authored with William Irwin Thompson), 'Blessing: The Art and the Practice', 'The Story Tree', 'Manifestation: Creating the Life You Love', and 'Apprenticed to Spirit'.

James Morton, dean of the Cathedral of St. John the Divine in New York City, once described David as "a highly regarded advocate of spiritual empowerment" who is "both down-to-earth and a genuine mystic". David describes himself as a "household contemplative", admittedly fond of chocolate and games, although not necessarily in that order.

David regularly teaches on-line classes for the Lorian Association

on spiritual development and on working with inner contacts – classes that can range from a weekend workshop to six weeks in length to even a year-long, depending on the depth of the training.

David lives near Seattle, Washington, with his wife and four children.

I should first say that, philosophically, I have a challenge with the term 'guides'. It is a carry-over from spiritualism and implies the idea that the reason inner beings may contact us is to give us guidance and wisdom and, even more so, that they are qualified to do so. While this is certainly true in some circumstances, it is, in my experience, not true in all. The relationship between physical and non-physical beings is or can be complex – every bit as complex and varied in terms of motives, consequences, potentials, and so forth, as any relationship between two or more physical individuals. We do not call everyone we meet here on earth a 'guide'... why do so with non-physical beings? The fact is that it is simply a convention we use. Using it conditions our expectations about inner plane contacts and, in numerous instances I have encountered, can lead to unwanted and debilitating dependencies as physical individuals give over their wills and choice-making capacities to their real or projected inner contacts. My own understanding is that no inner being of any quality or competency will ever accept such a dependency on our parts, and may even avoid contact with us in order that it does not develop. The terms I prefer to use are 'inner contact' or 'colleague', or, if the relationship is a close and ongoing one, 'ally' or even 'partner'. The term 'soul companion' is also a very lovely and appropriate one.

This is not to say that an inner contact cannot or will not offer advice, insight, wisdom, speculation, opinion, guidance, comments and the like, appropriate to the nature of the relationship. They can relate to us like any friend or acquaintance can. It's just that giving guidance of any kind is not necessarily their primary function and, if a being claims that it is, I would question the contact or one's own need in seeking out that kind of relationship.

Having said that, I have over the years – and continue to have – several regular contacts and some who are irregular. For twenty-seven years I worked primarily with a specific being whom I called 'John', for no other reason than that I liked the name! The name he used for himself was a vibrational signature, which is true for my other contacts – I know them through their energy patterns and don't use names with them at all.

Inner contacts have been as natural to me throughout my life as my outer contacts. My earliest memory is of dying in another life and being reborn in this one. Since childhood, I have been aware of subtle, non-physical dimensions of life, sometimes referred to as the Inner Worlds or the Spiritual Planes. It is a capacity I was born with, as many children are, and I took this capacity for granted and hardly ever talked about it. I most definitely was *not* a psychic child and had a reasonably ordinary childhood with the exception of this inner awareness, which I figured everyone had. When I was fourteen, I realized this was not the case, so I set about to understand it and refine it. Much of what I contribute as an educator and lecturer in spiritual development has grown out of my efforts to understand my inner perceptions and from my exploration of the inner dimensions and the beings inhabiting them.

Even though I have always been aware of non-physical beings and have had communication with them, it was generally a background awareness as I was growing up. I did not have a disciplined practice nor did I have means of journeying into the inner, making new contacts, or navigating the inner worlds. Although I always had the *capacity* to do so, I didn't have the knowledge or the skill. This changed when John came into my life.

The first three to five years of my life with John was definitely a time of training as he helped me from his perspective and his side of life to develop and hone my natural inner capacities, greatly expanding my range and ability to interact with non-physical reality. He acted as coach and mentor. But much of his training was 'Socratic' in method – giving me hints, clues, asking me questions, giving me exercises to do, but then letting me work it out or make discoveries largely on my own. Like my father who, when I would want to know the meaning or spelling of a word, would hand me a dictionary and tell me to "look it up", John largely had me train myself (or discover ways of doing that). Much of the teaching work I do is based on that training as I work on ways of extending it to others. My book, *'Apprenticed to Spirit'* goes into the details of my training with John.

My first encounter with John occurred in the late spring of 1965. I had been living in Phoenix, Arizona and attending Arizona State University, working for a Bachelor of Science degree in biochemistry. However, I'd been feeling a call to a different kind of work, one that would be more directly based on spirituality. I'd been doing a small amount of lecturing in the Phoenix area drawing on my experiences with inner contacts for my material, and I'd been invited to come to Los Angeles to give a series of lectures. I accepted the invitation as a way of trying out this inner calling I was feeling. This was one instance when I was given direct guidance from my inner colleagues saying that my path was not going to be working in a laboratory.

One morning while in Los Angeles, about a week after I'd arrived, I was having breakfast with a friend discussing some classes we might do together when we were both aware that an invisible spiritual presence had entered the room. I 'saw' with my inner senses a powerful sphere or aura of light that radiated a most embracing and inclusive lovingness. This light resolved itself into a middle-aged man dressed in slacks and shirt, and a tweed jacket with leather patches on the elbows. He looked exactly like my image of some college professor and, while I knew that this image was projected for my benefit, it provided a familiar and comfortable form that I could relate to at that time. The name of this being was contained in his energy signature, but he said I could call him John as that was a name I liked. He said that he and I had worked together in the past, sometimes with him being in the realms of spirit and me on earth, as at the present, and other times with the roles reversed. We had work to do together again, if I were willing. He said that I should think about it and then let him know.

I thought about this for a couple of days and realized that I was indeed willing and told him so when he next appeared. That began, as I have said, a relationship that lasted for 27 years. John was a friend and colleague, and in the early days of our time together, he was a mentor and coach, basically training me in the use of my inner senses and towards my calling as a spiritual teacher.

Anything, from the smallest pebble to a tree to a bird to even our sofas and chairs, can be a spiritual companion or ally, as everything is imbued with sacredness and with presence.

I have a view of the inner worlds as a complex ecology and, for that matter, I view the physical world as one of those 'inner worlds', or spiritual worlds, as well: the spiritual world that is most readily accessible to our everyday senses. Otherwise, it is one world among many in an ecology of mind, beingness, and dimensions.

Inner allies can come from a great many places – post-mortem worlds, teaching realms, what I call 'collaborative realms', or spiritual realms. They can be human and non-human. They can be planetary, in that they are connected in some manner with the evolution of life and form upon the earth and carry within themselves a vibratory signature that marks them as participants in the World Soul, or they can be 'extra-planetary' or 'cosmic' (these words can be misleading, so I use them with some trepidation), though the latter are fairly rare and not easily contacted, mainly because, in my experience, their mode of thinking and being is so different from the human norm.

Some of my inner colleagues are non-human, or what in shamanic parlance would be called 'animal powers'. These are most assuredly and definitely not inner-plane 'pets' or cuddly inner-friends, but beings who are wild in the best and deepest sense of that word – belonging to themselves and part of nature as a whole. They interact with humanity because they share the holism of the world with us, but they are always partners on equal terms, never subservient to the human. Beyond a certain astral level of glamour and wishful thinking, there are no masters and followers on the inner planes, no dominance or subservience. Any being who would suggest otherwise or seek to establish such a relationship with you (with you being either the master or the servant) is to be avoided, no exceptions, for this is a delusion of the rankest sort... though unfortunately one to which human beings are particularly prone.

There are also astral forms, thought forms, deceptive entities, inner plane busybodies and the like, as there are non-physical realms close to the physical plane and thus close to human consciousness that contain either projected material arising from our own unconscious (and conscious!) thinking and feeling, or beings who are, in the fairly accurate Spiritualist term, 'earthbound'. Appearances can truly be deceiving on the inner, and I feel a significant percentage of what we feel are inner contacts are actually projections of our own unconscious material and/or contact with collectively manufactured thought forms. Discernment is an absolutely key skill for any inner work to proceed safely and accurately. Such discernment is more than just a mental skill… it is an emotional, physical, and energetic one as well.

While it has been my experience that the inner worlds are generally safer than many people fear they are and certainly a great deal safer than certain religious denominations would have us believe (there simply are *not* demons waiting to grab us at every turn), there are risks. Most of these risks do not come from inner beings per se but from the nature of the inner worlds and their sometimes profound difference from sense-based thinking and feeling. They are risks of misinterpretation, overstimulation and confusion.

As to why inner allies come to us, the primary reason from my point of view is that the ecology of realms that make up the planetary wholeness, both physical and non-physical, constitute a holism – a collaborative project, if you will. Allies come to us because they are colleagues… they wish to help and be helped, they share the 'earth project' with us, and so on. Incarnation is a joint effort in many ways, not unlike a moonwalk in which one astronaut walks on the moon but thousands of people are involved in getting him there and keeping him safe. So some of our inner contacts are among our incarnational support staff. Actually, in classes I sometimes use a NASCAR model of incarnation and call them our Pit Crew that can keep us running and in the race.

Inner beings can have a variety of motives in seeking out physical humans for contact, just as we in our everyday lives can have different objectives in why we seek out certain people with whom to connect. Mostly they come because of love, a desire to be of service where possible, and a desire for partnership and collaboration in the projects of life. It is possible for some of them to come to deceive, to be mischievous, to exercise power and dominion and just to be busybodies, but these are not common unless a person makes himself or herself vulnerable. It's really the same principle that goes with conning a person; an honest person cannot be swindled. It's when we think that we can make an easy dollar or get away with something that a con artist finds our vulnerabilities. Generally speaking, when I have found deceptive entities at work with a person, it's because that person is vulnerable to practicing deception herself or himself. They want something for free – they want power, they want to feel themselves special, they want status, and so forth. Truly, the same principles that get us into trouble with ordinary human contacts and also that give us wonderful relationships that are co-creative and mutually empowering, also apply to our contacts with the inner realms. How could it be otherwise?

Having said that, I want to also emphasize that in my experience there is a class of beings – call them angels if you like – that do their darndest to protect us, to police the barriers and boundaries between the physical and non-physical worlds, and to keep 'nasties' away. But our own motives play an important role here… it's hard for anyone to protect us from ourselves.

All my inner contacts are friends and allies first of all. We are colleagues in a shared work together. I have had some contact with my mother and father who are on the other side now but, otherwise, none of my usual contacts are related to me in this life in any way. Some are part of what I call my 'Soul Cluster' – a group of souls that interact together in various ways throughout many lives, so that strong bonds of family and resonance are built up between them – I recognize that we have known each other in other lives. But most are simply co-workers with whom I am united in doing particular tasks; as the tasks change, so my co-workers can change.

These days, I have no single personage that is a 'main ally' like John was (he left to go on to do other work in which I could not participate), but rather a group of colleagues. As I say, we are involved in a teaching work together, among other things, so I interact with them much as a college professor and researcher would interact with his or her professional colleagues at the university or the laboratory. I am in constant contact with a 'communion space', something akin to a switchboard, I suppose, or a portal site onto the web (rather like having a DSL or Cable line in which you are always connected to the Internet, as contrasted to a dial-up link in which you have to dial up to become connected). This is normally a 'place' or state of loving energy, maybe like a faculty lounge, and it's from this place I can specifically connect with an inner colleague or it is from this place that they connect with me. Because I have been doing this all my life, it seems perfectly normal and ordinary to me and has the same effect any ongoing connection with friends and co-workers would have in the physical world.

Though there is an ongoing connectedness, it doesn't mean that I'm always talking to some inner being, but should I need to be in touch with them, or they with me, the means to do so is there. I do not need to meditate or do anything specific for this to happen, other than give them my attention.

I should explain that the mechanism for this is not what I would call a psychic one. I am not a very good psychic. If you ask me what you're thinking, or where a lost article is, or what is happening right now to Uncle Joe, or ask me to psychometrize something, I will most likely draw a blank. I have friends who can do things like this much, much better than I can. If the information is considered needful and I ask for it, then perhaps one of my inner colleagues will provide it, assuming they have access to it (and that is always an assumption; just because a being is non-physical does not mean they are omniscient!). Mostly what comes to me is work-related material, which makes sense when you think of it.

Receiving messages via synchronicities, dreams, journeys, or visions constitute major channels for communication. Actually, this is a bit misleading because it's from our end of things that we see a single holistic act of communication broken up into these different forms. It is due to the nature of our space-time world that for us is very particularized and sense-based. The most common form of communication on the inner-planes that I have experienced is a form of holistic sharing of 'beingness' – a multi-sensory, multi-channel exchange. But when that translates into our particularized universe, it gets broken up into what appear to be different modes to us – some of it comes in dreams, some in synchronicities, some in a vision, some in words or thoughts, and so on. Yet, each of these, in truly holographic fashion, contains the whole communication if we can resolve it and understand it. I might fail to see the synchronicity but catch the dream or hear a word or see a vision, and so on… each fragment I get is a holograph in itself which can contain the whole message or lead me to it.

But for practical purposes, it's useful to say that there are many channels through which communication with inner allies can take place, so we should learn to pay attention across a broad spectrum and not just focus on having a telepathic experience or a visionary one or a special dream, etc. Each person is a unique act of communication with creation. As such, how any given person experiences contact can be unique to them and different from any other person's experience or methodology. As I said earlier, while I have been a researcher of the inner worlds in a very conscious and deliberate way for over forty years now, I am still just a 'universe of one'. I see things through the lens of my experience, personality, history, capacities, and so forth, and those are not the same as yours. So everything I say needs to be understood with that caveat as being one person's perspective.

To me, the relationship with most inner beings is that of a Soul Friend, what the Irish monks used to call an *Anam Chara*. The idea of a 'Soul Companion' says the same thing, I believe. There are times when guidance is important and needed, and there are beings who can appropriately and lovingly and wisely give it to us – but mostly we are all partners, companions and friends together doing the 'project of life'. I use the term 'ally' because, for me, an ally means a co-equal partner. An inner being may be vastly more accomplished than I, have access to much more powerful energies, insights, wisdom, etc., than I do, but we are still equal in our sacredness, and I have something to contribute as well. It's like an alliance between the United States and Switzerland – the former is a good deal more powerful than the latter but both are sovereign countries. The idea of sovereignty is very important to me, and was one of the ideas that John stressed in his training with me back in the Sixties. So I think of an alliance as a co-creative partnership and companionship between sovereign entities, and that describes how I think we best work with inner beings.

When I travel around our country, it teems with life both visible and invisible. Much as our ancestors may have seen and sensed – mountains and prairies, rivers and forests, all share overlighting presences that mediate the flow of vital energies through the landscape. They are the spiritual part of the ecology that nourishes all living beings. A good friend of mine, Dorothy Maclean, one of the founders of the spiritual community of the Findhorn Foundation in northern Scotland, sees these beings as angels. They are certainly sources of blessing for all who live within their influence.

And it is not only natural features or places that have such beings overlighting them – cities, towns, villages and other places of human habitation, work, and worship can and usually do as well.

Many of these beings who embody the energies of the land as well as of spirit, long predate the coming of humanity to the North American continent. They are beings of great antiquity for whom a single human lifetime is like the passing of an instant. Some of them may be only dimly aware of the existence of humanity. Others, such as those overlighting the cities of America and Canada are fairly recent and have awarenesses more attuned to the rhythms and timing of human life. They participate in their own way in the life of human society, usually to our benefit and blessing since beings of their stature and nature truly are angels dedicated to drawing out the best in humanity. But there is one presence that I have seen that is of particular importance to the citizens of the United States. It is part of the land but it is much more besides. Some people have called it the National Spirit of the United States or the Angel of America. I believe it is an angel of vast power and love – holding and nurturing the vision and values that shape our country, and working to mediate spiritual qualities and energies into our national life, for both our well-being and that of humanity and the planet as a whole. I think of it as the 'Soul of America'.

'Soul' is a word with many meanings. It can mean the life within something or its spirit or essence understood in an artistic, psychological or mythic way – such as the soul of a baseball team or the soul of jazz or the soul of a painting. In a religious context, it means the eternal part of a human being, that which survives after death in some form and continues on the journey of its life in a postmortem realm of spirit. It can mean the divine spark within us, the holiest part of us, the essential part of us, without which we lose, if not our life, then our connection to all that is good and beautiful and empowering within life.

I use the word 'soul' here to mean a consciousness operating at a level of life and intelligence that is attuned to sacredness and love and the spiritual forces of creation. It is a consciousness that knows the potential of a particular manifestation of life, holds a vision of how that potential may be best unfolded and expressed, and can mediate and coordinate vital creative forces to support and fulfill that vision. In this sense, my soul knows what my potential as an incarnate human being may be. It holds a vision for my life and is a source of vital living energies that can enable me to fulfill that vision. It is a presence that holds my life-vision clearly so that I can attune to it and thus be enabled to make choices and decisions that will fulfill it. Of course, I may not attune to that inner presence or vision, and even if I do, I may choose to ignore it or make different choices.

That is the challenge of incarnation. I learn and develop capacities of mind, heart and spirit by making choices and experiencing the consequences. I discover what works and what doesn't work. From this I develop wisdom. Wisdom is food for the soul.

In some ways, I am a throwback to an earlier time. Had I been born into a Native American tribe, chances are I would have become a shaman or medicine person – one who talks to the spirits of the land and of the inner realms. Or perhaps I am a 'throwforward' to a time that is coming when our capacities to see and relate to the spiritual worlds around us will once again be a shared heritage, expressing perhaps in a newer and more refined way than they did for our ancestors. I suspect the latter.

photo credit: Johnny Rozsa

ICE AND SNOW

Denise Linn

Denise Linn is an international lecturer, healer and author at the forefront in raising consciousness about the benefits of working with subtle energies, Feng Shui, and space clearing. She has been teaching for over 35 years.

She has written 15 books, including 'Soul Coaching', 'Feng Shui for the Soul' and the best selling 'Sacred Space'.

Denise is of Native American heritage and, although she wasn't raised in a traditional way, feels called to connect with the 'old ways'. This calling occurred in a profound way at age 17, when she went through a very traumatic incident resulting in a near-death experience. During those few moments when she was thought to be dead, she glimpsed a realm beyond the ordinary view of life – a remarkable place of great beauty and great peace.

The way Denise perceived the world around her changed dramatically after this experience. She began to sense energy fields around

plants, animals and objects and discovered that her ability to be aware of energy flows was not new – in ancient times, those who lived close to the earth knew that the world was comprised of energy.

After this realization, she began her quest to understand more about the ancient ways. Her training – which included learning from such varied teachers as a Japanese Zen master, an Hawaiian Kahuna, a Pueblo Native American elder, Australian Aborigine elders, a New Zealand Maori Tohunga and a Zulu Sangoma – has allowed her to access ancient wisdom that she uses to teach and inspire thousands of people worldwide.

Denise believes that within each person lies the ability to reach inside themselves to find sought-after answers to life questions. She believes in the majesty of every individual and, in her seminars, creates a safe and sacred space where that majesty can unfold.

She lives on a ranch on the central coast of California with her husband, David, and with their robust ranch-dogs Pepper and Sadie.

The main guide that is working with me now came to me in a very dramatic way. In 1983, I was in Melbourne, Australia, teaching a series of seminars. One evening after class I returned to my hotel room to meditate to connect with my guides. During my mediation, I saw a huge free-standing door that suddenly flew open and a huge Viking burst through in a blizzard of snow and ice. At that exact moment, something remarkable happened… the series of light bulbs on the ceiling directly above my head exploded, covering me in glass! I instantly snapped out of the meditation – I was shaken, because I didn't know what had happened – but this event seemed to validate the arrival of my new guide!

He was robust, strong and earthy, which is the last thing I would have expected my guide to be. Why would I get such a burly male guide when I was leading workshops for women? I had been sure that any guide that may appear would be female. When I asked the Viking why he had come, he told me that his presence would help keep me grounded for the work that I was doing.

I feel that my guides are always around me, but they work in different ways – different guides will come through depending on what is needed at the time. They also have different ways of communicating with me. The Viking comes through with specific messages during meditation, and my other guides make themselves known by way of synchronicities and symbols, or by hearing the sound of an 'inner' voice.

I believe that we have many types of guiding spirits on our journey through life. We have ancestors who are always watching and guiding us. Spirit animals may have a message and can be our guides and helpers. Also, angels can give advice and guidance. Throughout history, angels have been recognised as messengers from the Creator. In Native cultures throughout time there has been a belief in angels – they are called the Feathered People or the Bird Tribes.

I have been honoured by the presence of angels many times in my life. Once, when I was attending university, I was walking home one night after studying late at the library. Suddenly, a man jumped out from the bushes with a large hunting knife. He grabbed me and started to pull me into the bushes. I was terrified. Just as I started to panic, I heard a voice very clearly say, *"Talk to him"*. The voice was very insistent and a wave of calm washed over me. Instead of struggling or fighting back, which probably isn't a good idea with someone holding a knife to your neck, I calmly said, "It's nice to meet you". I'm sure that was the last thing he expected me to say and somehow my words changed his state of mind. Although he seemed surprised and even a bit bewildered, he let me go. I am grateful for the angelic presence that spoke to me and protected me that night.

One of my guides is a Taos Pueblo Native American Indian called Dancing Feather – I studied with him when he was alive and he became one of my most important teachers. I was with him at the Santa Fe Indian Hospital when he died. His last words to me were, "Wherever you go, wherever you are, I will be there".

After his death, feathers began to mysteriously appear in the most unusual places… One morning, I was taking a bath and there was a feather floating on the water. Another time, I wanted to buy a car and I opened the door and there was a large white feather on the seat. On a couple of occasions when I was giving a lecture a single feather floated down in front of me.

Every time a feather appeared, it seemed to have a message for me. Sometimes the message indicated that I was on the right path and other times seemed to indicate a new road I should take.

During my seminars, feathers also began to come to other people. One day I joked, *"Don't be surprised if feathers start appearing for you!"* The next day, a woman came to me holding a huge long feather she had found in the sleeve of her coat that morning. She was visibly shocked, and couldn't understand how it got there – especially as she lived alone!

I am Cherokee on my mother's side and my spirit name is 'White Feather'. Over the years, many people have seen me appear to them in a dream as White Feather, giving them a message.

During a seminar in Norway, a woman approached me insisting that I knew her. She became very upset when I didn't remember her as she told me that, many years ago when she was very depressed and suicidal, I had appeared to her in a vision. She said that I told her my name was White Feather and that I had come to help her. She told me that I said that everything would be all right and then I disappeared – vanished into thin air! She had never heard of me before she came to the lecture and didn't know what I looked like, so she was very shocked to see me.

At first, this unsettled me. I didn't want to take the credit for something that I couldn't consciously remember or perhaps hadn't even done. But over the years I have come to understand these kinds of events. I now believe that there's a divine part of our being – a 'higher self' – that is helping others unbeknown to our conscious minds. In that sense, perhaps we are all guides in ways that we may never know…

photo credit: Diane Arcieri

THOMAS

Alan Arcieri

Alan was born on July 22, 1952, on a military base in North Carolina. After two years, his family moved to New York, where his father was a police officer. The oldest of three children, his first psychic experience at ten years old had a profound impact that started him on a spiritual path.

Alan and his wife Diana have worked with the Hope Hospice Organization, helping people and their families who to cope with terminal illness. They have also worked in an Intensive Care Unit with a coma patient. Using a combination of Therapeutic Touch and telepathy, he was able to communicate with the patient, who would regulate his heartbeats in order to answer yes and no questions. This very rewarding work propelled him forward on his spiritual quest and helped hone his ability to communicate with the spirit world.

As a young boy growing up, ever since I can remember I had communications from spirit. Being raised in the Catholic religion, I was familiar with the concept of guardian angels. Although my teachers did not elaborate on how they interact with us, I assumed that perhaps this was 'the voice' I was hearing inside my head. I never really talked to anyone about this, simply because I thought they would think I was a little strange… so I kept the voice I was hearing to myself. Granted, this was not happening on a daily basis, but it was happening often enough.

It wasn't until I was much older that I started looking beyond the walls of dogma I found in Western organized religions, in search of truth. Once I got past their tall dark walls of fear and guilt, I was amazed to see what was on the other side. I began exploring early Christianity, Judaism, Hinduism and Buddhism. I learned that we *all* have spirit guides.

At the same time I started this spiritual quest, a very special spiritual teacher appeared in my life, Michelle Gellman – it was through her that I learned the practice of meditation. And it was through meditation that I was able to tune in and hear the voice clearer and more frequently.

One day while meditating, this soft familiar voice began speaking to me. After listening for a minute or two, I asked the voice in my head who they were. "*You can call me Thomas*," the voice replied.

"Well, Thomas, how do I know you are real? How do I know I am not just making this up in my head?"

"What is it you want me to do to prove to you I am real?"

I thought for a moment, and replied, "I want you to show me a dove... no black spots, no grey feathers, only a pure white dove."

"So be it," was his reply.

After the meditation, I had a strong desire to listen to a song I hadn't heard in years. I knew I had this particular song in my music collection, but I did not know exactly where I had put it. I opened the drawer and reached in to begin my search by pulling back a row of music albums I had filed in alphabetical order, when I looked down at the picture on the front of the first album I had just exposed – it was a picture of a pure white dove held in the hands of a naked black man. I was absolutely floored! I couldn't believe how fast it happened... I honestly didn't know what to think.

The next day, Thomas began speaking to me while I was meditating. I said to him, "That was really good, Thomas, I'm very impressed... but it all happened so fast. I need another validation, I just want to be sure this is real."

"What do you want me to do this time?" he asked.

"I want to see someone bring a single red rose into my house – not a picture of a red rose, not an artificial rose, not a dozen roses… but a single red rose."

"It is done."

I ended the meditation and went about my day. Seven days went by without a single word from Thomas... not even during any of my meditations. I had all but forgotten about the red rose validation I had requested and life went on as usual, with a visit from my sister Debra and her family. They rang the doorbell and I went to greet them. I opened the front door to my sister and she was stood there with flowers in her hand – a beautiful bouquet of white carnations, surrounding *a single red rose!* I was absolutely speechless. She handed me the flowers as she walked in and I immediately went around the room showing everybody the flowers, telling them to remember this single red rose... I'm sure everybody thought I was little strange for getting so excited (and I don't blame them), but my feet didn't touch the ground the rest of that day!

I asked my sister why she brought flowers, as it was something she had never done before… she said they caught her eye while shopping that morning and thought it would be a nice gift. She was right – because it was a gift I will remember for the rest of my life.

The next day while meditating, Thomas reappeared. *"Was seven days long enough?"* he asked.

"Yes, it was definitely long enough, Thomas, and now you have my undivided attention! What is it that you want from me?"

He then told me he was my spirit guide, here to guide, protect and help me reach my spiritual goals in this life. Not knowing consciously what my spiritual goals exactly were, I needed as much help as I could get! Thomas did not let me down. A short time later, I was guided to some other very special spiritual teachers and I was taught how to hone the skills I had acquired over the last twenty years while on the spiritual path. This was a major turning point in my life. Since then I have met a few other spirit guides that work with Thomas my 'master guide', and two guardian angels as well – Maria and Clair. I also know that there are many others I have yet to meet! It is comforting to know that I have such a great spiritual support team that I can rely on for guidance and protection.

Thomas and I have been together before in previous incarnations. Although I don't know all the details, I do know that there is a strong spiritual connection between us that transcends many lifetimes. Thomas has a lot of patience with me… I know I've put him through a lot. Reflecting upon my past I can clearly see his hand in guiding and protecting me.

Thomas is from a higher level of awareness and has completed many incarnations. He knows what the earth school is like from being human. He knows the trials and tribulations of being human firsthand. He knows pain, suffering, heartache and despair. He knows the powerful illusions of the five senses. He knows the ego. He knows the powerful physical sensations and urges the human body has. He also knows unconditional love, compassion and forgiveness.

The earth school is sometimes severe, with many trials. In order to learn the spiritual lessons we came here to learn, attention is paid to these student and teacher matches. You remember when you were in school how well you did in the classes if you liked the teacher? It's the same thing here. They know how to get the most out of us and which way to guide us.

They can also have more than one student that they watch over. Some of them have millions! Thomas is also my mother's spirit guide. When I first told her about my experiences with him, she almost fell out of her chair when I mentioned that his name was Thomas. I am very close to my mother and I know we have been together in past lifetimes many times before, playing different roles. But for some reason she never told me that she had a spirit guide who's been watching over her named Thomas! He does validate our strong relationship and our many incarnations together.

Although our spirit guides cannot tell us what to do and what not to do, they do need to know how to guide us in such a way that we will get the most out of the lesson or experience. The master guides are with us from birth to death. We also have secondary guides that come and go as and when they are needed. Our needs at five years old are different than at 25, and our needs at 55 are different than at 85.

Even our spirit guides have spirit guides and they have theirs too. They are also learning spiritual lessons by serving as our teachers and guides. When we end our incarnations, we will be given the opportunity to become spirit guides ourselves, if we want. Some higher evolved souls choose to come back to earth as sages. They serve here on the physical plane as guides and teachers.

I know that my spirit guides and guardian angels are watching over me every step of the way through this life. I communicate with them daily to do my work as a medium. This is my calling, my 'greater work' – reuniting family, friends and loved ones living on this side with loved ones who have crossed over, bringing them healing, comfort and closure. I work directly with my spirit guides every day in order to do this work and they have shown me different meditation techniques to use which have helped tremendously with my spirit communications.

I use clairvoyance (clear seeing), clairaudience (clear hearing), clairsentience (clear sensing) and clairalience (clear smelling) during my communications with the other side. I also use psychometry regularly to gain insight and information – by holding personal items such as a ring, bracelet or watch to connect with and 'read' energy that is stored in the object. This is a special ability I am proficient at and is a useful tool to help make a stronger connection during some of my spirit communication sessions.

There's a special meditation ritual I use to turn the spirit communication process on and off. Before I do any clairvoyant psychic reading, I spend up to one hour in prayer and meditation, preparing myself to receive the clearest spirit communication possible. This way, I can make the best spiritual connection in order to pass on names, dates, messages and other information during a reading. I use a different meditation ritual in order to close this connection to the other side... I need my private time too!

Our spirit guides were the last ones we saw in the spirit world when we were born, and they will be amongst the first ones we will see when we go home. It takes a lot to come into the physical world and we want to get the most out of those experiences. Our master spirit guides are here to help us do just that. They help us to stay on track, and get on with our greater work. No random matches here… nothing is left to chance.

A MESSAGE FROM THOMAS

The most important thing to remember is that you are divine beings. You are not only the actors, but also the writers and directors at the earth school – you have all the powers, abilities and tools you need to to accomplish your spiritual goals. Make every effort not to get lost in the illusion and remember who really you are and why you came here...

We are here to guide and inspire you to understand there is a divine order behind everything you see as senseless suffering. You benefit from knowing the cold that makes you appreciate the warmth, from knowing hunger that makes you appreciate having plenty. We are here to help you master yourselves and to trust the inner guidance we provide with patience and determination. You are never alone, we are always here to help you... all you need to do is ask.

NUDGES FROM SPIRIT

by Leo Rutherford

Leo Rutherford is the founder of Eagle's Wing Centre for Contemporary Shamanism and author of 'Way of Shamanism' (Thorsons) and 'Shamanic Path Workbook' (Arima Publishing). He received his MA in Holistic Psychology from Antioch University, San Francisco, and has studied with many gifted shamans. 2007 was his 24th anniversary as a practitioner in the UK.

I remember the day the roof fell in on my life…

One Saturday morning in 1973, I was standing in the center of the factory for which I was responsible and the roof about 20 feet away from me, for no apparent reason, began to collapse. I was spellbound as one bay after another came down in a hail of metal, tiles, concrete, dust, all with a ghastly thundering noise. A portion of the building, about 3000 square feet, became rubble in moments. Under this rubble people were working – a moment before it had been a thriving department.

By some miracle no one was injured, never mind killed. It turned out that someone had driven a forklift truck carrying two tons into a roof stanchion and smashed it. That brought down the roof of one bay and then there was a domino effect as other bays followed. For me, it was as if I was watching the roof fall in on my life. Inside myself the decision I had been avoiding was made. My life must change radically…

Years later, looking back on that seemingly catastrophic moment with more open eyes, I see that it was a culmination of many things and not an isolated event. I had become less and less happy in the life I was leading but had ignored the signs and signals – Spirit's nudges – that had pointed me towards change. Finally, I was given a big, momentous, unavoidable *nudge*. The fact I was standing there when it happened rather than in my office or away for the weekend feels significant. I was destined to see, feel and hear this event!

Reflecting on the theme of Soul Companions, I have written about those moments in my earlier life when 'something' nudged me away from robotic thinking and living and gave me guidance on my journey. Regarding my current life, I have written about how I have worked to develop greater ability to hear guidance, to actively listen and let it assist me in seeing where I am going, what for, and what step to take next. The way I see it now (a very long way from my world view at that far-off time) is that my Soul Companion/Guardian Angel/Tutelary Spirit/Power Animal/Higher-Self, expressing through the medium of karma, had pointed out to me very forcibly that it was time to take a serious change of direction. It was one *big* nudge!

Education or Injure-cation

I grew up in what feels to me like the middle of middle-class England in a family of very straight-thinking lawyers and housewives. I was given the 'best education money could buy' – which meant I was sent away to boarding school at the age of eight (an experience I liken to jail) 'because we love you'. This made 'love' a very conflicting emotion.

By the time I had learned to survive that school, I was nearly 14 and it was time to go to a 'public' school (a more advanced jail). The school was Church of England with pious services every morning and evening. My parents did not thrust religion at me, yet the amount of guilt and negativity I picked up from religious teaching amazes me still. It was like a cancer – like being in a negative energy field and absorbing judgmental soul-destroying garbage from all around without realizing it was happening.

At the school, there were furious punishments if one stepped out of line, and the degree of control on our thinking was extraordinary, mainly from the embedded belief system constantly reinforced by the other boys and the masters. Much later, I found out just how conditioned I had become by the guilt, blame and shame of 'churchianity', the insane 'injure-cation' I had endured, and how much fear I had absorbed of becoming anything faintly like the real 'me' – or even daring to find out who the real me was!

'Something' – my Soul Companion again, little did I know at the time – told me I could make a bid for freedom when some people from the Ashridge Business Academy came to the school. With their guidance and help, I grabbed the chance to leave school a year earlier than parentally planned through finding myself an engineering training. I left both school and home in one coup and took myself off to a future full of new possibilities… or so it seemed. I had not realized that I would take all my problems, fears and hang-ups with me. I was so shy and fearful that I walked the world on eggshells. After ten years of Britain's 'best education', I had emerged a social and emotional cripple.

Searching for a different way – Christianity

At the age of 19, feeling quite desperate about myself and my miserably pointless life and that my bid for freedom had somehow backfired, I stumbled into a Billy Graham rally. He wasn't there but he was on a big screen pounding away about the iniquities of man and the goodness of Jesus. At the end of the service, I felt so bad that my feet took me to the front and I did whatever it was to, nominally at any rate, 'accept Jesus as my savior'. I was handed over to some nice people who called themselves 'The Brethren'. They were very 'Christian' indeed – so much so that the women didn't wear make-up and they spent their time being 'good', thinking of God and reading only the Bible. I was initially impressed and spent some time going to their Gospel Hall, but I kept finding beliefs I was supposed to take on and ever more narrowing rules and laws and limitations I was supposed to accept. It was not considered good to try to make anything of your life – one should spend as much as possible of it studying the Bible and praying and repenting your sins. After about three weeks, I went on a day out with them to hear Billy Graham in person in London, and the shine wore off. Underneath all the piety they were just as bitchy and competitive as the rest of the (from their point of view) more lowly mortals.

I then tried the Church of England. The girls were definitely a whole lot more attractive (and when you are 19 that is remarkably important!). The vicar was pleasant enough too, but the religion still didn't make the slightest sense to me. This 'god-chap' who supposedly created and runs the world sent his only son to sort out the mess we humans made, and what did we do? Murdered him and sent him packing, so we should all feel guilty and bad because we must be a bad lot to do something so horrible. We are a fallen race, rejected from the Garden of Eden, and furthermore only proper Christians get to heaven. If you are not baptized, or you happen to be unlucky enough to grow up in a country that isn't Christian, then God help you.

And so all good Christians should be converting other people and conquering unchristian countries for their own good. Life is really about getting to Heaven at the end of it however miserable a time you have down here, so repent, pray, be good, don't have any sex until you're firmly married, don't masturbate, don't have dirty thoughts, don't chase girls – don't, don't, just *don't*, because 'God' is watching you, judging you, seeing into your darkest thoughts… and as a hot-blooded, fit and healthy 19 year old, I had lots of those! Oh, guilt, guilt and more guilt!

I came to not like this 'God-chap' and, furthermore, his 'son-chap' seemed to me to have been a total abject failure if he was supposed to have sorted us out because the world was clearly no better after 2000 years, to say nothing of two lunatic world wars. But I wasn't supposed to have thoughts like that so I kept them to myself!

That Didn't Work... So What Next?

By the age of twenty, I gave up the search and struggled on to try to at least make some vague sense out of my existence. I felt I was living in a madhouse full of sick and miserable people, who were only happy when they drank too much, smoked like chimneys, blamed others for their problems or else had extra-marital fun-sex. It was quite clear that marital sex was a pretty miserable thing, as married people didn't seem to have any of 'that' energy for each other.

Remember – this is a lost young person's vision of the 1950's! It felt to me in those days that three of the rudest words in the language were 'love', 'family' and 'home'. 'Love' was what got you into trouble and trapped into this foul thing called marriage where your soul was destroyed, 'family' was the dumping ground for anger, bad feelings and ghastly manipulations from one member to another, and 'home' was the prison in which all this happened! And 'God' was the foul judge up there somewhere in the sky who ensured that you suffered hell and torment every possible day of your life unless you pledged yourself to believe in a whole set of impossible things and not have any sex or even think about it.

Surely somewhere – no doubt over a very distant rainbow – there was another way…? There was, but it took me another twenty years and a massive mid-life crisis to find it.

Unrecognized Nudges

At the age of 28, I was given the opportunity to take over a going-bankrupt little company that made metal containers. I only got the job through my father's influence, certainly not on my work record, but I realized that this was an incredible opportunity – a magical life-opportunity, a soul-growth opportunity… it was, in fact, *a Soul-Companion-nudged opportunity!* There was no question in my mind about this and I even turned down an offer to go professional as a musician (I played traditional jazz clarinet) just before taking over the factory. I 'knew' the factory was a lifetime opportunity and that the band, fun as it might have been, was really more appealing to my ego. I was a good natural engineer but, at best, a third rate musician.

I became managing director of the metal container company and ran it for ten years using all my available energy and skills. In many ways, it would be more true to say that I had run it for about eight years and for the last two it had turned round and run me! No longer could I keep up. By then I was physically, emotionally and mentally exhausted and living an emotionally isolated life which simply did not satisfy my cravings for a deeper sense of purpose and chronic desire for intimacy.

By the age of 37, my health was suffering from my unbalanced, work obsessed, overly mind-oriented life. I remember having a vision of myself reaching 45 and having my first heart attack. My family 'illness of demise' is heart disease and my mother managed 20 heart attacks over 20 years. I felt I was aiming the same way and would become a sad and decrepit old man well before my time, probably by the age of 50. I certainly felt sad and heavy, and was living an existence, not a life. It was clear that either I did something to change or else life was going to change me.

Now I look back on this period and reflect that it is because it felt like such a frightful madhouse world that I set out to find this other way – and have never stopped that search! Quite a *mega-nudge!* I used to think I was lost, unguided and out of touch through that difficult time, but I see now that without it I would not have developed the sheer determination and will to create another life no matter what.

The roof collapse in 1973 was a *VERY BIG* nudge and finally I took heed of the guidance I was being given!

A New Start

Over the next few years, I took many of the building blocks of my life apart and started again. I was able to support myself financially for a time and anyway I was quite unfit to work. I could not even go shopping and remember what I was doing. I would get home and find the list in my pocket and that I had maybe a quarter of the items I had intended to purchase. My memory was shot, my body was unfit, I was always tired and I was a depressive with a big belly (I got to over 14 stone with a 40 inch waist) and little energy. I had no loving relationship… how could I? I didn't have a relationship with myself, or even have time for one, so I couldn't create one with someone else.

I started going to therapy and groups in 1975 and '76 but after a year or so began to feel I was an 'unsuitable case for treatment'. I was too screwed-up for the therapy and the therapists! At least, that was the feeling I was left with. It felt as if my old life had not worked and now my attempt at a new life didn't work either. I felt I was being led up a garden path by the ethics of the groups in that those who were seen to be 'growing' seemed to me to become more and more like spoilt-brat-children rather than maturing adults. This was not how I wanted to become.

The fall of '76 was my nadir and that Christmas I felt so awful I almost tried to eat myself to death. My sister made quite wonderful Christmas spreads and I felt so rotten inside that I thought I would get some pleasure out of my life if it killed me. So I ate and ate and ate again! Fortunately there was so much food no one noticed my greed, but I had stomach pains for a month afterwards. I never went to the doctor – I was far too bloody-minded to do anything that sensible!

I did have *a nudge*, however. I kept hearing about this mysterious place in outer Scotland that grew enormous vegetables and where people communicated with plants, devas and what have you. Well I didn't believe a word of that, but enormous veggies must mean something, so at least I would get to see *them*. Anyway, I had nothing else to do and who knows, I might meet a nice woman. So I booked a fortnight at this place, the Findhorn Foundation, expecting to find myself with a bunch of loony phony-holy tree-huggers but what the hell, might as well do something before I'm dead. What I got was a total surprise. Findhorn was not phony, not loony and held for me those pieces that had been missing from the therapy I had done – a wider and spiritual perspective. Here was an altogether more encompassing worldview. My stomach pains went, my depression lifted and I came alive again. Wonderful! Now that's the kind of *nudge* I like!

And the nice woman I wished for turned up too! She lived in San Francisco and that is how I came to go to California that summer. When I got there, San Francisco 'called me'. Quite literally, it said, *"Come and live here. All you need to heal yourself is here"*. This was a serious mega-nudge. At last, I was now beginning to find a path out of the old guilt and soul destruction way of life. I had no idea of where it would lead but the feeling of absolute rightness was there. It was a matter of trusting it.

Back in England, I rented off my house and at the end of '78 set off into the great unknown of a new life in California. I kept hearing recommendations of something weird called Fischer-Hoffman. It seemed Fischer was dead but Hoffman was alive, yet they had created this process together. *Another nudge.* I went to see Bob Hoffman and he convinced me. I signed up for this heavy-duty highly-intensive three-month therapy (now called the Hoffman Process). It was about working through childhood mother and father relationships, and heaven knows I needed to do that.

The process took me through a great deal of early trauma and showed me much of my stuck places and helped me release voluminous amounts of buried emotion. In fact, it was the beginning of getting re-acquainted with my emotional body, so much of which I had had to bury in order to survive. I cried many tears and yelled, screamed and raged… quite a series of miracles.

Then *another nudge* came my way. I had wanted to visit the Esalen Institute, which I had heard so much of back in the therapy scene in England. I pored over the catalogue because I was determined not to find myself in one of those encounter-dump-anger type workshops that I had found so un-therapeutic. One person stood out right away – Gabrielle Roth. She worked with dance and movement, though it didn't sound like any dance I had experienced. It turned out to be quite wonderful. *Bullseye!* I was getting the habit of listening to my guidance! The workshop got me back into my body in a really magical way. Esalen truly is a wonderful place, perched on the rocks above the Pacific ocean with natural hot springs to lounge in, a beautiful location in nature, nice people, and healthy food. The whole experience was so great I signed up to return for Gabrielle's next workshop. I worked with her regularly up to her first-ever training course in 1982.

It was a couple of years later that I did my first venture into the wilderness. I had considered joining a vision quest group – three days and nights alone on the mountain, but I figured I wasn't ready for something that challenging. Instead, I signed up for a 2 week wilderness trip with the Esalen Institute, which sounded much more gentle. Lo and behold I received another *nudge* – now I was thinking of them as Coyote Moments (Coyote is the trickster of Native American mythology). I found out when I got there that a three-day vision quest would be part of it, along with sweatlodge and peyote ceremonies, all of which was new to me. They were at it again – my Soul Companion had tricked me into facing just what I thought I was going to avoid!

On the vision quest, I had quite an extraordinary experience. I had been given a dried peyote button and I chewed it (ugh, foul tasting it was too!). Relaxing in the moonlight that evening, I 'saw' the mountain on the other side of the valley. It was as if I saw the lines of energy, the earth-lines, which structure the physical mountain from inside. The nearest I can describe is that it was like a gigantic electric transformer with massive windings. Everything was normal in all other directions, but not the mountain across the valley. I squinted, changed my focus, and tried all manner of things to see it differently. I still 'saw' it the same way. Finally, I fell asleep and in the morning the mountain was just a mountain.

These experiences led me to a serious study of shamanism and it was here I started to feel truly 'at home'. The description of the world taught through the medicine wheel feels so superior to the western psychological models as it encompasses the earth, the sky and the greater forces that act upon us and through us. Another big nudge! A nudge for a lifetime.

Back in England in '83, I set about putting my skills to work under the umbrella of 'Play-World', a mixture of interactive games, improvisation, dance, chanting and voice-work, and then I 'dared' to offer the occasional mini-workshop on the little I knew of shamanism. It was in 1986 that a changeover happened in my self and my work. I went on a pilgrimage to Peru with Alberto Villoldo and don Eduardo Calderon, the Inca shaman with whom he was apprenticed. I can't say for sure what happened, but I came home from that trip different. I think that at last I was walking more solidly on the earth. Also, that year, Harley Swiftdeer, founder of the Deer Tribe Medicine Society with whom I had studied a bit in my California days, came to Britain and I absorbed from him a lot more of the medicine wheel teachings from a deeper perspective.

My shamanistic work took off in a most surprising way in '87 after I was invited to dinner by a dance teacher friend to talk about her work and to discuss whether or not I thought she could do a year-long course with her students? I listened to her and felt a resounding 'yes'. It wasn't until I was driving home that I got the nudge – and a *big nudge* – that *I* could do a year-long course, too. I remember to this day arriving home in the highest of high spirits and staying up planning out ideas and possibilities! My logic said to me that if it's not easy to get enough participants to make a weekend workshop happen, then it must be far more difficult to get a year-long course together. But logic had no vote in this! I put a two-line note on the bottom of my spring program and a couple of months later had a list of over 60 interested people. A giant Coyote Moment and one from which I have never looked back!

The Present

So what has changed for me? Well, I am no longer 'looking for God'. He/she/it is all around and alive here and now. The judgmental old man in the sky with a white beard – 'Father Christmas for adults' – is gone… the old control-freak patriarch has dissolved back into the dark abyss from which he was invented. I continue to look for how to live in greater peace and harmony, balance, and alignment with all of life and its many turns and changes and challenges. I seek all the time to stay in tune with my Soul Companion who I have learned to see and relate to, quite often as a 'power animal' as per many shamanistic traditions. I attempt to 'walk in beauty', to keep the old demon ego in check and to remember I am not actually trying to go anywhere except 'here' and 'now'.

And that, I found, was the hardest thing of all. Surely I should be trying to get somewhere, become 'someone'? (As if I am not 'someone' already! We are each 'someone'!) One of the many medicine wheel teachings I have taken very much to heart is to 'never make up my mind' about anything ever again! To be guided whenever possible by 'Spirit', by my soul companion. To allow and encourage my deepest essence to be the guiding force in my life.

In my early life I had no map – just Christian guilt, blame and shame. Now the multi-level maps of the medicine wheel are my guides and I experience life in terms of the four directions – physical, emotional, mental, spiritual = earth, water, air and fire. So much of life that used to be a hopeless puzzle to me has become clear through the medicine wheel.

The other big thing that has reversed for me is to know that the inner life is the real one. In my old engineering days, I had a life-aim to become boss of a substantial company making something useful. I thought that maybe if I worked hard enough and was clever enough I would get 'there' – somewhere with enough money and prestige to have the 'good life'. The 'good life' meant having the exteriors all looking good and then the interior would 'obviously' be just fine, so said conventional 'wisdom'. Now my aims are reversed – to find peace, love, harmony and balance inside and then to let the outside follow and mirror, as it naturally does, what is on the inside.

All our experiences happen inside, the thought or 'dream' world creates our experience of 'reality'. Imagination comes first. A beautiful building is first a thought, a 'dream' in someone's mind, then it is an architect's plans and detailed drawings… only lastly do the builders come in and create the 'reality' of the building. So to create a life, *dream* it first and then call the experiences to yourself. This is active co-operation with my Soul Companion, higher-self, inner being, who no longer has to create catastrophes to gain my attention!

We are spirits learning how to live in a body given by Mother Earth. That's why we are here, to learn to live in a body and to bring the whole of our-self – body, mind, emotions and spirit – into harmony and balance with All-That-Is. We are not in a body to get out of it and escape by becoming 'spiritual' or 'religious' – we are already spirits. We are here to learn how to be in a body – our vehicle-of-experience – and to bring matter and spirit together in harmony.

CHAPTER 2

DREAMS, JOURNEYS AND VISIONS

Those who have compared our life to a dream were right....
We sleeping wake, and waking sleep.
~ Michel de Montaigne, '*Essays*', 1580

One of the most frequent ways that spirit beings communicate with us is through our dreams. Dreams are a very effective way to receive messages from Spirit because the logical mind stays out of it! When we dream, we enter other dimensions of existence. We can visit these parallel worlds and enter the world of spirits – and they can enter our dreams, too. (But who is the dreamer and who is the dreamed?)

For instance, while I was writing this book, I awoke remembering the following vivid dream:

I was staying in an old Victorian house with some friends. Whenever they went out, leaving me alone in the building, I saw the spirit of a young boy who told me his name was John. He had brown, shoulder-length hair and wore a simple, long white 'gown'. It became apparent that he wasn't cared for very well, and I didn't want to be left alone for fear of seeing him again. So, the next time my friends left the house, I went with them. I stepped outside, and who should I see waiting for me, but John! He seemed happier outside the house and greeted me enthusiastically with a big smile, proudly declaring, "I'm an artist!" He then proceeded to show me personal 'scenes' from his life, like home-movie clips. He had many sisters who were very fond of him, but his father had been very cruel.

I couldn't figure out what this dream meant, so I didn't think too much about it until some weeks later, when I met the renowned psychic artist Patrick Gamble to request his contribution to this book. As we got chatting, Patrick explained that he channels an artist in the spirit world called *John*. This instantly triggered my memory of the dream and I was compelled to share this information with Patrick. I'm almost certain that's what John intended. The message was for Patrick, not myself.

Prior to this dream, I had always assumed that my dream life was 'mine' – that everyone and everything in my dreams had a personal message for *me* alone. This experience taught me that this is not the case at all. Throughout the ages, indigenous people have held council to share important dreams in order to benefit a specific individual or the community as a whole. Great decisions and actions were often made solely on the basis of a dream message. Sadly, in our modern Western society this rarely happens, if at all.

Most of us learn to dismiss our dreams at an early age, after experiencing nightmares as children. We were comforted by our concerned parents who, well-meaning in their intent, told us, "It's okay dear, it's *only* a dream". And so we began to believe that dreams are unimportant and that we probably only have them to keep us entertained while we sleep (lest we get bored!).

We generally tend to regard dreams as garbled nonsense because we are not taught to interpret the language of dreams, which is largely metaphorical and symbolic in nature. Dreams often arise from your subconscious, and to bring that into conscious reality is a powerful way to understand yourself and awaken to your full potential. Seeing as we spend roughly one-third of our lives sleeping, I think we would all benefit from learning how to make the most of these nightly visits.

Ancient and indigenous cultures understood this, which is why they consciously worked with and honored their dreams. In ancient China and Greece, they built special chambers in which they would 'incubate' dreams to give them answers to specific questions. They practiced the art of learning how to 'wake up' in a dream – of how to dream *consciously* – gaining the ability to intentionally maneuver through dreamscapes. This is often referred to as 'lucid dreaming'.

In our dreams we experience reality in a different way than we normally perceive it to be – things can shapeshift, we can talk without speaking, and we can even *fly!* What is that if it is not an altered state of consciousness? You've been doing this every night since you were born! *That's* how easy and natural it is to communicate with and travel to other dimensions.

Another way to consciously visit other dimensions is to 'journey' to them. This is the way of the shaman and is very similar to dreaming, the main difference being that you aren't sleeping while you have the experience. Instead, the shaman enters a heightened state of awareness through the use of sound, usually via the steady rhythmic beating of the drum, sometimes with the additional help of psychotropic plant allies, and *always* with the help of a spirit, or power, ally. In this way, he or she is able to safely enter and navigate other dimensions to seek insight and information.

For the uninitiated Westerner, journeying can be difficult if the logical mind cuts-in to negate the experience. The first few times I journeyed, this was indeed the case. I wondered if I was just 'making it all up'. The nearest thing I could equate the experience to was rather like having a 'guided daydream'. Now, I always enjoyed daydreaming as a kid, but I got the impression that this was mere fantasy and illusion, plus I was always getting into trouble for doing it at school. Whether it was 'real' or 'not real' became an issue for me and a barrier to the process. Realizing that my logical brain would always win the argument, I told it that, yes, I was imagining it all. Paradoxically, journeying then became easier for me. These days, I feel that my logical mind has quietly acquiesced to the simple fact that whether I decide to journey, daydream or dream, I enter the same space. That's all I need to know.

Visions are akin to journeying and dreaming in that most people usually 'see' them in their mind's eye… not with their physical eyes. (Having said that, many people have experienced visions with their physical eyes – the bible is full of such alleged encounters!) Personally, I receive visions in 'mind's eye', when I am in a very relaxed state, either during meditation or prior to sleeping. My physical eyes are usually closed. Sometimes these visions are like photographic images… other times they are like home-movie snippets.

It is difficult to explain how a vision differs from the hundreds, if not thousands, of random memories or mental pictures we experience on a regular day-to-day basis. In my experience, what they all seem to have in common is that they spontaneously appear outside and in front of my head, like a holographic 3D projection from my third-eye. It always surprises me because I do not expect to 'see' what I, quite clearly, 'saw'. The pictures feel significant at a deeper level than I have conscious access to, rather like an elusive *knowing* that I can't quite place. Even so, I am beyond doubt that every vision I have had has been a pictorial communication from my guides and allies in the spirit realms.

photo credit: Glenn Capers

NUINN

Philip Carr-Gomm

Philip Carr-Gomm lives in Sussex, England, with his wife Stephanie and their children. From an early age Philip studied with Ross Nichols, the founder of The Order of Bards Ovates and Druids. He has a degree in psychology from University College London, and trained in psychotherapy for adults at The Institute of Psychosynthesis, and in play therapy for children with Dr. Rachel Pinney. He also trained in Montessori education with the London Montessori Centre, and founded the Lewes Montessori School. In 1988 he was asked to lead The Order of Bards Ovates and Druids, and he combines his role as Chief of the Order with writing, and giving talks and workshops.

Ross Nichols was 61 and Chairman of the Ancient Druid Order when I first met him at the age of 11. His Druid name was *Nuinn*. He was Principal of a college in London where my father worked as a history teacher, so would often come to the house for supper and became a family friend. He was like a kindly uncle with a slightly teacherly air who could sometimes become crotchety, so we weren't 'pally' and never had any 'personal' conversations about anything.

Ross founded the Order of Ovates, Bards and Druids after the Chief of the Ancient Druid Order died. He didn't get on with the new Chief... they were two different characters. Ross was a poet and storyteller who was particularly interested in Celtic Mythology and he wanted to celebrate all eight seasonal festivals, but, at that time, the Ancient Druid Order only celebrated three.

One of the peculiarities of recent Druid history is that the Druid revival of the 17th to the 19th centuries occurred in England – not in the Celtic countries of Wales, Scotland and Ireland. English Druidry, which was quite formal and Masonic, wasn't particularly interested in Celtic literature. There are actually three different kinds of Druidry – there's some overlap, but not much. There's cultural Druidry, like the National Eisteddfodau of Wales, Cornwall and Brittany, where Druidry is used as pomp and ceremony to promote language and culture. Likewise, fraternal Druidry, with its male-only lodges, ritual and ceremony, gives people a sense of feeling they belong to something and provides them with financial help but, again, Druidism is merely used as coloring for the event. Neither of these are 'spiritual' groups, and most members would call themselves Christians.

The Ancient Druid Order and, following on from that, Ross Nichols were responsible for the revival of a third type of Druidry based on connecting to the earth in a very deep way as a source of spirituality. Ross and Gerald Gardner, who was a friend of his, were two of the seminal figures responsible for the modern pagan revival – Ross Nichols for Celtic spirituality and Druidism and Gerald Gardner for the modern pagan Wiccan movement.

When I was 15 or 16, I became interested in Druidry – I started to visit Nuinn regularly and gradually began my apprenticeship. He was interested in my progress – my intellectual progress in particular. Because I was young, perhaps, or because it was 'meant to be' I never questioned it or felt it was unusual. We just knuckled down to work together. I was initiated into the Order of Bards, Ovates and Druids on Glastonbury Tor when I was 18.

After my teacher died unexpectedly of a heart attack in 1975, when I was 23, the Order went into a sort of Winter sleep…

Do we carry on after we die? Well, none of us really know until we take the journey ourselves – but, a few days after Ross died, I was staying in Glastonbury for the night and I dreamt I was lying on a tumulus surrounded by a ring of people holding hands, directing energy at me. Nuinn was with the group. I woke up as the dream was happening, and an energy was poured into me – the voltage became so intense I had to ask them to stop because I thought I was going to explode… it was like having ten thousand volts run through me!

Nine years later, I was married with a little boy, taking a degree in psychology and doing a BSC Science degree in London. Druidry wasn't part of my life at this point. I hadn't thought about Ross Nichols for years. I was very busy, dashing about, but my whole life was about to change because of what followed. I received a series of three invitations and a whole string of extraordinary synchronicities and co-incidences, which resulted in the re-founding of the Order.

The First Invitation

I was meditating one day, simply experiencing a deep state of relaxation. Suddenly, quite by surprise, I became aware of Nuinn standing about 10 to 12 feet away from me. It wasn't like I saw him with my eyes open, as an apparition, but it was the equivalent of having your back to the door and 'knowing' that your husband or father or somebody you knew had come into the room – you'd be aware of them as a presence. I was really astonished because it was totally unexpected.

In a telepathic transfer of information, he said to me that I should look at Druidry again because it's not anachronistic – it's really relevant to today's world and all the problems that the world is going though.

"What I would like you to do is put all the teachings in a form that's accessible to people, because when I taught you, I only taught people who could come and visit me, which limited it hugely for obvious logistical reasons. I'd like you to put Druidry in the form of a course, where it can reach people all over the world, wherever they live. I would like you to lead the order again, but don't worry – all will become clear."

Nuinn had spent the last five years of his life working on a book – his definitive statement on Druidry. He'd put a lot of work into it, so, obviously, he was on the Other Side and was anxious to see his book published. He said to me:

"I'd like you to find the manuscript for this book and to get it published and I'd also like you to get the rest of my books as well, and put together the teachings."

A prolific writer, Ross had published five books – he'd given me two of them, so there were 3 that I didn't have. I hadn't been in any hurry to acquire them because I didn't expect him to die so suddenly.

After my 'visitation', it was around seven o'clock in the morning… I had to help get my boy to school and rush off into town. I was running a travel company at the time in Covent Garden and, in my lunch hour, I remember walking into a second-hand bookshop opposite my office – it was a smart one, an antiquarian bookshop. I asked, "Do you by any chance have any books by Ross Nichols that were privately published during the war?"

"It's very unlikely," the man replied, but, all the same, he went downstairs to look. He came back about 10 minutes later with a little book tied up in a parcel with string – also containing letters and pen and ink drawings from my teacher. In itself, this is an extraordinary co-incidence if you think about the number of second hand bookshops in London!

I walked around the corner to the Atlantis Bookshop by the British Museum. As I walked through the door, straight ahead of me was a twin-volume edition of *'The History of Magic'* by Paul Christian, of which my teacher had written the foreword and had had privately printed in a special edition with a slip case, marbled end papers and gold leaf on the tops of the pages.

That weekend, I went to have tea with a chap called Colin Murray, who's since died – he and his wife wrote *'The Celtic Tree Oracle'*. I was excitedly telling Colin that already I had two of the three books that I didn't have.

"Well, I've got 2 copies of the third book – you can have one of them," he replied, handing me a copy.

I made several telephone calls and found the manuscript to his unpublished book.

The Second Invitation

I spent the next four years gathering the information and putting it in the form of a course – but I held back. I thought that maybe, despite all these coincidences, I had imagined everything. When you study psychology, you realise how clever the mind is and how many tricks it can play on you. However real and objective and tangible an experience with the Other World might be, you can always say to yourself, "Well, actually, perhaps it's just my unconscious."

Out of the blue, in February 1988, I got a phone call from some people who had been connected with the Order when Ross was alive, 13 years previously. They visited me on Valentine's Day and asked me to re-found the Order and to lead it again. The extraordinary thing is that they knew *nothing* about my experience four years previously – they had waited all those years before telephoning me… I mean, how odd is that? It was extraordinary. When I got this invitation, I thought, 'Well, I'm going to accept this, because it's obviously for real'. This was too unlikely a co-incidence of events to dismiss.

I started the Order again and we date its re-founding to that day in February 1988.

The Third Invitation

Very soon afterwards, I met Caitlin Matthews and told her the story, and she introduced me to a publisher. I was asked to edit Ross' book and it was published two years later, in 1990, entitled *'The Book of Druidry'*. After this book was published, I was asked to write my first book, *'The Elements of the Druid Tradition'*, and ever since then, I've been asked to write books by various publishers. For the past 16 years, I've been writing about Druidry as a path that really has value in the world – that isn't just a bit of superficial dressing on something, but is really very deep and connected both to the land and the needs of our time.

I don't really agree with channeling – where people say, "I've been *told* that I must do this or that." I am uncomfortable with the idea that spirits tell you to do things. I think that it takes away your free will. Ross Nichols asked or suggested to me that I do a bunch of things that had life-changing consequences for me. But in all his subsequent visitations, he didn't ever tell me to do anything.

All the really deep contacts I've had with Nuinn have occurred spontaneously and have surprised me with their intensity. They have occurred roughly once every two or three years and have occurred either in lucid dreams, in meditation or in a hypnagogic state, on falling asleep.

I remember one dream… I was at a party and there he was and I was astonished to see him and blurted out, "But I thought you were dead?"

"Of course I'm not dead," he laughed, "you know that!" and then he gently pressed his forehead to mine, by way of greeting.

The Order of Bards, Ovates and Druids now has around 10,000 members worldwide – I've made many friends and travelled all over the world – and it's all the result of sitting quietly in my bedroom in Kew one day, experiencing someone from the Other Side visiting me.

THE SPIRIT OF SHAMANISM

Sandra Ingerman

Sandra teaches workshops internationally on shamanic journeying, healing, and reversing environmental pollution using spiritual methods. She has trained and founded an international alliance of Medicine for the Earth Teachers and shamanic teachers. Sandra is recognized for bridging ancient cross-cultural healing methods into our modern culture addressing the needs of our times.

Sandra is a licensed Marriage and Family therapist and Professional Mental Health Counselor. She is also a board-certified expert on traumatic stress as well as certified in acute traumatic stress management. She is author of many books, including: 'Soul Retrieval: Mending the Fragmented Self', 'Medicine For The Earth', 'Shamanic Journeying: A Beginner's Guide', and 'How to Heal Toxic Thoughts'.

I was always a spiritual child. Growing up in Brooklyn, New York, I had many different spiritual experiences. Understandably, I kept a lot of that to myself as I didn't live in a culture that would have understood it! To me, everything was alive and had a spirit, which is one of the basic premises of shamanism. I loved being out in whatever nature I could. I would come home from school every day and sing to the trees and the birds, and I loved to go out at night and talk to the moon. I also had experiences of spirits coming to me. Every night when I went to sleep I saw Jesus standing in my room, and I was not raised Catholic so that was not something one would expect.

I have had several near-death experiences in my life. The first was at the age of seven, when I was hit by lightening. Then, when I was about 19 years old, I drowned in the ocean at Mazatlan in Mexico and was brought back to life, and in my late twenties I accidentally drove my car off a cliff. As I was a child of the 60's, I also had a lot of experience with psychotropic drugs. All of these things helped me expand my perception of reality and realize that we really limit ourselves in our understanding of what life is about.

During one of my near-death experiences, I went out of my body toward what I perceived as a giant light – a light more illuminant than any light on this earth. It permeated love and I was completely filled with it. The light didn't recognize me as a personality or as an individual. If Hitler were standing next to me, he would have gotten as much love as I did, because there was no judgment. There was only an experience of oneness and love.

I realized that a lot of the suffering we experience as egoic beings with a personality was an illusion. There is another level of life where we can open up into a place of unity with the power of the universe, the Divine, the Goddess, God, essence of Light… whatever one wants to call it. Because we've forgotten about the principle of unity and the power of love, we think of ourselves as separate beings that are not connected to the rest of life. We have moved into what I call a 'trance state'… we're asleep. We've forgotten about the magic of life and we've forgotten about our interconnection with all of life. I think that people are slowly starting to wake up to realize that there's more than we can see, hear, feel, touch, smell, and taste in the tangible world – that there are many spiritual realms and that everything is alive and we are all connected.

When we're in that state of unity, we move past the egoic states of separation of fear and anger, jealousy, hate and greed – all those things that keep us in this trance state in our lives – and we can really open up to live from a place of love and peace and bring light into the world. Love comes when we remember that we're connected to an entire web of life and that nobody is separate. I have a spirit helper who gave me a wonderful metaphor of this. She said, "Imagine a hand, where one of your fingers drops from the hand to the floor and it thinks it has a separate life of its own!" She said that is a ridiculous concept, but that's what is happening to people on the planet today… we have all these fingers running around thinking that they're not connected to one body or part of the greater whole.

One of the big perceptions that I learned from my near-death experiences was that we came here to experience what it's like to be in a physical body but yet be spirits who can manifest things into form. We have so much unlimited creative potential. My strong feeling is that we really came here to learn about creating and manifesting spirit into form through love… not for personal gain but on behalf of all of life, to caretake the earth and create beauty on the planet.

Part of our mission and destiny of being human beings is to be a bridge between the worlds, between heaven and earth. The way to do this is through our hearts. What I wrote about in my book, *Medicine For the Earth*, was that my spirits taught me that heaven *is* on earth and that our perception creates our reality. As we move into a place of love and appreciation for everything that happens in our lives, that's how we start to experience heaven on earth. We have to wake up to a much larger reality than what we limit ourselves to with our mental thoughts and in our beliefs of what society has told us is real. We can work together as a community to create change on the planet.

Shamanism is a practice of direct revelation where we receive information from our own helping spirits. The practise of shamanism is cross-cultural. The word shaman itself is a Siberian word, but shamanism was practiced all through Asia, Europe, Australia, Africa, North and South America. If you're alive today, you come from an ancestry that has shamanic roots, so the practise of shamanism itself does not belong to any one culture… it belongs to everybody who's alive at this particular point. But I feel it's important to find our own ceremonies – not to go into an indigenous culture and copy theirs. I've been invited to speak to Native American communities, but I'm very clear with all of them that I'm not taking any of their rituals and that everything that I'm sharing came to me from direct revelation.

You have to be called by the spirits to be a shaman. It's not a profession that you choose, and it's not one you'd *want* to choose either, because it's the path of the 'wounded healer' – there's a lot of suffering that goes with it in order to have compassion for suffering in the world. I later learned that being hit by lightening is one of the ways of being chosen, but I didn't grow up in a spiritual family or a spiritual culture – I grew up in New York City… I wasn't to know that I was being called.

I believe that in the shamanic and spiritual traditions in the ancient times there was no separation between this world and the spiritual realms. As we started to move into trance states of believing science over spiritual teachings – that if you don't see or hear it in the tangible world it doesn't exist, it's in your imagination – we created veils between the spiritual worlds. Our minds closed down to them and so we became disconnected.

In shamanism, there are intermediary spirits between ourselves and the power of the universe that recognize us as individuals and can share their wisdom and their healing knowledge with us as individuals. They can appear as what we call 'power animals', teachers in human form, plant spirits, tree spirits or guardian spirits. In different cultures, the Gods and Goddesses that are aspects of the Divine are also intermediary spirits who have compassion for the suffering of beings here on the earth.

Shamanism provides a way to work with these spirits who do recognize you as an individual and can help with the personal issues, growth issues and challenges that you have in life.

I have found that I can't go to that kind of expansive energy of oneness to get a personal solution to something going on in my life. The only time the Light ever answered a question for me was when I asked, "Why do I only experience you when I'm having a near death experience or I'm on drugs?" I really didn't expect an answer to that question, but I felt the answer come to me in my journey… that as long as I have a body, I have to travel as deep inside of myself to experience the light as I traveled outside of myself in my near death experiences and my drug experiences. It's time for us on the planet today to experience this power of the universe within – not outside ourselves as we've been doing.

For me, there are different ways that I receive information from the spirit worlds. One is through shamanic journeying, where I use drumming, rattling, and singing to enter an altered state of consciousness. I journey out to my spirits and ask them questions or ask them for help with a client. Another way that I receive information is through working with omens – where you take a walk outside holding a question and the spirit world will give you answers by things showing up in nature. Even if you live in a city things show up… all of a sudden you'll see a sign, a person comes by and says a sentence to you, or an animal shows up to provide the answer to the question that you're holding. Sometimes, I just have a 'knowing' that's coming from another place… I didn't use the drum, I didn't use the rattle, I didn't use singing, but I just *know* that I've gotten spiritual information. For me, writing is a way of connecting to the spirits – I tend to go into very deep altered states while I'm writing. A lot of the messages that have come through my books actually came from dreams. I do a lot of work in my dreams… I've had healing dreams where I've been healed of physical conditions through a dream and I've also gone to people and done healing for them in a dream.

What I teach in my workshops is that one of the ways that we gave our power to authority figures in society was to stop singing. When we were growing up, most people were told, "You can't sing, you don't have a good voice and you're hurting people's ears". I think that that's how many people lost their power. Physiologically, what I've found is that when you really *sing*, you get in touch with your own personal power. When you sing, your energy expands. If you're depressed or if you're angry or you're experiencing a problematic state of consciousness – sing! If you either sing a song coming to you or sing a song that you already know, and *really* sing it, energy starts to flow throughout your entire body, creating healing for those negative states of consciousness. Singing helps you move out of a separate, powerless, negative state of consciousness and it opens up your heart and brings energy into your body so you really *do* feel your connection with all of life and you really *do* feel your connection with your own personal power.

Some songs come *through* you rather than from you. When you go out into nature and just ask for a song to come though, I think that nature sings through you at that point.

From a shamanic point of view, when a shaman sings a power song or sings before he or she does journey work for another or healing, it helps to dissolve the ego – the part of ourselves that keeps us separate from the power of the universe. The shaman becomes what in anthropological literature is called the 'hollow bone', where you can really bring through the power of the universe, because your personality or ego is not in the way. In singing a power song or soul song, it really helps you to move into an altered state of consciousness where you can experience oneness with the universe.

In the 1980's, I took a vision quest in New Mexico. I ate only fruit for 30 days beforehand, so I was pretty clear when I went into the quest. A Native American medicine woman created a large circular space around me using cornmeal to make the boundary. Enclosed within my circle was a sweatlodge. Although I had wanted to sit in a very small space in the traditional way, she had given me more land to be on as she felt I needed to learn flexibility. It was very hot and I was sitting in my little spot, when I saw a vision of a grandmother coming to me who said, “Go into the sweatlodge, sleep and your vision will come through a dream.” After resisting what she had said, because I really wanted to sit there in the traditional way, I finally went into the sweatlodge and I went to sleep. In my dream, the Egyptian goddess Isis told me that she was coming to me as a teacher to help bring peace and harmony to the planet again. Since then, Isis has been a teacher of mine in all of my journeys – she helps me write my books and I feel her merge with me when I’m teaching and when I’m doing lectures at conferences. She doesn’t show up when I’m doing individual healing work with clients, as she’s more interested in helping me heal and work with raising consciousness on a global scale.

I have always had an interest in Egypt because it’s such a mysterious magical place and I’ve always been drawn to that energy. Since she has become my teacher, I have become more interested in Egypt and Egyptian mythology and have taken groups there.

What I’ve learned in over 25 years of studying, practicing and teaching shamanism is that spirit helpers share their wisdom through metaphor. If you look at all different religious and spiritual traditions, you see that all the texts are written in metaphor – the bible is *completely* written in metaphor and that’s why we’re in so much trouble today with it, because people have taken it literally.

I think that the reason that the spirits share through metaphor is because they’re trying to give us many different perspectives. When you look at something on a very literal basis, there’s only one road to walk down with it. Our spirit helpers are trying to get us to evolve and grow – they’re constantly trying to get us to expand out of a ‘one road’ way of looking at things to be able to consider things on many different levels. When we look at something through metaphor, we have to look at all the different possibilities instead of getting locked into one way of thinking.

One example of this was when I journeyed to a power animal many years ago, back in the early 90's. I asked my power animal the general question, "What do I need to do in my life right now?" And his response was, "Go out and garden." I took it very literally… at the time, I was living in a place that was real rocky and wasn't really supportive of a garden, but I got out there and gardened. It was very healing to do some gardening work but at the end of the summer, I had this epiphany of realization – my power animal never meant that I should literally be gardening! He was asking me to look at my *life* as a garden – at what seeds I was planting in the world. He was asking me to look at how I worked with clients in my healing practise, my teaching and workshops, and to make sure that I was always moving people into a place of hope, love and inspiration.

For me, getting introduced to shamanism gave me a form to work in. Before that, I had a lot of spiritual experiences but I didn't know what to do with them. When I teach shamanism, it's amazing how many of my students say to me, "Oh, I've been doing this all my life… I didn't know there was a name for it." It helps people to realize that there is actually a practise that fits into what they have naturally been doing throughout their lives.

We're always connected to the spiritual realms and I don't think that there is *ever* a disconnection, but that doesn't always mean you can always get information from your spirits. I can always journey for clients, but I find for *myself* that there's an ebb and flow, where I have to experience life and stop asking so many questions. I find that there are times in my life when I know that my spirits are around me, but they're not available to me for answering questions. I think that it's a natural cycle to just experience life. But the spirits are always there – we always have spiritual support, even if we're not conscious of it.

My spirit helpers really teach me how to live life from the fullest of my potential. They're always getting me to stretch and expand. They inspire me to continue learning and that we all have unlimited potential. They've been teaching me step-by-step how to use my creativity for myself and for the planet. They have taught me healing practices to help other people. They help me move from a place of depression to a place where I really appreciate life and the preciousness of life and I'm very grateful for that.

A MESSAGE FROM ISIS

All the pain and suffering that we experience physically, emotionally, and in the world today comes from the belief that we are separate from the web of life and separate from each other. It is crucial for all of us to find daily spiritual practices that we can engage in that create unity and also that keep us connected to our divine light.

It is crucial to remember that everything we experience in our outer world is merely a reflection of our inner world. As we engage in spiritual practices that help us to transmute and transform our negative states of consciousness into love, light, peace, and harmony our world will reflect that consciousness back to us.

During these times of transition on the planet, the news can be so distracting. We must focus on not getting lost in the chaos of our times and continue to tend the garden. New life will be born out of the chaos. Our role is to stay focused on tending.

A SUFI MASTER'S BLESSING

by Master Ali Rafea

Born on April 7th, 1950, Master Ali Rafea is the son of a sheikh (Sufi Master and spiritual teacher) – Master Rafea Muhammad Rafea. After his father's passing, he was entrusted with the position of spiritual guide of the Spiritual Islamic Circle. He asks the followers of the order not to consider him a sheikh – he is only the symbol of the Circle. He continuously confirms that they are not to take his words without thinking, rather they should think hard and find the truth themselves. This attitude in itself is a renovation of the guide-disciple relationship and a breakthrough in Sufi orders.

Master Ali Rafea is also a Computer Science Professor at the American University in Cairo, Egypt. He believes that it is possible to feel God's presence with oneself at all times – not just during prayer, meditation and contemplation. This is how he became a prominent scientist and a spiritual leader at the same time without any contradiction.

The spiritual vision of Master Ali Rafea, which he has been

conveying in his speeches over the years, is presented in an Anthology that has been compiled and translated from Arabic into English by some close members of the spiritual Circle, entitled 'Islam: Living in Harmony with the Laws of Life'.

I believe that everyone has some sort of guidance from the unseen part of the world. This guidance could be from our higher consciousness, another person who lived on earth sometime ago or from unseen creatures, like angels, or by any other means that we cannot imagine.

My father, Master Rafea Muhammad Rafea, was the spiritual leader for the Spiritual Islamic Circle. Master Silver Birch was the Circle's spirit guide. He communicated through the medium Muhammad Eid Gharib (known as Abu-Sri'I) in spiritual sessions that were attended by the Circle members.

Silver Birch had previously told his group that a Sufi man would come and 'take the lead'. The members of that Circle were searching for that man. They met other Sufi leaders but Master Silver Birch had told them that the expected one was still to come. The spirit guide welcomed Master Rafea to the circle and gave him an assignment – to be a human guide for the circle.

My father learned that Master Silver Birch's mission is that of all religions. In other words, he found no contradictions between Islam and the guidance of Silver Birch. The language of the spiritual call is to remove the barriers between East and West, and the false barriers that are put between religions.

Some of my father's talks were collected, printed and distributed in his circle. My father also wrote two spiritual-fiction books – *'Memoirs of Khabridis'*, which anticipated the manifestation of the spiritual message on earth, and *'From the Revelation of Yathrib'* – about a sheikh and his disciples who came from different parts of the world... each of these disciples choosing a specific subject to deal with, sharing his insights with others.

The spiritual guide, Master Silver Birch, also has many books in the West which talk about the Divine Law of life – how man's behavior on this earth has its effect on his spiritual life... how every moment a man lives on this earth is intimately related to his future life… how that if praying is not sincerely addressed to God or is aimed at attaining spiritual or moral gains it is without meaning or value. These books played a great role in softening the materialistic outlook of Western Societies, which didn't believe in the extension of life beyond death. These books have also helped the Islamic Society to reinforce the beliefs of the Moslems and all those who seek spiritual values and meanings to cultivate a deep appreciation of the meaning of life's extension beyond earth.

After my father's passing, Master Silver Birch asked the Circle members to renew the pledge with me as their guide. I was not interested in being a guide and was in conflict between acceptance and rejection. I finally decided to accept based on the simple reason that my rejection would lead to the destruction of the Circle, which I could not morally accept.

Even now, I do not accept myself as a traditional Sufi guide. I am an ordinary person who is trying to think freely and go deeper in understanding the wisdom we have on earth coming from different sources. I feel, however, that one should not be completely dependent on outside sources and that knowledge should come from within, from one's own experience. I tell the members of the Circle that everything I am saying is not absolute and can be discussed – that they are only hearing wisdom from me because of their love, confidence and belief in me. We are all one… if I am the tongue, they are the ears. If I am the mind, they are the heart and body. We complement each other by love, desire for knowing the truth and a wish to improve our earthly lives and to be exposed to the mercy of God. I accepted the role of 'guide' to the group under this new definition.

I do not usually remember my dreams, but not long after I accepted my role as guide, I had a vivid vision that I felt was reality. In this vision, my father was holding my hands in the same way he did when a new 'brother' came to join the Order. In Sufism, this called *Kabada* – it is like a pledge that is made after reading a specific verse from the Koran.

This vision gave me the feeling of a new start. I felt comforted that my father was satisfied with my new approach. As I did not personally receive the *Kabada* from my father while he was on earth, I felt that he had visited me in my dream to give me his blessing and the power to continue his spiritual work.

Six years after my father passed away, the medium of our Circle, Mr. Gharib, passed away. Since then, we have not had another medium to communicate with Master Birch as we used to. This was another turning point in my life, when I suddenly found myself without direct guidance except for my inner consciousness and intuition.

Deep in our hearts, we sense another dimension of self that is unique to each one of us, yet it is beyond limitations. We cannot experience inner peace unless we nurture this spiritual core, this divine part within our own existence – the primordial nature, the Self, the inner messenger, or inner voice. The Self is sensed but cannot be defined. Sensing the Self is the gateway to inner peace. The Self sees its reflection in everything, and evokes love in the heart of humans. It harmonizes with the rhythm of divine law, and achieves a balance where peace becomes its expression. Unless we awaken this divinity within, it is hard to be able to listen, to understand, to tolerate differences and live in harmony.

On the spiritual level, the more we are in harmony with the purpose of our existence, the more we are able to take messages from our inner Self and the more we realize that human beings are endowed with divine source that links them to one another. That realization widens our scope and enables us to see beyond our limited interests.

Purifying the heart from negative energies is a process that is cultivated through spiritual training as well as good deeds. I feel that meditation helps me to purify myself to be better exposed to mercy, knowledge and wisdom. Sometimes, I experience external signs and co-incidences in my life… an unexpected event may occur to explain an issue I am thinking about, confirm an idea I have or inspire me with a new idea. Mostly, I feel guided by an inner sense of 'knowing'. When I talk to brothers and sisters in a gathering, some ideas come into my mind that I might not have previously considered. I sometimes raise a question and I really do not know the answer in advance, but I try to go through analyzing the question piece by piece until, suddenly, the clear answer emerges. As we always say, spiritual contact is an ongoing message because every man can go through this experience in different ways. I believe that God is transcendent and, for sure, all guidance comes from Him in the end.

In collaboration with close members of the Circle, we set the goal of the circle as the dissemination of knowledge about the oneness of all revelations, prophetic and natural, conducting research in that area. We feel that throughout history, the basic concepts that underlie the teachings of all revelations have been misunderstood, misused, and misrepresented distorted and overlooked. We are attempting to clear up the misconceptions as we see them departing from a belief that the aim of all revelations is to guide man through his earthly journey to make living spiritually fruitful.

The knowledge we have gained through our experience and mutual learning has been reflected into the basic premises and ethics of our spiritual Circle as follows:

- Each individual has a unique way of experiencing the divine spark from within one's heart.
- All revelations provide humans with spiritual training systems in order to help them experience their spiritual being.
- No one has the right to value, judge or impose one's beliefs on others.
- Each person has the freedom and right to choose for oneself the suitable way to develop spiritually.
- Spiritual development is reflected in one's daily life and behavior.

• No particular revelation is superior over others.

• All revelations came to liberate human beings from illusions that hinder their spiritual development.

• All revelations support humans in their search for equity and justice.

The teachings of Islam assert all the previous points and more. Because we are all spiritually connected, the great teachers of humanity are expressing the same path to inner peace in different words. We pray to God that the world will awaken to realize that there is One Religion, and that humans should not stick to false racial prejudices, and insist on ignorance. The world should realize that the shared goal among men is to know God, seek His face, and to gain Truth. The world has to realize that human brethren should talk to each other with open minds, discussing their shared goal: how to be real humans *whatever* their nationality, civilization, origin, or environment. Spiritual knowledge is not meant to be for a certain creed, religion or culture. It is for every one.

FROM BUSINESS TO BLISS: DAILY LIFE WITH THE SPIRITS

Dr. Geo Athena Trevarthen

Dr. Geo Athena Trevarthen is both a shaman and an academic. She received a PhD from the University of Edinburgh for her ground-breaking work on Celtic shamanism — the first to academically prove the existence of a full spectrum of shamanic features in Celtic cultures. She has also studied transpersonal and Gestalt psychology, theology, anthropology, art and film.

Geo teaches with wisdom and humor, sharing ancient chants and shamanic practices to reveal Spirit's presence with and within us. She is a registered Marriage Celebrant in Scotland through the Scottish Pagan Federation and an ordained minister in the Circle of the Sacred Earth.

She's spoken and taught at institutions ranging from St. Andrews University to the Omega Institute, and was the first scholar ever invited to speak on Irish shamanism to the Trinity College Theological Society,

Dublin. She's written widely on shamanism and spirituality, including the section on Celtic Christianity in the 'Encyclopedia of Religion and Nature'.

Geo currently teaches at the University of Edinburgh's Office of Lifelong Learning, where she developed the first academic course devoted to examining the deeper layers of meaning in the Harry Potter books. The class forms the basis of a forthcoming work from O-Books on using Harry's story as a guide for our own spiritual growth.

I grew up in a Celtic Shamanic tradition. My family are hereditary shamans. Of course, 'shaman' is a Siberian term. Traditional Celtic terms include *Druid* and the *Áes Dána*, 'People of Art,' encompassing 'arts,' sciences and shamanic practices.

According to the mythopoetic histories, we can trace our ancestry back to the High Kings of Tara in Ireland and the Scottish Chiefs of Clan Cameron and Clan Lamont. My ancestors came to Scotland in the 10th century. We continued to practice openly until the late 1600's, when we became more discreet for obvious reasons.

My Scottish and Irish family tradition came through my mother. My grandmother named her after the goddess Athena in the hope that she'd embody women's wisdom and power. As well as being a very spiritual person, she became the first woman to graduate in Roman Law from Cambridge, and had a career in public interest law. My father was a Hungarian Jewish scientist, philosopher and cosmologist, so I grew up with a mix of spirituality and hard-line, common sense. For me, the metaphysical stuff has to 'bear fruit' in physical ordinary reality or it's not a lot of use.

The first really clear memory I have of connecting with a spirit guide was in a dream when I was about seven. After that, I would journey to them, meditate and chat with them sitting on the beach. I connected with a wolf totem when I was little, and he's stayed around.

Because I grew up in a shamanic tradition, I didn't have anything I had to un-learn in order to communicate with the spirits. Children have such a great co-creative, imaginative faculty anyway – they are natural shamans. I just continued doing what I did as a child.

I have a lot of different beings that I would call spiritual guides and I have different relationships with all of them – I'd say I probably have a fair number of spirit guides. Some are totemic animals and others are spirit teachers.

On one level these beings are my friends and I have humor and fun in my interactions with them, but I was taught that these are what the Irish theologian Eriugena would have called *Theophanies* – they are manifestations of Deity. I was always taught to respect them. I find it a bit off-putting when some people start talking about their guides as though they've got them in their pocket. A totemic animal isn't your 'fuzzy little pal'. That attitude worries me slightly, because it feels irreverent.

I would describe myself spiritually as a Panentheist, which essentially means that there is one God who manifests through everything. One of the Old Irish Apocryphas depicts God as an upside-down tree with a single root in heaven and a myriad of branches growing downward. It describes this tree as Christ, the branches as Angelic Orders and the birds singing in the branches as the 'souls of the just'. It's the idea of God beginning at a single point and manifesting through a myriad of different forms. I like the term 'theophany' and the image of the downward growing tree, because it's a non-judgmental way of describing the level of energy when I interact with my guides – whether I'm dealing with more of a branch or more of a twig!

I use any and all methods of communication with my guides. It's no different to any other relationship – do you receive information from your friends by e-mail, text message, phone call or in person? Sometimes I specifically decide to journey to one or the other of them and at other times I just get a real strong sense of their presence. Sometimes I talk to one of my spirit teachers when I'm going for a walk in the countryside. Their messages come through in a variety of ways.

I have what I call a spirit mate, Divine Beloved or Spirit Husband. If I were to describe myself as a little leaf on a branch, he's more like the branch itself. He's closer to the trunk of the tree than I am. Our relationship has evolved over the past 15 years through dreams, physical and spiritual journeys, synchronicities and research into ancient languages, so I won't go into it in great detail here – that's a book by itself!

The experience of a manifestation of Deity as a Divine Beloved goes back to ancient times throughout many cultures… Sumerian and ancient Celtic kings married the Goddess, shamans in many cultures have spirit mates, Nuns have experienced Christ as the Divine Beloved, St. Bernard of Clairveaux talks about the marriage of the soul to Christ, and Sufis talk about God as the Divine Beloved.

The incredible love and the intense connection with my spirit mate is quite euphoric and is often present. It's not constant, but has intensified over the years and continues to be accessible. I think a lot of people only get to experience that for the first two months with a new lover. That's something that I'm incredibly grateful for, because it's a very blissful, sustaining experience and it stops me becoming over-attached in physical reality in the wrong kind of way.

A lot of the time, we expect the husband, lover or girlfriend to be God for us all the time, 24 hours a day. You can't cram 100% of God into a person – God's too fat for anyone's house! I'm grateful for the fact that there's something for me beyond the material, physical reality. That sustains me and it helps me cope with the fear of change because, although we love things to stay the same, life changes.

In the Old Celtic tradition, the primary conflict is often framed more as one between chaos and order than one between good and evil per se. I once went to my spirit mate with the question, "Is there absolute justice?" I was expecting to hear him say, "Yes", so I'd already bulldozed on to the next question before I'd realized he'd actually said "No". He went on to say, "If you go blundering around doing things coming out of your personal, ego-based attitude, completely unaligned with Deity… do you think that God doesn't have anything better to do than to run around playing tit-for-tat about every insult you happen to receive?"

Although I was initially shocked at his response because of all the injustice in the world, it suddenly made total sense – the more we align ourselves in such a way that we desire what Deity desires *through* us… the more aligned we are, the more justice we will experience. But if we're just blundering around doing whatever we please in a completely unenlightened way, then maybe there isn't absolute justice for us. Somewhere in there, there's got to be scope for a little bit of chaos that comes in sometimes and a little bit of freedom of action on the part of various different people. Our thoughts influence reality, but the trick here is, *other beings are thinking too!*

When something bad happens, people may think their spirit guides have abandoned them. People are always blaming God for all the terrible things that happen in the world, but what about the miracles of absence? We don't know how many times God's interceded in our lives, through His or Her Theophanies. Every once in a while we know what missed us. I think that it's important to bear in mind that this intercession is going on all the time. If God and the spirits are going to get the blame for something going wrong, they should get the credit for something going right! 'The kingdom of heaven is spread out upon the earth and men see it not', to quote the Gospel of Thomas. I think you have to work quite hard to miss it. It must take a lot of blind faith to be an atheist.

Russ – My Spiritual Business Advisor

Around 1995, the same man kept appearing in my dreams. He was an American – a southern, New Orleans-type gentleman in one of those white 'ice-cream' suits with a white hat. He was very striking and unusual-looking with big eyes.

Now, if a new spirit seems to be coming through in my dreams to work with me, I always check them out with one of the spirits that I've been working with for a long time and can really trust. I went to my spirit husband and was told, "Oh, he's somebody that we've found for you to be your new business advisor, because you're not doing very well with that and we thought you needed someone to help you out." Evidently, he's a businessman who died in New Orleans in the 70's. He was involved in various dodgy dealings, so he's helping me to improve his karma!

When I took a spirit journey to meet Russ and introduce myself properly, he said in this New Orleans accent, "Oh yeah, I met your husband… nice guy, but he sure dresses funny!" (He wears elaborate, ornate priestly robes!) What I always say in workshops is, "You can't tickle yourself." There are things that my spirit guides say that surprise me in a very genuine way. I wouldn't have thought to make that one up!

Russ definitely knows a heck of a lot more about business dealings than I do and it's brilliant to have his mind on that. He has advised me so many times over the years…

I write screenplays and I've got a Masters Degree in film. I was working on a few different ideas that I wanted to pitch to Star Trek Voyager, because I love science fiction programs. One day, I stepped into the elevator and Russ appeared. (I see him in my mind's eye – I've seldom seen a spirit with my physical eyes). He said, "Look – when you get home right now, if you phone up Paramount, you phone up the Voyager offices and begin the process of arranging for your pitch, you will sell your screenplay. But if you don't, you won't." So I went upstairs and did just that. Out of 4,000 freelance submissions, my storyline was one of the two that was chosen that year! It was called, *'Sacred Ground'*.

Then there was the whole process of trying to sell my first book at an auction. I had gone through the whole 'dog and pony show' with the big publishing companies. I had meetings with marketing teams and I got an agent who was good at selling books. The weekend before the book auction, we started getting phone calls from different publishers trying to close a deal beforehand, and the offers were starting to get enticing – one of them was quite a large sum. My agent came to me, asking, "What do you want to do? Are you going to take this? This is a lot of money!" So I said, "I've got to go and ask my business advisor first," and I went out on the balcony and had a chat with Russ. His immediate response was, "Don't take it!"

"Are you sure?" I replied.

"Yeah," he said, "Absolutely do *not* take it. I can fix this for ya, but I can't do it till Tuesday."

The auction was on *Monday*, but my experience of Russ had been so good that I'd learned to trust him completely. I told my agent not to take the offer. Come Sunday, we got a phone call from two of the publishers bidding to say that they couldn't make it on Monday and would we move the auction to Tuesday! It turned out that we got over three times the amount that the initial offer was for, which enabled me to get through my PhD.

I would describe my relationship with Russ as close to being very good friends. When he was incarnate he loved to play pool, and that's one of the ways I thank him for helping me – I'll go to a place where they have the full-size pool tables and I'll drink some Jim Beam, which I don't drink otherwise, and he plays pool through me. It's like if someone wants to come and sit on the settee next you, you would move aside a little bit. That's what it feels like to me internally and spiritually. He's giving me all this help, so the least I can do is give him the experience of enjoying being in a body again on occasion, although he complains because I'm not nearly as tall as he was – my arms and legs aren't as long so he can't play all the shots that he used to! But I still play a lot better when he's playing through me!

I've done different levels of acting as an oracle for a spirit or a Deity before when it's been done in a religious context to help others receive healing or information. There have been times when a bigger Theophany has taken me over and I don't even remember what's happened, so there have been times when it feels like a complete displacement.

Manannán

Another of my guides is Manannán mac Lir – son of the sea god, Lir, in ancient Irish tradition. I'd say he's one of the more urbane of the Celtic deities! He's interacted with my ancestors in some of the legends so in one respect he's an ancestral deity. I go to him when I'm looking for clarity and common sense. On a symbolic level, the sea represents our emotions, which can cloud our minds the most.

For example, I once met with a few people to do some spiritual work at a particular sacred site. We'd come together through amazing synchronicities from all around the world, but there was another person who had an interest in the site who was being very possessive of the place. This is kind of comical when something's been around for 5,000 years!

We found ourselves spending far too much time discussing the weirdness of this person. I went down to the beach to ask Manannán what was going on and what we should do. The first thing he said to me was, "You know, sanity is a choice." He was right. The person we were interacting with was choosing not to be sane. And those of us who had come together over thousands of miles, to work at this particular site for a limited time were spending that precious time talking about how 'not well adjusted' this person was, which was *also* insane! So I went back with that message and it just cleared the whole situation.

One of the other major lessons that Manannán taught me was about the different levels of Theophany. Modern physics theorizes that there are probably lots of different realms of being. Shamanic cultures tend to believe in different levels of reality, layered like a cake. What we're in now is the middle world and you can spiritually journey through layers of the upper and lower worlds like floors in a building.

I think the first levels of the upper world are where lots of people have their heaven. It's basically like here, but a bit nicer – if you've got your semi-detached house in this reality then maybe when you go to the upper world, you'll have your semi with a conservatory! (Russ has his own pool hall!)

Some guides are on a closer level to you, like totemic animals or ancestors. There is also an Absolute Deity, who's probably beyond any of our abilities to understand It, at least in the earthly context. That Absolute Deity is with all of us all the time. It moves through everything and rests in nothing. This Deity is paradoxically the 'furthest' from us in terms of Its perspective, and yet is also nearer than our breath.

After Manannán discussed these two polarities, he cautioned me about the 'in-between' deities. Manannán told me that one of the most difficult kinds of spirit to work with is a being who is at a very high level – one who is very powerful and may have lots of things they want you to *do*, yet not high enough to have large measures of divine compassion and understanding. Manannán termed them 'Jehovah class,' which I found rather amusing, kind of like how you'd describe a type of battle ship or space ship or something. To this 'class' of spirit or deity, you are in fact 'a flea' and some of them can really use you for their own purposes. They're not necessarily meaning to do bad, but they effectively chew you up and spit you out again, because your individual well-being is not important in their particular plan. Others' well-being may not figure high in their priorities either.

This is where the absolute hard and fast rules come in, whereby if a spirit tells you to do something you know is wrong – *don't do it!* That's where the moral standard 'don't do harm to anybody else' comes into play. There are a lot of people who do some silly things because they believe that spirits or God is telling them to do it and it's bad news. You don't do what a spirit says willy-nilly.

I think that there's a perception that everything out there is benign and that everybody's on the same side, but I've even journeyed to archangels where it's clear from what they're saying that there are differences of opinion between them – not about the ultimate goal of positive change on Earth, but how to go about it. There are different beings that have different opinions as to what kind of road we need to be on.

The method of getting in touch with all varieties of spiritual beings is basically the same. In all shamanic traditions, you withdraw your attention from the physical realm (from the denser level of being), and direct your attention towards the subtler levels of being. You enter the state of what I call shamanic trance or the 'awareness state' – the state in which you can become aware of spirit.

In Old Irish, this is called *Súan*. It's an interesting state depicted as part of a trinity, often described as different types of music. There's *Gentraige* – the music of joy or happiness, *Goltraige* – the music of sorrow, and *Súantraige* – the music of trance. The state of spiritual trance is one in which you can experience joy without clinging, and sorrow without despair – it's a state that balances us and puts our feet firmly on ground that's strong enough to stand on in the Other World. The Old Irish term for the Other World is *Síd (pronounced shee-thuh)*.

It can also mean 'peace', and 'tumuli' – the ancestral burial mounds and places where people would go to have contact with the ancestors in the Otherworld. The word *Síd* implies that the densest level of the Otherworld is right here around us, so it's that idea of a very grounded spirituality that works in and is connected to this reality. It's not about going off into 'airy fairyland'… it's about being engaged with spirit guides for the purpose of having a better, stronger connection with life, a deeper engagement with life on all levels, and being of benefit to other beings.

I think the biggest reason why we have spirit guides is that we're all in this together to try and improve things – to create a situation where there's a lot more love and a lot less misery in the world. Just as you want to do your bit to help improve things, there are also various beings or entities who want to do their bit, too. If they can guide somebody towards more constructive behavior, then they will. Although a lot of beings are interested in what's going on, I don't think that humanity, or even this planet, is necessarily the sole focus of every metaphysical entity in the universe

– many of them don't have anything to do with us or have any particular interest in us.

Sometimes, spirit guides can briefly turn up just to teach you one particular lesson… Once, I was going out with a man who was a real killjoy – he was really not a lot of fun. I had a very strange dream about Lawrence of Arabia, where I was just being shown in no uncertain terms what an incredible wet blanket this man was! It was the most vivid experience on every sensory level. Lawrence was really short and had dark hair. His face looked really sunburned. He put his arm around me at one point in the dream and he was wearing scratchy robes and smelled really weird – a 'goaty' smell. I certainly don't make up those kind of details in every dream! The only thing I'd seen or heard of Lawrence of Arabia was the Peter O'Toole film. In the movie, he's wearing silky-looking Bedouin robes, but when I did a bit of research I found that he actually would have worn goat wool an awful lot more. He was also dark, not fair like Peter O'Toole, and had fair skin that sunburned! He was the image of the man I'd seen. In that particular dream, he told me that in a past life I had been a little Arab boy who chased him around. I feel that he helped me because we'd had some kind of connection, however small, in that particular lifetime.

Some spiritual beings are awesome, amazing deities. You get a sense of the incredible scale of them. I've asked them, "Why do you even *bother* with us?" What comes home to me, is that if these huge amazing spiritual beings are stooping to help us, we should be helping everybody else. We need to take every ounce of our energy and devote it to being of benefit to other beings on this planet right here and now, because we're never going to get this chance again, not as physical beings.

Manannán has told me that *this* is our chance. In some respects, you have a better opportunity for spiritual growth as beings physically incarnate on earth than you do when you're disembodied and in spirit in the Otherworld. The physical form is a denser level of being so we have this incredible ability to *focus* and to really take leaps of faith. Because here there's risk, here there's danger… or at least there *appears* to be. The Divine spark within us can't die, but this life, this theophany, this manifestation in the physical, can and will end. When we're out of a body, it's not so much of an issue. We experience our immortality. Here and now we have a chance to really be of service and help other beings. Just doing concrete things. Praying or sending light is good, too, but being of physical assistance to other beings comes first, because that's what we're here for, that's the level we've chosen to work on right now. On that level, we extend our lives in physical reality.

Of course, part of that process for me is offering my ancestral shamanic tradition to my children. My three year old can already sing songs in Old Irish! It's up to them whether they want to continue in it, but I'm giving them the tools that have been most helpful to me in my own life. Ancestral wisdom means that we don't have to reinvent the wheel every generation. Gratitude towards Deity has always been central to Celtic tradition. One way I encourage my children (and myself!) to remember to be grateful is by keeping a 'gratitude journal', where we write down a few things that we're grateful for at the end of the day. This is an example of how I expand on what I was given in harmony with my tradition. The traditional principle I grew up with was gratitude, but I learned this particular practice from Sarah Ban Breathnach's book, *'Simple Abundance'*.

To me, the gratitude journal is one of the best things you can do to support your spiritual connections. It changes your consciousness and extends you to the world in a much better way, because if we're not grateful for and if we're not acting on what we're already receiving, what's the point of the spirits interacting with us any more? I hope that this kind of practice will stand my daughters in good stead for the rest of their lives. If I was to tell anyone to do any single thing to improve their lives, that would be it.

Obviously, the whole idea of having spirit guides is based on the idea that

God isn't done talking to us yet! There's always fresh learning and love coming to us from Spirit and from our spirit guides.

My guides have given me an incredible amount of resilience, for which I am enormously grateful. I've gone through many different, often difficult, transitions in my life. It has been reassuring to feel that I had someone to turn to at those points, and also to feel that there's someone to go to *now*.

What I really want to say to people is that, although I was very blessed to be trained to connect with Spirit from an early age, I am no more 'special' than they are. Even if they feel alone, they are not. There are many beings who care about them and can be sources of love, joy, guidance and help in their lives.

photo credit: Colleen Brescia

'Yeats in the Magic Cottage' by Robert Moss

A FRIEND IN THE HOUSE OF TIME

by Robert Moss

Robert Moss is a world-renowned dream explorer, a shamanic counselor, a best-selling novelist and a former magazine editor and professor of ancient history at the Australian National University. His deep engagement with the Dreamtime springs from his early childhood in Australia, where he survived a series of near-death experiences, and has deepened through his visionary encounters with his Celtic ancestors and an ancient Native American woman of power. He teaches Active Dreaming – his pioneer synthesis of dreamwork and shamanism – all over the world and is the founder of a contemporary mystery school. His many books include 'Conscious Dreaming', 'Dreamgates', 'Dreaming True', 'Dreamways of the Iroquois' and 'The Dreamer's Book of the Dead'. He has also produced an educational DVD series, 'The Way of the Dreamer', demonstrating the core techniques of Active Dreaming.

The souls of enlightened men return to be schoolmasters of the living, who influence them unseen.

~ W. B. Yeats, 'Swedenborg, Mediums and the Desolate Places'

"What better guide to the Otherworld than a poet?"

The question was put to me as I embarked on writing *'The Dreamers Book of the Dead'* by a dead poet. I did not know, up to that moment, that a modern poet and his efforts to envision and create a Western Book of the Dead were going to figure as the central panel in the triptych my book was to become.

It seems to me that the true poet has two gifts that are vital for a reliable and effective psychopomp, or guide of souls. The first is the magic of words: passwords that open gates, and the power of naming that can bind or appease gatekeepers or even bring things into being. Shamans and initiates of all traditions know that poetic speech is important.

The second gift of the poet as Otherworld guide is that poets live by metaphor and are therefore friends of metamorphosis – inclined by their calling to shapeshift realities, averse to being penned in any routine concept of what is solid or 'real'.

What better guide to the Otherworld than a poet? The more I think about it, the more the answer seems clear: *none better*.

The question was put to me (as you may have guessed) by a poet – not one of my contemporaries, but a poet who died seven years before I was born. You know his name: William Butler Yeats.

Our conversations took place in a space that was outside the physical world, but quite real to me and to others who have learned – and been invited – to go there. It is a place like a library, inside a complex building I have come to call the House of Time. There are fierce guardians at the gates of the building. If they let you through, you may proceed through a number of rooms and passages to reach the library on the far side of a vast atrium under a dome with an oculus high above, a window onto a sky full of stars.

The librarian often appears to me in the form of a gentle, donnish Englishman of an earlier era, but when his form casts a shadow, it is that of a being with the head of an ibis bird.

This is, of course, a magic library. You can find a book on any subject that pleases you, and – as in the children's movie 'The Pagemaster' – when you open any book you may be transported into the scenes or dramas that it concerns. You can fight with pirates on the Spanish Main, or talk to Julius Caesar about how he dealt with a deadly accurate seeress advising hostile tribes, or study landscape gardening with Inigo Jones. Your call. Or, if you are brave enough, you may look at the book of your life, past and future, which may open into other life experiences. You may even be able to read the terms and conditions of the life contract you entered into before you came here.

Yes, the magic library is a 'made-up' place. But so is the Sears Building or the Eiffel Tower in the sense that they are products of thought and imagination. The magic library may outlast either of those physical structures. It has its own stability, now that generations of visitors have been here and contributed the energy of their own imagination and passion for study. It is a real place in the imaginal realm, which for initiates of many traditions is *more* real, not less real, than the physical plane. Here you are not confined to books that have been published in ordinary reality. You can examine books that might be written and published – maybe by you – and books that may never be caught on printed pages because their comments are too subtle.

I have led many group journeys to this locale, using shamanic drumming to help travelers switch frequency and move from the physical to the astral or imaginal plane. I can no longer recall whether I was thinking of Yeats on the day I met him in the library on one of these group journeys, or whether he made an entirely spontaneous appearance. Maybe it comes to the same thing (a shrink would no doubt say so). Either way, Yeats was no stranger. I had met him many times before, in dreams and reverie. On that particular visit to the library, while I was drumming for the group and helping to hold the space for what Yeats called 'mutual visioning', I found myself drawn from the ground level of the library up a corkscrew staircase.

I found Yeats lounging at a table on a mezzanine. He appeared as he might have in his prime, broad-shouldered, his hair flowing, gold-rimmed spectacles on the bridge of his patrician nose, wearing a loosely knotted silk bow tie and a three-piece light-coloured suit. I sat with him at the table and we had a mental conversation – no need to speak aloud here, and anyway libraries are meant to be quiet – about a whole range of things. I wondered whether Yeats could advise me on publishing problems I was having at that time. No sooner was the thought shaped in my head than he was introducing me to a pleasant man I had not noticed before. Maxwell Perkins. I was incredulous. I knew the name; it's proverbial among authors. 'Maxwell Perkins' means the author's editor, the one who will nurse you through your funks, save you from your creditors and your wildest fugues, and get you to keep on writing and deliver no matter what. I could not recall the details, but I knew that Max Perkins was reputed to have performed such services, and more, for such famously difficult authors as Thomas Wolfe and Ernest Hemingway.

'But you're dead'. This was a terrible faux pas, of course, even as a thought not spoken out loud. I hastened to redeem myself. I meant, of course, that the very idea of Maxwell Perkins had vanished, at least from the big-city publishing world that I knew. I thought, *where in the world am I going to find an editor like you?* Quick as thought, the message came back that I couldn't find what I was looking for. I needed to begin by cutting old publishing ties based on business calculations, and trust that as I opened myself to a new kind of relationship – centered on creative and personal affinity rather than money up front – I would draw the right editors to me. This was wonderful advice. When I found the courage to follow it fully, my life as a writer was transformed. I did not find Max Perkins in the physical world, but I found editors equally passionate and caring.

I had enjoyed a lifelong relationship with William Butler Yeats. I had always loved his poetry and have been able – since elementary school – to recite long passages from memory. I have had dreams and visions of Yeats and his circle for as long as I can remember. He was not only a marvelous poet; he was a Western magus, one of the leading figures in the Order of the Golden Dawn.

Yeats began to appear in my dreams at night as well as my daydreams and willed journeys in consciousness. In these dreams, I sometimes seemed to be living in his era – sometimes I seemed to meet Yeats in another reality altogether. Many years later, I dreamed I received a message from him inviting me to visit him at home. I was not sure where 'home' for Yeats might now be, but it did not appear to be in Ireland. In a subsequent vision, in that promising state of fluid awareness that sometimes develops in the hypnagogic zone between waking and sleep (or vice versa), I found myself floating above my body, up through the ceiling, and then through some kind of mesh that looked like an intricately woven fabric or netting. I was drawn up as if a traction beam had been turned on. I was under no compulsion, but I let myself rise on the intention of the one who was calling me. I had no doubt who that was. His lines were running through my head:

I shall arise and go there, and go to Innisfree...

Oh, yes, the early poem that has been quoted so often that Yeats himself got bored and irritated by it, vastly preferring the maturity and complexities of his later work. But its rhythms helped me travel, helped me swim through the subtle air. You don't reject a wing song that works (and indeed, Yeats wrote many).

I passed through many landscapes, perhaps whole worlds. They were separated by dividing partitions that were sometimes like cloud-banks, sometimes like membranes that stretched to let me through, and sometimes like woven fabric or netting. I came at last to what appeared to be a pleasant country cottage on a winding path. The flower beds were bright with colour. It seemed to me that, as I glanced around, the colours at the edge of my peripheral vision would change. Behind the cottage was a gentle river, and on the banks of the river, spires and towers that might have been those of Oxford. I began to drift along the path beside the river and saw another town beyond the first, this one quite certainly Italian; the architecture was that of the Quattrocento Florence or the Urbino that Yeats had loved and sometimes threatened to make his sanctuary from the critics and civil unrest in Ireland.

I was thrilled that scenes the poet's words had often conjured in my mind in lesser, drifting states of reverie were now so vividly and palpably available to explore. I hurried toward a palazzo worthy of a Medici that looked as if it has been constructed that day.

But again there was that tug of another's intention, and I allowed it to pull me back to the cottage. Did the cottage really have a thatched roof before, or was that detail changed while I was looking elsewhere?

Through the door, along a hall, and there was Yeats, sitting at a broad table covered with books and papers. Through the leaded glass window at his left hand I saw the cities along the river; they changed from one to another at the blink of an eye. I was excited to see that Yeats was continuing to study and to write. I wondered whether it hampered or helped his craft that his new work would not be published on earth. He was patient with me, letting me gradually awaken to the understanding that, from his new perspective, the most important form of publication might be to inspire others, to operate as one of those 'teachers of the thirteenth cone' he wrote about in *'A Vision'*.

He showed me a large blue crystal lying on his desk. He was most insistent that I should use this blue stone for creative inspiration and to open and focus the third eye of vision. This blue crystal was a place in which to see, and a connection between the two of us.

He gave me some personal guidance and an update on certain psychic crosscurrents involving individuals and groups that had been caught up in psychic battles in the past, in the time of the great rift within the Order of the Golden Dawn and in the darker times of the struggle between British magicians and the Nazi occultists. I asked Yeats where exactly we were.

He told me very precisely: "We are on the fourth level of the astral plane". It seemed this was a neighborhood essentially reserved for people of creative genius, for writers and artists and musicians.

I felt immensely privileged to have been given this tour of Yeats' environment. It was not clear to me whether he lived in the cottage alone; I was not shown the private rooms. I did feel quite certain that this Yeats was embarked on a vast new project, though its exact nature was not yet made clear to me.

Since I grew up on Homer and Virgil and struggled to read Dante in medieval Italian when I was a student, I was aware that poets are extraordinary guides to the Other Side, not least because they are masters of "magic words", often required for safe transit through these realms.

All the same, I was shocked when Yeats made a spontaneous appearance, on November 18, 2004, and proposed that I should let him be my guide to the Other Side. He suggested that my fieldwork should include interviewing quite a few dead people previously unknown to me – but not, perhaps, to him – on their post mortem experiences.

I was on the Connecticut shore on a blustery day in mid-November when Yeats made his proposal. I was leading an advanced group of dream travelers, by common agreement, on a group journey to the Library of the House of Time. I was drumming for the circle and watching over the group both physically and psychically, allowing myself to enter the astral locale quite deeply, but with no fixed personal agenda. I checked on our dream travelers. Some were meeting a favourite author, or consulting the librarian, or opening books and traveling into the worlds of knowledge and memory and adventure that each one contained. A couple of brave souls were inspecting the books of their own lives, looking into the future or to things beyond time – for knowledge of the soul's purpose, and the connectedness of one life in time to other lives in other times, and to personalities beyond time. Everything seemed to be going well. No need for me to intervene to help someone overcome their fears or open the vision gates wider.

So: my body is circling the room, my arm working the beater against the drum. My mind is tracking inside the dreamspace. And in that space, I feel the tug of a transpersonal intention. It is not coming from another member of our circle of thirty dream travelers. It is coming, quite specifically, from the figure who appears at the top of the spiral staircase that leads to an upper level of the library. It is Yeats, inviting me to join him up there, where he had previously introduced me to Maxwell Perkins (and others). It is here that he makes his astonishing proposal: "Virgil was Dante's guide to the Underworld, and I am willing to be yours."

The poet's manner is quite brisk. He sounds rather like a tour guide announcing the schedule we'll follow before a pub lunch. Next time we meet, Yeats advises me, we'll visit the place of an ancient king. Later, we may delve 'into the realm of Maeve'. Most certainly, I will need to interview quite a variety of people on their experiences of the afterlife, because these vary so greatly.

Yeats insists on the need for me to understand the importance of Ben Bulben, the 'bare' mountain under which he had wanted to be buried – in Drumcliffe churchyard – with the following inscription carved on his tombstone:

Cast a cold eye
On life, on death
Horseman, pass by

Those lines had been with me since childhood, so I was a little wary of what I was receiving. I have a vivid imagination, and it seemed rather likely that it was weaving from half-buried memories. The idea that Yeats could play the role for me that Virgil played for Dante was absolutely thrilling, but was this anything more than a pleasant fantasy?

The creator's answer moved through me: *Just let it play*. Enter the game, and let the results be judged on their own merits. Whether you are talking to the actual Yeats, or the part of yourself that so loves him, or some daimon or essence of personality that is using the mask of the poet is of secondary interest. What is primary is what you bring through.

Need I say that this offer was quite impossible to refuse?

No sooner had I accepted the offer than synchronicity came into play, as may be counted upon when emotions are running high and bold ventures are unfurling their sails.

I drove home from Connecticut and found a message waiting for me from a friend who had travelled in Yeats country in the west of Ireland the previous year. She had decided, for no obvious reason, to share with me her feeling that the barrows and faery mounds of Ireland had been used across the centuries as sites of shamanic initiation and interdimensional communication – even as launchpads for star travelers, coming or going.

I shivered with excitement as I recognised the link with Yeats' inaugural itinery, involving two ancient tumuli (a cold name for the Mounds of Wonder) in his own landscape. I hurried to research the names that Yeats had given me. My excitement deepened when I found that 'Queen Maeve's Tomb' – a huge cairn that has never been opened – is right opposite Ben Bulben, at whose foot is the churchyard where Yeats wished to be buried.

In Yeats' early book '*The Celtic Twilight*', I found a passage in which he says that there is a gate to the Otherworld in the side of Ben Bulben, *"famous for hawks"* – *"the mountain in whose side the square white door swings open at nightfall to loose the faery riders on the world."*

I called the friend who had sent me the message, out of the blue, about the cairns of Ireland. She described how, as she drove by Ben Bulben, her Irish guide had pointed out a strange shadow moving across the side of the mountain and declared that Yeats believed that this marked a door to the Otherworld of the Sidhe and the ancestors.

My encounters with Yeats guided me to dream at several ancestral sites in Ireland that were places of vision for him and portals to the realms of the ancestors and the Sidhe. My full report on these sites – and what was revealed there – must be reserved for another book.

When I shared some of my encounters with Yeats, [my friend] Elizabeth asked, "Is Yeats available to lead anyone through these realms or is he *your* guide? I would like to know how to connect with Yeats or someone like him. Or is it more a matter of the Other Side contacting us, and we just have to be ready?"

I responded: "I think mutual affinity is the key. That, and being ready to do the work and making oneself available to the work whenever one is called. And recognizing, above all, what entertains our guides and makes them want to spend time with us."

I recalled that I had read Yeats aloud for most of my life. I have written poems of my own under his influence and have always had the sense (or memory) of a shared connection with a magical order in Britain in the period between the world wars.

I remembered many, many dreams and visions of the poet and his circle. "I feel I have been dreaming of Yeats all my life." As I spoke, the vision returned to me of a radiant Otherworldly woman who has also appeared to me to invite me and guide me on journeys into ever deeper and higher realms. I call her simply the Blue Lady.

Elizabeth commented, "Ah, so there is another very important reason for honoring our dreams – to let our guides know we take them seriously and want more!"

When we go dreaming, we step through the curtain of ordinary reality and wake up in a deeper world. Through the play of synchronicity, the powers of the deeper world push a finger through the veil to prod or tickle us awake.

CHAPTER 3

THE ARTIST'S WAY

Music gives soul to the universe, wings to the mind, flight to the imagination, and life to everything.
~ Plato

Where the spirit does not work with the hand there is no art.
~ Leonardo da Vinci (1452-1519)

Art is an expression of the creative energy of the cosmos. It is everywhere. Its most breathtaking works can be found in the natural world – a sky washed with brilliant hues of orange, pink and red shot with purple, the undulating curves of a hillside as the sunset illuminates it 'just so', a spider's web on a frosty morning, sparkles on a turquoise ocean, the iridescent hues of a dragonfly's wings, a clear starlit night… The same creative energy is also expressed in the works of *all* artists – be they painters, dancers, writers, poets or musicians.

When a great creative idea comes into our heads, we feel really pleased with ourselves – we own it and call it 'mine'… but perhaps our best inspirations are not 'ours' after all, but are suggested and encouraged by the invisible presence of Spirit.

We often label a person a 'genius' if he or she produces a fantastic new invention or wonderful piece of music, yet even the most famous of these creations are often communications from Spirit, using the so-called 'genius' as a channel – for example, the poet and artist William Blake claimed to have received artistic guidance from his departed brother Robert, and Robert Louis Stevenson wrote *'The Strange Case of Dr. Jekyll and Mr. Hyde'* after spirits he called 'Brownies' gave him the central idea for the story in a dream. Beethoven composed a canon after falling asleep in his carriage on the way to Vienna – on waking, he couldn't recall any of it, but he returned the next day in the same carriage, resumed his dream-journey (this time while remaining awake), and was able to transcribe it.

Many people in this day and age would much rather have you believe that they are the sole proprietors of their creations. People who become famous rarely acknowledge that they are merely a vessel through which 'their' ideas and inspiration flow. It was refreshing that John Frusciante – high-profile musician and guitarist of the Red Hot Chili Peppers – released a statement on the band's website in March 2006, stating that their latest album, 'Stadium Arcadium' was a product of a year-and-a-half of channeling 'messages from beyond'.

Music and sound have always fascinated me because (unless it is a recording) it is purely of the moment. It flows from and to invisible spaces. Unlike most other forms of art, it is not something tangible you can physically see or hold onto (again, with the exception of a CD). Everyone knows that just one word can have a lasting effect on a person. Sound vibrations are very powerful… they have the ability to transform and create change at a very deep level. We are conduits of sound, yet the energy and intent of its source comes from a mysterious place.

Indeed, the more you open up and allow energy to flow *through* you, rather than come *from* you, the more you align with the creative powers of the universe and the more wonderful those creations will be. In my own experience as an 'arty person' – I sing and play music, draw, paint and write (among other things) – I know that whenever 'I' *try* to create something wonderful, it just doesn't happen. But if I stay out of my own way and simply be open to it, it can spontaneously flow. It is a *natural* process that cannot be coerced or ordered to perform 'at will'.

Interestingly, the times in my life when I have experienced this creative flow at its most intense were when I gave birth to my children. I felt like a straw and that there was a huge balloon of energy trying to pass through the top of my head. It was the most overwhelming and powerful feeling I have ever experienced in my life. I intuitively knew I had to open and 'surrender' myself to this energy, which was so much bigger than I. Giving birth is the ultimate illustration of the creative process, but when we sing, dance, or create anything, we open ourselves up and surrender to *the same source of energy.* Ultimately, by our very existence we are all individual creative expressions of the universe.

When I create something beautiful and somebody tells me how wonderful it is, I say, "Thank you", and I pass the thanks on to the Source, my spirit helpers and allies, as, in truth, all my creations are 'co-created'. I believe in giving credit where credit is due. Although I'm responsible for my part in 'birthing things' – for transforming creative energy into physical form – I do not 'own' them… they are a gift from Spirit to the world. These creations would not exist in all their beauty without the intervention of Spirit (*especially* the writing of this book!) and I'm very thankful for their assistance.

The following experiences are from artists, writers and musicians working consciously and creatively with Spirit to affect the positive spiritual development of others…

painting by Patrick Gamble

A BRUSH WITH DREAMTIME

Patrick Gamble

Born in Cornwall in the U.K, Patrick was a builder by trade until a spiritual experience changed his life. He now works full time as a professional psychic artist and is also a registered healer. His unique and inspiring work acts as a catalyst – helping others consciously connect to those aspects of life that are usually unseen and ignored.

Thirteen years ago I was an atheist. I kept my life simple. I believed that you're born, you live, you die and that's it… nothing more. I became this way from observing life. Because of all the trouble and strife in the world, I was convinced that there couldn't possibly be anything more to it.

One day at work, a box of junk came along by accident (that's how I viewed it at the time). It contained a canvas and other bits and pieces. My immediate thought was, 'I'll never use that because I can't paint'. So I took it home, put it in the garage and forgot about it.

Some time later, I was having a 'clear out', and loaded my trailer with rubbish. As I emptied this box, my eyes were drawn to three tubes of paint. I picked them up and suddenly had an overwhelming urge to put oil onto canvas. In my builder's kit, I had some white spirit and small brushes that I used for painting behind radiators – and that's what I used. I sat in my kitchen and began to paint…

After two hours, although it only felt like ten minutes, I propped the canvas up to take a look at what I had painted *(see page 97)*. There was a very elderly gentleman looking back at me! I wasn't comfortable with the face. It was a very strong image – a very serious face, almost frowning at me. It was very positive, but it didn't mean anything to me. It was later that I learned that this man is one of my guides.

I can't remember painting it. The only way I can explain it is when you're driving along in a car and you can't remember driving the last five or six miles… the painting was very much the same.

I didn't understand how it got there and I didn't *want* to understand how it got there. I didn't even know what guides were! Why would I? I wouldn't have even wanted to know. I guess, being truthful, it was quite frightening. So the picture was put away.

Until that day, I had no sight of spirit but the experience opened a doorway where this ability gradually developed. I began to experience unfamiliar sensations… I would feel 'shivers', like there was a draught in the house, and I would go round checking all the doors and windows, but they were shut. I also began to see what I call 'flickers and shadows' – out of the corner of my eye, I would see something move very fast, and think, 'Did I just see a mouse, or no?' It's like when a bird flies past the window and by the time you look, it's gone and you dismiss it. I would have a feeling that someone had just walked past my window and I waited for a knock at the door… but it never came. It was nothing more than that, but over a period of time I experienced too much of it and began to wonder what was going on.

I talked to my immediate family who gave me some support on it. My partner at the time believed that there was more to life, so when this started to happen she encouraged me to buy some oil paints.

After a while, I began to have dreams and would awake from a restless sleep with the urge to paint. Not really knowing or planning anything, I would put colour onto a canvas and images would appear. It was really as simple as that. At the time, I restricted painting because I was busy with building work and I didn't really understand, so it's been a very gradual process.

I began to meet mediums and they gave me information about my guides. The first time I was told something I thought, 'Hmm'... Then someone else told me the same thing and I thought, 'That's odd'. Six months may pass, a year might go by, and a different person would tell me something very similar again. So that's how I began to know...

My guide's name is John – without him, I wouldn't be painting. He is an artist from London in the 1800's and is the one who works through me when I paint, although he refuses to work in anything other than oils... I *have* tried using other artistic medium, but he refuses to come through!

John himself has never been painted. He gave me a lot of struggles with this, because, although I 'see', I couldn't 'see' him. He stands to my right, slightly outside my focal point – so I can't paint him, because I don't have his detail. For me to be able to paint John, he would have to show himself to me. I have asked him to, but he won't! This really used to bother me. It filled me with a little bit of fear for quite a while, because I used to think, 'What on earth does he look like? Is he disfigured? Would his physical appearance frighten me?'

To this day, John has not stepped forward. But now it doesn't matter... it's not important to me anymore. Regardless of what he looked like, I'd put my arms around him.

As a guiding energy, John is fantastic because he's my best mate and he's also my workmate. To me, the relationship is no different than the one I have with my mate Roger, who's a building mate of mine. I treat them both the same. There's very little difference whether it's spiritual or physical.

I don't mix words when I'm talking with John – I talk very bluntly to him, because I have to be true to myself. By being true to myself, the greater my connection is to him. As I grow older and develop further, I'm bound to have struggles with myself as a person – I struggle with my weaknesses… everyone has struggles somewhere with one's self – but I have to remember that I can only be myself.

That very first painting was actually a portrait of one of my other guides – he is very wise and has an air of determination and philosophy. He's the boss… the main man who oversees the others – a bit like the head teacher of a school. Depending on what you need to learn, certain teachers teach specific things. Some may leave the school and new ones will take their place. The head will interview a new teacher, see what he's made of and decide who comes into his school and teaches. In a way, they are like guides to your guides!

I had three guides for a long time, which I thought was plenty enough, to be honest with you! – but I acquired another one, a medieval knight, about 12 months ago. I also have a Native American guide. One stands in each corner. This gives me structure, which is very important to me because, for one, I'm a builder – I've grown up with it. I can't do away with it completely because it's part of me. Structure is like building a house – it's like putting scaffolding up… it's there to give us some form of help, assistance and support. If there is no structure then it really becomes quite pointless.

Each of my guides has their job to do. Whether you are aware of it or not, we all have a team of energy. Each person does a specific job. They can all overlap, of course, but specialize in certain areas. Working together, we get the job done!

I ask many times a day for guidance and help. I feel it's very important to remember to ask. Sometimes I even *demand* what I want from them! Being firm and direct becomes very positive. There's no point in being wishy-washy – I have to get myself across the country, turn up and be ready to work. Over the years, I've painted thousands of spirit pictures for people all over the world. I have also painted around 150 huge canvases. Because I make this effort, I need the same from them. They respond by sending signs, but I don't see a great vision in the sky that says, "GO THAT WAY!" I might ask for a sign, walk straight past it and not even realise until a week later! We all miss these signs at times because we're not always so 'tuned in', but we have to keep asking. If we don't ask, we don't get.

Sometimes people say, "Oh, you're brave to give up your day job! Did you go through some trauma coming into this?" and I reply that I wasn't brave at all… I had nothing to lose. My life was fantastic. I had a wonderful life – I was married with a beautiful son and we'd just moved into a new house, so I didn't have any trauma. My test came with spirit five years ago, after I was already involved with this…

Five or six years ago, I was asked to go to Canada to paint – a trip that took two years to organize and plan. When I got there, I found that people wanted proof of life after death… the only way I could give that was to paint a relative, a loved one. The trip was very successful, although I couldn't reach everyone. Sometimes it's just like that.

I was only away for three weeks and two days, but, when I returned, everything in my life had changed – my wife had an affair, it was a struggle to see my son, I lost a beautiful home and I was in debt, which I'd never been in my life. All I had was six bin-bags full of clothes. To add insult to injury, I'd always had long hair and went to the hairdressers for a trim but they cut all my hair off! People didn't recognise me… *I* didn't even recognise myself!

I felt really let down, so I told Spirit, "On yer bike, I've had enough of you! I'm going back to just being an atheist again and getting on with life!" I handed in my notice… I'd had enough of the job. I was really struggling, and that's when John pulled in – he pulled in very, very close and I felt *his* hurt and pain. And I really do feel he felt mine.

After a period of time, I said to John, "Look, I've made a decision. I'm going to paint full time." It was almost like a contract. I've never worked again building, I've been painting ever since. Until then, I was building full time and only did a little bit of painting. I could have gone back to building… even now, I could make more money building, but I choose to do this instead because I feel that this is my direction. On saying that, if the work stopped, which is possible because I depend on this team of energy to be able to do this, then I could go back to building – no problem!

I'm only able to do the work I do now because I don't have the responsibility and commitment of looking after a family. I can devote my time to this, whereas before I would not have. I did consider that perhaps Spirit had manipulated the situation… it did cross my mind. But now I believe that everyone has a pathway. My son has his pathway. I thought my wife was my soul mate, we'd known each other a long time and we had everything in common, but she's also got her pathway. It's taken me a long time to accept this because I was full of anger, but that's gone now. I wish her all the best in the world.

This is where we learn spiritually. We don't learn through the easy times! We cannot. It's the same for everyone. That's why we all have these challenges… they pull you apart, but you come through it a different person. We get disorientated and we know we've changed, and that makes us even more frightened because we don't even know who we are anymore. But we always have to be aware that we only have the pieces, and it's the bigger picture that matters. I have come to believe when one's heart weeps for what it has lost, the spirit smiles for what it has gained.

As I began to 'see' energy, I also started to perceive auras and Spirit. The essence of Spirit is an energy of being, which we all have. It's *not* a form and shape. We're asking it to take a form or shape to give us some understanding. It's very hard for Spirit to show themselves. They have to take on a physical image in order to make their presence known.

Most of the time, a picture starts with color, like an aura, around the image. Sometimes this is delicate and may alter in appearance, through ageing or sometimes even different characters. If this happens I must go with these changes. It's like looking into a still pool of water… you can clearly see your reflection until someone drops a pebble and your image moves. The bigger the pebble, the bigger the ripple. I have to work with that movement and sometimes it's very difficult. It's like having a conversation on a mobile phone that starts breaking up – so I move around and try to get the strongest signal. It's trying to keep the connection going… sometimes it's like a candle flickering in the wind.

To see an image is a language. Spirit is trying to give me an understanding. If it can show me a strong image, then that will tell me something. If it shows me a very gentle image, that would tell me something else. I've learned to 'read' it – to get a sense of feeling from it.

I've got to be careful that I don't mis-read the message… but sometimes I do! That's what makes it hard. I try to understand the message and make my message clear, so that you know what I'm talking about. It's like having 3 people in the room that all talk different languages and we're trying to get right down to the nitty-gritty of it all.

Part of the message is to say 'Hey – hang on, there is a positive here.' Everything has a positive, but when life presents itself with a number of negatives, sometimes it's hard to see the positive. We just become blinded by it.

I am conscious of what is going on around me when I'm painting, and I do look at the painting when I'm working. I see the image above the person who has come for a sitting with my own eyes – it has to physically appear. If it doesn't appear then I won't paint anything. This doesn't happen often – it may happen a couple of times a year, but it does happen. I think it keeps me in place. It makes me very aware that I depend on my guides, which is very humbling. It makes me pray and gives a great respect to the process. I don't take it for granted… I daren't.

People can be quite nervous about having a painting done. When someone comes for a sitting, I firstly say a prayer to ask for permission, help and guidance.

Everybody carries an abundance of energy, that's the truth of it – and I mean *so* much. We open up a doorway and paint whoever shows themselves. I have no influence on who comes through… I just sit and paint. Animals, family members, guides and helpers can show themselves.

Of course, some people want pictures of their loved ones. A mother may ask me to paint her son who has died, which is a *huge* responsibility. I feel her expectation, yet I know there is a chance that her son won't be there. Why can I paint a child for someone and not for another? I nearly stopped painting because of this.

Families can be very complicated! There are a number of issues with painting family members – there's a loving, joyful element to it, but there's also a difficult side…

A lady once came for a sitting. I had already started painting, when she suddenly said, "I don't mind who I have, but I *don't* want my mother!" When the painting was finished, I turned it around… and it *was* mum – the one person she didn't want! I guess maybe mum had given her a difficult life, so she had come through to say, 'Look, forgive me'. It *is* a healing process, but it's quite a shock for someone to know that a particular spirit is around, when that's the last person they want!

All the visions that materialize into finished paintings are for a purpose. There is a personal connection between the painting and the individual, which can relate strongly to the subject and the feelings that took place when it was being created. Many times people have felt spiritually uplifted and encouraged, with a feeling of well-being. This has encouraged me to experience more of the spiritual, opposed to the materialistic, side of life.

At first, when people came for a sitting, I would say very little… basically just, “Sit down” and then, “Here’s your picture”. That was it – there was nothing else, because I had nothing else to give.

About 4 years ago, I started to include ‘readings’ in a sitting, using cards based on a portion of spiritually inspired paintings I have produced over the last eight years. These images came to me either in dream state, as visions or through my meditations. Some of these paintings have been painfully difficult and a real struggle. The paintings have meanings – some of them mean something to me personally, and other people have helped to interpret those that I didn’t understand.

I ask the person who has come for a painting to shuffle the cards, keeping them face down and to intuitively choose six cards without looking at them. Then they can turn over the remaining deck and choose six more. The first six cards represent the subconscious, intuitive and spiritual… and the second six represent the logical, conscious and ‘worldly’ approach. It creates a balance – because I ‘read’ between those two sets of cards… the space in the middle is what I’m trying to understand.

The painting of your guide also gives me some understanding. How much, I don’t know… some paintings can be very hard to read. Sometimes there is really so little connection to the painting, that it may come just from the cards. It’s similar to reading something I’ve written and then painting a picture in my mind from those words, except it’s the other way round… my challenge is to take that feeling and put it into words. This is a skill I’ve had to learn.

I say to people, “If you don’t understand what I’m talking about – tell me.” It’s important for me because a lot of our past and a lot of people in our past we don’t really remember. That’s why sometimes we have to speak to mum, dad and grandparents and it can be very hard, because those people aren’t even around for us to ask anymore. A lot of knowledge is lost. A lot of it is also buried inside ourselves.

I measure my life like beads on a string – each bead is a memory of events and people in my life. If I really focus on that memory, then I can take it back to a certain year. The smaller beads represent the memories that we've got to think very hard to remember anything about… so much is forgotten and buried under all these layers. That's why you're not going to recognise all of what is said in a reading. If you tell me you can't recognise it, at least it makes me try to look harder, so you have something more to work with and work upon.

I feel that a lot of people are 'shut down'. They don't want people to look at their personal lives. Our culture wants to make us look 'over there' to learn – to discover… I say you've got to look to yourself as a person, yet sometimes it's the last place we want to go. Sometimes, even when I'm leading workshops, a person might be doing something they don't want anyone to know about, and they're frightened. They don't know what's going to come up. Respect of a person's space is very important, because I may touch on something – but I am sensitive to that. That person will *know* what I'm saying without me telling everyone else in the room what's going on!

We don't need help when things are great. That's not to say that I can't paint guides around you when things are terrific, but people often come and have a sitting because they're searching. We're all human. We're all learning and discovering.

Painting has made me more aware of color. I have come to realise that color is a medicine – it helps us to harmonize with our natural rhythms and remedies and to become more balanced. The eyes are a gateway to color-healing. It goes back to nature, because the colors of the oils on the canvas are taken from the colors of the earth.

Color is strong, powerful stuff… it has a great influence on us. It's a known medical fact that if you're placed in a red room, it will raise your blood pressure and a blue one will lower it. If you have a blue filter and a red filter and you put a glass of water on each one, the 'blue' water will stay purer longer. Red can be seen as a very passionate or aggressive color – it's an energy color, so you've got to be careful with it because it can be overpowering. Blue is softer… it's gentle. If I've got a job to do, I don't want a nice 'powder blue'… what good is *that?* But it's just what I need when I've had a tough old day and I want to sit down and try to relax.

All colors can be 'felt'. Some colors work for us – although we can be physically attracted to certain colors, their energy doesn't always work for us. If you place a colored cloth over your shoulder (not into your hands, because you'll be distracted by the texture of the fabric!) and close your eyes, you can 'feel' the effect of the color – sometimes a favorite color will make you feel physically sick. Healing is the same – you 'feel' something. You can't always explain it, but it's an energy that you are experiencing.

My life has totally changed. I can't say my life has become very peaceful because of this, because it hasn't – it's become very challenging. One part of it is exciting and one part of it is very demanding… it's both sides of a coin. I have mixed feelings on it, if I'm truthful.

A lot of the answers, they're in tomorrow. We want answers *now* – we want to be told what to do, or what not to do… but you've got to walk your life, because that's where your answers are. You've got to keep moving forward. It's very, very important for everyone.

I don't class myself as a religious person, but I feel that everyone has their truth. Faith is like a truth. Religion is like one's own truth. Whatever my life is, I don't know how long things are going to last. I'm dependent on John and the rest of the gang. Because I'm not in charge of it, I have to trust.

Ultimately, my job is to strengthen the awareness of the influences that are around us. Some people are very aware of their own energy and what's around them and I confirm that it's there – and, at other times, I introduce the awareness of a particular guiding energy around you. *Know* it and call upon it to assist and help.

photo credit: Denise Schwartz-Logan

SPIRITUAL FRIENDS, FRIENDLY SPIRITS

by Jessica Macbeth

Jessica (or Jesa as she is also known) has almost completed seventy trips around the sun, during which time she has practiced as a hands-on healer, medium, spiritual counselor and teacher, Coyote poetess, fabulist, wordsmith and storyteller, and doting grandmother. She is the author of 'Faeries Oracle' (illustrated by Brian Froud), 'Moon Over Water', 'Sun Over Mountain', and many articles, essays, and short stories. She is currently working on more books on Faery, healing, and natural magic.

Jesa enjoys gardening in the costal forest of Western Washington State, observing miracles everywhere she goes, grandmothering, and dropping pre-blessed pennies for people to find (thus winning themselves a fortunate day). She is presently being trained by the Green Woman and Coyote, with the aid of many others, and is a Zen Pagan – Zen as in 'a Buddhist follower of the eight-fold path', and Pagan in the original sense of 'arising from the earth'.

If she doesn't get everything all done on this earth tour, Jesa hopes to return as a silver birch dryad on a Scottish hill, a mama raccoon in a cool northern forest, a giant sequoia tree high in the Sierra Nevada mountains, or as her granddaughter's granddaughter.

From my earliest memories, I was aware of the presence of otherworldly beings. I believe that most, perhaps even all, children are – but we are taught to disregard that awareness and then we forget. I wasn't very good at learning that particular lesson, although I did learn to keep quiet about it!

I can't remember a time when there were not presences available to share and play with and to act as mentors. I can, however, clearly remember a powerful moment of affirmation for my understanding of the world…

When I was two years old, we lived on my grandparents' farm in Oklahoma not far from the then-small town of Stillwater. When the new film *'The Wizard of Oz'* came to town, we all went to see it. You know the place in the film where the farmhouse lands in Oz and Dorothy opens the door and suddenly the screen is flooded with color? I stood up in my seat and shrieked! I'd never seen a film with color before and I was overwhelmed by this unexpected and entirely unforeseen blaze of glory. For me, this was an absolute confirmation that there *was* magic in the world, and nothing has ever been able to change my mind about this magic. Now, you might think that is very mundane, but to me now, it confirms that we are given what we need when we need it. We can use it or not, but it is there… just as this sense of clear magic was there for me through all years of early childhood, even though people in general were so busy trying to teach children that it did not exist.

Over the years, I have had so many invisible friends in my life – faeries, nature spirits, human spiritual guides, and others. When I was healing and counseling professionally, I also came into contact with a great variety of guides and the spiritual friends of my students and clients.

Now that I am more or less retired, the Fae have pretty much taken over, saying that the present need is to focus on rediscovering and growing into my own true nature. They have a way of teaching and helping that is very joyful. That joyfulness is also something they are trying to help me with – the capacity of always being aware of the bedrock of being (which is joy), no matter what is going on at the surface of the world.

At this moment, I seem to be primarily under the supervision of the Green Woman, the Faery Godmother, the Sage, Coyote, the Bees, and Raccoon. The Green Woman has long been a mentor, and with her feisty, frisky, not-old-not-young nature, she is like an elder sister teaching me about the nature of process and how nothing is really a thing, but everything is a process within other processes. We earth beings all fit together, though our eyes are not always big enough to see that. From her, I'm learning what growth, in all its phases, including spiritual, is really about.

Coyote teaches fun (one of the more important things in life), reminds me that I'm not always as clever as I might like to think, and is a very protective and able guardian. The Bees know the news. Raccoon is wise and busy and playful and, along with Coyote, a bit of a trickster. She knows when to stand her ground, when to give way, and when to dash up the nearest tree. She also understands about a lesson I'm being forced by age to learn. She would like me to be a better student!

The Sage has been teaching me a lot about human relationships and the wisdom to be learned from them. He has been very patient and loving about this, and we often sit on a hill, under a tree, or beside the water as I learn to unravel some of the knots in my thinking and see certain human processes more clearly. He also has a way of putting his head in one hand, closing his eyes, and saying, "Are we *really* going to go through this again?" that brings me up short to think, reconsider, and to look past the obvious in whatever is happening. And when I don't get the message right away, this patience and love eventually carries me through.

Most of my guides are mentors and friends, regardless of the origins of the relationship. We have a very relaxed, informal community here with many beings popping in and out as they feel it is appropriate or fun to do so. Sometimes, they bring a friend who visits briefly and, sometimes, they stay for a long time, becoming a valued part of the family.

There is pretty much a constant interaction with the spiritual realm, even when I'm around other people and doing 'mundane' things. They are always there, frequently commenting on or calling my attention to something I might be missing. But, in addition to that, there are times when we sit down together and focus on some sort of inner journey (see my book '*Sun Over Mountain*') for a deeper communication. And of course, meditation time every day is something we share, even if none of us are talking during it – or at least we aren't *supposed* to be talking.

My spiritual friends are very big on cultivating what they call 'deep listening' combined with an open heart. Silent meditation is one of the easiest to learn keys to this. They nearly always recommend the practice of simple, one-pointed meditation for others as well as a key to opening the doors to the unseen realms. This is so important to them that they actually arranged, with some help from human friends, for a publisher to ask me to write a book on meditation. To give you some idea of how amazing this is, I had never written a book before. I knew the publisher as a friend, but wasn't thinking of writing a book. One of my students, unbeknownst to me, took some of my class handouts on meditation to him, saying that he should get me to write a book on it. He did, but I know who was *really* behind the whole process.

The Fae really do think this is very important. If we can't be still, we can't listen, and most of us have never learned to stop babbling in our own minds. When we first try to meditate, we can feel overwhelmed by that babble. It takes a lot of practice just to be quiet, but people who do take the time and effort to practice it find that it makes a huge difference in all aspects of life, especially in our openness to inspiration and insight and intuition – the three 'I-eye-ayes' of spiritual communication.

The messages that spirit sends through synchronicities, dreams and visions are often the ones that I most need to hear but am not listening closely enough to clearly hear in everyday life. Their oft-repeated motto is that we just need to, "*Be Awake and Aware*" of what is happening. Sometimes I'm not sufficiently present in the here and now to get it, and then they really have to whack me over the head somehow.

My spiritual friends have always insisted that the practice of any kind of creative activity (from cooking to art to gardening to writing to... well... anything) helps us to develop in many ways. We become more aware, we see more, we understand more as a result of doing creative things. They prompt, they provide inspiring ideas, and they even suggest new approaches to old activities, new ways of doing the old things. Creativity *is* magic – *real* magic, *natural* magic… magic that is available to all of us.

The important thing, they say, about creativity is NOT the result. They don't actually care if we produce beautiful paintings or write epics that will live forever, or cook absolutely astonishingly delicious meals. What they do care about is the *process* – the thoughts, insights, and inspirations that pass through the mind while the hands are busy. Creativity is often about seeing old things in new (and sometimes surprising) ways. Also, it is about letting the subtle energy of the universe flow freely through us, just as the practice of healing or channeling does. Like meditation, creative activity is one of the main keys to the door of spiritual communication.

In fact, doing something creative, simply responding to whatever inspiration we have, *is* communication with spirit – that of our own spirit (or our own true nature, as they would say) and the spirits of others. *Go for it!*

As far as their influence in my life is concerned, I could not manage without them. It's that simple. They have literally saved my life more than once. I've been in accidents where none of us 'should' have survived, yet we all did. And once, when I was sitting for a time on Death's doorstep with illness while the doctors shook their heads, one of the Fae brought me a cup of scintillating, foaming medicine. It had the most astonishing effect on me, fizzing and sparkling through my entire body and aura, and right away even the humans around me could see that something had changed… just like a miracle. I smile at that phrase now. 'Miracles' are one of my favorite things to watch. If you have a noticing eye, you will see little ones and big ones often and everywhere.

Every day is made more productive, more joyful, and just plain old better for their companionship and guidance. 'Expectant gratitude' is a part of my meditation practice, and there is so much to be grateful about.

photo credit: Keven Erickson

THE UNIVERSAL ENGINE ROOM

The Barefoot Doctor

Barefoot Doctor is Stephen Russell, maverick expert in Taoist techniques for remaining sane in a mad, mad world, with a flare for color, warmth and controversy in imparting his information that has won him worldwide acclaim, as well as occasional opprobrium. Author of 11 books, he has a daily online wisdom-busking platform which attracts over 4 million hits monthly and, as well as doing one-man spiritual stand-up theatre shows around the world spends most of his time now making music with his band, Barefoot Prophet.

I was about six years old when it happened... I was lying on my bed one afternoon watching the clouds go by, when I spontaneously found myself hearing a deep chanting sound multiplied by at least ten million and way deeper than normal human hearing can detect. I knew that I wasn't imagining it, but I also knew that I was the only one in the house that could hear it. In my frame of terminology at the time, I knew it was 'God talking'.

My later interpretation of the experience was that I was hearing the sound of the engine room of the universe. I couldn't formulate it at the time, but I feel that this divine presence, which is essentially made of sound, was telling me that my role in the world is to help everyone remember, possibly through the use of sound, that we all have that connection.

I suspect that all children are connected to this divine presence, unless their parents distract them from it, which (unfortunately) usually happens and did for me. I don't know why that connection wasn't damaged in me at an earlier age, but it just seemed to be there. Hearing this sound was the confirmation of this presence and was a big formative moment for me, which isn't to say that afterwards I became a 'weird spiritual kid' or anything… I was actually quite raucous. In fact, I was a real little yob in some ways – I used to love fighting and I was constantly getting into trouble. This, in turn, led me to martial arts. My dad introduced me to Aikido when I was 11 because a friend of his was studying with an old Japanese guy who took me on and, as well as Aikido, taught me how to meditate and how to heal people by channeling *ki* (energy) through my palms.

Between the ages of about eight to 19, I sensed I'd lost my conscious connection with the presence and would find myself wondering, "What was that thing I used to have? I used to have this 'thing'… this relationship, this 'thing'… where's it gone?" It was the connection to the source of that sound, not the sound itself, which was important to me. It wasn't until I was 24 in the mountains of New Mexico that I got the key to unlock the door to wherever that sound had come from when I was six years old…

After travelling around the world for about six months looking for 'the spot', I found myself at Miami airport feeling utterly disillusioned and booked myself a flight back to England. I was about to go through the metal detector and board my flight, when I felt the presence of, and clearly saw in my mind's eye, a Native American with a full clichéd feathered headdress standing behind me. He put his hands on my right shoulder and physically pulled me round, as if to say, "Don't go". (At this point, I have to qualify this by saying that I am one of the biggest skeptics on the planet when it comes to this sort of thing – if I was reading this story, the chances are that I'd now be thinking, 'Oh, what a fucking wanker!' but I really, truly promise you that I felt this presence and the physical tug on my shoulder). I couldn't resist the pull, the feeling was that strong, so I turned round, walked back through the metal detector, forfeited the money I had paid for the flight and walked out of the airport. I followed what he was telling me to do and that's when I ended up back in New Mexico, where I stayed for four years. I sensed that the same presence had been urging me to leave London in the first place a few months earlier – I'd hear it whispering, 'go, go, go…' Although I hadn't perceived him as visually in my mind initially, in retrospect I feel that it was the same being.

My whole life transformed and changed in New Mexico, and I became who I am – I began the process of dropping into my skin on all levels, from the spiritual down. From then on, I started crystallizing the connection again, fully and consciously. It was still quite a novelty and I had to use my discipline, as I still do, to keep it active – but I got it back. I retrieved my connection through various methods, one of which was experimenting with healing sound, which is why music and working with sound remains my greatest passion and driving force (for my sins).

I would be being lazy if I said I'm a Taoist because I find that a bit of a silly, limiting concept, really, calling myself an anything, but I've found that the Taoist template is the one that seems to fit me the most comfortably. I've also had quite a deep long-term relationship with Buddhism, as well as studying Kabbalah and Western Occultism. I lived with the Native Americans in Taos (New Mexico) and took on the model of the Great Spirit and the way of animism, and I've done yoga for many years as well, so I've also got a bit of a Hindu thing going on too… I'm a bit of a 'spiritual libertine' in that respect.

I practice Taoist techniques on a daily basis – I do Tai Chi and a series of Taoist exercises called Red Dragon Yoga, at the end of which I do one or another form of Taoist sitting meditation. At some level I believe that wherever the Taoists got their techniques from it was not from this planet – and that I got it from there, too. I get a sense that I was in that place, wherever that was… right back in the origins. Because it does seem like coming home every time I drop into the zone and always has ever since I first spotted two guys doing Tai Chi in the park back in the early 70's and, though I'd never seen or heard of it before, knew instinctively that I had to take it up. As soon as I did, it was like stirring an ancient memory. It was the same when I studied acupuncture – it was like reconnecting with something I already knew. My teacher often remarked at the alacrity with which I was able to soak up the information – like a duck to water.

During the 80's when I was well into astral travel and channeling, I seemed to be receiving guidance for quite a long time from a being composed of blue light, looking quite like those statues of the pharaohs, who I assumed to be Isis, or at least some presence from the Sirius star system. Apparently I wasn't the only one – there were many people experiencing telepathic connection with what they felt was Sirius or some planet somewhere around Sirius at the time. Though I respect these peak experiences, I also take them with a pinch of salt – but that's because I'm from the holy hills of North London and it's the way round these parts.

So, while I do feel that my interest in Taoism and eastern philosophies has to do with past lifetimes, I don't dwell on that. Mind you, on a good day, when I'm practicing Tai Chi and am so 'in the zone' that the Tai Chi is doing itself canceling me out altogether for a brief and welcome respite from myself, it seems as if I've been taken over by the presence of some ancient Taoist master or other, who managed to attain spiritual immortality (the attainment of which is the underlying promise of Taoist practice) and decided to jump into my body to enjoy the Tai Chi form that day. He seems to coach me from within, correcting posture, reminding me of basic principles and revealing secrets of the art. It's like having two people in me at the same time.

My belief about spirit guides is that everyone has one, at least. Even those who don't believe they have a spirit guide get guided. I have no idea where they come from… I don't care. What I *do* know is that when I ask my spirit guides to be there for guidance that it works for me, and I believe it works for other people, too. Whether we're all deluded or not doesn't matter, because it does work.

It would be arrogant to the point of utter ignorance to assume that the only beings that exist are the ones that we can see with the naked eye. We can only see a very small part of the spectrum and so it stands to reason that there are energies and forms that are too refined, vibrating at too high a frequency for us to see. On the other hand I'm sure that, just like people, there are some pretty stupid ones out there, so I get the sense that some discernment is required. Maybe people who go mad are following the guidance of really silly spirit guides… who knows?

My belief is that the whole universe is a unified field of consciousness, energy and love, which manifests itself as everything we see around us, including each of us as individuals, and therefore connects us all on a deep level. We're here playing this game of 'hide and seek', where the goal of the game is to see beneath the surface of everyday reality to be one with that field of consciousness that we are all an expression of.

I think that we create reality with our thoughts. If I was being more precise, I'd say that the Creator, the Tao, Unified Field of Consciousness – call it what you want – is creating reality with it's thoughts and when we access that level of the creator of the Tao within us, then we are co-creating or, if you prefer, creating reality with our thoughts from that level. It definitely is absolutely connected with tapping into the Higher Self, which is the Tao, and then whatever you're thinking or intending, if you do it clearly it will manifest for you. In fact, it will anyway… it's just that many people aren't conscious of what they're intending, so quite a lot of the time they're being driven by the negative thoughts that are buried in their unconscious, thus creating a negative reality.

I have an almost constant dialogue between the Tao and my universal self, where I'm being guided by a voice that seems to arise in the center of my brain and comes up through the center of my spine to give me messages. It's an internal presence that guides me like a Master would, saying things like, "Remember, today is all about accepting the play of yin and yang, young Barefoot", or, "Ah, there you are panicking – breathe, now… relax!" Sometimes I'll romanticize it or see it as a separate entity, but, essentially, it all boils down to one big consciousness that seems to be urging me with prompts from my belly, pictures in my mind and synchronicities.

What guides me is belief. Not a directed belief, but belief as a pure preatomic quality or essence – it's the way I describe the feeling I have in my chest and my belly that compels me to keep exploring and moving along the path. What drives me is a playful sense of adventure… it's the same excited anticipation, the "What am I going to find today?" that I felt as a small child and combines with a feeling of love in my heart area, because the excitement of following the adventure somehow in itself makes me love everyone else and want to help people who are not doing that to do it, and to 'big up' the ones who are. That's the feeling that drives me to get out of bed in the morning – that and my abject fear of failure, death and dissolution… but it's mostly the excitement.

'Alain' by Lyn Allen

HOLDING THE LIGHT

Lyn Allen

Lyn is a Light Worker and a Hermetic Alchemist – she puts the energy of Spirit onto paper. Lyn's destiny-work is her Art. She has used this process over the last 20 years, painting Spirit Guides for herself and others to be used as stepping-stones for personal growth.

She lives in South Australia, with her wonderful 'long suffering' hubby of 37 years. They are blessed with two beautiful daughters and six grandchildren.

About fourteen years ago, I took my daughter to an obstetrician as she was having her first child. On the way there, we stopped at a New Age bookstore so I would have something to read whilst she was in the specialist's rooms. The book I chose to read was called *'An Act of Faith'* – The P'taah Tapes, channeled by Jani King. I did not get much past the first chapter, because in the first few pages she stated something she experienced when she was 2 years old or thereabouts – she disappeared for several hours and no-one could find her. Well, my hair stood up on end because, you see, the same thing happened to me at the same age…

We were living in the hills at that time – my parents searched the property for me and I was nowhere to be found. I finally turned up at the back door several hours later, covered in ants. They thought that a cow must have knocked me down a hill onto an anthill or something. I don't remember what happened, although I do remember there being a 'diamond' shape filled with brilliant light. Reading this book put me on a very real trail of discovery, I had to get some answers…

I went to a close friend who is an exceptional medium, and asked him what had happened to me when I was young. He said I'd gone somewhere I shouldn't have, and that there was a craft there, but the 'beings' did not want me, so I'd been placed in 'safe-keeping' by my Spirit Guides. As ridiculous as this may sound, I wondered why on earth 'they' did not want me, and why I was 'rejected'.

I have since found out where these 'beings' come from – the Horsehead Nebula, which is about 15,000 light years away. I feel that they are like the 'keepers of the Earth', and that they are assisting in the healing of this planet. They have visited me every 7 years since I was 14 years old. I haven't always been aware of their visits, but have pieced together bits of information through various deep trance mediums, speaking directly with Spirit in many cases, and by reaching deep into my own subconscious with the aid of meditation.

The first time I was truly 'aware' that they were present was about 14 years ago, when we were living on a property in the southern vales area of South Australia. It was midnight, and my small dog (who was shut in the laundry room) began to bark crazily.

I got out of bed and looked out of a back window to see what was going on. It was a strange evening – the air was thick with energy and very, very still. I could see a reflection of red light that 'bounced' off some sort of object above the ground at the end of our house. This red glow was amazing… it was coming and going every couple of minutes and was pulsating. I watched it for a while, became consumed by my own fears and then raced back to my bedroom, jumped into bed, pulled the bedcovers over my head and promptly fell asleep!

I know that these beings do not mean me any harm because they have never harmed me. They appear as very tall funnels of white light, and I feel they come back to check up on me – to see what I am doing and whether I am working with my 'gift'. I have had energy circles appear in the paddocks of our previous house, and have found that these energy circles were actually tapping into the energy deep within Mother Earth, allowing that ancient energy to rise up to the surface to assist in the healing of the planet. Around the edge of these circles, the grass grows differently, and there would sometimes be a circle of mushrooms around them. When I first encountered this, it was like walking into a wall of energy that went far up into the sky and deep into the earth. Walking into the center of this circle was like going into a vortex, and the feeling was incredible.

Although I had an enormous amount of fear to work through because of my experiences, I was also plunged into a trail of discovery, which was amazing in the extreme. I have overcome my fear now, and feel very much in balance with it all. I have an acceptance that 'All is One'. It is because I have gone through these processes that I am able to do my paintings more objectively and without judgment.

I channel other people's guides when I paint them. These paintings are also healing for people as they touch them on a soul level, and are a tool for that person's development. When I paint, I step out and allow the person's spirit guide to come through me. I am still conscious but, until the painting is done, the spirit stays with me until I have finished it. When the painting is finished – poof! – they are gone.

I feel that many of our guides have been with us in past lives, and that they are a part of us – part of our energy, like another layer in the aura. I believe that we are everything we have been before and everything we will be in the future, right here and now – that our guides are an aspect of ourselves.

I have a Native Indian gatekeeper. A 'gatekeeper' is the spirit who was with us when we were born, is with us when we die, and through whom all others must pass.

One of my main guides is a bloodline relative of mine – his name is Alain and he is a Capuchin monk. He has spoken to me through a trance medium, where he undertook a healing on me in full Latin mass. It made my hair stand up on end, but he got my attention! The love and light that emanated from his energy was magnificent. He said he "always holds the light for me".

I feel honored that Spirit wishes to work with me in this way. Nothing gives me greater pleasure than to see people grow within themselves, drawing upon their own knowledge and the realization of the Divine Spirit that exists within them. We are, in truth, only limited by the limitations that we place upon ourselves.

I have found that to add Spirit to your life makes it fuller. Just remember never to allow it to replace your Life.

CHAPTER 4

HEALING THE SOUL

***Healing is something you** are, **not something you** do.*

~ Rev. Warren A. Wise (quoted by Jessica Macbeth in *The Faeries' Oracle*, 2000)

Healing is a two-way process… a flow of energy. A healthy person is balanced within – mind, body and spirit, is at peace with their environment, and One with Spirit. This is an ongoing process, as the universe is in a constant state of flux – of growth, movement and evolution. No pill, or drug you can take, will 'make things better forever' because, as both human and spiritual beings, we are part of an interconnected whole. Everything affects everything else and, for the whole thing to maintain equilibrium, there will always be minor (and sometimes major) adjustments and 'tweaks' that need to be made along the way, no matter how 'evolved' we may be. All beings, even those in the spirit realms, need healing from time to time – some more regularly than others.

Although conventional medicine and surgery save many lives, those in the medical profession are trained to treat the symptom, not the cause. There is one vital element missing from this system – the premise that being human is a physical experience for a spirit being… that, first and foremost, we are Spirit. The ailments of our bodies merely *reflect* the wounded soul.

Louise Hay's 'little blue book', *'Heal Your Body',* explains how every physical problem, including so-called 'accidents', reflect our mental and emotional imbalances. This superb little book provides a list of positive affirmations to counteract the negative core belief that may have caused the problem in the first place. The thoughts and feelings we have are powerful things indeed… not only do they affect the state of our mental and physical health, but they shape the very world we live in. The daily events in our lives are good indicators of our mental and emotional health on a personal level. If we take a step back and look around us at the world today to get an overview of the bigger picture, it is clear that there is much collective healing to be done.

The revolutionary work of Japanese scientist Dr. Masaru Emoto, (detailed in his book, *'The Hidden Messages in Water')*, shows how crystals formed in frozen water reveal changes when they are exposed to specific, concentrated thoughts. He found that water from clear springs and water that has been exposed to loving words show brilliant, complex and colorful snowflake patterns. In contrast, polluted water, or water exposed to negative thoughts, form incomplete, asymmetrical patterns with dull colors. Homeopathic formulas are based on the theory that even when a remedy is diluted with water to the point where no starting material remains, the water will retain a 'memory' of what it was once in contact with. Incidentally, 75 % of the human body and 85% of the brain are composed of water…

To be healed is to become whole. When we experience trauma in our lives, we experience an imbalance, or sometimes a loss, of life energy – of Spirit. This results in dis-ease, which manifests as a mental, emotional or physical condition. In shamanic terms, this is often called 'soul loss'. When the soul feels threatened, the part that was wounded or neglected can become separated and stored in a fragment of consciousness, hiding itself in the spirit world for safekeeping. However, it maintains a connection with our main consciousness, and it is this link that makes the recovery process possible.

A shaman can journey to the Otherworld and, guided by their spirit allies, retrieve the lost part of the soul. The fragment is then invited to return, and must be welcomed and reintegrated; otherwise it may depart again.

Soul fragmentation is not healed by death, whereupon the newly deceased spirit – the discarnate entity – remains fragmented. By the same token, the soul can also be born fragmented. The incident causing the fragmentation could be located in another lifetime – in which case, past-life (and perhaps future-life?) therapy may assist in recovering and healing this fragment, healing the soul and restoring balance.

Plant spirits are powerful healing allies. Many of the wild plants and unwanted 'weeds' in our gardens are, in fact, remarkable plants that have beneficial healing properties, every plant a specialist in its field with a unique gift – for example; the dandelion (a wonderful tonic for detoxifying the system), stinging nettle (a nutritious and a fantastic tonic that strengthens and supports the whole body) and cleavers (excellent for inflammations, taken both internally and as a poultice). In fact, most manufactured drugs are originally derived from a botanical source – aspirin's plant origin was the bark of the white willow tree, morphine is derived from the opium poppy, and wintergreen is a source of methylsalicylate, the active ingredient in topical ointments and liniments to relieve muscular pain, lumbago, sciatica and rheumatic conditions. To connect with the spirit of the plant itself is more beneficial than ingesting the synthesized plant-based drug. The spirit *is* the medicine.

Like humans, plants have a spirit and a purpose that needs to be honored. Scientific studies have proven that plants respond to loving appreciation – most famously those of scientist Cleve Backster, whose thirty-six years of laboratory research into biocommunication with plants (using a polygraph machine) shows that they respond electrochemically to thoughts and threats. This has led to his theory of *primary perception.*

It is the soul, or essence of a plant that heals, which is why vibrational medicines that contain no physical part of a plant are just as effective as remedies. Dr. Edward Bach developed Flower Remedies based on the theory that the vibration or essence of a plant or flower had specific healing properties that could be captured in water and energized by the sun. Similarly, stones and crystals are vibrational healing tools. Specific stones have specific properties, or vibration, that can help rebalance a body's energies, and have been used as healing tools for thousands of years – in ancient Egypt, China, and India, as well as in indigenous shamanic cultures.

Spirit guides and allies can and will assist with the healing process, but it must be noted that nothing and no-one can 'make you better' without your willing participation, both consciously and subconsciously, to release the cause of the problem. This certainly requires courage and determination on your part.

We all want to be healed, to be whole – yet if only we would realize that, as Divine beings in human form, this wonderful healing potential is within each and every one of us at any time. We each have the ability to heal and be healed – the two go hand in hand… for, ultimately, when you heal another, you heal yourself.

CURANDERISMO

by Elena Avila

Elena is a first generation Chicana born in the barrios of El Paso, Texas. Her parents were born in Mexico and brought their medicine with them out of Mexico... medicine passed down through time. Elena's first language was Spanish, and her family's health care included Curanderismo as well as western medicine.

After graduating from the University of Texas in 1976, with a Bachelor of Science in Nursing, Elena obtained her Master's degree from the University of Texas in 1981, and specialized in mental health. She began her research into Curanderismo in 1974, gradually incorporating native folk healing into her work as a nurse.

Elena has held many administrative positions in nursing, including Head Nurse of Psychiatry, Director of Maternal/Child Nursing, Clinical Nurse Specialist at UCLA, and Director of the Albuquerque Rape Crisis Center.

Renowned throughout the United States and Mexico as a Curandera, Elena is an international speaker on the subject and has

taught at various universities on cultural diversity and Curanderismo. Elena was awarded the Martin de la Cruz Medal, and international honor for excellence in the practice and research on Curanderismo, **and she** ***is a member of the International Congress of Traditional and Folk Medicine.***

Her book, 'Woman who Glows in the Dark', is a National Bestseller, and the only title ever published in which a Curandera reveals the ancient tradition of Curanderismo from an authentic practitioner's point of view.

Elena combines Curanderismo with western medicine in her private practice. In addition, Elena is a poet, writer, playwright and actor. Elena has 4 children and 5 grandchildren.

When I was a child, I could predict when my father was going to come home drunk. My stomach would ache and I could just feel that he was. I just 'knew'. Sometimes he would spend half the paycheck, which was always a bad thing because he and my mom would fight. This used to upset my little sisters, so they would want to know what state he would be coming home in – they felt that I had the answers, so I felt very responsible for them when I was little. Those were very uncomfortable feelings, just knowing something bad was going to happen and not being able to change it.

I was a sensitive child. I had a natural talent to heal and to help people, and I was the neighborhood healer from a very young age. I also loved rituals – as a very young girl I was 'marrying' the neighborhood kids… I was the 'priest' and I would create very elaborate weddings!

I was the first in the whole family to be born in the United States. If I spoke Spanish at school, my little hands would be hit with a ruler. We were really punished for being brown, for being mixed-race. I felt that who I was and where I came from was not something to be honored and respected, so there was a time when I didn't want to know anything about my culture.

My grandparents lived in Mexico. I loved my grandmother very much. She died when I was seven, but I had an incredibly strong connection with her. When I went to stay with her, they would literally have to drag me out of the house screaming, as I did not want to go home! All I remember is the incredible love that she had for me, and I had for her. It wasn't until I started nursing school that I started to remember my roots, my culture and my past…

I was asked to write a paper on Curanderismo, which really stimulated my interest. During my studies, I remembered my grandmother doing healing work and realized that she was a Curandera. I made a conscious decision to retrieve my grandmother's medicine and headed to Mexico.

Our emotional, physical, and spiritual health depend on a healthy relationship with the ancestors. I feel that being a Curandera was passed on to me through my grandmother. When she was alive, she taught me about love – she didn't teach me about Curanderismo. My grandmother is still very much with me as one of my spirit guides.

I tend to hear and sense the awareness of my guides, rather than 'see' them, though my guides have come to me through lucid dreams. They are always there to help me through creating synchronicities in my life. Sometimes they work at a very subtle level. Other times, I'll be working with someone and I get a sense – a push or a pull – to say this or do that. I couldn't do this work without them.

One of these is La Virgen De Guadalupe, who is a brown Madonna and the patron saint of Mexico. On December the 12th, there's an incredible pilgrimage to Mexico City, where hundreds of thousands of people go to the Basilica to pay homage and dance – I've danced as an Aztec dancer there to honor her.

I've just gotten over an illness and the guide who was constantly by my side was the Virgen De Guadalupe. What I went through was so traumatic – they found a tumor on my left kidney and they had to remove it. I was in a lot of pain. She really helped me through that, there's no doubt about it. When the pain was unbearable, she would envelop me in her green robe and hold me like I was a child.

Another of my allies is Coyolxauhqui – she's the Cosmic Aztec Mother, and she's the moon. She has five names and one of her names is Mother That Glows in the Dark. She teaches us that even though sometimes we have to go through dark times, there's an ember of light still there. I wrote a poem after my father and my two younger sisters died, asking her to guide me through that dark period in my life. I asked her that if I went through this period of grieving in a good way without getting too out of balance, if I could be called 'Woman Who Glows in the Dark'.

The way I mostly connect with my spirit allies is through rituals and ceremonies. I work with the sacred directions using the ceremonies that my ancestors used to use. Sometimes, if I am with other helpers they might beat the drum and I can go into a deep trance state.

When I'm doing a healing and I want to get in touch with my spirit guides, I first travel physically to the directions. I always start in the east.

Depending on the state of development that you're in or where I am working, if I just want to thank the divine energies for my breath and my body, then it's just a matter of saying, "Thank you". But if I want to invite them in because I'm going to do a healing for myself or for somebody else, then I place symbols in all the directions and I stand in each direction and call and invite the spirits in. This is done in Nawat – the Aztec language.

I went very deeply into the medicine and culture of the Aztec people – I joined and still belong to an Aztec tribe, where I learned ceremony as a dancer. Every step is ceremony. A male Aztec warrior has been seen by one of my teachers on my right-hand side, assisting me during ceremony.

When the natural and the spiritual are not torn apart into disjointed entities, there is a balance between human and nature. Human beings have a spiritual nature as well as an individual soul, and the body cannot be cut away from the soul and spirit. Humans are members of the natural world

– animals, plants, minerals, earth, and all living things found on earth. Illness occurs when one does not live in harmony with all these aspects of 'self'.

In Western medicine, the body goes to the hospital, the mind goes to a psychiatrist, and the soul/spirit goes to church. In Curanderismo, there is no such severing between the emotional, physical, mental, and spiritual realms. There is no separation between the nature of humans and their environment. The totality of the person is the patient. The folk healer does not withhold her own religious and spiritual beliefs from her treatments.

A soul that is off-balance is said to be suffering from *Susto* (fright), and the treatment involves a 'soul retrieval'. If one's spirit has lost faith in God or the Divine, one suffers an illness as real as a physical or mental illness. All aspects of the 'self' will suffer, and one will experience diseases that affect one's body, mind, emotions, spirit, soul, family, community, and nature. The Curandera understands this concept of illness and will have knowledge of how to guide the patient back to balance.

Curanderas also have insight into the way the patient perceives his own illness within the context of his culture. The patient's values, family, society, and culture must all be taken into account. No treatment goal can be envisaged that does not involve a value which is itself culturally determined.

My guides and this medicine inspire me to heal in a creative way. I don't know where these guides and helpers come from… I don't want to get lost in my linear brain trying to figure that out! All I know is that we're on a tiny planet whirling through space in a galaxy among millions of galaxies, and that it's a miracle to be a tiny speck of humanity in this universe.

'Abraham' by Pattie Greenberg

HEALING HANDS

Gary Mannion

Gary is one of the youngest professional healers in the world – at the time of writing he is 19 years of age. He is an 'Indigo', which is a term referring to those who are born with psychic, empathic and telepathic abilities. Gary is an established clairvoyant and Medium, Hypnotherapist, and Indigo Child Specialist. He is especially renowned for his work as a Psychic Surgeon, and is asked to perform demonstrations of Psychic Surgery all over the world. With the help of his Spirit Surgeon, Abraham, Gary aims to bring this form of safe and non-evasive surgery within the sphere of the National Health Service (NHS). He lives in the U.K.

As an Indigo, I've been psychic all my life. Unfortunately, my parents weren't very understanding – my mother was an atheist and my Dad was into Spiritualism… he would regularly take me to a Spiritualist church from an early age. One day, I was watching the medium tune-in, and I heard a voice in my head say, "*You* can do that." Dad just didn't believe *I* had the gift, so I didn't get a lot of encouragement and support. I was very much left to my own devices.

I grew up with my abilities in high school. I really distanced myself from a lot of people because I knew what people were thinking, and what someone was like when I first met them before I'd even had a chance to say hello to them. It was my big secret – I didn't want to share this with the world because I didn't know how everyone would take it. I remember saying, "If I was given the choice, I wouldn't be psychic. But now that I am, I couldn't live without it."

I know that I 'inherited' my gifts from my grandmother. I didn't get to see much of her because she lived in Ireland, and she died when I was about nine or ten. But, even now, if I ever have a problem psychically, it's her who comes through to help me.

Because of the laws here in the UK, I was considered 'too young' to be a medium, so nobody would teach me how to use my abilities… how to close down, or how to do things properly. Because of that, negative spirits came to me as well as positive. It got to the point where I couldn't tell the difference, and I almost felt schizophrenic.

You see, these negative spirits would start off being very friendly. As an Indigo child who was different from my peers, I thought that nobody liked me. So when a spirit came along pretending to be my friend, I would listen to it. Over time, when that spirit had really latched onto me, it then became negative and manipulative.

Not knowing how to deal with this, I completely stopped all the spiritual work I was doing. Nevertheless, I still felt a 'calling', so eventually, I said to Spirit, "What am I meant to do?" Thankfully, Spirit responded by offering to teach me first-hand how to do it properly. And so I've been completely spirit-taught. Nowadays, I can just tell by the energy if something is negative.

At the time, it did mess me up. The positive side is that, having experienced that negativity myself, I know how to help others who are getting possessed. I have no fear of negative spirits now.

A lot of psychics won't even *talk* about anything negative because they have a fear that doing so will bring it on. But you don't feed negative energy by talking about it – only by fearing it. If you can talk about it and understand it, then there's nothing to fear.

When I first started doing psychic readings for people, I knew the information was coming from *somewhere*, but I didn't know from who or where. Whenever I'd go to the spiritualist church, the medium would come to me and say, "I've got a 'David' with you." And I would reply, "Well, I don't know anyone called 'David' in the spirit world." Eventually, one night a medium came to me and insisted, "You've got a *guide* called David with you," and so I started referring to David when I came to do clairvoyant readings, rather than just opening up to anyone and everyone.

Abraham

The head healer of my church saw that I was psychic, but that, at my age and being an Indigo, I was all over the place. She introduced me to healing in order to calm my energies down. Eventually, I was given special permission from the SNU (Spiritual National Union) to start healing others two years before I was legally allowed to do so. She always said to me, "You'll be a healer, not a clairvoyant." I didn't find healing that interesting – I wanted to be a clairvoyant! And yet, here I am now doing healing for a living.

I'd only ever done spiritual healing up until the day I was asked to try out a method of healing devised by the renowned psychic surgeon Ray Brown… As soon as I put my hands on the woman, I simultaneously felt a strong spirit presence behind me. Now, I'd done clairvoyance and that was one thing, but when this spirit came through it was ten times stronger than any other spirit contact I'd ever had. All of a sudden, I saw some hands reach inside her and pull mold out of her stomach. I didn't know what to make of it, and I told her about what I'd experienced. "Yeah, I have a digestion problem – food doesn't always digest in my stomach, so every now and then I have to go to hospital to get it removed," was her reply.

After that, every time I did any healing, I would see the same hands going inside the person's body, but I still didn't know whose hands they were! Then, one night, I was sat at my computer listening to some music, when I felt my hands start typing of their own volition. The words were a message from a spirit called Abraham.

Abraham has told me that I've known him spiritually for a long, long time – we're on the same level and our souls are very well connected. Working together was something I had agreed to do before I came to the physical plane. It was a choice I was given.

When I perform a surgery on someone, I always say to Abraham, "Right, it's over to you." He'll then assess the area, I am able to 'see' inside the body and know what he's looking at. Then I give him full control of my hands. To feel my hands move 'by themselves' was quite intense at first. However, although they're moving themselves, I can still *feel* what my physical hands are doing. I can also see other hands going inside the body and I can feel them, too – it's quite squeamish at times, but I am getting used to it. The only thing I really can't stomach doing is eyes!

When people come to me for surgery, a lot of people do feel that the process has started beforehand. All Abraham does is use me to do whatever he needs me to do – he passes his energy though my body, which acts like a portal. When he is working through me, my body vibrates at a different rate than it's used to, and it does sometimes make me feel physically tired. Abraham continues the healing process afterwards as well. A lot of people feel him working on them at night. I don't 'own' Abraham in any way and he will come to anyone who calls him.

David is my main spirit *guide* and Abraham is my spirit *helper*. I see 'guides' as spirits that owe you karma in one way or another, whereas Abraham is 'past his karma' and he doesn't owe me anything – he chooses to work *with* me. Although I know David is still with me, I don't often refer to him at the moment. Nowadays, I tend to refer most things to Abraham.

From what Abraham tells me, we can never fully pay off our karma while we're in a physical body. While we're paying off some karma, we're earning more. He says that the only way to fully pay off your karma is to be a spirit guide – to enter the physical plane and pay your karma to someone you owe it to, but not take on a physical body to do it. This is why guides can change, because once someone pays off a certain amount of karma, they move out and someone else comes in.

When Abraham first started coming through to me, I would feel him on my left-hand side, 24 hours a day. Nowadays, I feel as if we are a part of the same soul. There are so many facets of the soul… you could simultaneously be living another lifetime somewhere else as someone else, because time's irrelevant to Spirit. The guiding spirits that are part of your higher-self, or soul, tend to be much higher than the 'average' spirit guide. 'Becoming more Light' is what the definition of 'higher' is – just less crap to hold you down, really. The lighter you get, the more closely you merge back with the wholeness.

When I've asked Abraham, "What's it like where you are?" He says, "I'm aware of millions and billions of souls around me all at once – but yet I'm still my individual soul as much as I'm connected with every one of them." He tells me that there are ten 'planes' or dimensional levels – that he moves between the sixth and seventh. But he's not an angel… he says that angel's spirits are very different.

Before Abraham came to me, I would go to clairvoyants and spiritualist churches all the time, hoping to get a message. But when I turned 18, I said to spirit, "Right – I'm putting my life in your hands. I'm not going to worry about a single thing anymore. I'm going to give you complete trust as long as it's a spiritual path, my life's yours." I've not worried a day since, and I've not felt the need to. However, Abraham does advise me of a lot of things and he does give me warnings and keeps me well-informed on what's going to happen and how things are running.

When Abraham talks to me through thought, it's a different type of sound. You know how when you talk to yourself in your head you've got that one voice? His voice is very different and I can also feel his energy more strongly, so I definitely know it's coming from him.

With me, when Spirit comes through they will either do one or more of the following – show me something, tell me something, make me feel something. Sometimes, I could say a bookload just from a feeling, because I know what it means and what they're trying to imply with it.

I really need physical proof that something is real. If I just hear a voice telling me something, I would probably just shrug it off, but if I get a strong gut feeling with it, or an external sign, I know that I have to listen. Spirit knows that the only way to get a message through to me is to do so in a way that leaves no doubt in my mind. For example, when I started psychic surgery, everyone around me told me that I was going too fast, even though I didn't feel that I was. I said to Abraham, "Right, I need an answer today, in a way that I'm going to believe, that I'm not going too fast." I just so happened to run into another psychic surgeon, and the first thing he said to me was, "I've got to tell you… you're *not* going too fast."

The feeling I get from helping someone through a healing – to hear someone say, "You've given me my life back" is indescribable. And to think that I was selling windows to people when I was 16… there's a big difference.

photo credits: Chelynn Tetreault

TEN YEARS UNDER THE YEW TREE

by Michael Dunning

Michael first became aware of his latent shamanic abilities in the far north of Scotland during an encounter with a powerful earth spirit that almost took his life. His state of health slowly deteriorated. Several years later, he was struck down by a bolt of light from the sky and became seriously ill. This marked the beginning of his ten-year shamanic initiation that took place under the vast enclosure of a sacred 2000-year-old yew tree in his homeland of Scotland. Michael believes that the spirits at the yew tree were passing on a sensory and experiential knowledge that once belonged to the indigenous shamans of Scotland. He leads shamanic workshops throughout New England and teaches and runs a practice as a Biodynamic Craniosacral Therapist.

Michael is also a musician and a visual artist. In 1999, he was invited to compose and perform as part of a concert in Edinburgh celebrating the reconstruction of the Deskford Carnyx - the Celtic war horn depicted on the Gundestrup Cauldron. His composition, 'Taxus

Baccata' is a musical interpretation of a possible meeting between the yew tree and the carnyx. Michael has also been awarded two musical study grants from the Scottish Arts Council.

Michael currently lives in Western Massachusetts with his wife Chelynn and Wallace the cat.

The Tree Surgeon

I stood fragile and still inside a darkened and tangled cocoon vault, gazing into the contracting afternoon liquid light that slid through gaps in an intricate weave of branches, casting mottled washes of gold, Turner watercolor fragments against the south western profile of the yew tree. To this day, I wonder that this perfectly inverted cauldron of branch contortion could admit any illumination at all. Moody dark for most of the day, and certainly during nights without a full moon, the great yew goddess would sip in the last light of each day as her delicacy… a taste of potency to be gathered and bound only during those dying moments. But the true light source of the yew came from elsewhere.

The previous night, I had climbed to the top of this sacred goddess, guided by the light of the moon and a local tree surgeon named Bob who had dragged me from the village pub after I admitted both ignorance of yews as a species of tree and that I had never visited the 'cathedral' in my own Scottish back yard. At that time my illness was advanced, so walking any short distance could exhaust me for days. But there I was, blind drunk, in the middle of the night, stumbling over broken branches and jagged bushes to visit a tree I had neither heard of, nor, if truth be told, was interested in. The effects of the alcohol, the tree surgeon's animation and something else, a curious feeling previously unknown yet irritatingly familiar, had compelled me.

After about ten minutes Bob stopped. "Here we are… you first!"

"What?"

"This is it," he whispered…

I couldn't see any tree at all – only a small, dark and circular opening in what looked like a huge bush. I laughed pathetically. “You’re kidding, right?”

“In you go!” He waved his hands dramatically, feigning impatience.

I had to bend almost double to get into that black hole. It was cold. I shuffled forward without lifting my feet off the ground. I realized that this was a narrow tunnel because each time I tried to raise my head a few inches, it touched a ceiling of sharp, pointed branches. I encountered the same spiked barrier on either side as I reached out with my arms. The ground of the tunnel rose gently and evenly for the first 20 feet, then began to incline more steeply. I shuffled another 25 feet and began to make out what looked like a doorway of sorts. I reached forward with my left hand and touched a cold iron rail, feeling tiny flakes of rust sticking to my palm. I found the partner rail on the other side and using both hands hauled myself through an entrance. The ground seemed flat and I raised my head tentatively – no ceiling this time. I stood up slowly, waving my arms around in front of me and took a tiny step forward. Repeating this bizarre sequence, I advanced two or three steps further and then stopped. My eyes had adjusted to the darkness and by the light of the moon I could make out my position at the edge of a large, and enclosed circle perhaps 50 feet across. In the middle of the circle was a huge black mass that I took to be the trunk of the tree. Moving closer and looking up I followed the trunk to the buds of its massive branches, but instead of continuing horizontally into space they swooped back down to the earth in long graceful arcs forming an inverted basket shape.

As my eyes traveled the underside of one of the branches on its descending trajectory, I almost fell over backwards. Righting myself, I walked some 15 feet from the trunk to where one of the huge limbs reached the ground and, squatting, ran my hand around the area where it met the soft earth. The bark came away in flakes. I rested my hand there for a few seconds and my head began to feel heavy. I felt sleepy. At first it seemed that the branch had actually entered the earth. On closer inspection, I realized that it turned at a right angle just under the surface of the earth, and continued half buried along the ground. I rose and walked another 10 feet or so alongside the slithering shape toward what appeared to be one of a multitude of smaller trees that made up the internal circumference of this vast enclosure. I couldn't see a way in or out other than the tunnel I had just navigated. The ground seemed a writhing mass of snakes tripping and snagging at my feet. 'How could a tree do this?' I wondered. I didn't even hear Bob coming up behind me.

"Bloody amazing, eh? What de ye think?"

"I don't understand it," I whispered sharply, "Is this all the same tree? I mean it can't be... right? It's all different trees mixed up!"

"Nope, just the one tree," he declared proudly, "All 400ft in circumference of it, biggest in the country *and* it's a *she*."

"A '*she*'? Come off it!" I rebuked.

"Oh yes, she's a she a'right. Yews are dioecious which means they are either male or female. Not only that, but you are in the presence of the oldest female you are ever likely to meet so you'd better mind yer manners!"

"How old is it… err, she?" I asked.

"Could be over 1000 years old!" was his reply. (This turned out to be a modest guess – the yew is considerably older).

I was stunned.

"Anyway, welcome," Bob said, "to an unknown wonder of the world."

The next afternoon, sober and alone, I returned. At the threshold entrance of the yew tree I smiled briefly for the first time in many months. I felt that I had finally come home. Flexing my body almost in half, I crossed the threshold and entered into the twisting, cathedral plexus – the great enclosure of the sacred yew tree. Upon entering the main chamber for the first time in the partial light I began to weep, and wept uncontrollably for over an hour. Then I slept, curled up against the tree roots.

The convulsions woke me up violently, my body whipping up into the thick, musty air above the serpentine roots, my back arching well beyond its physiological limits as if pushed from below. The space within the enclosed area had become dense like water and was pushing painfully against my body, arching me upward and then slamming me back onto the ground. My head and chest felt compressed, making breathing extremely difficult, and my left eye was burning as if an acidic solvent was being applied directly to my retina. I can't say how long this lasted… I lost all sense of time, but just as it was passing, I saw flickering lights and sensed many presences around me. I had no idea then that this was the beginning of a ten-year journey of pain, transformation, learning and, ultimately, healing. This is the story of my shamanic initiation in Scotland under the Whittingehame yew tree.

The Whittingehame Yew

Let me tell you about the yew tree before I proceed any further because without getting a sense of the magnificence of this tree, my story makes no sense in the telling.

The Whittingehame yew almost entirely obscures the circular mound on whose apex the central axis of the tree grows. It is clear to me from my experiences that the yew was deliberately planted on a system of closely-grouped earth mounds forming an essential part of a telluric geometry involving underground water, related earth works, burial sites, single standing stones (most of which have been moved from their original positions), and a nearby sacred volcanic hill called 'Traprain Law'. There is certainly a sacred spring beneath the tree that can be evidenced by the remaining sunken stone with its hollow center, most likely the base of a Victorian pumping system.

There are at least 25 well-sites across the British Isles marked by yew trees. I have always felt an overwhelming presence of water at the yew and during part of my initiation was shown that the tree gathers-in the stray souls of the dead to a great well that flows into a river to the place of the ancestors. I was eventually to work with the spirits connected to this well and river many times and intensively during 'natural' and not-so-natural global disasters. The 'well of souls' comprises just one of the yew's many dimensions and functions. The earthworks surrounding the Whittingehame yew are now almost invisible and possibly of Iron Age or earlier origin, but no archaeological survey has been carried out to my knowledge.

Female yews bear Autumnal berries, or arils – the seeds of which are reputed to be toxic, as are yew leaves. However, there are numerous accounts of the healing properties of yew trees – tea made from the leaves and bark, and healing powders made from the bark as a cure for heart problems, hydrophobia and even viper bites according to Claudius in 1st century AD. In 1967, a new drug to combat cancer called *taxol* or *paclitaxel* was developed from a complex of alkaloids found in the bark of the Pacific yew – now an endangered tree. Used mainly to treat lung, ovarian and breast cancer, the drug effectively surrounds the cancer cells with microtubules that starve the cells.

It is very interesting that this enfolding of space occurs at all levels of the yew's organization. For just as the cellular action of the microtubules encase cancer cells, so the yew creates a 'sealed cavern' by arcing its branches into the earth, and many hollow yews grow an aerial 'root' within, to form a new trunk encased within the old.

The Whittingehame yew is only 12 feet in girth, leading many locals and tree experts to underestimate its age. It is as if they are blind to the fact that the yew has enfolded space, embryo-like, around itself in order to grow a 400 feet expanse of sensory branch fibers! The old Lord of the manor (now deceased), whose land the tree inhabits, estimated the age of the yew at 750 years but, according to recent research into the trees and, more importantly, from the tree itself, I estimate an age of at least 2000 years (and this could be a conservative estimate). Some of the branches could be over 750 years old!

Yews go to sleep, sometimes for over 60 years, and they grow very slowly, particularly in Scotland, with some national growth rates recorded at 0.02 inches per year. The yew conveyed to me that it had been sleeping for a long time before I came. Not that it hadn't been loved or cared for –

far from it, as is obvious from the marks of regular trimming and maintenance – but nobody had bothered to try, or knew how, to speak its language. Even the birds preferred other roosts. The language of yews cannot be spoken from the head, only from the body. The yew taught its language to my body through initiation, and an ancient practice was reawakened. Eventually the birds returned. I 'saw' that the yew tree was a place of initiation, ceremony and healing to the indigenous peoples.

Carbon-dating methods to age yews have been demonstrated to be inaccurate by over 600 years – for example, a tree with a known planting date of 1,000 years was carbon-dated at 187 years. Yew trees cannot be dated accurately because their heartwood rots and the new growth keeps up with the rot. This is one of the simplest and greatest lessons from the tree – its continual genesis, a constant renewal according to a cosmic principle. This is the yew's secret of immortal life in this dimensional reality. If we learned nothing else but this from the tree it would be enough. But the yew has so much more to offer us – so much more wisdom, guidance, and even a re-patterning of our neural pathways.

That there was a widespread cult of the yew tree in Britain I have no doubt – York in England was known as Eborakum, meaning 'yew town', and there are countless place-names throughout the UK that are derived from the word 'yew' in its older forms. The Whittingehame yew gave me a vision of many yew trees and groves spanning vast areas of the countryside… sadly, most of these have been destroyed. I was also shown detailed ritual and events that took place under the yew canopy.

I witnessed her being ceremoniously planted some 2000 years ago by a man dressed in a grey tunic of rough material covered with unusual signs like arrow heads, and I witnessed the passing ages and the passing of the many protectors of this sacred tree, as it was known through time. They each died and were replaced one after the other, and I saw a time when the last protector fell and none came forward. This seemed to be around the 17th century, significantly around the Age of Reason. Although I had thought to remain in Scotland to be the guardian or protector of the yew and had been prepared for this role, the tree explained that she is one of the last of her kind and for that reason she pushed me onward to the USA, to offer some of the language of health and rejuvenation that she inscribed into the parchment and space of my body.

The First Stage of Initiation: Luminous Yew Fibers

It was enough back then to simply get to the yew tree. Even now, I wonder that I managed even that, given the state of my health. I continued to feel empty and utterly depleted. I had spent time in hospital on numerous occasions, but the doctors could find absolutely nothing wrong with me. They eventually diagnosed me with 'Chronic Fatigue Syndrome' and sent me home. My own local doctor pursued the depression angle, recommended anti-depressants and sent me packing from his office. I did not take the anti-depressants.

As soon as I entered the vast canopy of the yew, I would make for the central trunk and sit with my back against it. Nestling into the tree, gently wriggling my exhausted spine to find a comfortable position between the gnarled lumps, I began to feel a quality of pull from within the yew itself – a suctioning inward of my body into the tree. My eyes would begin to vibrate and torque painfully in their sockets, as though the muscles attaching to my eyeballs had received some warped instruction to turn the eyeballs backward as if to fold vision in on itself. Apart from the obvious pain, this was a subtle experience and, in any case, I was unable to follow it for long because I would be lulled into a deep sleep. I quickly saw a pattern of activity emerge, beginning with the pull of the tree against my spine, followed by an intense burning sensation, particularly in my left eye, violent shaking and convulsions, then, finally a deep sleep. I would then experience further convulsions after I woke. I now understand this as the first stage of my shamanic initiation that lasted for about three years. It was during this time that I began to see the dancing tendrils of light under the yew – at first, merely a glimpse here and there, but then rapidly a web of light-fibers continually on the move, appearing and disappearing around the space under the tree. It was also during this time that the light tendrils began entering my body.

The tendrils would not appear until my convulsions had ceased and I lay still. The atmosphere was always changed after these convulsions – there was a clearing, a clarity, the way people describe how they feel after an epileptic fit or seizure. This clarity gave me sight from a deeper place and the fibers would appear, dimly at first and at a distance, occupying the circular inner circumference where the first line of huge branches entered the ground to form the inner, vaulted sanctuary of the yew. Time slowed and the air felt thick. Both eyes would sting horribly but, strangely, my vision was clear. The fibers would appear and vanish, leaving a trace on my eyes like the effects of lightning on the retina right after it strikes the sky. It was so beautiful to watch these tendrils – it was a dance unlike any other.

Over the next few months, I took to visiting the yew tree everyday, and often during the night. The exquisite dancing light-tendrils became more numerous and began to approach me directly. The light-fibers would hover around me, shimmering wisps of silver smoke that, with a flash, would find shifting nodal points on my body, entering to become expansive, pushing not against the opposing outside force but rather into deeper internal 'spaces'. The pressure pushing against my body from the environment remained the same – uncomfortable, but unchanged during these early stages by what was happening internally.

The internal and viscous pressure began to build as an intense pain in an organ – in my liver, for example – and I would initially feel my liver physically stretch and expand far beyond any physiological possibility until I lost all sense of anything that could be felt or described as a liver, partly because of the pain. Then a visual-visceral language would emerge… milky-white luminous strands that wound like rivers, like grooves in a gel-like landscape that ascended into thick air or took incomprehensible crystalline geometric shapes that never stayed still because they were talking with my body.

My entire body was affected this way – every organ, every bone, every muscle – literally every cell seemed to be transformed and yet somehow identical with this luminous, viscous language. As the complexity of this language developed, it became impossible to define what was happening inside from what was happening outside of my body. The pressure remained but now spread everywhere with no clear boundary.

It was as if the space under the tree had a specific function – that its dark and resonant chamber existed to close it off from outside influences. The yew tree – as a sentient survivor to the ancient yew groves – knew exactly what it was doing because it had done this many times before.

The light-fibers filled me at the same time as taking something away, something dying and broken. As I expanded from the inside out with this light energy or 'white-darkness' (a phrase I borrowed later from a shamanic account), I began to sense the guiding presence of the yew behind the actions of the light-fibers. The fibers of light now seemed as emissaries of the tree, purifying me of my illness and preparing me for something I could not begin to imagine. Despite the pain, my consciousness was expanding.

The Second Stage of Initiation: Rituals and Tests at the Yew

It was during this next phase that I began to actually 'see' the yew tree and its myriad of spirits. I was pushed to my limit by these yew spirits – on the one hand feeling stronger, while on the other, increasingly aware that I was entering into a contract with forces that I didn't understand nor could refuse. Whenever the light-tendrils appeared, the wind would gather outside of the yew enclosure to form a whirling membrane of weather around the outside of the tree. It was as if I was sealed-in with no prospect of getting out until whatever needed to happen had happened. I often remained under the tree for seven or eight hours at a time.

I sensed that the tree not only knew when I was coming but had summoned me. By that time, I had given up any idea of myself as an independently-acting subject and often 'decided' to go to the tree during my worst bouts of illness, which made no rational sense.

The second stage was marked by the sudden appearance of barn owls under and around the yew, even during the day but particularly at night when they would perch only a few feet from me. The owls were the first birds to return to the yew. I would catch a glimpse of an owl almost every time I set off from the cottage to the tree. The appearance of the owl was usually accompanied by a faint orb of light that darted around my head.

I sit, exhausted, with my back against the yew tree. I push my head back against the dry, crumbling bark and look up. A large white owl has appeared above me and is moving rapidly through the branches. Its black eyes flash and it rushes at me, ripping into my chest and causing me to double up in pain. I watch in disbelief as it disappears into my chest cavity at the same time as appearing in the space around the tree. "How can this be happening?" I manage to ask myself feebly. At that instant, an invisible force drags me downward towards the earth and I collapse painfully, twisting around the exposed serpentine roots. I feel nauseous and, at the same time, feel a tugging at my body from the ground and a simultaneous pressure bearing down on me from above. The forces abruptly recede and, for an instant, the unbearable pressure ceases. I lay on my side in the fetal position with half my face pressed into the cold soil beneath the yew. My fingers claw up the earth into tight fists but I can't open my hands. I am frozen. Beyond my body, I sense a gathering of forces as if from a single focused point in space somewhere higher up, spiraling and expanding, and I begin to feel a searing hot pain throughout my nervous system. A force slams into the exposed side of my body, igniting every single nerve so that I can smell an acrid burning. The force keeps pushing. I am being pushed into the ground. The skin of my face is now raw with the crush. My internal organs sense a gathering potency until I feel an intense nerve pain and, with incredible speed, I fall downward into the earth. I experience an alarming duality as I sense two *bodies – two 'Michaels'... one laying slumped and immobile on the ground, the other moving at blinding speed into the deep earth. My nausea increases as I begin to spin faster and faster. I can't tell if I am going up or down. I see the owl calmly flying close by me – a brilliant white blur with motionless black eyes. The stillness of the eyes draws me. It doesn't fly in any way I've seen a bird fly – rather it seems to remain precise and crystalline in form, while at the same time forming a rhythmic on and off series of successive images of itself at an impossible speed. I can't reconcile the two readings and yet I instinctively know that they are the same thing. Our pace slows and the spinning stops and begins to take on the features of a landscape. Its saturated colors reminded me of a 13th Century painting I have seen in the National Gallery in Edinburgh. I see beautiful blue flowers growing from multi-colored and cracked earth, almost like a stained glass panel. I sense an animal nearby and see blurred faces. I can feel the weight of many hands on my body and begin to feel heat. I try not to panic. A golden-colored flat disc appears on the ground and I stare at my own head upon it. A voice seems to speak from within my body, or I hear it within my mind, saying, "This is the canter of life," and I am shown an almond-shaped glowing object with serpent-shaped bright filaments within that seem to vibrate at high speed. Involuntarily, I am drawn into the filaments. I feel intense, unbearable heat. The owl presence feels strong and I feel protected by it. Then I lose consciousness.*

The Old Woman and The Sand Painting

Crawling my way through the entrance to the yew, I catch the briefest glimpse of a figure but it moves beyond me at a rapid and instinctual animal speed. (This is the first time I have seen anything vaguely resembling a human at the tree.) *Then I see it again, sliding around the base of the tree like a shadow, rising up the trunk and peeling itself off the bark to manifest into human form. It is an old woman. Her hands whirl and arc through the air as she inscribes invisible maps in space and her nimble fingers flick a sign language that is incomprehensible to me. The light fibers follow her every move.* (Later, I begin to understand that she is teaching me a skill to be able to harness some of the power from the light tendrils.) *Then she gestures for me to lie down. I watch several pairs of hands being lain on a swollen belly whose skin is leathery and black. As the hands settle, the belly turns to sand and the hands, now grasping short wooden sticks make marks in the sand creating beautiful geometric symbols. Holes suddenly appear at specific points in the sand drawing and the hands enter the holes. At that exact instant, I feel pain in my own belly and realize that I am seeing myself, my own belly. The hands pull me inside my own body and I experience an intense surge of nausea as though I am turned outside-in. I look up at what appears to be a network of vaulted arches, like Gothic architecture but more organic and stained black with a thick slimy coating that drips a black oily substance. Incredibly, this is the interior cavity of my chest but not as simple anatomy – more like a space that opens into other spaces. The outside-in feeling intensifies and I find myself entering between the oily vaulted ribs to emerge into a deeper space. Ahead of me I see four huge pillars of bone with a black orb on top of one of them. Instinctively I swallow the orb. Immediately the top of my head burns like fire and I break through an opening in my own head into the sky. A fountain of white energy streams out from my head into space and I collapse around the tree roots. As I come out of my trance, I catch another glimpse of the woman but now younger and with thick black hair.*

The old and simultaneously young woman appeared many times and each time my ability to work with the light-fibers increased. The orb I swallowed was also to serve a particular purpose, involving three other orbs that I was to take into my body at later stages.

Badger and Bird-Shaman

Around this time, I began to find tools that I would later use in my shamanic work. The experiences at the yew tree although exhausting had, at the same time, given me enough strength and purpose to take to the outdoors again and I began to explore the countryside of East Lothian. Very soon, I was to get to know that land in a deep way. I often walked along the edge of a river near to some old Scot's Pines in an area of hidden hills and valleys that seemed magical to me. One day, I had ventured far along the river and had become exhausted. I stopped and stood for a few minutes and noticed I was standing on something. Lifting my foot, I looked down at a beautiful deer antler. This antler is now used during healing sessions.

Soon thereafter, I came across an enormous dog-fox lying dead in a ditch. I lifted him up, slung him carefully over my back, his tail almost reaching the ground, and took him home. Fox was the first of many animals I was to bury at specific locations near my home. I always seemed to know exactly where to bury the animals and which ones to dig up for shamanic purposes. Many of them are still there. Every one of Fox's bones is used in my work and I have given many people a claw or rib for their own healing. He is a powerful spirit.

Soon after this, I found a badger that had been hit by a car and I arrived just as the last breath left his body. Stooping over him I sensed that his soul couldn't entirely leave his body. I can't say how I knew this. I decided to ask the yew tree for advice and, after laying the badger in my old coal shed, set off for the tree. It was already dark with no moon, so getting to the tree was a challenge. (Later, I was able to walk to the tree in the pitch black without making a sound.)

The old woman who is also a young woman has come to me many times since that first occasion, but, as I enter the yew enclosure, I see a different figure – male and very stern. *He wears a rough-textured dark cloak covered with the arrowhead symbols not unlike those on tree guardians. As he steps nearer I shrink back in alarm – his face is not human but bird-like, and this is certainly no mask. His frontal bone is very square and flat and beneath it two pearly-black eyes peer over a large beak that protrudes and curls downward to a sharp point. He wears a headpiece that seems more Egyptian in style than anything recognizably 'Celtic'. Strangely, I feel the weight of the dead badger in my arms even although this is impossible, and the Bird-Shaman motions me to lay the corpse on a stone table that has simply appeared under the yew. Bird-Shaman deftly slips a hand into his cloak and pulls out a collection of odd-looking tools. He begins to dissect the badger. I can't see any blood, but in a few moments he has the badger's heart lifted aloft in his right hand whilst muttering a rhythmic verse in a language I have never heard. He then gestures to me to lift the remains of the badger and to set him on the ground next to a semi-circular opening that has appeared next to the base of the Victorian pump. I hear water rushing and, looking down at the opening, see black water flowing directly into a groove in the earth that seems to run deep below the yew tree. The black river flows toward Traprain Law, the volcanic hill nearby. Badger is sucked into the hole and is gone. I do not see what the Bird-Shaman does with his heart.* I met Badger's spirit again many years later when he came to me as a helper.

Bird-Shaman pulls my arm roughly and I am suddenly standing with him at the summit of Traprain Law. It seems that the black water from the tree connects directly to the hill. (The geometric patterning of spirit lines and subterranean waterways in the landscape now form a major component of my shamanic work.) *Many people stand on the hill, mostly old women and four pillars of intense light surround us. Bird-Shaman leads me to the edge of a quarried section of the hill that was sliced away during the 1950's to create the local roads. He is extremely unhappy about this and I feel his words with my body as he explains that this violence has upset the spirit of the hill. Then, without any warning, he pushes me violently off the edge. I experience an incredible confusion in my senses – simultaneously lying under the yew whilst plummeting like a stone toward the ground. I am scooped from the air by an owl and within moments we are back at the yew tree.*

I needed to find some way of understanding what was happening to me but I had no idea who to ask for advice. I finally decided to confide in a friend whose husband happened to be an anthropologist. She related some of my story to him and we arranged to meet. He listened carefully to each detailed account and gave me some photocopied notes to read. He had recently returned from Africa where he had spent several months with a peripatetic tribe learning their ways and customs, so his awareness was tuned to the non-Western world of spirits and ritual. I was stunned by what I read. He had given me accounts of shamanic initiations from around the world and on each page I read about myself – mysterious illnesses, encounters with spirit, bodily dismemberment, spirit helpers – and for the first time I read the word 'shaman'. "Is this happening to *me*?" I asked myself. The notes gave me some much-needed clarity around some recent happenings under the tree involving Native American spirits. At the time, I thought it extremely unlikely that a Native American 'medicine man' would appear at a tree in Scotland. Surely the spirits at the yew would be somewhat 'Celtic' and indigenous? And they were, but not always… shaman-spirits were to appear from many other cultures and continue to appear to me. Nowadays, I often work with South American shaman spirits and occasionally with Siberian shaman-spirits. The South American shamans are mainly involved in my work with people and appear during my Craniosacral work – testament to the fact that the nature of the yew tree is in no way bound by the concepts of space and time.

White Bear and Dismemberment

Several weeks earlier, I had a direct encounter with a powerful medicine man who called himself White Bear amongst other names. White Bear is the least complex of his names so I have decided to use that here. For about six months he had watched me at a distance, but on this occasion he had stood right at the center under the yew and around him were several other spirits who remained unclear and surrounded by a thick mist.

In one stride, White Bear reaches me and strikes me hard in the face.

I fall to the ground and the vaporous spirits attack me in a blurred frenzy. I swing my arms wildly in sweeping motions in a futile attempt to protect myself. I feel searing pain and experience a tearing sensation from my abdomen to the base of my throat. I begin to lose consciousness; or rather I enter a different state of consciousness, more a form of trance where I see a green snake inside my body. The snake opens its mouth and a blackish-green liquid oozes out in a thin stream that runs into a landscape stretching far into the distance, and which I somehow feel as continuous with my own body. I see a symbol of two animal heads facing each other just as my body wrenches upward. A pressure builds in the torn cavity of my chest and I see what looks like a black seed pod there. The pod is swollen and bursts, spewing a foul-smelling black oil that fills my chest and spills into my throat and out from my mouth. I begin to convulse violently and am pulled further from the ground into the higher canopy of the yew. My body is pulled outward from every point as though ropes have been attached all over my skin with hooks. As I am pulled all at once into every conceivable direction I feel my flesh tearing apart and it seems to transform into an expansive crystalline fluid. Within this gluey crystalline form I expand further and further and feel a blurring of my identity, a shift into an expanse that has no words other than a sense of infinite continuity with space. I pass beyond what seems like our galaxy and am moving at a speed that is inconceivable. Even although my body is altered I continue to feel immense pain and pressure. I see worlds flashing beneath me, planets, entire star systems, comets and a place in space with geometric structures of an organic-synthetic intelligence comprised of living cell forms and fluids and inorganic material combined. (This is very hard to describe and as perplexing to me now.) *Then I enter a crystalline world of mountains and recognizable landscape features and I see a massive white orb ahead of me and speed toward it. I enter the orb, which seems both infinitely vast and at the same time so small that I can place my hands around it. I become very confused since the orb appears to be an aspect of the yew tree and as my awareness spins into the globe I arrive back at the yew tree taking the entire globe into the cavity in my chest. As I do this I feel my flesh return and a new skin forms over the wound in my chest. I am lying face down at the foot of the tree. I sense another spirit and it seems that the ritual is not yet complete. I see an old man with thin white hair who also looks Native American. He seems kindly and tells me his name and where he was born and other personal details that I cannot share. Then he shows me a white fish bone with a hole at the end of it. He pushes a thread through the hole and pulls the loose end down tying a secure knot. Without any further explanation he stabs the bone into my lumbar spine and begins to sew the thread through each vertebra.* (I cannot even begin to describe the pain so I will not even try.) *This process seems to take an eternity but finally it's over. I am crying now and not simply because of the pain but because I feel a renewal, a rebirth and a surge of health that I have not felt in a long, long time.*

The Third Stage of Initiation: Working With the Light Fibers

My heath gradually began to improve and I experienced a vision shortly after this last ordeal that was to show me that it was not my time to die. From this point onward, events in my life began to turn in a positive direction. The process of initiation continued unabated and involved painful 'dismemberment', the learning of new skills and visions of other worlds, and complex, multi-dimensional beings. The tests and rituals are far too numerous and detailed to describe here, but there was one initiatory test within a series that I would like to share because it led me to train as a Craniosacral Therapist. This therapy has offered me a structured practice able to support my work as a shaman in a modern and more socially acceptable form. Today I run a busy Craniosacral business alongside my work as a shaman.

I am sitting in my usual position with my back against the yew tree. The wind has gathered around the perimeter of the tree as a sign for me to prepare. The owls appear, followed by the old woman. She seems more bent than usual, and I notice that her hands are clasped and drawn in to her chest as if holding something extremely precious. She moves directly toward me without looking. As she gets nearer I see that light is escaping from tiny gaps between her interlaced fingers. Her pace quickens. The light is the color of molten gold and almost too bright to look at. I sense her struggling to contain it. She reaches me just as the light begins to spin like a small sun and without hesitation she thrusts her hands directly into my body. This is agonizing and I scream falling to the ground and convulse, every muscle twitching involuntary, like a series of electric shocks. When I regain consciousness, Bird-Shaman is waiting for me. There is no time to recover and in an instant this has transported us to an enormous stone circle. We move rapidly beneath the circle and into a network of transparent veins of light that reach a huge orb whose nature I cannot identify – seemingly a semi-organic, but also synthetic intelligence. I struggle to keep my bearings, since I also remain at the yew and can read the two places simultaneously. I watch my hands push into the white veins deep within the earth below the stone circle and, strangely, at the same time, beneath the yew tree. I draw liquid up from the veins into my hands and body like a syringe. The liquid has a crystalline quality but flows like water. I draw the liquid out from the earth and up the edges of the tree into points in space. The liquid is suspended there. My body begins to expand and I look down at a barren landscape with rutted and blackened earth. The water in my hands becomes more crystalline, hardens and then fractures into a powder of tiny crystal fragments that shower down onto the landscape. I feel euphoric as an immense power flows through my body. I sense a great healing on the earth below as the crystal rain touches the atmosphere and drifts to the denuded land. I can hardly contain myself. I feel a joy and sense of absolute well-being unlike anything I have ever felt.

The old woman under the yew had been trying to teach me to use my hands to work with the light tendrils and I was beginning to understand what she meant. Now, as I moved under the tree the tendrils moved with me, mirroring or inducing my own movements. I began to experience the light fibers as a source of power and healing and more importantly as inseparable from myself. The light fibers had become a part of me. I call this the 'luminous body' after other shamanic traditions.

I repeated this technique many times and eventually found that I could use it with the land in Scotland, paying particular attention initially to the quarried section of Traprain Law. I don't remember exactly how it happened, but one or two people had somehow found out about me and had approached me to work with them or with their land. My work as a shaman had begun…

My shamanic tool bag, or crane-bag, had been filling up rapidly with all manner of animal bones, feathers, stones and crystals. The Bird-Shaman and White Bear had shown me how to use many of these objects in various combinations for healing – mostly at that time for myself – and for constructing medicine-wheels for specific purposes. I was now shown how to use my hands and my own body for healing.

The Whittingehame yew gave me rebirth and I began a new life. I had taken to drawing during my shamanic illness as a way of retaining my sanity, and continued this practice. In 2000, I won the Acharossan Award for painting, which took me to Vermont. There, I met my wife Chelynn – a talented artist. In 2003, I emigrated to the USA where we were married – first living in Boston before being drawn to the spiritual heartland of Western Massachusetts. Here I have found great power in the land and a great spirit in the people. The land here asks for support and the spirits are more than willing to engage with an 'alien' – as it states on my Green Card – like myself. The spirit of the yew tree walks with me here in the U.S., and for that I am blessed.

ORIGINAL THOUGHT

Julie Soskin

As an author, intuitive, and university lecturer, Julie has worked in the field of spiritual self-awareness for over 25 years. Julie's passion is in the transformational process of self. She is highly respected in her field and has been a lecturer at all the major centers in the field of personal and spiritual self-development in the UK, as well as lecturing abroad. She was employed as a teacher and intuitive at the College of Psychic Studies in London for 12 years during which time she created many innovative courses. In 1996, she set up the School of Insight and Intuition where she is principal. The School runs an accredited Spiritual Healing Practitioner course and a Psycho-spiritual program. In February 2005, a module of this program was implemented as part of a BSc degree in Integrated Health at Westminster University in London – the first of its kind in universities in the U.K. Her latest book 'Insight Through Intuition: The Pathway to Spiritual Self-development' includes current thinking in science and psycho-spirituality, some of which was drawn from her research at Surrey University,

where earlier last year she was awarded a Master of Philosophy.

I feel I have a link to Source that I can interpret, but I don't ever say I've got a guide… I never use that term. In 'New Age' terms, you could say that I link with a 'Light force'. I don't like using the word 'guide', because I think it's misleading. I work with energies, but not with what I call a personality. My view is that, because the way our mind works and we need to give things shape, we tend to personalize these energies. There's nothing wrong with that in itself, but it can lead people to think that they're actually in contact with an individual person, and I don't really see it like that. There's a little bit of a danger in getting too personalized – like somebody who won't even buy a dress because their guide told them to buy blue or something, which I think detracts from individual choice and responsibility.

My attitude is that no benevolent being tells us what to do. When people say, "My guide tells me…", I'm very suspicious, because that's not the job of those energies… to tell us what to do. I think that sometimes it can be an excuse, sometimes it's an unconscious thing and sometimes I think people are just in contact with another aspect of themselves – and all those things are valid. But if you believe that they're something else, you can get into trouble sometimes. On the really negative side, you get people who say a voice told them to kill someone – that's clearly *not* a benevolent spirit, and yet the voice to them is real. I always say to my students, "Listen to the song, not the singer". If you're getting messages that are in any way controlling or fearful or telling you something that you know is not right, then no matter what sort of communication you have, it's not a good energy.

I first became aware of my psychic abilities at the age of four, when I realized I was able to perceive things that others could not. As a teenager, I developed the disconcerting ability to read other people's minds as clearly as a telex. Naturally, this trait did not endear me greatly to others.

I instinctively knew I couldn't discuss this with my family or friends and, although I was happy, for the greater part of my formative years I felt apart from others.

I trained as a medium years ago at a development group run by a lady from the local Spiritualist church and later at the College of Psychic Studies in London, where I eventually became one of the College's own mediums and teachers. I was giving people messages from their departed relatives and that was a joyous thing to do, but then, in June 1989, I experienced an almighty shift in energy over a period of a few weeks. I was in contact with something 'different' from what I'd experienced before – it was like my vibration went up a couple of notches. At that time, a lot of people were experiencing similar shifts. I'm not going to give any wild and weird ideas about why that should be – it might be astrological, or it might be a shift of consciousness on the planet… who can say? I sat down and tried to find out what was going on. I set aside a regular session each week to find the highest level of truth, and that's how I came to channel the *'Wind of Change'* trilogy.

The energy that I channeled was a 'Light energy' that pervades all… it's part of everyone, every living thing. At the time, I did ask what I was linking to, and the reply was quite nebulous… it was the words 'Original Thought'. Now, if you ask me what Original Thought is, it's a very difficult thing to describe, other than it's part of the Source – maybe a higher level of thought.

A lot of people thought I had channeled 'beings from outer space', but that certainly wasn't my experience! I felt that I was linked to a higher level than myself, meaning my 'little self'. I prefer to think of it as an alignment, rather than having some kind of e-mail to little green men or something!

When I was writing the fourth book, I decided that I would never do another book that was labeled 'channeled by', because it was too problematic. People started treating me like I had all the answers for them. Certainly I do what I can to help people on a spiritual level, and I hope my books are inspirational, but I don't have all the answers and I'm not plugged into something that is absolute like that. And, frankly, I'd be very suspicious of somebody who said they were.

I wouldn't suggest that anyone takes all of the channeling that I've written, or indeed anyone else's, absolutely on face value – I think that's dangerous, because everything is so open to personal interpretation, plus the information is filtering through many levels and layers into the human mind, which isn't always that failsafe, is it? Look what trouble we've had with religions… it's caused us no end of problems. I feel you've just got to take what's best for you and what you feel is right from it and if it rings true to you then, great, follow it. I just do what I feel is right.

I set up a spiritual program in 1996, which is now part of a BSc degree course at Westminster University. The difference that following a spiritual path makes to people is extraordinary. I'm much more interested in being a better person and helping others to have a better life and seeing opportunities and possibilities, than I am with the 'Wow-factor' that I might be channeling some weird and wild guide, which doesn't interest me.

Every living thing has a spirit counterpart – just as we have spirits that we usually call guardian angels, you could say the sun and the stars and everything else also have them. I don't understand it in scientific terms, but my impression is that some*how* those energies are allowing us to be present in the material world – that there's something holding us together that allows us to be both spirit and matter. They oversee things, but I don't think they have control over us in the sense that a lot of people think they do. I think they are literally there holding the energies together and, yes, they can give us healing and comfort and guidance – but they don't control us and nor do we control them.

There are very few people that *aren't* conscious of it somehow… people walking in the woods or somewhere quiet, even if they don't have any sort of spiritual notion, will talk about the atmosphere of a place and how good they feel. I think they pick it up, even if they're not consciously aware of it in our terms.

Sometimes, in various situations, I feel that there's a presence with me. When I give healing, I definitely feel there's a presence with me. When I'm giving sittings, sometimes I *do* speak to people in Spirit, and there's a very definite feel about that, but I don't ever refer to this energy as 'my guides'. Functionally, I'm a medium in the literal sense – I'm a go-between, if you like… a medium between my sitter and whatever is coming through for them. Usually, the message is very personal to that person… something will be related to them in a way that they understand, that's peculiar to them. Obviously, this information comes through my own mind and I interpret it in the best way I can.

When I'm 'on key', I have an intuitive 'knowing' about things. Unfortunately one isn't always in that space – if one's emotionally all over the place or there's some mental thing going on, it's very difficult. I am an advocate of meditation and that certainly helps, but I often find that if I ask for help and guidance during a meditation, I receive messages perhaps 24 hours later and not at the time. I often find that I get a lot of clear inspiration when I'm driving the car or doing something mundane like washing the floor – it's almost like my mind gets out of the way.

I have no doubt that mankind is on the brink of a massive shift of consciousness. Certain scientific discoveries (like, for instance, in genetics) are going to alter our lives forever and we had better raise our consciousness to meet it. This does not mean finding some mantra, master or meditation – it means the hard work of understanding self, dissolving aspects that are unhelpful and being true to ourselves. It's one thing to think about this but its quite another to live it and, quite frankly, very few have. The possibilities are extraordinary and I don't believe we've reached even half of our capabilities. The human mind is amazing and, in terms of consciousness, I think we're all babies… we have hardly begun.

CHAPTER 5

YOUR PAST, PRESENT AND FUTURE SELVES.

We are the ones we've been waiting for.
~ an unnamed Hopi Elder, Hopi Nation

When your Infinite Spirit and local self converge, there is an explosion of consciousness. The pieces scatter to all parts of existence, transforming your reality from the roots, and you know with all your heart, soul and might, that you are me and I am you and that nothing will be the same again.
~ The Barefoot Doctor

There is an aspect of ourselves that guides us. This is sometimes referred to as the inner, 'higher' or core self… the part of us that intuitively *knows* what is right. In many ways, the wise all-knowing soul that you are (beyond your persona or who you have been conditioned to believe you are) is your ultimate soul companion.

We are 'programmed' by society – the education system, parenting, T.V, advertising and the media – to believe that everything we need exists outside of ourselves, when it is exactly the opposite. We have lost touch with the Divine within. It is as though we have collective amnesia… we can't quite remember what it is we have lost, so we spend a lifetime searching externally for the 'perfect' partner (or car, house, latest gadget, alcohol, drugs, etc.) to fill the void. We frequently seek advice from others perceived to be far more enlightened or wise than ourselves… we are even willing to pay them large amounts of money to tell us what we already know but forgot to remember.

The truth is, you are a multi-dimensional being. You are capable of being in more than two places at once. You may not be consciously aware that this happens, but consider, for example, when you dream... your physical body may be lying in bed not going anywhere whilst you experience adventures in an alternate reality every bit as real (and often more exciting) than this one.

Taking this concept one step further, it is possible that many spirit guides are in fact *ourselves* in our previous and future incarnations. We may even be living many lifetimes simultaneously. Linear, sequential time is a man-made concept. As Albert Einstein said, "The distinction between past, present and future is only an illusion, even if a stubborn one."

Perhaps premonitions, 'gut feelings' and hunches are memories of events that have already occurred? Says Cornish healer Robbie Wright:

"At various times throughout my life, I have been given insight into forthcoming events concerning my own future. With the benefits of hindsight, this 'knowing', as I call it, has proved to be extremely accurate. I often wonder where this knowing comes from... Could it be some type of divine intervention given to me directly from the Great Spirit? Could it be my spirit guides impressing it onto me? Could it be coming from my higher self? I'd like to think that it's a combination of all three, but I'm also starting to believe that there may be a fourth alternative. I wrote a meditation called 'Healing Your Past', where you send back love and strength to your previous self. Now, I know, not just from my own experiences but from the reports that I received from other people, just how well this meditation worked and I was struck by an idea... if the Robbie of the present was able to send back healing thoughts to the Robbie of the past, could it be possible that the Robbie of the future is already sending back not just healing thoughts, but impressions and guidance as to the way my future's going to unfold to the Robbie of the present? If the Robbie of the present knows that at a given time the Robbie of the future will be sending back healing thoughts and images, it could well be possible to tune into

this energy and maybe the present Robbie could gain some insight of things to come. Who better to have on your side than your own future self? So, I created a new meditation that could help others live in the moment by taking away the fear, anxiety and uncertainty about the future... trusting that your future self has already been there, done that, got the t-shirt, and will send back these images and reassurances for you to tune into."

Who are any of us, *really?* Our bodies and our personalities are transient. What it boils down to is that we, and everything else, are all merely vibrating energies of varying frequencies. Interestingly, we often say when we don't understand or gel with a person, that he or she is, "Not on my wavelength." And we are probably literally right. Each of us, as a vibration of energy, has a note. When we are in harmony, we get on well with others. When there is discord, we don't.

Scientists tell us that the whole universe is made up of atoms. These atoms are not 'solid' – everything, including the chair you're sitting on, is mostly 'space'. We are all made from the same stuff – from planets to plankton. There is no separation and we are all connected to everything in the universe, including what we call 'God'. If we are all inter-connected, then is it not possible that we are co-creating it all? That the physical world around us – everything we see and experience – is not 'real' or 'solid' at all, but projected consciousness? Just a thought…

Ultimately, we are our own guides (even when the guidance appears to be external) because we are one small part of everything – *nothing* exists outside of ourselves.

photo credit: Andrew Einspruch

THE TRIBE

Billie Dean

Billie Dean is a professional psychic animal communicator with an international clientele. She comes from a natural therapies background, and is partner in the filmmaking company Laughing Owl Productions.

Over a 30-year writing career, Billie has written children's books, and has also written extensively for stage, television, newspapers and magazines. Her most recent television credits include writing for children's shows, notably Cushion Kids and the award-winning Hi-5.

Billie has also performed as a stand-up comedian, and with her husband, Andrew Einspruch, as a comedy duo, both in Australia and in the USA.

Billie was the writer, director and lead actress for her debut feature film, Finding Joy, which won her an ACT Film and Television Industry award (AFTI) for Best Actress. Along with Andrew, she has produced and directed numerous documentaries, corporate and music videos, and

programming for cable and experimental television. Billie was recognised as an Emerging Producer by the Screen Producers' Association of Australia in 1999.

Billie and Andrew's most recent film is the dog-umentary 'Seven Days With Seven Dogs' (2007). In 2005, they documented the development pressures on the heritage town of Braidwood, New South Wales, which, in 2006, was granted with a State Heritage listing.

Billie is an activist and a strong supporter of animal rights.

As a child, I was considered 'too sensitive'. Of course, now we know that being 'sensitive', often means we are psychic. But anything psychic was strictly between me and myself as I was growing up, because I realized early on that others didn't feel, see or hear what I did. I was very attuned to nature and animals and had a strongly developed intuition. I would 'know' things that others didn't understand.

I guess I first encountered my spirit guides in the early 1980's, when I became aware of the presence of a young female Native American during meditation. I learned that she was myself in a previous incarnation and that if I carried her with me when I performed stand-up comedy, I performed better as she was so grounded and clear. She was a healer and very serene and sure of herself – a far cry from who I was in those days… I was much more anxious! My low self-esteem led me to study all kinds of personal growth techniques and it was great fun to hang out with other people in the personal growth/consciousness movement, many of whom could see Native American presences around me. So it was all good!

Later, I was travelling in the UK and was staying in a healing B&B on a leyline doing some Reiki on a woman, when a whole tribe of spirit Native American warriors on horseback thundered into the room. They couldn't speak English and I couldn't speak their language, so they rode away in frustration. During this time, my mother, who passed away when I was eight, was also around me and offering me guidance.

My work with the Tribe really began in the early 1990's, when I came down with Chronic Fatigue Syndrome. During this time, I underwent what I call an ‘initiation into stillness’. I meditated every day and lived a life with this tribe (who now spoke English for me) while I was in a trance state. They gave me tremendous teachings and guidance about my life direction and after six months they told me I was ready to go back into the world working as an animal communicator because I was “woman with twin tongues”. Even though I spoke telepathically with animals and nature, I was worried about doing this professionally. I was in the entertainment industry and, while many people there were open minded, it was still considered very wacky to be psychic or ‘New Age’. So, I began very timidly, telling a few people I could help them with their animals. At first it was just my natural horsemanship circle of friends, but word quickly spread and soon I had a lot of work from people around Australia. The work I do now is in what I call a ‘light trance’ state. But really it’s just concentrating on the intuitive and inner vision, sounds and feelings with focus and intent. I love trance work, however, and often take shamanic journeys.

The Tribe is my soul family and is also the tribe I belonged to in a previous incarnation. I learned recently that my husband Andrew, who is also my husband in the Tribe, is our daughter’s spirit guide. So, to be clear, Andrew’s Native American spirit self, is taking care of our daughter, whilst his physical self is still alive and living with us. Tamsin, my daughter, was recently intent on getting a spirit guide painting. When the artist drew this wonderful Native American man, I immediately recognised him and started crying… we were deeply in love then, as we are now.

A guide I call Grandmother really encourages me to become skilled in horsemanship and riding – we have 28 horses in permanent sanctuary at the moment and I’m sure that’s her doing. Grandmother also gives me guidance about diet and health. I’m not supposed to eat sugar and am to have more water and flaxseed oil. This is on top of me already eating a vegan diet, non-drinking, non-smoking and non-drug-taking. I even had my amalgam fillings replaced without drugs! Grandmother nods and tells me "this is appropriate" as I write this. It helps to be a clear channel for the animals if you live this way.

A man I call Grandfather helped me create a meditation CD *'Time of the Drum'*, to help people reconnect with nature and animals and to remember and reawaken their own telepathic ability, essentially allowing people to enter light trance to journey to a magical world. Grandfather is also a healer and assists me to heal both myself and other animals in his uniquely shamanic way. He came 'out of retirement' to heal my dog Suki of tick poisoning and then turned up to support me and my adrenals when I was making my first feature film *'Finding Joy'*.

There are others in the Tribe, all with their own gifts and guidance. They also encourage me to write stories and share my experiences with people. I've been a bit slow, but I'm doing that now. And when we fought against the inappropriate development of our town, they told me the outcome and they were right – we ended up getting the town and its pastoral setting State Heritage Listed and the land was saved, as they said it would be.

My big challenge in life is to learn to be still enough to listen and channel all that the spirits have to say. Sometimes they scold me to go outside and sit in stillness by my pine trees where we all like to meet. They know I'll pay really good attention then, and will take notes. Sometimes a guest guide will come through with surprising information and wisdom.

I am always encouraged to teach and share the knowledge – to 'dream the dream awake'. This work is needed now among humanity, so many of whom are so disconnected from nature. It is always my great honor to teach what I have been given.

I asked them what it was like being my guide and they said something in their language that roughly translates into 'affection'. They said I was a bit slow to get started, but that I am on the right track now and there are plans to "make up for lost time".

The Tribe is always with me and I don't have to meditate or sit by the pines to hear them… I just have to listen. If I am doing something that is right on my path, they look joyous – big smiles and lots of dancing. They are a loving, warm family who offer advice and wisdom, and I am so grateful they are there for me.

photo credit: Eli Lund

INVISIBLE FRIENDS FROM VARIOUS DIMENSIONS AND TIMES

by Joshua Shapiro

Joshua is American and was born in Chicago. He has been active with crystal skulls since 1983 and is the co-author of the book, 'Mysteries of the Crystal Skulls Revealed' (with Sandra Bowen and the late F. R. 'Nick' Nocerino), and 'Journeys of a Crystal Skull Explorer'. He is chairman of the board for the World Mystery Research Center located in the U.S. and Holland, and the director of the Crystal Skull World Foundation, also located in Holland.

A note about crystal skulls:

Crystal Skulls are considered to be one of the world's greatest mysteries. Simply defined, they are human-shaped-and-sized skulls made from various types of quartz crystal. They have been found over the past 150 years within ancient ruins in Mexico and Central America. Researchers believe they are receptacles of great knowledge created by very ancient cultures, and were gifted to various indigenous people at some time – for example, the Tibetan Buddhists, Mayans and Native Americans. Some of these artifacts have even been researched by Hewlett Packard and continue to baffle the modern scientific community.

After I graduated from College (from the late 1970's till the early 1980's) a change occurred in me, where I felt that the physical world and the reality that surrounds us is not the totality of what exists within this universe. An inner part of me sensed that there was more to life…

I started to study all kinds of metaphysical and esoteric subjects, including reincarnation and past lives, UFOs, spiritual gifts... you name it and I was either reading about it or meeting people involved in such studies. Eventually, I even quit my regular job so that I could devote my full time to these studies.

A spiritual teacher in Chicago, where I lived at this time, told me that my first two inner gifts were the ability to feel vibrational frequencies or energies and my intuition or inner voice. It is my solid belief that every person has such inner abilities, but some may be stronger than others. Thus, it makes sense that your guides will utilise the inner gifts that work best for you in order to communicate with you.

For me, there is no doubt that, in our essence, we are spiritual beings who have taken on a physical 'spacesuit' we call a body to experience this particular planet (or classroom) in the infinite universe we find ourselves in.

Since we don't all have the absolute memory of being infinite beings, most of us forget about this divine aspect of ourselves. So, to help us along, we have these old (but seemingly invisible) friends who are only separated from us by the vibrational spin of their molecules versus our molecules. They are there to silently and subtly offer us advice.

In effect, we are never alone – there are always very loving beings around us, encouraging us to move forward, to challenge ourselves and to go beyond what we think we can do.

As I learned about the existence of these helpers, they began to contact me. I found they would whisper to me in my own thinking voice and I would also feel a presence around me. Sometimes I would see pictures in my mind's eye associated with the guide or message or information they wished to convey.

A key question then is – how can I tell when a spirit guide is speaking to me or when it is my *own* thinking voice? Well, I think it works like in the movie 'Always' (directed by Steven Spielberg and starring Richard Dreyfuss) – the main character dies and becomes a spirit guide, helping a young man by giving him silent suggestions that he believes are his own ideas! This is how I feel my guides work with me – I feel the presence of spirit as kind of a pressure upon my body and then ideas or thoughts pop into my head. I've learned over time to distinguish between my own thoughts and those communicated by guides.

I believe that my spirit guides have been instrumental in guiding me in the spiritual work that I am doing with the crystal skulls, which is indirectly connected to the transformation of our planet (to be completed at the end of 2012). I believe that the crystal skulls are not our possessions – they are from Mother Earth and we are just their guardians and their hands and feet to take the skulls and share them with all the people of the world.

It was during the writing of my first crystal skull book, '*Mystery of the Crystal Skulls Revealed'* (by Bowen, Nocerino & Shapiro, published by J & S Aquarian Networking, Pinole, Calif. 1989), that I first came into contact with Master Li – a Tibetan master who, according to my co-author Sandra Bowen, was the Dalai Lama's teacher in about 400 A.D.

Based on past-life hypnotic regressions Sandra undertook with F. R. 'Nick' Nocerino (deceased – considered to be the foremost expert about the crystal skulls while he was alive), she remembered in vivid detail a lifetime that we, the three co-authors of the aforementioned book shared together in Tibet. In an excerpt from page 71, Sandra details:

"*In appearance, Master Li (in this lifetime) was very old. (He had) a gray-white beard almost down to the top of his legs. He also had a moustache and sideburns. Master Li had long thin fragile fingers, a brilliant golden aura around him and he wore a Tibetan Style hat.*"

Sandra was told that, "*The Skulls would help to open people's memory banks of knowledge and wisdom gained in past lives. Master Li was considered a very holy man. When he was young, he went into the mountains and spent many years in silence. After he returned, he came as a Master. Master Li had a staff with a small Crystal Skull on top and there were snakes etched into the wood in the shape of a caduceus (two snakes intertwined)*".

We constantly felt his presence around us during the writing of our book and were told by Master Li, through the channel Kathy Reardon, that he had come for our protection and to offer assistance to us to publish our first book. In final parting at this channeled session, he said, "*With the planting of belief in self is the key to available knowledge to all.*"

Years later, we still feel Master Li's presence. I believe he is a guardian spirit for the work with the Crystal Skulls. He is an example of a being that is interested in helping humanity raise its level of conscious awareness and thus he supports special projects on the earth plane that can assist people to remember who they truly are. We are grateful to have his help, that's for sure!

I have another guide who helps me specifically in relation to a crystal skull that I know exists, but has yet to be discovered. He is my guiding and protective spirit in this quest…

During the excavation of a pre-Inca city in the northern part of Peru in 1987 (near the city of Chicaylo), the tomb of a king was discovered. In his tomb were five other people buried with him – four surrounding him and one above in a meditative pose, with his feet cut off. The ruler was wearing twelve layers of clothes and copper sandals. They called him the

'Lord of Sipan', because he was the ruler of this ancient city connected to the Moche or Mochica people who, according to archaeologists (based on carbon-dating of the artifacts he was discovered with), lived in this part of Peru somewhere from the time of Christ up to 200 A.D. and that he died at about the age of 40.

How I came into contact with the Lord of Sipan is through a strange run of co-incidences. In 1990, I went on a tour of Peru (50 Brazilians and one American) with my ex-wife, Vera Lopez. While I was eating my breakfast at a hotel in Lima as we prepared to go to Machu Picchu, our guide Marino Sanchez (who had written a book on his theory about the origins of Machu Picchu) for some reason that I still don't understand to this day, looked at me and said, "Joshua knows where there is a crystal skull in Peru!" And I thought to myself "I do? What on earth is Marino talking about?"

But then, suddenly, I had an inner vision in my mind of a group of Indians traveling in a procession through a tropical or jungle area – the person leading the group was holding in his hands what looked like a crystal skull. As I was seeing this vision in my mind's eye, I felt myself being pulled to the Northern region of Peru – an area I have never travelled to, nor did I know anything about.

I thought to myself, 'If this crystal skull exists, then I think it would be sky blue', as this has been my favourite color ever since I can remember. From that day, I started to see in my mind's eye, a sky blue, very transparent, crystal skull that appeared to be floating above my head on my left side at about a 45-degree angle in front of me. When I had this vision, I inwardly asked myself the question: "What did this crystal skull have to do with me and was I supposed to come back to Peru one day and look for it?"

My contact with the Blue Skull is always there – although, at certain times it changes its position in relationship to how I perceive it around me. In this way, you could say the Blue Skull is also a guiding 'spirit' in my life.

Over the following years, as I continued to offer public crystal skull talks, I felt inspired to speak more about the Blue Skull. With each passing year, the desire to go back to Peru to look for it in the North became stronger and stronger. A few other people have 'seen' this skull and describe it exactly the same way I do… a very human-looking skull with a movable jaw, similar to the famous Mitchell-Hedges Crystal Skull, but a transparent sky blue – the colour you see in the bottom of a plastic bottle containing spring water.

Another time I journeyed to Peru, I asked my friend Erik Mendoza – one of the owners of Peru Mystic Tours (the company that always helps us with our tours within Peru), "If a crystal skull exists somewhere in Peru, where would one go?" Erik is very knowledgeable about the various ruins that are known in Peru and spoke of several locations in the North, but he mentioned one in particular… the ancient Moche city of Sipan near Chicaylo. I never forgot Erik's suggestion and in 1997, I quit my well-paid job as a computer system administrator, and Vera and I arranged a trip to Sipan in northern Peru in search of the elusive Blue Skull.

All we knew about Sipan was the tale of the Lord of Sipan and the city they were excavating there. We were able to speak to two local archeologists and neither knew of any crystal skulls having ever been found in the ruins. However, when we arrived in Chicaylo, some strange things began to happen…

After we checked into our hotel, we went to a restaurant – the interior décor contained imitations of artifacts found in Sipan. While we were waiting for our food to arrive, my thoughts drifted to the ancient city of Sipan we would be visiting the next day. Suddenly, I felt the presence of a man – a spirit with great strength – standing behind me. He told me his name… but I didn't believe it! I asked Vera, who is very sensitive to energies and to spirits being around (she is Brazilian and was trained by the famous psychic artist and spiritualist, Luis Gasperetto), and she said, "Yes, there is… it is the Lord of Sipan" – which confirmed what I had heard inwardly. Why would the spirit of the Lord of Sipan care about a crazy gringo who is searching for some crystal skull that might or might not exist?

Part of the answer came the next morning when I woke up and saw the 'Lord' (as I called him) around my bed at the hotel. My right hand spontaneously shaped a strange formation – my index and middle finger forming a V pattern, my ring finger and thumb forming an "O" or circle pattern and my pinky sticking out at about a 45 degree angle. I felt "The Lord" (as I called him) had something to do with this crystal skull… that he worked with the skull somehow. I later learned this is a type of 'mundra' pattern for energy used in the Far East. When I do it, it helps to balance the energy in my body.

It felt like his spirit had come to help guide and protect me on my quest. He didn't talk to me much during this trip, but he was always around. To cut a long story short, I was eventually guided to camp out for three days near a sacred lagoon about 15,000 feet high in the Andes mountains called the 'Laguna Negra' (the Black Lagoon), near the mountain city of Huncabamba – not far from the border with Ecuador. I felt the Blue Skull was in this area, inside the mountain next to the lagoon, but it was not my time to see the skull.

On the last day of my visit to this area, I felt pulled to walk by myself to a certain location not far from the lagoon. As I sat in this space near a circle of stones, I 'saw' that a long time ago there existed a temple during the time of Lemuria. (It is speculated that part of Peru was part of the legendary continent of Lemuria, which existed in the Pacific Ocean – that when Lemuria sank, this caused the Andes Mountains to be formed.) I felt that I had been a priest in this temple. I saw glass cases on the wall of a circular room, and in each glass case was a crystal skull… the blue one I was seeking had been in this room before. After my vision, I had a very bad headache and returned to my tent to rest, but felt compelled to sit and write…

According to what I wrote down, the Blue Skull first originated in Lemuria and when it sank, the skull was transferred to Atlantis. Again, when Atlantis was destroyed, the skull came back to this area (now a mountainous area) and was protected by some people who lived inside the mountain. During the reign of the Lord of Sipan, some tall strangers came and gifted him this skull. He used it to help his people and to heal, and eventually requested his high counselor to take the skull and return it.

It makes sense that if the 'Lord' had the Blue Skull in his possession when he was alive, that he might be interested to see how it could now offer assistance for humanity and to the person or persons the skull was calling to (as there is no doubt I was being called for some reason).

The spirit there told me I was not ready to see this crystal skull – I had to work on some personal things to purify my energy first – and that I would return to Sipan one day with my wife. I had also felt that during the 'Lord's' lifetime, I was there… but I was not sure of my role. When I left Peru, the contact I had with the 'Lord' was energetically broken.

In 1999, I acquired a crystal skull made in Brazil, which has the name of *'Portal de Luz'* – which is Portuguese for 'Portal of Light' (see my title picture). This was a gift from Vera, earlier that year. When I meditated with Portal (as I call him), I heard that I must return to the temple area in Peru again, on August 26th of this same year, to meditate with the crystal skull for world peace. I dutifully returned to Peru, stopping at the museum near Sipan, where the bones of the Lord of Sipan were stored.

I asked if it would be possible to do a meditation with this crystal skull around his bones and was told that we could do so after the museum was closed to the public. Erik and his life-partner Edith, accompanied me on this adventure, along with a friend from Utah. Several people working at the museum also joined us. We formed a circle around the glass display case holding the bones of the 'Lord'. After we finished, I was charged with so much energy that it took me 10 minutes to ground myself. Some who touched the crystal skull said it was filled with a very powerful energy and was 'vibrating'.

The main purpose for this ceremony as it transpired was to fully link with the essence of the 'Lord' in order for him to be present wherever I am in the world. He integrated into my energy field completely. During this time, it was suggested that I might have been his counselor, who was buried with him when he died – the one who had returned the Blue Skull to the tall people, leaving it at the mountain by the Laguna Negra.

Desy Rainbow, my special friend and my third wife, gifted me another trip to Peru in 2002. It was while we were in the area that we were spiritually married by a shaman trained in the old traditions (a ritual that is probably hundreds if not thousands of years old), fulfilling the prophecy given by Spirit that I would return to the Laguna Negra with my wife. As it turns out, she was also my wife in a previous lifetime in Peru – she was the Lord of Sipan's daughter and I his counselor… he married us. He had treated me as if I was his own son, which is why it was important for him to reconnect with me, to assist in helping in rediscovery of the Blue Skull once again, so it can be shared with all the people of the world and, of course, DesyRainbow is also connected to this skull as well.

We still don't know when the 'Blue Crystal Skull' will emerge to the world but the 'Lord' is ever present around both of us… waiting for that day to occur.

Back to the Future…

Finally, let me pose this question: Is it possible that one of your spirit guides could be an aspect of yourself that comes from the future? Well, what do you think? Perhaps I should first speak about the concept of time and how time really works, as I believe, so that if I tell you that I am speaking to a future part of myself, it makes some sense.

It is stated that we live in a three-dimensional world that includes measurements for height, width and breadth. And that within our world is another dimension, which we call time. We believe that time functions in only one dimension – going forward – but I believe that time also has three dimensions so that you can travel forwards or backwards in time as well. Each moment of time is interconnected and exists in an energetic state of being which we can touch with our inner or spiritual senses, but not with our physical senses. When we go to sleep and dream at night, I believe that our consciousness travels to other levels where time (as we know it) doesn't exist, making it possible to travel into the past or the future.

Furthermore, I feel this next statement is absolutely correct, which is that all time and all realities exist in the simultaneous now. What this means is that all events and activities are happening at the same time but through our physical senses we cannot differentiate this (if we did we could become quite confused). For example, just as we use a radio set or a TV to tune into broadcast frequencies that our physical ears or physical eyes cannot detect, our souls have the ability to tune in to any part of our existence in the past or future at any time.

If it is true that we have these 'past selves' and 'future selves', then we could converse with that part of the soul residing in any moment of time… I, myself, encountered an individual who says his name is 'rJis' (pronounced *'are-gis')* – his name comes from the initials of various names I have used throughout my life. He says he is my future self in this current lifetime. RJis is living some years beyond 2012 - 2013, when our world has gone through a complete and total transformation – a time he calls 'The New Dawn'.

Also known as the 'Story Teller', rJis showed me a vision through his eyes of what the future world looks like. I am working on a story that I hope one day will become a feature film entitled *'Crystal Skull Chronicles'*, where I introduced the character of rJis. When I re-read this story, I am a bit surprised where the ideas come from especially when it describes a potential future. Could the description of this future really be where we are heading? This is what he had to say...

A MESSAGE FROM rJis

April 17, 2037, the 25th year of the New Dawn:

The world of 2037 is very different… We no longer have countries – we are united in every sense of the word. Our world is organized more on a community level, as each person has a choice to decide which community is right for them at a given moment and for how long they decide to stay. Our communities, or what used to be termed cities, are normally based upon a theme such as a community for artists, technicians or spiritual philosophers. I recall in the Pre-Dawn days that each city was filled with a random grouping of people with no discernible common thread to connect them. The people in our communities live and work together and usually host at least once or twice a week what we call 'Celebrations of Life', that gives the citizens of the community a chance to commune and joyously share with their fellow citizens.

Each citizen of the New Earth offers to our world and their local communities exactly what they love to do. Thus our citizens happily offer their unique gifts and talents, which is not considered work but a sacred trust. On most days, it is not uncommon to see people singing or dancing in our streets with almost daily celebrations (or parties) with friends and family in the evenings … People generally do not go to bed till late hours in the evening or into the early hours of the morning, as they stay outside talking and sharing with each other. Time has no meaning to us... there are no schedules to be met, yet each person intuitively knows when their tasks must be completed.

Hunger and greed no longer exist. No one is without. Ever. In order to truly live in peace we have joined together to provide for every being on this planet. There is no form of currency. If you need or desire something, it is yours. We attach no monetary value to 'things', nor do we expect anything in return for services rendered. All things are completely free. Not one child in our midst has ever known the feeling of hunger or thirst for anything, physical or spiritual.

Our small communities all over the world are interconnected to each other via our various forms of communications devices. We are able to travel quickly throughout the world using extremely fast transport aerial ships and, we are told, within the next two years we will have teleportation machines for almost instantaneous travel to anywhere on the New

Earth. We still have various communities who have chosen to honor and live the way of their ancestors in the 20th century, keeping the traditions of the old cultures. We also have special centers, where our citizens can learn about the member worlds of the Federation of planets that the New Earth belongs to.

Our homes are very simply constructed, using some of the new light materials given to us by our Space Friends. Usually our homes will take on a dome-like shape or is beautifully carved from pure (absolutely clear) quartz crystal. The inside of our homes are designed to not only be simple in form and attractive but the geometry of the home provides a healing and uplifting energy. We use specific combinations of color in our rooms in combination with music based upon the individual's unique energetic vibrational signature. For over 20 years now, in coordination with this home design, we have been using color and sound therapies to help heal people of any type of illness or pain (which does not happen too frequently now). We even have flying crystal cities (which has just been incorporated recently and is pretty fascinating for us), which use a form of anti-gravity beam to hold the city in the sky. Temperature is moderated all over the planet to always be pleasant (never too cold or too warm), again using a simple form of weather control technology. Yes indeed, the people of the planet Earth have finally been able to create a Paradise that is absolutely amazing.

The openness we have has allowed us to fully experience our spiritual selves. In older times, many people were frightened by their ability to sense the feelings of others. We have embraced this fully. There are some who have allowed their 'inner' being to develop to such an extent that they feel no need to speak aloud – instead they communicate telepathically. There are no longer any language barriers for we all speak the same language. Some of the elders and those who are nostalgic still speak in the tongues used during the Pre-Dawn times. We are all able to understand what they are saying because we can feel what they want to convey to us. When the Mother Earth shifted its vibration into this higher octave, many of the so-called psychic or spiritual gifts that only a few people demonstrated in the prior century became commonplace for us. Once, they were looked upon as being curious, fascinating, and even frightening. They are now beautiful, enlightening, and something to be truly cherished by all. Though it is a 'normal' thing, these abilities are still precious to everyone.

Thus, through the combination of our wonderful technologies and the loving vibrations that surround our world, all physical needs of each citizen of the United Earth is taken care of. When I think back to the events of the past several hundred years or so, it is truly a remarkable story of how quickly our world changed from one of great challenges and conflicts to one of total peace and calm. I can scarcely believe it myself!

photo credit: Debby Kaplan

MOLECULAR RE-STRUCTURING

Joel Kaplan

On October 17th 1996, Joel died in a car crash after having a heart attack. He was brought back to life with a defibrillator machine after being shocked seven times – the procedure prior to this was only shocking a person three times. He became a national case study and changed the life-saving procedure in using defibrillator machines across the United States.

Joel is now able to look at an individual and see very clearly into their reality. He has also been given the gift of telepathy to be used only in a positive manner. Internationally recognized as a medical intuitive, clairvoyant and healer, Joel is currently involved with many individuals, assisting them to grow and become more of who they truly are. He looks forward to serving all others at their highest level and for their highest good.

Joel lives in Boston, Massachusetts, with his wife Debby.

We're all spiritually guided, every one of us. We all have guides. In my early childhood, I used to see things that the naked eye shouldn't see and this was the beginning of an awareness about my guides…

When I was about eight years old, I saw different patterns and molecular structures in different colours form in the air. When you're that age you're free, so there's no restriction on what you see and what you know. Society moulds and shapes us, so that it goes against principle to see things that you really, truly, *do* see. The brain gets convinced that those things don't exist, and so you tell yourself that you never saw them. You block the memory. I always had an ability to communicate with the unseen world, but I was afraid of it. I blocked it out for many years, and then hit a point in my life when I gained a lot of self-confidence and made a choice to try and find out what it was that I was seeing. Fortunately for me, I was able to re-enact the memory in a much bigger way, which enabled me to connect much more to who I am.

I believe that we're all a lot more than we understand ourselves to be, which has made me try much harder to bring that 'who I am' through me in a conscious way. That's something I've been dedicated to doing for the last 23 years and has caused a lot of change in my life, opening the door for a whole lot of spiritual experiences to occur.

Ten years ago, I was driving home from work and I had a heart attack. It was totally out of the blue… I had no warning, no prior pain or problem in any way, shape or form. This caused me to pass out and to die in an automobile accident. I had no blood or oxygen to my brain for nine and a half minutes – usually after three minutes you have brain damage.

I found myself surrounded by a tremendous white light – a light so bright that you couldn't describe it. This was beyond bright… this was illuminant. I was overwhelmed by the light, but that wasn't anywhere near as impressive as the feeling of a tremendous presence. If I put my finger on your shoulder and I pushed down on you and it weighed 20 pounds, then you would feel it, but if I put my finger on your shoulder and it weighed *20,000* pounds, then you'd *know* something overwhelming was touching you. And I *knew* that it was God. I *knew* that I was dead. I *knew* I wasn't in a body anymore.

I was awestruck being in the presence of God. It was the most profound experience I have ever had. I felt euphoric. Human words could never describe the experience – it's beyond any words I could ever create, it was that unbelievable, powerful and loving.

The next thing I knew, I was looking down at my physical body and it was in Massachusetts general hospital. I had 19 machines hooked up to me and I was whirling around in energy form looking down at my body. I woke up inside my body and I felt tremendous pain, but the pain actually felt good because it was something I could relate to. Being outside of my body was not easy for me – it was an uncomfortable sensation, because I wasn't used to it.

Now I have no fear of death. I am really happy to be alive and to enjoy life's simple pleasures. It took me two years to physically recover from the reality of what happened. After my accident, I went back to the work I had been doing as a businessman selling auto parts. I had also been doing some healing work, and I found that this radically changed and became more enhanced.

My reality was radically expanded. When you die, you leave your physical form and, if you're dying a violent kind of a death, then the molecules that you are made of get forced apart in a real dynamic way – so this has enabled me to have a much greater perception, sensitivity and understanding. I believe there are no accidents. I believe everything happens for a purpose. My body totally let me down and that was part of my learning. That's what was chosen for me to experience in order for me to change in a very big way.

Pictures come to life for me ever since I died. Everything I look at comes alive. I 'see' in my minds eye. We all have 'minds eye', but we also have 'brain', and 'brain' tends to dominate and control 'minds eye'. My brain has surrendered to my truth (and that's not easily accomplished), so it enables me to focus more on whatever that is that truly is of benefit to others or myself. What I can 'see' visually enables me to perceive much more of the multi-dimensional frequency that exists around us. Everything is frequency.

I am able to take a person's molecules and re-structure them. Molecules are part of structure and we're all made of them. It's something that I'm more dynamically working with now. I have also been given the use of telepathy, to be used only in a positive manner.

My belief is that we're operating in a multi-dimensional way of being, even though consciously many of us are blind and don't understand that. I also believe that we're operating not only in the present, we're operating in the future and in the past all at the same time. I believe that each of us runs on a frequency that harmonizes with our past and future lifetimes. Consciously, we are not able to interfere with it, but in a sub-conscious way, I feel they're all connected and work on the same timeline.

For example, I was in Nepal. I went into a square and a lot of people came running over to me, wanting to be my tour guide. So I said to them, "Wait a minute – how about if I'll be *your* tour guide?" I walked over to a building and I started to describe what had occurred in that building. Now, consciously I had never seen the building before… but the truth was that I knew all about it, because I had had another lifetime there. The memory came to me when I arrived there. The locals were in total amazement that I knew all about it!

I've been in other places in the world where the same thing has occurred. I was in Peru and I went to Machu Picchu. I walked into the place and turned my head and I *knew*… as soon as I saw it that I had been there before. I started to cry and I couldn't stop crying. I jumped down about eight or nine feet into this place and I sat with my back up against the rocks and felt a tremendous energy field come into my reality.

You see, time is really an illusion – consciously we're living in time, but sub-consciously, we're *not*. You're operating in more than one place at the same time. You're here, but you're also someplace else.

Consciously, I'm just a small extension of who I *truly* am. And who I truly am is a whole lot more than I'll ever know. Who I truly am chooses to move through me consciously to assist all others. He is me and I am him – we're one and the same. He operates multi-dimensionally, while I'm his reflection here on earth. As an energy form, part of him is always here in my reality but part of him is also elsewhere. I know what I know about myself, but there's a whole lot more about me that I don't know. He knows *everything*. What guides me is who I truly am.

One of the purposes in my going to different places is to re-ignite, within my own true self, aspects of myself from other lifetimes that can be brought into this lifetime, because they're actually part of me. It's almost like a regression – going back into an experience of another life where these aspects, being the essence of who I truly am, can be brought into this life. This helps me to consciously undertake certain things that I might desire to do here in this world and in this life. The more that we acknowledge truth, the more our truth comes into us.

Everything that I do is done through guidance. I am guided by my ancestors and by other spirit beings – sometimes they're on the earth plane and other times they're not. I can tell you that their desire is to help me to succeed in my life's mission and, because they want me to succeed, they send me telepathic messages at times. Their communication is subtle, but my feeling is that they're trying to express their love for me in an assisting manner. In and around full moons I feel more presence and activity with my guides. When the moon is in a particular phase I feel that perhaps it's easier for some beings to enter and leave the earth.

I've been given a new life and my purpose here is to assist all others. I've committed my reality to the purposes of serving and, as a result, I'm where I need to be when I need to be. I open my heart to allow love and truth do whatever those things are that I'm truly here to do. I reflect the essence of who I am, trusting and aligning that reality through me to others when it's appropriate. I seek only to trust and use my intuitive ability to access the appropriate information to do what it is I truly need to do, and it's simple for me.

I'm *still* expanding the real purposes of my being here. My healing work has taken me around the world. I've worked with thousands of individuals that have come to see me. I've done things in groups. I've also done and do things in the moment and just allow things to happen that need to happen – I put myself into the moment and play my part. I feel very blessed to be here.

ENCOUNTERS WITH THE SHINING ONES

by Andras Corban-Arthen

Andras was adopted into the practices of a Scottish family of witches in 1969. He is founding director of the EarthSpirit Community, and serves on the board of trustees of the Parliament of the World's Religions. Andras teaches about Earth spirituality throughout the U.S. and abroad. He lives with his intentional family in the midst of a forest in the Berkshire hills of western Massachusetts.

I don't remember exactly when they first appeared... perhaps they were always there, from the moment I was born, or even before. For all I know, I may have come from them, or am, in some way, related to them. I have never been quite clear about the precise nature of our relationship, despite its longevity. If anything, the ambiguity has deepened over the years, not the other way round.

My early memories of them are like facets of a landscape enveloped by dense, swirling fog: bits of momentary clarity, some less fleeting than others – revealing enough to provide a sense of the scenery, but not of how the glimpses quite fit together with each other. Those memories are a blend of some things I've never forgotten, of other things I've later remembered, and of things that others (my family, mostly) have told me. Starting with the latter, my story goes like this:

Sickbed Companions

I grew up in a Spanish family, though when I was small we mostly lived in the Caribbean. Throughout my childhood, beginning when I was still an infant and lasting almost to the time of puberty, I was beset with some regularity by bouts of sudden and exceedingly high fevers lasting several days, which had no apparent cause and which would disappear as swiftly and mysteriously as they came. Sometimes I'd have two or three feverish episodes in a year; at other times, a year or more might elapse between one bout and the next – there was no clear pattern of predictability.

The first few times they occurred, my parents, as might be expected, became quite alarmed (according to my mother, I almost died during one early bout). They took me to several specialists and insisted that the doctors perform every possible test available at the time to determine the nature of my illness. This took place during the early nineteen-fifties, in the midst of a widespread epidemic of poliomyelitis, which my parents understandably feared might be related to my condition. But all the test results proved negative, and the fevers, despite their intensity, were otherwise asymptomatic, so the doctors were at a loss to find a satisfactory medical explanation for them.

After a few years, the fevers simply became a fact of my existence. My parents, though they still harbored some trepidation, came to accept them as unwelcome periodic disturbances in my otherwise unremarkably normal and healthy life. I, on the other hand, grew to look forward to each successive episode with great anticipation, for I quickly learned the fevers meant that *they* would be coming to visit.

They were my friends, my 'special friends', although, even at my young age, I understood quite well that 'friends' was a designation that did not begin to do justice to the nature and complexity of our relationship. They were friendly enough, to be sure, and would come and sit upon my sickbed for hours – keeping me company, regaling me with fascinating stories, playing unusual games, and teaching me things. But in so many ways they were totally different from my ordinary friends from school or the neighborhood – they were not human, were invisible to everyone but me, could take any form or shape they wanted, had all sorts of magical abilities, and would sweep me away on whirlwind voyages to distant lands and mysterious locations. I came to call them, in Spanish, '*los brillanticos*', or 'the dear shining ones', since, no matter which shape they assumed at any given time, they invariably had a soft, glowing quality about them, as if they were lit from within.

Naturally, most of my family regarded the accounts of my encounters with my 'friends' as being merely the feverish hallucinations of a sick child, perhaps combined with the pattern, common among so many children, of inventing imaginary playmates. There was not a doubt in my mind, however, that my 'friends' were real; I understood that there was a very clear distinction between my experiences of them and the imaginary or pretend games and characters that were also a part of my life, as they are in the lives of most children. For one thing, they appeared only during the unusual episodes of fever (they would not come during fevers that were directly related to ordinary illnesses such as colds, mumps, measles, and the like). I could not engage them at will or control their behavior, as I could easily do with the clearly imaginary characters that my neighborhood friends and I often embodied in our games. Moreover, my experiences with the 'shining ones' had consequences in my life that went far beyond those of any mere children's game.

As an adult, during a conversation I once had with my mother about that particular aspect of my childhood, she remarked having noticed at some point that the fevers appeared to be related to developmental and cognitive changes in me. I had learned to speak – and, later, to read and write – and developed quite a strong sense of self-assurance at a precociously early age, apparently in a very sudden and surprising manner, and my mother had come to realize over time that those developmental spurts seemed to follow particular episodes of fever. This was something I had implicitly understood, but had been unable to verbalize, as a child.

My precocity was a source of both pride and amusement to my family. At our frequent gatherings, they would often pull me out of playing with the other children and insert me into conversations about 'grown-up' topics – politics, literature, philosophy, etc. – in order to impress our relatives and friends with my intellectual abilities and poise at such a very young age. For me, however, there was nothing unusual or special about that – if anything, all the fuss was embarrassing and also rather confusing, as it seemed that the things that most impressed my family about me were those I had been taught by my 'friends', yet they steadfastly refused to accept 'them' as real.

I understood, for instance, that my early verbal facility which my family considered so remarkable – the use of extensive vocabulary, intricate imagery, and the ability to go off on lengthy and complicated tangents and yet return smoothly to the main point, for instance – was simply the direct result of the long conversations in which my 'friends' and I would engage using their unique language, which I can only approximately describe as symphonic: multiple sounds, images, colors and other sensations – each of them carrying a strand of primary meaning or subtext both simultaneously made and perceived, and understood both separately and collectively, providing an extremely complex yet elegantly precise form of communication. Somehow, I could perfectly understand and communicate in this language through what was, essentially, a telepathic process. Even though in the ordinary world there was no way for me to even come close to reproducing their language accurately, given the limitations of the human speech apparatus, in my febrile states I apparently attempted to do just that.

Needless to say, to my family, I was merely hallucinating and babbling incoherently due to the fevers; except that, once, when I was thus afflicted, a relative of my father – a professor of linguistics at a university in Spain, who had come for a visit – overheard and then carefully listened to the sounds I was making, and told my parents that I was actually speaking some sort of coherent language, although he could not decipher it. During other feverish episodes I was also overheard speaking, with apparent fluency, recognizable languages such as French or Italian although, in actuality, I only knew a scant few words of each at most. Those, I'm sure, would have been times when my 'friends' took me traveling.

Our trips were one of my most favorite aspects of my interactions with them. I never knew when or where they would take me next – all of a sudden there would be some sort of shift, and somehow we'd find ourselves in other places that would seem completely and physically real to me. Some of those places were actual geographical locations, which I would instinctively recognize despite never having been there before. My 'friends' would point out various features of the landscape to me, and teach me things about them. They would also introduce me to certain local people, and I would have no problem communicating with them in whichever language they spoke. The vivid memories of these journeys, and the ability to understand foreign languages, would often carry over into my ordinary life quite a while after the fevers had passed.

Once, for instance, a relative who'd been living for some time in Germany came to visit, and brought us a bottle of wine from that country. The bottle came in a fancy box that had some printed text in German describing the wine and the region from which it came. My father asked the relative to translate the writing for us, but, before he could do so, I seized the box and promptly made an accurate translation, even though I spoke not a word of German and had never had any exposure to that language.

Another time, we went to visit an elderly couple who were friends of the family; he was Spanish, she was French. During our dinner conversation, the woman told us a story of her childhood growing up in a certain neighborhood of Paris. After she'd finished, I spoke up and said that I knew her neighborhood quite well, as I had just been there shortly before. My parents became rather upset at what they perceived to be a barefaced lie, but the woman engaged me further and I proceeded to describe the environs in great detail, including the locations and names of streets and shops which I had to spell out, since I did not know how to pronounce them. Afterwards, the woman scolded my parents for not having told her of our recent visit to Paris, and it took a great deal of awkward explanation on their part to convey to her that my trip had been merely 'imaginary'. I will never forget her response: "There is simply no way this child could have imagined all of that. One way or another, he *was* there."

As an adult, I have traveled to several of the places that I visited on those trips during my childhood, and have almost always experienced a very strong sense of recognition – knowing ahead of time, for instance, what I would see upon turning a certain corner, or being able to find a desired location without needing a map. To this day, I sometimes feel confused as to whether I physically traveled to a certain place as a child with my parents, or with my 'friends'.

The overall sense of my interactions with the 'shining ones' was profoundly spiritual, though that is not how I would have described it as a child. In typical Hispanic fashion, I was raised as a devout Roman Catholic, and that fact, combined with my lack of years, prevented me from being able to make a distinction between religion and spirituality, and hence to articulate the nature of our interactions. Yet, with hindsight, most of my conversations with my 'friends', most of what they taught me, most of what they helped me to experience, fundamentally dealt with questions about the mysteries of the universe, about the nature and meaning of reality, about life and death, about the fitness of things and the right course of action to take in a variety of situations. My encounters with them, long after each bout of fever had passed, left me not so much with a belief, but with an experiential certainty that there was far more to life – to what was possible, to what was real – than we are ordinarily able to perceive. That certainty was to inform and steer the rest of my life in ways that, as a child, I was unable to really understand or anticipate, and eventually lead me away from the religion of my immediate ancestors and toward the mystical practices of my more remote forebears.

Beings of 'Light'.

I mentioned earlier that my 'friends' were not human, and realize that this may seem much too facile a statement to make. As a small child, however, I accepted this fact easily and implicitly. They seemed to be made essentially of light, or at least of something I perceived as light. It was not a dazzling brilliance, though at times, especially when they merged with one another, there would be blinding flashes resembling lightning. Rather, theirs was a sort of modulated, viscid luminosity, almost as if light itself could take a substantial, gelatinous, malleable form that could, in turn, assume any desired shape without losing its gleam.

Sometimes they appeared as glowing, floating globules that resembled soap bubbles, only denser. At other times they took on a variety of asymmetrical shapes, which I find quite difficult to describe in words. When they so chose, they could easily assume the shape of humans, animals, plants, rocks, etc. Yet, particularly when they took human form, there was usually something about them that subtly hinted at their otherworldly nature – some slight detail that somehow did not quite fit, almost like the sense of seeing someone wearing an ill-fitting hairpiece. In my interactions with them, they would frequently morph from one shape to another right before my eyes, though I was never clear on their reasons or need for doing so.

They appeared to have individual identities, and at the same time they could easily merge with one another, whether in pairs or clusters. I don't recall their having names, as such; rather, their identities, their presences themselves, seemed to be the equivalent of their names, almost like fingerprints or some other unique, indelible mark that defined each of them regardless of whatever shape they had taken, or whether they had merged with one another. Those 'mergers' had their own distinct definitions as well, composed of all the individual identities that had combined, plus some additional sense that defined that particular configuration as unique. It may sound rather complicated in the telling, but, to my recollection, I never had any difficulty or confusion with this process.

Some of them presented themselves exclusively in animal form, and of those, the one that appeared most frequently was a large grey wolf who was especially dear to me. During our encounters, the wolf remained mostly in the background, as a strong but inactive presence. At some point, however, he would climb onto the bed and lie on top of me as if he were a blanket – his muzzle inches from my face so that our breaths touched – and take away the fever.

I must confess to a bit of hesitation in writing about this as, in recent years, wolves seem to have become exaggeratedly romanticized and popularized as the 'totem animals' of choice. Back in those days, and particularly in the cultural setting in which I lived, there was nothing at all romantic about wolves – they were only feared and hated as ruthless predators. My grandfather, who lived for several years in the Basque country and was something of a storyteller, would often use the wolves of the Pyrenees as the villains in his horror stories, much to my dismay and loud protestations in the wolves' defense which, in turn, apparently caused some consternation among my family. That wolf has remained the closest and most constant of my 'friends' over the years, and at times his presence has been strong.

I have been asked many times whether my 'friends' used any particular term to define or name their kind, but this is not a question that I can answer easily. In their language, there was some sort of construction that came close to a type of definition or naming, though it is very difficult to describe because of the multidimensional, layered nature of their communication. It was, fundamentally, a relational term – one basic sense of it was 'the others', except that the common meaning of the word 'other' implies difference and separation, whereas their sense was something more like "the others of you" or "the others like you," despite the obvious fact that most human beings would probably not identify what I have been describing as being 'like us' at all. Other layers of that term approximate our concepts of kindred, lovers, beauty, friends, and companions.

I realize that other people, in different times or cultural contexts, might well have labeled these entities as fairies, angels, gods, spiritual guides, or, perhaps, extraterrestrials (and I have no doubt that still others would have called them demons, despite the fact that there was never anything sinister or malefic in my interactions with them). I have always resisted those labels in the assumption that, should they have wanted to apply any such predictable moniker to themselves, they could have easily done so. The fact they did not is, in itself, significant. In retrospect, I find it particularly curious that, despite my religious upbringing, I never had the remotest urge to force my 'friends' into a Roman Catholic context by defining them as saints or angels. Rather, as I gradually realized that there was not much point in talking about them with other people who simply could not understand, I kept my 'friends' in a very separate, protected niche in my life.

The question of whether or not they had genders has also arisen over the years. Given that they had no specific form, much less a human form, the topic would seem irrelevant. My sense, although I have no memory of ever witnessing any obviously reproductive act among them, is that, rather than being sexless, they incorporated within themselves not only both the masculine and feminine genders, but also other permutations of gender and sexuality that are beyond human comprehension. Indeed, there was an underlying quality in all our encounters that was quite sensual, even erotic. Being in their presence was very stimulating in a multi-sensory way, and, as a very small child, I had not learned to make a distinction between genital and other forms of excitation – it was all the same to me. I have previously mentioned their ability to merge with each other, but they were also able to do the same with me, and the experience of such a merging was one of indescribable bliss, as if I could feel every cell of my body, every part of my being, caressed by wave upon wave of overwhelming pleasure, joy and peace. I believe that, as I grew older and my sexuality became more defined, my attitudes toward gender, sex and pleasure were deeply influenced by my experiences with the 'shining ones'.

A Fateful Transition.

One of the surprising things I learned from them was that I was part of another family that lived in the United Kingdom, who were as much my 'real' family as was my family of birth, and that I needed to learn to speak English so that I could find them and communicate with them, though I had no idea who they were or how I might locate them. I casually informed my parents about this (much to their dismay), and promptly set out to collect and attempt to read every English language book or magazine that I could get my hands upon, and plastered the walls of my bedroom with photos of various places in the U.K. which I cut out from the magazines. Little by little, and without my consciously realizing it, the photos became more specifically focused on Scotland.

Just before I turned twelve, my parents made plans to move back to Spain, but a series of unexpected circumstances forced us instead to relocate for a few years to the U.S. (where I finally was able to learn English) and eventually to Puerto Rico. The move seemed to put a stop to the feverish episodes and, for the next seven years or so while being caught up in the complexities of adolescence, I essentially went through a period of selective amnesia during which I don't recall even giving one passing thought to my 'friends'.

Throughout my secondary school years, I found myself growing increasingly distant from Catholicism and from Christianity in general. I began to ask a lot of questions about religion and the meaning of existence, as so many young people are wont to do at that stage of their lives, but the answers I received from my teachers and from the priests of my church seemed very simplistic and unsatisfactory. By the time I turned sixteen I decided I could no longer be a Christian – a very difficult decision to make, considering that all of my family and friends were deeply Catholic.

Still, I remained with a very strong yearning for some type of spiritual practice, for something that would fill the void I felt within. I began to study other religions, mostly Asian and Middle Eastern paths such as Buddhism, Hinduism and Sufism. I also began to read about Spiritualism, Theosophy, and Native American spirituality, but, other than books, I could find no actual practitioners where I lived who could teach me about such things.

Toward the end of secondary school, I decided, clear out of the blue, to go to university in Boston, Massachusetts. I had no particular school in mind, knew no one in that city, and had no good reason for making that choice other than an odd sense of utter certainty that it was the place where I needed to be. Arriving in Boston toward the end of the nineteen-sixties, I was very glad to find, among other things, that the city was home to a wide array of alternative religions and spiritual groups, including all the ones I had studied and many others that were totally unfamiliar to me.

I proceeded with great zeal to visit as many different groups and centers as I could, in the hope of finding what I was looking for. One of the places I frequented, the Theosophical Society in Boston, offered a variety of esoteric courses on mysticism, psychic development, astrology, and so on, and as a result I also began to develop a casual interest in such topics. Unfortunately, none of the various paths I explored – for all that each had to offer to a young seeker – felt like the right one for me.

Then, one day, barely six months after I'd arrived in Boston, a friend who had just learned about my curiosity regarding the occult suggested that perhaps I'd like to meet a married couple he knew. They were from

Scotland, he said, and they were witches.

At the time, all I 'knew' about witchcraft were the very same things that most people held as true: it had all been about evil, about devil-worship, but in the enlightened years of the twentieth century witches only belonged to the realms of fantasy and superstition. I no more believed in them than I did in unicorns, and the idea that there might be modern people claiming to be witches seemed downright laughable. Still, my curiosity got the better of me, and I arranged a meeting with the couple.

They turned out to be quite intelligent, attractive, and personable, and not at all what I had expected. In answer to my questions, they explained that they belonged to a family of Scottish witches that had originated in the Highlands and been in existence for many generations. Then, in an exchange that lasted several hours, they proceeded to dispel most of my prejudices and misconceptions regarding witchcraft. They told me, for example, that originally witches had performed a variety of beneficial roles as healers, seers, magicians, midwives, and even primitive psychotherapists, in service of the common folk among some of the tribal societies of our pre-Christian pagan ancestors. With the arrival of Christianity and the imposition of a new social order, the function of witchcraft gradually became eroded and eventually marginalized, until almost all that remained were the unsavory stereotypes – the result of religious, cultural and classist prejudices – that eventually led to the persecution of witches, and which have survived until the present day.

As the conversation progressed, I began to experience a strange sense of agitation – a mixture of both excitement and dread. There was something about what those two people described as witchcraft that appealed to me and made sense in a way that nothing else had, and at the same time instilled in me a deep sense of foreboding, as if my life were about to end. I also realized that I felt an unusual familiarity with the witches, as though I had known them well for years. By the time I returned home I was so agitated that I could not sleep for two days.

Before our next meeting, which took place a few weeks later, I made sure to read all that I could find about witchcraft, in order to be better prepared. Our conversation proceeded in the same fascinating vein as our previous one. At some point, one of them made reference to certain spirit beings with which their family had been connected for a very long time. I asked them if they were talking about fairies, as I had read that in folklore there had been many connections between witches and the fairy-folk. They replied that the spirit beings had been called by many different names, but that their family referred to them as the Shining Ones.

As they spoke those words, I immediately felt very faint and nauseated, and it seemed as if the lights in the room had suddenly been turned way down. The witch couple's voices sounded quite remote and echoing, and as I attempted to remain focused on what they were saying, an overwhelming wave of long-forgotten childhood memories swept over me, and I began to weep uncontrollably.

My companions did not seem at all fazed or surprised by my reaction. They simply stopped talking and looked at me very intently through half-closed eyes, as if they were trying to see me from a distance, and waited until my sobbing subsided. Then they asked me to tell them the reason for my tears.

I immediately launched into a long and rambling account of my relationship with my childhood 'friends', punctuated by bursting feelings of yearning for them, along with a disturbing sense of disbelief that I could have forgotten about them for so long. I must have ranted in a nonstop monologue for well over an hour, but the witches smiled and nodded and listened very patiently, exchanging an occasional glance, until I could talk no more.

Then, very guardedly, they told me about some of their own experiences with the Shining Ones – experiences that were quite similar to mine. For the first time in my life I had met others who not only accepted the reality and validity of my childhood encounters, but who also could help me to understand them better, and to put them in a perspective larger than my own. As I listened to their stories, the strong sensation of familiarity with them which I had felt on our previous meeting returned even more pointedly, so that by the time our evening ended, I realized that despite having just met them I somehow felt as close to those two people as I did to my own family. The very next week, I had my first bout of fever in more than seven years, and with it my 'friends' – including the wolf – returned, as though they had never been away.

A short time later, I did what I could never have imagined doing, and asked the Scottish couple if they would train me to become a witch. Thus began a rigorous and extremely challenging apprenticeship that lasted several years, during the course of which I had to undergo a rite of blood-binding in order to formally become part of their family. As part of that ceremony, my teachers told me that, about a year before we had met, the Shining Ones had let them know that a young man would be coming to them from across the sea, except that they had assumed the sea in question was the Atlantic Ocean and that the person would be coming from Europe, not from the Caribbean. And so it was that I found and joined my 'other family' from the U.K.

What my teachers called 'witchcraft' was quite different from what has popularly become known by that name (or, synonymously, as 'Wicca') within the modern pagan movement. It was not a religion in the conventional sense of that word, as it did not involve any worship of deities or reliance on faith and beliefs. Rather, they described witchcraft as a practice mainly focused on the three areas of magic, divination, and healing (or *sorcery*, *seership*, and *skeelery*), which required that the witch enter, by means of deep states of trance, into what they called 'the Invisible World' – a transcendent dimension of existence which nevertheless intersected in places with the ordinary, physical world. By making repeated sojourns into that Invisible World, the witch learned how to interact with the various forces and beings encountered in that dimension, and to bring those powers to bear onto the ordinary world when necessary (some years later I would come to realize that their practice of witchcraft amounted, in effect, to a form of Western European shamanism).

But the journeys to the Invisible World proved quite difficult to undertake, as they required the ability to let go very deeply of the controls that keep us anchored to the ordinary world. As a result, for roughly three years of my apprenticeship I underwent a series of very intense and often terrifying psychic experiences that took me to places bordering on death and crossing over into madness, that shook and shattered my sense of my own self, of the world, and of what was real. These experiences were magnified by my interactions, under my teachers' tutelage, with a very powerful but unrelenting being who, in the physical world, generally takes the shape of a certain mushroom.

Throughout this process, I was often keenly aware of the presence of the Shining Ones around me; as far as I can tell, they never intervened directly, even during my most desperate moments, but, rather, seemed to confine themselves to act as witnesses. Yet, other than my teachers' wise ministrations, what held me together in the midst of the most overwhelming madness, anguish and despair – when more than once I was literally on the verge of committing suicide – were the memories of my childhood encounters with the Shining Ones. It was as if, at the last seeming possible moment (and there were several of those), I would somehow manage to find some tenuous foothold to enable me to avert disaster, and I could always trace those footholds back to some thing I had learned from the Shining Ones. In retrospect, it seems that during the course of our interactions they had laid down some kind of foundation to prepare me for what would eventually come.

The Guidance of Spirits.

In the ensuing forty years, my relationship with the Shining Ones has changed considerably from that of my childhood. Most of the time now, when they appear, there is no fever to herald or accompany their presence. They don't come nearly as frequently as they did when I was young, though when they do, they tend to remain actively present for months at a time. I am much better able now to engage them at will than I could as a child, but for the most part their presence is strongest when they contact me of their own accord. And I am no longer alone in seeing them – many of the people to whom I am closest have encountered them in some form, even people who've professed for years not to be at all 'psychic'. Indeed, during one particularly intense period of manifestation, they were perceived several times by casual visitors who had no inkling of what they were seeing. One of them was even recorded for posterity in a digital photograph.

I have long come to recognize that their appearances invariably signal some important transition in my life. Such changes have not always been easy or pleasant, though they have proven, in the long run, to have been the right courses of action. In the mid-to-late nineteen-seventies, for instance, the Shining Ones began to send me messages – gradually at first, and then much more insistently – to the effect that I needed to devote my life fully to my spiritual practices. In dreams, and later in a series of very vivid and complex visions, they showed me what some of that would entail – speaking and teaching publicly about the pagan spiritual paths, bringing people together in large gatherings to learn and practice those traditions, and building an ongoing community which would not only support that work, but would focus it on promoting certain necessary changes and developments in the world.

I resisted those messages vehemently at first. Given the 'fuss' that my parents and teachers had made over me as a child, I had developed a very strong aversion toward anything that would place me in a leadership role or in the limelight. In addition, I am by inclination something of a hermit, and the idea of being actively involved with hundreds or thousands of people was utterly distasteful and unimaginable to me. At that time, moreover, I had been for several years ensconced in a very satisfying existence, with an interesting circle of friends and lovers, a comfortable job at a prestigious academic institution, a good and steady income, and had just embarked on a plan to achieve greater material success – a plan that did not include any of the Shining Ones' designs. I also kept my spirituality, quite deliberately, as a very private and separate part of my life.

Yet, over a couple of years, their messages became more specific and compelling, and I began to feel some sort of shift happening within me in response. Eventually, within the span of just a few short months, I left my job and my home and withdrew from most of my social circle, organized one of the first pagan gatherings in the United States, accepted an offer to teach public classes on paganism and witchcraft at an adult education center, met my life partner, and together we developed an organization – the EarthSpirit Community – which for the past thirty years has grown to include several thousand pagans and others interested in nature spirituality. Those choices took my life in a totally different direction than I had anticipated and also involved a great deal of struggle and personal sacrifice, but, looking back on it now, there's no question in my mind that they were the right choices to make.

Similarly, during frequent visitations during the early nineties, the Shining Ones communicated to several of us, with great urgency, that we had to move to a new home somewhere in the countryside, and, once having done so, that there were several other things we needed to accomplish. At the time, we had been living for many years in the suburbs of a large city. Our community, our jobs, our children's schools, and most everything else that was central to our lives was located within that metropolitan area. To make such a sudden, drastic move involved taking huge risks on many different fronts – risks that, under different circumstances, we would most likely have chosen not to take. Yet, again within a matter of a few months, we found a small farm in western Massachusetts, sold our homes, and eleven of us – eight adults and three children – moved together to the country. Uprooting our lives in such a fashion, and for such a reason, was not something most people could understand, and many among our family and friends warned that we were making a grave mistake. To be sure, we experienced some degree of emotional and financial struggles at first, but for more than ten years now we have been living literally in the midst of a forest, in a natural environment much more suited to our spiritual practices than a city, and our work has grown in unexpectedly fulfilling and important ways.

I imagine that there may be those who will read what I have written here and conclude that it's simply a fabrication or the product of an overactive imagination… perhaps even of some sort of mental illness. I have at times come across those and similar reactions over the years, and fully realize how, to someone who has not actually experienced anything comparable to what I have described, my account may quite reasonably seem spurious. It's unfortunate that, outside of the realm of deliberate fiction, modern culture essentially sanctions only two acceptable choices – falsehood or delusion – for categorizing such experiences. Yet, having spoken about these topics with a great many people throughout the U.S. and in other countries, I know full well that my encounters with the Shining Ones are far from unique. I hope that this book, with the many and diverse perspectives it presents, will encourage those who perhaps have felt too vulnerable to speak openly of their own encounters to take heart, and that it will also serve as a reminder that, for all the vaunted progress and advances of modernity, we remain nestled in a vast and ineffable mystery, abounding with fascinating possibilities, remarkable beauty, and infinite wonder.

CHAPTER 6

ANIMAL MAGIC

If you talk to the animals they will talk with you and you will know each other. If you do not talk to them you will not know them, and what you do not know you will fear. What one fears one destroys.

~ Dan George, *'The Best of Chief Dan George'*

Lots of people talk to animals.... Not very many listen, though.... That's the problem.

~ Benjamin Hoff, '*The Tao of Pooh*'

Humankind has had a deep kinship with the animal kingdom since ancient times. Although this was probably often more as a result of hunting them for food rather than any conscious spiritual connection, our forebears came to acknowledge that different animals display different characteristics and patterns of behavior. Consequently, certain animals were 'adopted' as protective guardians, and to represent the strengths and power of a clan or family group. Countless examples of this can be found in heraldic motifs and coats of arms, as well as on the flags of nations and countries. This symbolism is also used today on the logos of businesses and organizations worldwide, though I sense that, in most cases, the true significance of this often goes unacknowledged.

The shamanic and magical cultures of the world have long honored and respected the spirit in all animal beings, knowing that they bring their own particular sacred wisdom and lessons, or 'medicine'. During an altered state of consciousness, or trance state, the Shaman 'journeys' to other worlds to bring back information and healing, which is often achieved with the help and protection of a Power Animal, or ally, in the Spirit World. The Shaman will often wear or make ritual and sacred objects from parts of an animal that represents his or her ally in the Spirit World, to attune to the vibration of their totem.

I believe that we all have a spirit animal that guides us – much like a guardian angel. If you feel an affinity with or admiration for a particular animal and wonder (as I did) if this could perhaps be the one, you may be surprised (as I was) to discover that your Power Animal is not at all what you had expected! One important thing to remember here is that *you* do not choose *it*… *it* chooses *you*.

The way we treat animals reflects how we honor the spirit in all things. Looking around, this is not encouraging… In our quest for control and domination, certain species are extinct and others – the giant panda, humpback whale, jaguar, chimpanzee and gorilla, to name a few – are endangered. We test products on them, use them in scientific experiments and also in warfare. We hunt them and breed them to fight against one another, all in the name of 'sport'. We even genetically manipulate them by cloning their DNA – we recently combined the DNA of human and goat to form a 'chimera'.

Most farmed animals live in appalling conditions. For the consumer, meat is something you buy mostly from a supermarket, wrapped in plastic and resembling nothing like its former self. Are we, too, merely flesh and bones? What makes us different from them? The answer is, I believe – *nothing at all*. Ultimately, each life has a consciousness and a soul that needs to be honored.

Happily, many people do enjoy a wonderful closeness and companionship with certain animals they refer to as their 'pets' (yet, curiously, they wouldn't dream of eating *them!*). My belief is that this bond is at a deeper, soul level than is often acknowledged. They choose us (although it may *seem* like the other way round) for a reason. The love and joy they bring into our lives should never be underestimated.

Even some of the most loving of 'pet owners' treat their furry friends as an inferior species. Because they don't speak aloud or behave as we do, it is assumed that we are more intelligent. Yet have you ever seen a person learn tricks or obey commands from their dog? How is it that we often don't understand *them* but they know perfectly well what *we* are saying? I feel that this is because they are naturally telepathic – a skill that perhaps humans would have developed more fully if they were more open and honest. If you communicate telepathically, lying is not an option. Most people prefer to use the telephone for this reason.

I have a strong bond with my dog – a collie/Alsatian cross called Sheikyer. He's an old boy now, but in his younger years he was quite wayward. He once took off on his own during one of our afternoon walks together, which wasn't unusual, but many hours later he had still not returned. I spent most of the evening sending him mental 'commands' to come home, and asked Spirit for help in guiding and protecting him on his way. At 1am in the morning, I was relieved to hear him bark outside! I believe he got the message (and, for once, actually did what he was told!). There are times when his doggy antics totally perplex me, but I'm sure he feels the same way about us humans.

Since childhood, many of my pets became dear friends and companions. In my college days, I had a white rat named Ringo who was my confidante. I would often take her with me on the train in a zip-up bag to visit my folks. One day, while waiting at the bus stop I noticed that she had eaten through the zipper – yet she chose to stand by my side rather than scamper off into the fields. We were good buddies. She had a wonderful habit of peeing on unwelcome visitors! When she died, I *knew* before I 'knew'. I was heartbroken. For months afterwards, whenever I wore my favourite jumper I could physically feel her moving around inside the sleeve (as she loved to do when she was alive).

In those days, I wasn't familiar with the concept of animals as guides but, in hindsight, my pets often taught me something about myself or showed me a different way to handle a situation. Although I didn't consciously hear them speak to me in my head, a communication passed between us. Even so, I have often made mistakes… on occasion, I've neglected to take Sheikyer out for a walk because it's raining or I'm feeling tired. Yet he loves me unconditionally. I feel that this gift of 'unconditional love' is the ultimate lesson that our animal companions show us.

photo credit: Shamanism & Healing Association, Munich, Germany

WHEN THE POWER ANIMALS BECOME VISIBLE

by Ailo Gaup

Ailo is a Sami, born in 1944 in Kautokeino in the northern part of Norway. He is a journalist, poet, and author of two books, including 'The Shamanic Zone'. Ailo resides in Oslo, Norway, where he teaches shamanism as a world heritage, based on his deep experience and knowledge of Sami history and traditions, rituals and symbols, and his own personal experiences and explorations.

Animals' senses are specialized and their incredibly-developed senses by far surpass our capabilities, but the human ability for creative thinking surpasses that of animals. Within us, we have sacrificed much of the animals' sense power and energy in order to develop our brains. We have come out of the 'animalism' to become humans. Although this has separated us from them, we still carry that link to them within us.

My culture has a history of working with power animals that shows how humans have an inheritance from the animal kingdom. That inheritance makes up a collective system whereby different animal energies and temperaments are transferred to us, according to what we need to become balanced and whole individuals.

It is good to be connected to at least five power animals – one for each sense, one for each element. Our animal allies can pop up as if by themselves within us when we need them. The many gifts we can receive from this animal inheritance include a beating heart, sharp senses, flying thoughts and many unique talents and temperaments.

The Bear

The bear is an important animal in my culture. It is described as both king and grandfather.

The bear dreams in the earth through the winter, and when spring comes it is called out by the sun. She-bear comes out of the cave with her young cub, who has two mothers – mother bear and the earth herself. The bear gives an earthly power to the body and the sun gives power to the soul, because the sun sent its beam into the sleeping bear's heart. So, bear represents the giving birth and the power of waking up, touched as it is by the sun.

In nature, the bear is a meat-eater, fisherman, and ant-eater. Their diet also includes roots, nutrients from the surface of the earth, and grass. If they can't find any of these they will eat rubbish. For dessert, they pick berries and love honey. They use their left paw best, people say. Bear walks with big paws on the earth, which in itself is a symbol of the earth element. They can also stand on their hind legs, swim in icy water and climb. Bear's only predators are humans.

Bears have adjusted to several climate zones. There are many types of bears… the black ones are dreamers, the brown ones are earth bears, and the white ones are heaven bears with footprints like star pictures. Lots of grand mythology can be made from this.

Due to its adaptable, earthly way of life, the bear is a versatile master of the soul. Spirit Bear is birth-helper – it is protector of children and is safety and security itself. Bear carries the shining heart, is mysterious, visionary, intuitive, strong and wise, gives nourishment to the soul and helps us along the roads of our dreams. Mother bear and child, the big and little bear in the sky, can guide the soul further when the 'last journey' is imminent.

In the Sami tradition, the bear ritual was in a league of its own. It was a life/death/rebirth ritual that renewed an individual's and the whole clan's life and power. Bear's power is strong and this energy was transferred to the person who directed the spear and killed the bear for the ritual. If you looked directly at that person you would injure your eyes.

Spirit Bear is virtually all-knowing and almighty and can be called upon in nearly all situations. All this makes him powerful but also dangerous and shrouded with taboo. Bear power could enchant a person and make them unfit for life in the village. Every Sami knows of stories of women who went off with a bear and, after a while, came back with a child.

One should not call Bear by his proper name – he hears he is being spoken of, so one must also be careful about what one says. If a person said something disadvantageous about Spirit Bear, he can trouble that person.

Bear is a bringer of happiness, a big eater and lover. A highly developed sense of smell is the bear's power – therefore, as power animal, the bear can sharpen your sense of smell.

Bear holds a reservoir of energy that can be used for healing and to allow a powerful development in numerous areas of life. Nearly all parts of the bear's body were medicine. Bear penises were big life-givers and were given as gifts. In previous times, the teeth, claws and bones were also held dear as amulets. Today, bear bile is very sought after medicine in the East. Spirit Bear is a holistic energy. It is strong medicine. The shamans collect this medicine from spirit bear's body – there is thus no need to kill the bear to receive a part of it.

I love the bear. I have drummed myself into the form of a bear many times and I have close relatives in the bear clan. I also know many other people that shape-shift into bears. You don't believe it? No, not before you see it. Are you sure your eyes have the ability to see?

The Dragon

Spirit Dragon is as old in our minds as the bear. I have no problem with the dragon only being a creature of mythology, or even if dragons as we think they look even existed. What's important is that it's an energy form that inspires us in our minds and our mythology.

Dragons and their relatives are the power animals for emotional and sexual energy. They symbolize the element of water. Dragon's power is connected to puberty and sexuality and the loneliness that wakes in young people when they separate themselves from nature and the power of the bear. But dragon has a longing inside… the longing for a partner. It longs for the moment when its fire can be set free.

Dragon wakes later than bear from its slumber in the mountains, under rocks or deep in the ocean, and drinks sun-flames from bear's heart like a baby does from its mother's breast. When it begins to spit fire and lay eggs, it signifies that a young person has reached puberty.

Dragon has a lot of relatives including those that bite their tails and carry on the circle of life. It is also related to the adder, cobra, python snake and mamba – not to forget the anaconda. They all crawl along on their bellies and must be warmed up by the sun before they really can show their strength and power. Our homely grass-snake is related to the lizard, with rudiments of front and hind legs. Dragons, I guess, are overgrown lizards.

Dragon-power has played with humans forever. We are enchanted by them, and totally in their power. Dragon seduces us by playing with our hormone-mirror and keeps us locked in a breeding-agenda for years and years. It is no accident that the dragon is the family protector in China –

the world's most populated country.

Dragon encourages our individuality, freeing us from nature and our parental ties, and turning us into independent people who start from scratch. Dragon shows us a new world of warmth and wet dreams – a condition for many of the critical and obvious choices we make in life, that being to find a partner, stay together and, last but not least, procreate.

The Spirit Dragon seduces individuals into ecstasy – the 'little death'. To receive the dragon's gift, we have to 'shed our skin' in order for new life to occur. As snakes change their skin, we too can continually renew ourselves from the inside. This is how the spirit dragon can free us from our hormone dreams.

The dragon's breath lights a fire that brightens up the hunters' land. In the hunters' country, the fire element is central. Spirit Dragon's job is to ignite the fire in the hunter's belly. This is the fire, the spark, that fuels our engagement and self-development, makes us honor our power and show this to the world, and stimulates our desire to succeed.

The Wolf

In our part of the world, the Spirit Wolf is the perfect power animal to accompany us through the adult stage of life. The wolf is the here-and-now power energy we need when we reach adulthood and are supposed to manage on our own and stand on our own two feet. The wolf is in charge of the taste sense and is fuelled by the fire element.

The inner wolf-pack within each of us mirrors how our meeting with life can turn out. But the meeting with that power can also create fear if we get caught up in someone else's raw wolf energy and have not found our own. Leader Wolf… Bloody Wolf… Grey Wolf… Lonely Wolf… Injured Wolf… which one of them are you in your adult life, your professional life, your family life?

The Injured Wolf in our inner-self has been castigated, disciplined, or criticized by others. Sometimes this wolf has not had the courage to use its own power. The Spirit Wolf's power is used here and now. It must be directed and steered and be used for challenging tasks. If you meet the Injured Wolf on inner journeys, the challenge is to nurture it back to health and then that will heal your own wound. It is said that as we heal, we shall be healed.

The Lonely Wolf has become lonely because it didn't find its place in its family, or it was rejected. The wolf constantly seeks its own – it sings, seeks and roams the forests. What the lonely inner-wolf can teach humans is to carry on seeking, wander on and not stop and sink into ill-health or self-pity. It's difficult for both humans and wolves to survive on their own. Companionship can occur in the most unexpected situation. Together we become strong, though it is said that you must do it alone if you want to become a shaman.

The Grey Wolf needs color and character. If you are a grey wolf outwardly, you need to help the inner grey wolf step into the light, show its talents and display its elegance. The grey wolf often belongs roughly in the middle of the wolf hierarchy, but the one who shows its beauty and the power of its talent can bounce higher up the ranks.

The aim for humans in relation to the inner-wolf hierarchy is to be an Alpha Wolf. Then you can tame the power in the inner-wolf pack and make them work as one. Through this, the pack will express one will – yours. This is how many dilemmas get solved. The challenge is clear, the obstacles gone. Nature's power flows freely through you and you flow with it. Under guidance of the Alpha Wolf, the wolf pack does what it's best at – run together, hunt as one, play and bring up their own young.

The wolves sing to the moon, in reality a false God – one who borrows its power from another. The moon gives off just enough light to explore our own feelings and instincts, but not enough to see further. This is why the wolf pack must be steered or led, or it can falter. It can be tragic for a hunter clan that must kill to live.

The wolf can go mad in nature as well. It can become intoxicated by blood and kill for the sake of it. It has been said that a wolf pack can destroy half a reindeer herd and ruin a nomadic Sami family in one night.

Humans can also become like the most bloodthirsty wolf and kill for the sake of it.

These three power animals carry the energy from inside the earth – from the depths of the oceans and muddy lakes, from the valleys and plains. The alpha wolf is supported by them all and carries all these energies within.

Helping Powers That Come From Above...

Born as if from the sun itself, these power animals descend from the light down to our consciousness – through angel pictures, on eagles' wings, and in bird flocks that land on earth – and include those animals that live up high in the mountains and on the plains.

Birds are mighty soul guides. They carry the gift of sight and give life to the air. They govern the air element and are masters of the wind's energy and power. Birds fly freely and easily like the thoughts in our minds, but also like the movements in our hearts. The sparrow is a heart-bird – it stays around the tent all year and flies in and out of our hearts.

Birds are connected to perspective and freedom, intuition and sight. The third-eye in humans can awaken like a hawk. The owl is a good power animal for the one who wants to see in the dark. But the eagle is the soul guide that can fly the highest – it can look straight into the sun without blinking.

Deer

The reindeer spirit is my favourite, but in the same family is roe deer, stag, and their big brother, the moose. The reindeer is a horned animal with thin legs that hardly touch the ground and has an air of peace, lightness and beauty. The reindeer thrives in the mountains, high up on the plains where it has air and space around. It is so quiet that hearing is its strongest sense. Reindeer don't hunt or hurt other animals, but live on low grass. When you talk about reindeer you talk about cautiousness and beauty. The reindeer equals blessing, forgiveness, peace, fellowship, moderation and unconditional love. The reindeer is the Christ of animal mythology.

A shamanic ritual I sometimes do is called the 'Wolf Wedding'. Here the beauty and the beast meet… In mythological manner during the ritual, the wolf's bloodthirst and the reindeer's flight instinct are transformed to the opposite. Bloodthirst becomes infatuation and fear becomes attraction. The result is love.

The Alpha Wolf falls to his knees and proposes to the beautiful white reindeer. If she says yes, the wedding can take place. The opposites are cancelled between the beauty and the beast. The two become one through inner alchemy. The wolf wedding creates deep changes and transformation in the inner self.

It's the dance that is lovely – not the pauses. The pauses can have last way too long. In this ritual, you jump into the big life dance again… the dance for 'The One'.

THE PATH OF POLLEN

Simon Buxton

Simon Buxton is a recognized elder of the European shamanic tradition known as The Path of Pollen. He undertook a thirteen-year apprenticeship with a Welsh Bee Master and key aspects of this apprenticeship are detailed within his award-winning book 'The Shamanic Way of the Bee'. Simon is also the co-author of 'Darkness Visible', the British faculty for The Foundation for Shamanic Studies and an elected Fellow of The Royal Anthropological Institute. His organization – The Sacred Trust – is concerned with the teaching of practical shamanism for modern women and men and its application to health and other challenges of daily life. He lives in Dorset, England at The Sacred Trust Centre, where he conducts his writing, research and teaching work.

My earliest memory is lying in a pram outside at night, looking up at the stars and having some sense of knowing that I had chosen to be here, on Earth. I can't have been more than two or three years old, so I suppose I was still a very recent émigré from the starry firmament!

But that memory aside, my first dynamic and pragmatic contact with Spirit was when I was nine years old, living with my parents and siblings in Vienna, Austria. I had become gravely ill, although quite with what was unclear, as there was no watertight diagnosis. My condition rapidly deteriorated to the point where my mother and father were told to brace themselves for the very worst, and I was brought home from hospital so that I could spend what were considered to be my last few days and nights with them. As they were readying themselves for the death of their youngest son, in desperation they reached out to our neighbor. I should explain that we lived right on the edge of the Viennese forest and there was just one other property in the vicinity – a very simple, wooden Tyrolean-style structure – and within this charming rustic home lived a retired anthropologist. He was in his mid-eighties and had spent most of his adult life undertaking fieldwork in cultures where shamanism was still very much alive and kicking and, at some point in his academic career, he went from being an observer of tribal cultures to becoming a participant within them. In other words, he became a soul doctor – a shaman.

In desperation, my parents asked him if there was anything he might be able do with his so-called 'primitive' healing methods and he apparently responded – without hesitation – in the affirmative. That evening he undertook one of three shamanic healings that I was to receive from him and, put simply, a healing miracle occurred. Within a week I was back on my feet, tearing around and climbing trees like most nine-year-old boys, the illness having been 'pulled' out of me, just as it has always been done by shamans the world over.

Being a recipient of this astonishing healing allowed me more than a glimpse into the power and the beauty of Spirit and this undoubtedly changed the trajectory of the rest of my life. I became firm friends with 'Herr Professor' – as our now revered neighbor was known – and he became the archetypal Wise Elder to this little boy. Most significantly however, in terms of my later life, he introduced me to the world of the hive and the honeybee, for as well as being a shaman, he was also a beekeeper. It was a potent portent for things to come.

Well, jumping forward seventeen years – I was now twenty-six with a *suma cum laude* university degree under one arm, a whole lot of questions about life under the other and not much else! I was living in England and had adopted the habit of undertaking long walks across different parts of Britain, with a particular love of an area known as the Quantocks. Upon one of these extended hikes I chanced one day upon a beekeeper tending his hives. I say 'chanced' but, in actuality, at the moment of meeting him I was overtaken by the most all-pervasive sense of a fate being met. In what seemed a very casual fashion this gentleman took me under his wing, and reintroduced me to the art and craft of the beekeeper. What was unbeknownst to me at the time, was that there was rather more to him than being a keeper of bees, for he was also a 'Bee Master', that is, an elder from an obscure and ancient spiritual path known within the British Isles as the 'Path of Pollen'. I was eventually invited to join him and his companions within this 'Brotherhood and Sisterhood of the Sacred Hive' as it is also known, and went on to serve an apprenticeship with the Bee Master until his death – when he chose to walk out of his body.

Traditionally the male teacher, the Bee Master, teaches the male apprentices on a one-on-one basis. The women within the bee tradition work within a slightly different format, as a group of six students together with their teacher who is known as a Bee Mistress. The women in the tradition are known as *Melissae*, which translates as 'bees'. This is a term that was adopted by women within the bee tradition right across Europe, adopted from the Greek temple traditions, which held links with the great oracular center of Delphi, a center of great and ancient feminine powers ruled over by the dragoness Delphine. The Melissae are transmitters of an archaic impulse central to the Path of Pollen, which is based around the fact that Melissa – the name of the very first Melissae – was the Goddess of intoxication and sexual passion. These two themes continue to be drawn upon, and much of the teachings given by the elders within the tradition revolves around the use of these qualities in order to assist in our growth. Here we touch upon an approach to wisdom, little known or acknowledged in the West, which is the impersonal use of sexual power and energy and the act of *Hieros Gamos* – sacred, impersonal sexual expression and union, known technically as 'The Serpent Flight of the Honey-Bee'.

These teachings were transmitted to me 'from mouth to ear' as the old expression goes, but I should make it clear that the spiritual interaction with the tradition itself starts in a very humble way. It commenced for me by undertaking the daily physical duties with the hives, learning about the considerable gifts that the honeybee brings. After all, the world would be a very different place if there were no honeybees. Did you know that every third mouthful of food we eat has arrived onto our plates due to her gifts of pollination? They are, without dispute, our most ancient allies and let us never forget that without them humanity would – in short – have a very bleak future indeed.

As part of my daily duties, I was instructed to follow individual bees in their foraging – which is far easier said than done! This process itself brought about an enormous physical agility, because bees can travel up to 20 miles an hour and can happily fly over several miles as part of their foraging work. Over a period of several years, my body became honed and I developed a tremendously useful, very high level of physical prowess. I was able to move silently, stalk, and to see things that typically for most people would be invisible. Regrettably, we no longer know how to 'see' in the wilderness or in darkness because that age-old ability has atrophied in most people, largely due to living in a culture of instant gratification, literalist intractability and an absence of the sacred in the everyday.

Over time, I began to learn something of the energetics, the 'energy dance' that exists between the human being and the bee. This can be summed up by two expressions we use, the first being the old English adage "Ask the wild bee what the druid knows". The second is simply "Tell the bees" which reveals the practice – if not the method – to complement the first. So, on the one hand you're being told to *ask* the bees for something and the other you're being told to *tell* the bees. There's obviously a connection between the two and in time the connection was explained to me. Firstly one learns, through a relatively straightforward methodology to shift awareness – how to 'tell' the bees, that is, how to impart to them all the key realizations that occur within one's development and unfoldment upon the path. One is in effect *depositing* what has been learned into the beehive itself as a type of sacred depository. By invisibly depositing the realizations within the hive, they will be able to be accessed by your successors. How? Well that is the other side of the coin of hive communion: the student learns a method to *ask* the bees for information – information that will have been planted there by those who went before. Thus, in theory, the student may request of the bees information that has been deposited there by any of the members, any of those involved in the Path of Pollen, right back to the very birth of the tradition. How long ago was this? To quote my teacher, the Path of Pollen existed 'before Eve's apple had been eaten'. It is indefinitely ancient but simultaneously ever-new and therefore there are thousands of years of wisdom and realizations that have been given to the bees in sacred trust, which can be be retrieved by the current generation of practitioners, who in time will contribute their own knowings to this sacred depository.

Something that I wanted to mention to you was that within the Path of Pollen all our behavior, all thoughts, activities and so on, in other words *everything* within our daily lives is undertaken as what are called 'total acts'. A 'total act' is when every atom of one's being is utterly and completely engaged with whatever it is that one is doing. And no, that's not just when you're doing something that might be labeled as holy or sacred or entertaining, but also when undertaking things which might be considered mundane, like doing the washing up, sorting out the recycling or paying bills. *Everything* we do is met with a full and complete awareness and commitment, and in truth this is something that is all too rare in the modern world. I recall, when I first commenced my apprenticeship, being asked to make a list of anything that I had undertaken as a total act over the previous five years. Try it yourself. Well, after agonizing about it for several days, I had to confess that there was absolutely nothing that I could come up with other than when I had been chased by a bear in Romania! That was it. Nothing else. The point is, that if you begin to live your life as a total act, it brings about a level of intensity to life itself that ushers in a quality of magic and wonder that otherwise would be absent. But that's not the reason we approach life like this… no, we seek to embrace life as a 'total act' for the simple reason that we don't know when we are going to die. As a result, we choose to live each moment as if it were our last – fully and totally. From our point of view, we want to ensure that whatever it is we're doing – our last moment on earth – is being met in full, so that we can celebrate a life lived fully; not half lived, or lived in bits, but lived *fully*. The primary regret people have at the time of their death is that they did not lead as full a life as they could have done and I would encourage anyone reading this to start leading their life as if today was the last day they had.

Something else that may be worthy of giving mention to is that from the point of view of The Path of Pollen it would be considered absurd to live life as a 'total act' and then go to bed and waste half our lives sleeping. There is this massive reservoir of time just waiting to be drawn from – seven, eight hours a night, seven nights a week. Hence practitioners on the Path of Pollen engage in dreaming practices which include dream hunting, waking up within dreams whilst dreaming, bridging the dream world with the waking world, exploring little known regions of dream landscapes and meeting at pre-agreed dream locations with our companions, including teachers that have long since left their bodies permanently. When you're 'dreaming true', you are able to move your awareness behind the trembling veil into a state of non-ordinary reality – the same non-physical reality to which the shaman travels when they 'journey', where they meet and work with their spirits. As an apprentice,

I was given instructions on how to begin to become more aware of life when I was dreaming and to assist me in this I was made to sleep upon a hammock, which was a remarkably useful aide to the work – indeed, even to this day I only rarely sleep in a bed. Over a period of time, I learned to develop a self-control and self-awareness of my dreaming life where the dream world became as real, if not more real, than the waking world, and a good deal of my teaching was given to me by my teacher whilst we both slept. The next morning, having written up the night's adventures within my dream journal, the Bee Master would read over my work like a headmaster marking exam papers. Even after ten years into my apprenticeship I could never hand over my journal to him without a snake of unease moving around in my belly!

And with mention of my belly, one of the other matters that is very well understood within the Path of Pollen is that the human body is one of the rarest commodities in the universe. It is truly rare. Unfortunately, perhaps because they're ubiquitous – you have one, I have one, we walk outside and everyone else has got one – we don't acknowledge just how precious they are. Now, within my experience of shamanism, a crucial exchange is made possible between the individual shaman and his or her spirits (I call them *tutelary* spirits). When we ask the spirits to arrive into our bodies so we can do our work, we are technically merging with the powers of the universe and this merging typically brings about an ecstasy for the shaman. But what do the spirits get out of it in return? Well, they receive the opportunity, albeit briefly, to experience the one thing we have which they do not have, which is physical, corporeal reality. It's a beautiful exchange based on the principle of partnership, which is the basic principle of all shamanic work. In other words, the shaman can't work without his or her spirits, but, curiously, the spirits can't do the work without the presence and involvement of the shaman.

From my explorations of the universe, I consider that all human beings have made the decision to come to earth – there are no errors in this regard. Imagine before you were born, before you had chosen to accept this extraordinary gift of having a physical body… there you are out there in the Universe, pure consciousness and awareness, and you make a decision to move your awareness to earth. You plan to come to earth to express certain gifts, talents and your strengths – that's the big contribution that you're going to be making, to feed into humanity's evolution. And to do that, you're going to make certain appointments that you're going to try and meet. Your first appointment will be your birth, and your last appointment, of course, will be your death. In between that first and last appointment, you make a number of other appointments. Then you're born. You come into the world as a pure bundle of love. You've come to express these gifts and talents and strengths and you've made a number of appointments that will encourage you to do that… but you don't always receive the love or protection that you need and, as a result of that, you begin to accumulate wounds. These woundings within our personal lives can delay, distract and deflect us from meeting the different appointments we made in order to ensure that we do indeed express all the gifts and talents and strengths that we're here to express in this lifetime. Indeed, the vast majority of people become so deflected and deviate so far from why they are here, that they forget to even ask the key question. It is one of the perennial questions that we must return to again and again – "Why am I here?" – in the knowing that by bringing our attention to the question, cogs will begin to turn and revelations will, in due time, arrive.

I have absolutely no doubt that I had an appointment with my childhood illness, an appointment with Herr Professor and with the Bee Master. I also had an appointment with the Path of Pollen itself. The perennial questions that I ask myself when I look into the mirror of self-reflection are "Am I meeting my appointments?", "What may the next appointment be?" and "What do I need to change in my life in that I may meet my next appointment?". The great challenge is that we have to recover who we *really* are, not who we were told we were by our culture, our education and our parents, and we can only do that with any success if we undertake the quest as a total act.

Authentic spiritual and progress upon one's spirituality path is a meritocracy. In other words, it's strictly based on merit. It's based on how hard any one person is prepared to work – to toil the soil of the self – and what level of commitment they make towards their evolution. The great exploration to discover our potential is, by definition, in the place of the unknown. It's the unknown where our riches lie… not in the familiar place of the known. For us to have the greatest chance of embracing the fullness of the mystery of who we are, we have to liberate sufficient personal energy to explore the unknown landscapes. To do this, we need first to ruthlessly look at our lives and determine which things are depleting energy from us. And then? And then we release those things – be they addictions, patterns of behavior, relationships, possession and so on. Having done this, we need to ensure that we replace the released patterns of behavior, relationship, etcetera, with those that feed and support us. A ruthless look at one's life will typically cause radical changes to come about, as we realize, for example, that after many years a particular relationship is no longer feeding and supporting our sacred dreams – and, incidentally, if that is the case it won't be feeding *their* sacred dreams either. And the more energy that can be liberated from areas in your life that aren't serving you, the more energy that you will have access to which will support you as you move further into the unknown towards who you really are. We could say it is a matter of simply redistributing energy – a form of alchemy if you like.

One is being asked to, metaphorically, leap off the side of a mountain… but you don't get to know whether you're going to soar or crash until after you make the jump. It couldn't be any other way, because if you *knew* that you would fly like the wren or the eagle – there would be no personal challenge involved, no courage invoked. Daring to become who we really can be takes personal effort and courage and it is naïve to think otherwise. What we can do, however, is dare to put our trust in the universe and, in my experience, the universe wants one thing from us above all others – and that is for us to become *everything* we could be; to meet all the appointments we are here to meet.

People are sometimes wary of practitioners of bee wisdom, as they associate the honeybee with the pain of being stung, and that's fair enough! However, we use the venom and the sting as part of our work to bring about healing. The Bee Masters and Bee Mistresses are adepts at the use and application of bee venom that is held within the bee sting of all female bees within the beehive, with the exception of the queen. This is known as the Sacramental Venom or the Secret Fire. Much of the training given to the apprentice involves learning how to apply the venom onto the human body in the form of a type of acupuncture needle – in fact, it's well understood that the application of the bee sting was the forerunner of Chinese acupuncture. However, the application of Sacramental Venom is used not only as a phenomenally potent means of healing, including very severe chronic disease, but also can be used as a means of inducing certain transcendental states, allowing the students to move into certain spiritual threshold locations where they can meet with the spiritual denizens of the tradition itself.

At the very outset of entrance into the Path of Pollen, the male apprentices are typically given a ritual initiation that involves being stung in multiplicity on various parts of the body. This induces a shift of awareness from ordinary reality into a communion with the hive and the wisdom of the hive itself. If the apprentice survives, and I say that because it can be very traumatic, then the link that the apprentice has with the hive is rarely if ever unbroken, and the work proper begins from that point. Following that, typically the apprentice is put into physical darkness for a period of up to 23 days and nights. This period of darkness is both challenging and beautiful, for – paradoxically – darkness is understood to be a remarkable tool to discover and explore our luminosity. In other words by stepping into darkness we can achieve enlightenment! We call this work 'Darkness Visible' and darkness itself is known by us to be one of the great tools to be drawn upon. But, like owning a human body, because it is common and free of charge – it arrives every time the sun sets, every time we blink – its phenomenal value has been rarely understood by the 'outside world', as it were. One of my great joys in recent years has been taking people into darkness for a handful of days and nights. It is here where they have a chance to interact not only with their own luminosity but also with the most ancient spirit in the universe; the spirit of darkness; she who gave birth to all other spirits, including the pantheons of the gods of light.

I believe that we're coming to a time in history where the old apprenticeship systems are not necessarily the ones that best serve us anymore. In the old days, apprenticeships were the prevalent model for a variety of reasons – one was for preservation, of the self and the tradition itself. This is the fashion in which the Bee tradition survived in Europe when many of the other pagan ways did not, because it was effectively an enclosed order and was invisible to the outside world. This cenobitic, discreet way of existing and operating allowed the Path of Pollen to survive periods when persecution and missionization were rampant. The other primary reason for the apprenticeship system was to ensure the integrity of the teachings so that they were neither abused nor misused. The former reason has now gone and we live increasingly – with some notable exceptions – in cultures that embrace a spiritual democracy. As for the latter reason, well, if anything, there's too *much* information out there, not too little, and so the challenge for people in this day and age is to use their sword of discernment to determine a spiritual tradition that can truly help them, taught by *bone fide* teachers. And although my book describes a traditional apprenticeship, I was the final apprentice within the old system and the task that I was given was to seek to bring this material out to the public – to externalize what had historically been a very private body of work. In doing that, the apprenticeship system becomes broadly redundant as teachings that until recently were considered to be private and handed down from 'mouth to ear' are now available at your local bookstore and taught within seminars! Even a generation ago this would have been seen as absurd – madness no less! But, in fact, to my delight it has become clear that teachings from The Path of Pollen that are being shared to those who aren't involved in a strict and formal sense in the tradition, are as potent outside as within the format to which I was introduced to them.

I consider one of the poignant matters regarding this work is that so much of it involves working outside the circles of time. That's when you move through the veil, and arrive into the parallel universe of the shaman – you're working outside of time and space. But, even more interestingly, it's a place where everything that ever has happened and everything that ever will happen is happening *simultaneously*. And once you've been exposed to that kind of reality – no time, no space, that everything that's ever happened is happening at the same time – then you will have a somewhat different way of interacting with the illusion of linear time.

Upon the Path of Pollen we have a particular concern and interest in the concept of infinity. The symbol of infinity - more properly called the 'lemniscate' - is the 8 on its side, and is used as the basis of much of the work that we do. We call this practice The Dance of Infinite Flight or the *Lemniscatic Volatus* and it can most easily be described as 'walking the 8' or the Walk of Infinity. It harks back to and beyond the ancient dance of our forebears within the European witch cult – the dance that was known across parts of Europe as the 'Volta', based on the so-called 'waggle dance' of the honeybee. If you observe a beehive, you will see the bees dancing this symbol. Anyway, the Dance of Infinite Flight is introduced to the student not only in symbolic form, but also as a map – a comprehensive physical educational system, and an internal energy system that generates well-being, mental alertness, emotional balance and longevity. Beyond these applications, the lemniscatic dance of the *Analemma* is eventually revealed, demonstrating how it may be utilized to move between worlds and step outside and beyond the circles of time.

I invite you to try it… put 10 minutes aside, and, as a Total Act, walk the figure 8. What will typically be discovered is that after just 10 minutes you will find that your level of mental clarity and your sense of balance and well-being have been heightened to a noticeable degree. Simply by walking that figure – the figure that was a gift to us from the bees – has the effect of bringing a beautiful harmony and balance between the left hand and the right hand sides of the brain. The Path of Pollen walks equally in an impeccably balanced fashion, both the left hand and right hand paths, accessing the intellect and intuition evenly, and seeking to balance the feminine and the masculine within the physical body and within the psyche of the individual. One of the gifts that the hive has brought us is the opportunity to create a balanced life constantly exploring infinity itself.

This is not a matter of escaping – for spirituality can be and is misused as an escape route from the appointments that we are here to meet. This tradition is rooted in physical discipline, so there is much less chance of the aspirants becoming involved with abstract notions and theories, or indeed using – misusing – their spiritual path as an avenue of escaping the demands of incarnation and involvement in the physical world. Those who walk this way seek to embody spirit into matter upon this beautiful blue-green jewel that is our earth, our home – it is our only home. And because of our communion with nature, we have a particular awareness of the fragile, precarious times that we live in and how important it is for us to allow the honeybee to continue to do her work of pollination. When nature has work to be done, she creates a genius to do it – the humble honeybee, our most ancient ally.

I continue to be guided by my teacher from behind the veil. He spent so much of his life seamlessly moving his awareness from within to without his body, that when he died it was undertaken as conscious act, a conscious death – he simply chose to walk out of his body, his appointments all having been met. He seamlessly stepped from the role of elder to the role of ancestor, and his awareness continues to be with me as guide, mentor and friend – and indeed not just for me, but also for most of my colleagues and companions within the Path of Pollen. It is our birthright to have communion and guidance from Spirit and spirits – we simply need to open the door, to draw back the veil and then run forwards into the unknown as if it were our last moment on Earth. Why? Because it may be….

SPIRIT

by Laurie Lacey

Laurie is a writer, painter, naturalist, and traditional medicine-maker from Lunenburg County, Nova Scotia, Canada. He has worked for over thirty years with the plant and tree medicines of the North American Native peoples and has authored three books, including 'Medicine Walk: Reconnecting to Mother Earth'.

My brother found a young male crow, less than a year old, alongside a major highway – he had been struck by a car and was in bad shape. His beak and many of the wing feathers were broken, and his feet were also damaged. As I live in the country, in some respects I suppose I was the ideal candidate to care for him. I have an awareness of the roles birds play in many Native cultures and I was already familiar with crow legends from a shamanic and folkloric perspective, so I jumped at the chance to actually *live* with a legend!

Spirit was small for a young crow, as his growth had been stunted by the accident. After giving the matter of creating Spirit's own space much thought, I decided to keep him in a large cardboard box in my cabin and was delighted when he accepted his new home. He particularly enjoyed the dried grasses in the bottom of the box. This was where he spent the remainder of the autumn and the winter months that followed. In early spring, nature rewarded my two-winged friend with new feathers and mended his beak to its original shape and size. The latter was a miracle, contrary to the educated opinion of certain people, who had assured me that a crow could not grow a new beak. His feet were another story… they healed but remained badly disfigured, making it impossible for him to perch on a branch.

I struggled with my desire to maintain the 'wild' nature of the bird – to have as little influence in his development as possible. My attitude soon changed, however, as medical opinion confirmed that it was impossible to fix his legs and feet. I was forced to concede that this crow would live the rest of his life in close interaction with humans, especially myself, and I figured we were undoubtedly placed together for reasons unknown to both of us.

As I witnessed his effort to adapt to and overcome handicaps, to live a crow life within the confines of a human environment, I soon felt a tremendous respect for his spiritedness. For example, he quickly adapted to life within my cabin and to moving about in his straw box, contentedly pecking away at its walls. He was not averse to flying, despite more than one crash-landing. Eventually, he learned to land smoothly, despite his battered feet. Upon witnessing his determination, I realized that I should name him 'Spirit'. I thought this name was especially appropriate since, at some primal level, I felt he brought me closer to the spirits or devas, which legends say protect and nourish the minerals, plants and animals on their evolutionary paths.

This helped me to realize what a blessing he was in my life. I believe I was touched by deva magic one chilly November night, while asleep in the loft of my cabin. As I recall, I awoke to the sounds of the movement of Spirit's feet on his grass bed. When I peered downstairs to investigate further, I was struck by sparks of moonlight dancing in his magical eyes. It was as if the light of the moon was the medium by which something very special was communicated between us. I am convinced that this special 'something' was the primal soul nature of the crow. If one accepts the premise that we humans are not alone in possessing the quality of soul, then it is not difficult to accept this interpretation. The world is, indeed a magical place.

For as long as I can remember, my mind and emotions, as well as my spiritual feelings, concepts, and expressions, have been fostered by nature and the natural world. So, in this respect, you might say that living with Spirit reinforced my nature-based spiritual path.

I studied anthropology at the University of King's College and Dalhousie University in Halifax, Nova Scotia. Since I've always been an outdoors type of person, I was attracted to ethnobotany. At that time, Carlos Castaneda's books were appearing on the market – I was totally fascinated with them!

I studied plant and tree medicines with people from the Mi'kmaq First Nation of Atlantic Canada (Atlantic provinces) and would often hitch-hike to Reserves to speak with the Elders. I thought it would be a one-shot deal – that I would write my report and that would be the end of the plant medicine research, but then it took over my life. The medicines are like that... when you get started, they take you on a journey, and you don't know where it will end. I gave talks and field walks, and got invitations to attend Native powwows. Later, I learned that my great grandmother was Mi'kmaq, and that I inherited some Native blood through her and my grandfather. I suppose you could call me a Metis, because I have mixed heritage – I am primarily Irish, Mi'kmaq, and Swiss/French, but the Native factor seems to be quite strong in my mental and emotional life.

I didn't truly appreciate the full extent of crow intelligence, until Spirit came along. The entire experience of living with Spirit was a medicine journey. Because he was quite handicapped and required a lot of care, we became very close. I gained knowledge of many types of crow vocalizations, of how crows behaved in the dark as opposed to the light, of their playful nature, and their keen sight, their patience, and alertness. All those things gave me a splendid knowledge of crow characteristics. I learned that crows are sentient creatures – they have their own awareness and know very well what's going on about them. They have an awareness unique to their species.

What really 'fluffed' his feathers or annoyed him the most was when I came home at night and suddenly flicked on the lights in my cabin. The feathers on the back of his neck stood on end, while he gave me a severe verbal blasting with a series of low-pitched sounds, which I imagined were the equivalent of every four-letter word in the English language! He simply found it difficult to tolerate a sudden switch from darkness to light. I quickly learned my lesson and began to introduce light in a gradual fashion whenever I returned to my cabin in the dark. This practise proved to be much more satisfactory, and eventually he refrained altogether from verbal abuse.

Spirit was also very good at mimicking, mocking and replying to sounds. Over the years, I learned to communicate with him either vocally or thorough 'tapping' sequences. For instance, in the winter when Spirit was in my cabin, I would often listen for his movements when I awoke during the night. If there was silence, I would tap my knuckles three or more times on the floor, then listen for a reply. Spirit was somewhat of a trickster, and might remain quiet, though I knew he was listening. So I would tap again. Soon he would respond by tapping his cardboard box or some other object, sometimes with an exact copy of my pattern. When this happened, we usually continued our game until we became bored, or I fell asleep.

He was really quite funny! He made me laugh – a deep gut laugh, the kind that feels really good and brings tears to the eyes. We should all learn to cultivate this kind of laughter… it's good for the soul, and makes the world a more joyous place. It was like a gift that Spirit gave me, this laughter.

Spirit was a catalyst. As his full range of capabilities started to grow on me, I realized that he appeared in my life for reasons (many of which I didn't know), and that I should focus on our relationship more fully. More than anything, he made me aware of the importance of the crow in my life. So, that awareness made me pay more attention to things around me.

Having Spirit in my life made me realize that my relationship to crows was more than a passing fancy. It made me realize that my affinity for those birds was very similar to someone who feels a strong attachment to the desert, or to the mountains. I felt drawn to Spirit and to learning and sharing with Spirit on many levels. It felt like our souls or spirits were meant to meet, so that we could share life experiences – that I could have a glimpse of crow experience, while he was having a glimpse of human experience. I think we both fostered one another's evolution.

I recall a few times when I had dreams involving crows, which could have been a form of dream communication, but telepathy was a more frequent way of communication between us. I often knew in advance what he was up to, for instance, or where to go in order to experience other crows in the wild. He guided me on some of my forest adventures, in terms of learning about crows, or finding medicinal plants. He always seemed to be there in my mind.

Everything is connected – there is no separation between the physical and spiritual worlds. The spirit is present in nature. The plants teach you things and the crow teaches you things, and they can interact with their lessons and healings. The crow might guide you to a particular plant, for instance – it's just like the butterfly… perhaps the butterfly will land on a plant that you need as medicine. They are inter-connected.

I knew for years, prior to Spirit's arrival, that the crow was special to me, and a medicine bird for me, but it was totally personal – something just between myself and the crows. Spirit seemed to make me focus more on it, and to learn about what that meant in my life. I realized that it also went quite harmoniously with my interest in plant medicines. There wasn't any conflict.

I've been involved with traditional Native medicines for over thirty years, and am recognized by Native peoples as a medicine maker. I give presentations and also conduct nature awareness workshops. When I did a presentation, I would often see crows at propitious moments, so I knew the presentation would go well! I'm always on alert when a crow appears, wondering what it's telling me. As a result of my bond with Spirit, I began to integrate crow medicine teachings in my workshops.

Crows are social birds and have probably always lived close to human society. Humans have had ample opportunity to witness crow behaviour and to enshrine it in legend and myth. I like to believe that those legends and myths of Native North American peoples were, in part, created to express admiration and respect for the intelligent and cunning nature of the crow, genetically preserved and expressed in the actions, tendencies and behaviour of each generation of crows.

Crows can play a spiritual role in the lives of humans – they can be allies, and carriers of spiritual messages. Crow medicine is simply a willingness to be open to what you can learn from those birds, and the realization that they can learn from you. From that point, you then develop a deep affinity or attachment – when you meet a crow in the forest, it is like you are meeting a friend. Then, you have to be open to all the possibilities they offer as your ally. Perhaps they will show you the way out of the forest if you are lost. Perhaps a crow will suddenly appear and bring you a healing, or perhaps this healing will be in a dream. Perhaps you will see a crow before you do something important, and, if you are open-minded, will recognize its appearance as a good omen.

Crow medicine can also mean consciously imitating or assuming crow characteristics and applying them in our lives – for example, a person can observe the patience of a crow as it sits on a tree branch and emulate the same patience in his or her life experiences, or practice a keen observation of the landscape. It can also mean meditating on crow images, receiving crow visions and dreams or shamanic journeying, in which you journey with the assistance of your crow ally, or, psychologically, assume the nature of a crow during the journey.

Spirit and I became very close, and had the same sentimental attachment to each other that very good friends feel. I remember realizing that he was teaching me how crows experience things… I would observe and view things, thinking 'Yes! I'm doing it as a *crow* would do it!'

I felt, too, that through Spirit, I was unfolding a special spiritual connection to crows in the wild, and to crows as a bird ally. As I walked the fields and forests, I felt like I could relate to crows whenever I saw them – as if we were kindred spirits. I knew intuitively that Spirit came into my life to reinforce this connection. We silently communicated with each other, and this communication was a silent knowing that we were allies and shared a close bond.

Now, I wave at crows, whenever I see them along the highway!

TRANSMIGRATION OF A SOUL

Holly Davis

Holly works in the UK as a professional animal communicator, transpersonal interspecies communicator and animal healer. She runs the Nirvana Springs Healing Centre in Southwest Wales, where she lives with her family and a large selection of animals, many of which turned up in the form of rescues.

Holly has written a diploma course in Animal Communication for Stonebridge College – a distance-learning college based in the UK – as well as running an Energy Therapy For Animals and People diploma course from her Healing Centre. She is also a regular magazine columnist and is currently writing her first book, 'The Texas Highway – Animal Wisdom on a Road to Enlightenment'.

Sometimes animals come across as angels in disguise! Both animals and human guides communicate with me in the same way – by thought transference. It's my own voice I hear, but it takes on different attitudes. My understanding through the work that I do is that I read their thoughts as an energy vibration – like tuning-in to a radio station, which my subconscious mind then 'translates' into words. Sometimes, I am shown pictures, both moving and still, or feel pain in areas of the body that correspond with their physical or emotional discomforts. As this communication is telepathic (meaning remote feeling), distance isn't an issue. This means I am able to work with animals all over the world.

Most, if not all, of my animals communicate with and 'guide' me – also offering advice for other people and, of course, animals. All of them are interesting – but my horse Texas, well… he's just mind blowing! He advises me in my day-to-day life and is a true and dear friend. His words have picked me up when I've been down, made me laugh, made me cry and sometimes just completely taken my breath away! We help each other out – he gives me information and I take care of his physical and emotional needs.

Texas prefers to call this type of communication with animals *Transpersonal Interspecies Communication*. This involves connecting with the higher self, or soul – the part of us that has access to mass consciousness and is often able to get in touch with information on a much deeper level than the physical self. It is connected with the subconscious, which can enter and exit the physical body at will.

The higher self is also termed the psyche or soul. Psyche is actually a Greek word, meaning soul or butterfly. Several times when I have been working with animals I have been honored enough to witness a white butterfly flying either in or out of their physical body.

Meeting Texas

The first time I spoke with Texas his consciousness was in the body of another horse that I was asked to see by a client. This horse had what I would term 'self-induced autism'… he was completely emotionally shut down. While I was communicating with him he showed me pictures of strange things that I didn't understand – Indians on horseback and a woman riding bareback through long grass and other things that I hadn't seen before that were quite unusual. He seemed to have a deep attachment to me and, after my return home, he continued to communicate with me.

For the following ten days, every time I shut my eyes I would be bombarded with images – us walking through a tunnel and the walls closing in around us, being chased by knights in armor, people being beheaded and experiencing different horrific deaths… sometimes it made my heart beat fast, because it was scary. At times I was in a human form and other times I was a white Arab mare. We would stop for a rest on the American plains and graze before we carried on with our journey. At the very end of my 'vision', we were stood on the earth and it literally cracked and exploded. It was like being taken back into time, into blackness – into nothingness… right back to the beginning of time.

I didn't know what was going on, so I sought advice and was told to read a book by Stanislav Grof called *'The Holotropic Mind'*. I was absolutely amazed, because the process described in the book was exactly what I had experienced! I realised then what had occurred… this horse had taken me right the way back to my beginnings, re-experiencing all my past lives. The tunnel that had closed in around us was the birth canal.

After this intense experience, he continued to talk to me – he would pipe-in frequently when I least expected it. For instance, I had a stand at a fair… someone was stood in front of me but before they'd even opened their mouths he said, *'Ask her what's wrong with her shoulder'*. He was constantly right and always amazed me. He kept on like that for a long time.

Four years later, I received a phone call from an owner of a horse called Texas – a blanket spot Appaloosa, who had an old injury to his leg. As we were talking, he kept repeating, *"You know me. You know how to make me better. I have already given you my heart."* I was asked to have him, so my daughter and I went to visit him. There was an immediate resonance and I knew it was meant to be, although he insisted that, *"You need to make me better, but there's somebody else's horse I'm meant to be."* Not wanting my daughter to become too attached, I said to her in the car on the way home, "Look – he might have to go to somebody else after he's better." And she said, "But mum, don't you realise? He's meant to be *my* horse… I *know* him!"

During the two-week break between the visit and him coming to live with us, the penny suddenly dropped – I realised that Texas was the very soul that had been in the other horse, talking to me all this time!

When I started looking into things and understanding, I realised it's what is called *transmigration of the soul* – where that part of the consciousness that is not physical can come and go from the body. When we went on that ten-day journey, he had actually detached himself from the other horse and had left with me. When the time was right, he'd embodied into another horse that was going to come to me.

Funnily enough, I was told: "He will find his way to you. When he comes, he'll choose Polly (my other horse) to lead the herd", which is exactly what he's done.

Horse Sense

I can separate the physical horse from what's talking to me. Texas has told me that his spiritual name is Khazar – this embodies the true essence of who he is. However, he's still got a physical body, he's still got horse needs, and has to be treated like a horse! He's 15, and can be quite stallion-like in his behaviour – he's got a very male energy and will pull his head in and stamp his front foot.

Texas is very demanding and bossy in his personality, but he also has integrity. He has very high morals and principles. He also has a wonderful sense of humor… I shall never forget the day he told me to look out for a red lottery ticket. Of course, they are normally pink and white but the very next day I found one on the lounge floor that had fallen out of a magazine! I was so excited and all week I eagerly filled in the numbers. Finally the big day came and I won… nothing! When I asked him why, his answer was simple. *"I told you to keep a look out for one – I never said you'd win anything!"* Yet another lesson for me in listening, not presuming!

Texas won't answer what I'm not meant to know, and he won't tell me anything that might affect anyone in a negative way. He is one of the wisest, most honest animals it has ever been my privilege to speak with. He's also very sweet, because when he talks to me he always calls me 'my love' and 'my darling'.

Texas tells me about other animals and people, how they feel and what is going on for them in their lives. He has even warned of events before they have happened, and is very good when it comes to offering advice on emotional and medical or energy problems, as he appears to be able to see the energy patterns that surround people and make up their thoughts.

He talks a lot about the 'crystal children', particularly what he calls the 'amber children' and 'emerald children'. He likes to discuss how we can help them. There are so many children now with learning and behavioral problems, and not nearly enough is being done to help them. He feels that children need more time back in nature and learning to rekindle their imaginative and artistic abilities – he says that too much time is wasted on TV and playstations!

Texas often helps me with medical research involving energy therapy to do with the sedating of horses, trigger points for accessing a body-healing blueprint and other things that made no sense to me at the time, but now do. He gives me pages and pages of information which myself and a kinesiologist then go through, work out what it all means and start working with it.

There is a chakra that he showed me that is located in the flank of most animals – I can't find any information about it in any healing books at all – that he calls the 'second heart' chakra. Once it's activated in the larger animals, they are ready to facilitate the healing of others, but this chakra shouldn't be opened until they're ready to start doing that work, because otherwise it's quite detrimental for them to take on the negative emotions of people. This has changed how I work, as I now communicate with the animals incorporating the energy of this second heart chakra. I also run workshops called 'Healing With the Second Heart'.

All the healing stuff he's coming up with now – it's all thousands and thousands of years old. We're re-discovering, not discovering it! A lot of my work is to teach people this and how to work with it. He uses me in this way to share this knowledge with others.

Texas has also taught me about multi-dimensional reality and how this affects our day-to-day lives. We are *all* multi-dimensional beings. We're fragmented with different parts to us… some can be of a much higher consciousnesses and higher vibration. These different parts of you might come from other parts of, or beyond, the universe – but some of these parts of you, including some parts of other animals, will be guides to other people, even though we might not be consciously aware of it ourselves. I've got two spirit forms that I know of – one is a white Arab mare and the other a medieval-style armored white stallion. Other people have seen and been guided by these forms.

Time is not linear, as we perceive it to be. All time is now. We tend to think in terms of past lives and future lives but, really, everything is parallel life just playing out in another time zone. Something that happened from a past life could cause a problem for you in this lifetime because it's just happened – but it's happened within another dimension.

Kayleigh

Although I also have three human guides, I don't speak to them for months on end. Most of my work is with my animal guides. (I love animals and I prefer them to people, so it makes sense to me!) Texas is my main guide and alongside him is Kayleigh who was my mare that died. I can honestly say that between the two of them, my life has transformed.

Kayleigh was my first animal communication. She was very wise and quick and clever. She never questioned, just graciously gave herself totally to those she taught and loved. She was my teacher and always forgave me every time I got it wrong.

Kayleigh was still talking to me as the vet was putting her to sleep. During the day, however, I received *so* many messages from friends – she was going through everyone and anyone to pass on communications from her to me! One of these was this poem:

We are but one, I have not left…
I stand by your side and shall guide you.
Your dream is my dream
and I shall defend it till the last.
We shall walk together
side by side
I shall be the shadow
that follows where no one else wants to follow.
For you are my trusted friend
and I your guide,
stepping silently in the sand.

I have had many conversations with Kayleigh about healing. She tells me that holistic medicine, done correctly, should work on 'levels'. To rush in and treat a particular problem isn't always right… developing and using our intuition will help us identify this in many cases. She explains how one 'set' of remedies when given correctly will bring you to the next level. Once this is reached you are ready for the next stage of repair. It's like building a strong foundation for the body… how can good healing take place when it has nowhere to 'live'?

I had two particular instances where what I can see, hear and sense has been so heightened it's been absolutely phenomenal. When the energy is as high as that and I'm out with the animals, they react to it. They behave in a way that they wouldn't normally behave. I remember the first time that it happened I was out with Kayleigh in the field. I put my hands out and as her nose touched my hand she reared up and it absolutely made her jump! The expression on her face was one of shock… it was literally like an electric shock to her. This has happened to me about three times, and is just unbelievable! The horses will come over and stand in a semi-circle around me, just staring at me. You can see why they're reacting because they're feeling it themselves.

Belief isn't a pre-requisite for something to exist. It exists whether you believe it or not. Everything that I believe is based on experience, not hearsay – if people think I'm mad, let them carry on. I'm happy with what I do and I'm confident that it works. My work is very important to me and I wouldn't stop what I'm doing, even if I won the lottery tomorrow… I wouldn't change it for the world.

A MESSAGE FROM KHAZAR (TEXAS)

The grim reality is that many of you have forgotten how to feel. Destructive tendencies are rife. Feeling the need to justify one's actions is ego-induced. Allow yourself to stand back and see the true reality that one is all.

Animals have a giving as well as forgiving nature. When you learn to work with them they will show you the shadow of your soul, which you need to encompass. Love the hate and the dark as well as the light and the love – they are all part of you. You will then be able to address the balance that makes you unique. By opening up and *re-learning* your soul's true essence, you will become a true part of the planet's future.

CHAPTER 7

NATURE & ELEMENTAL BEINGS

The best place to find God is in a garden. You can dig for him there.

~ George Bernard Shaw

Planet Earth is alive – a living, breathing, sentient organism. It has a soul. It is also our source of life... it 'feeds' us in so many ways and we depend on it for our survival. Everything we are surrounded by comes from the earth in one way or another. It is so easy to forget this living in a modern world, molded and manipulated into a concrete environment filled with plastic 'things'. Yet, all that is 'man-made' (even this computer I am tapping away on) originated from the natural world and carries the vibration of Spirit.

For me, nature is a source of great energy where I receive healing, signs and information… where lyrics, complete with tune, 'pop' into my head and I get crazy ideas, like *'write a book!'* Even the stones on the beach guide and point the way – when I had 'writer's block' and needed inspiration, I found a stone with a fossil embedded into it that resembled a shining light bulb (like a cartoon 'eureka!' moment). When I was feeling confused and needing some insight, I found a stone with an 'eye' on it. Another time, I found a stone with a 'key' shape on it. Many people consider stones to be inanimate, lifeless 'lumps', but, in my experience, they are certainly not. Everything, from the smallest flower to the highest mountain, is imbued with Spirit, or essence, that will teach you if you are receptive enough to listen. The vibrant natural world we live in is our guide and our greatest ally.

In addition, there are invisible spirit beings that guard and protect the natural world. They are said to govern the elements of earth, air, fire and water – hence they are collectively referred to as 'Elementals'. Earth spirits are affiliated with rocks, minerals, soil, mountains and caves. The spirits of the air can be found in the wind, sky and clouds – assisting the growth of all plants, trees and flowers. Fire spirits govern heat and light, and the guardians of water are the spirits of springs and wells, marshes, lakes, ponds and streams, waterfalls, rivers and oceans – as well as mists and rain.

Every country throughout the world has their own myths and legends to tell of magical beings that live in an Otherworld within the earth – they are the *Tylwyth Teg* in Wales, the *Pobel Vean* in Cornwall, *Fées* in Brittany, the *Phi* in Thailand, and the *Alcheringa* and *Iruntarinia* to the Arunta tribes of Central Australia. Malidoma Patrice Somé, in his book, *'The Healing Wisdom of Africa'*, describes his encounters with the *kontomblé* in Africa, and it has often been said that Ireland contains two races – the visible human beings we call Celts, and invisible beings known as the *Sidhe* or *Tuatha De Danann*.

In particular, the Celtic lands had an oral tradition rich with encounters with these magical spirits – these remnants of ancient bardic tales were told for a perhaps a thousand years or more before they were eventually recorded in writing. A good example is the Welsh *'Mabanogion'* (1300–1425), where King Arthur makes an appearance. Incidentally, in the older Arthurian legends, Arthur is an incarnate fairy king with a mystic brotherhood known as the Round Table, his wife is Gwenhwyfar (whose name translates to 'white fairy'), and their son is called Llacheu ('bright one') who is credited with clairvoyant vision. Lancelot is the foster-son of a fairy woman, and Galahad the offspring of Lancelot and the fairy woman Elayne. The old Welsh legends say that Arthur lives in the Otherworld, and prophesy that he will one day return.

In *'The Fairy Faith in Celtic Countries'* (first published in 1911), the anthropologist W.Y Evans-Wentz shares a fine collection of testimonies from indigenous Celtic people regarding the existence of an invisible race of beings inhabiting the land. One of those, Mrs. Betsy Thomas from Wales, then aged 100 (in 1909) said, "I saw one of the *Tylwyth Teg* about sixty years ago, near the Tynymyndd farm, as I was passing by at night. He was like a little man. When I approached him he disappeared suddenly. I have heard about the dancing and singing of the *Tylwyth Teg*, but have never heard the music myself. The old people said the *Tylwyth Teg* could appear and disappear when they liked; and I think as the old people did, that they are some sort of spirits."

In the ancient tales, these beings are rarely described as the gossamer-winged dainty 'cuties' prevalent in children's stories today – on the contrary, they were extremely powerful, wild and often volatile. Respect and caution were essential if you ever encountered such a being, but, when not offended, they would become beneficent allies and guardian spirits.

I feel that perhaps these beings were the original native peoples of the planet, and that, long ago, human beings lived in harmony with these beings and were in unison with the natural cycles of the land. There have been many tales told and songs sung of human and faery beings crossing the boundaries between the worlds, and alliances – even marriages – between the two. At some point in history, that connection was lost or broken. Perhaps human beings, with their corrupt societies and pollution, did not respect these ancient ones of the land, so (with exception) they withdrew from their interactions with us – or maybe we lost our connection to the earth, and thus to the faery realms, as we constantly developed new towns and cities.

With the increasingly rapid technological advancement of humanity, we appear to be even further away from our roots – from the earth. It is imperative at this time that we remember our connection with and reconnect to the power within the land… our continued existence depends on it.

THE VINE OF THE SOUL

by Howard G. Charing

Howard G. Charing is a healer, a workshop facilitator, and a director of the Eagle's Wing Centre for Contemporary Shamanism. He has co-published numerous articles with Peter Cloudsley about shamanism in Peru as practiced in the Andean, coastal and Amazonian regions and jointly they have published a documented collection of chants and ayahuasca icaros on CD, entitled 'The Shamans of Peru'. He has also co-authored the book 'Plant Spirit Shamanism'.

For many years, he has been organizing plant medicine retreats to work with the indigenous peoples in Peru's Amazon basin, as well as Andean retreats with shamans of northern Peru who work with the visionary cactus San Pedro. Howard has been baptized by the Shipibo Indians, and ritually initiated into the lineage of the maestros of the Rio Napo region. Howard and his colleague Peter Cloudsley also hold Amazonian Medicine Retreats at their dedicated center in the Mishana National Reserve. As a protected nature reserve encompassing several thousands of hectares of primary rainforest, Mishana is home to many

plants and animals that are not found anywhere else on the planet. At Mishana, participants are able to work with indigenous shamans and experience the direct healing of nature through the visionary vine of the soul.

We are not talking about passive agents of transformation; we are talking about an intelligence, a consciousness, an alive and other mind, a spirit.
Nature is alive and is talking to us. This is not a metaphor.
~ Terrance McKenna

On being invited to contribute to the Soul Companions book, I considered the ways to approach this concept. This I know holds different associations and connotations for people. The word Soul in some respects is a technical 'gloss' for an extremely subtle and complex concept. For some it would be from the perspective of the *genius,* its original meaning inherited from the ancient Greek and Roman civilizations of a tutelary spirit or divine nature of a person, nourishing and inspiring us. These days in different cultural environments, this describes guardian angels, spirit guides, or an ally such as a power animal. The idea of *soul* is richly represented in our culture, language, and spiritual beliefs. It is a concept to describe the deep feeling at the core of our being, a feeling evoked by music, food, love, or just simply feeling ensouled.

I decided to write from my own personal perspective from my years of work and research in the Amazon Rainforest with the shamans and curanderos who drink the visionary plant brew called ayahuasca. I use the term 'shaman' as a convenience as this title has only been 'imported' from the West into the Amazon quite recently in the past thirty years or so. A more appropriate general term could be *'vegatilista'* or a seer and healer who works with plants, not only from the physical or medicinal aspect but also in communion with the soul of the plant. In addition, there are many 'sub' specialties, so a shaman who primarily works with *chonta* (a hard palm wood) is known as a *chontero*, a shaman who works with the aromas and scents of the plants is called a *perfumero*, and a shaman who works with ayahuasca is known as an *ayahuasqero*.

We humans have a special relationship and dependence on plants. Since our beginnings, they have been the source both directly and indirectly of our food, our shelter, our medicines, our fuel, our clothing, and of course the very oxygen that we breathe. This is common knowledge and generally taken for granted. Yet we view plants in our Western culture as semi-inanimate, lacking the animating force labeled soul, mind, or spirit. Many people ridicule and regard as eccentric those who speak up and say they communicate with plants. You only have to recall the popular reaction to Prince Charles's comments saying that he often did just that.

The biggest challenge for a Westerner undertaking this communion with the plants is to accept that there is another order of nonmaterial reality that a person can experience through his entrance into plant consciousness, and to do this requires a significant leap of the imagination. We are all born into the social paradigm that surrounds us, with all its beliefs, myths, and institutions that support its view of the world, and it is not within our worldview to accept the immaterial and irrational. Before we embark on this journey to the plant mind, then, we first need to examine some of our most deeply ingrained assumptions, assumptions still fostered by many of our religious and social institutions today. The starting place for this journey is within ourselves.

HomoSapien-centricity is a strange looking word, but perhaps an appropriate one to describe the concept that many of us, consciously or not, carry within us: that we humans are the most important and perhaps the only conscious and self-aware (or rather, ensouled) beings in the universe. For shamans, the world that we perceive through our senses is just one description of a vast and mysterious unseen reality, and not an absolute fact. In John G. Neihardt's book, *'Black Elk Speaks'*, Black Elk – the Oglala Sioux 'medicine man' – remarked that beyond our perception is "the world where there is nothing but the spirits of all things. It is behind this one, and everything we see here is something like a shadow from that world."

How can we enter into a communion (in the true sense of the word) with the plant consciousness or soul? This can indeed be difficult, as we in our culture have long forgotten this understanding and body of knowledge. However, we can learn from those peoples who still live within a paradigm that our physical forms are illusions, and beyond that we are all connected and no different from all things. Modern physics which recognizes the underlying nature of form and matter as an energy which pervades and informs the universe is saying the same as the ancient shamans, "reality is an illusion, albeit a persistent one" – Albert Einstein (*'The Expanded Quotable Einstein'* by Alice Calaprice).

These are the peoples referred to by the Alberto Villoldo as those who were never ejected from the Garden of Eden (unlike us). It is clearly a good way to learn and study from the shamans of the Amazon rainforest where this knowledge is still alive and from those who still live in the mythological Garden of Eden. One of the great plant teachers is ayahuasca, also called the 'Vine of the Soul'. Ayahuasca is a combination of two plants (although other plants are added to elicit certain visionary experiences or healing purposes). This mixture of two plants the ayahuasca vine and the chacruna leaf, operate in a specific manner with our neuro-chemistry. The leaf contains the neuro transmitters of the tryptamine family (identical to those present in our brain) and the vine itself acts as an inhibitor to prevent our body's enzymes from breaking the tryptamines down thereby making it inert. Science defines this as the MAOI effect (Monoamine Anti Oxide Inhibitor) and forms the basis for many of the widespread anti-depressant pharmaceutical medication such as Prozac and Seroxat. This MAOI principal was only discovered by Western Science in the 1950's, yet interestingly this very principle has been known by the plant shamans for thousands of years, and when you ask the shamans how they knew this, the response is invariably "the plants told us".

The Sacred Doorways to the Soul

In my subjective experiences, plants have been a doorway to finding my place in the great field of consciousness. I am aware that subjective experience is not regarded as scientific, but at the end of the day, all our experiences are subjective and reality is not always that consensual, as we believe it to be. It is somewhat of a paradox that the leading edge of modern science, Quantum Mechanics, has also arrived at this conclusion and describes a mind-bending reality in which we are all both alive and dead at the same time. Quantum particles (the very basis of matter) exhibit the properties of bi-locality i.e. exist at different locations in the universe at the very same time, transcending vast distances of many thousands of light years.

With the visionary plant doorways opening to the wider field of consciousness, my experience and personal revelation is that I am a discrete element in this great field, a unique frequency or wavelength amongst infinite others, and that all these are vibrating in a vast wavelength of ecstatic harmony. I understand the purpose of my human existence is to be just simply human, and embrace the unique experience of human emotions and feelings. I have learned that my soul is not separate and is integral to me. Expressed differently, I am part of this soul, which has the *appearance* of form. My soul is outside of physical time and space, and is itself a component of an ineffable and indescribable existence in infinity.

My first real encounter with the plant world of the shamans was when I arrived in the Amazon some ten years ago. The moment I stepped off the aeroplane in Iquitos it felt as if I had been hit by bolt of energy. I felt so energized that I didn't sleep for two days, my senses were at a heightened state of awareness, and it felt as if I could hear the heartbeat of the rainforest itself.

Iquitos is a city in the Amazon rainforest. There are no completed roads to it. The only way to get there is via aeroplane or by riverboat. The city in the 19th century was the center of the rubber industry but by the early 20th century the rubber trade had moved to the Far East, and the city had fallen into neglect and disrepair. It is now a place with no apparent purpose resplendent in its post-colonial splendour literally in the middle of nowhere – a true frontier town.

I recall my first moments in Iquitos standing on the Malecon at the edge of the city overlooking the river and some 3,000 miles of pure rainforest spread out in front of me, an exhilarating experience which still fills me with wonder and awe.

I had come to Iquitos out of a long-standing interest and desire to experience at first-hand the living tradition of plant spirit medicines and of course, the magical brew of ayahuasca of which I had heard so much about.

I was not to be disappointed; my first sessions with a shaman in an open jungle clearing changed my view and understanding of life, a spiritual epiphany. I experienced being in the very center of creation. I had the realization and experience that I was not separate but an intrinsic part, a discrete element in the vast cosmic mind or field of consciousness, and that we were all connected. All part of the one great mind, and our experience of 'separateness' was no more than an illusion, generated by our being in our bodily vehicle which housed our senses.

One of my most profound experiences was during an ayahuasca ceremony, when I found myself transported to what I felt was the center of creation. I was in the cosmos witnessing totality – planets, stars, nebulas, and universes forming. Everywhere stretched vast patterns of intricate geometric and fluid complexity constantly changing size and form. The chanting of the shaman was filling every cell with an electric force, every port of my body was vibrating and it felt as if I was being bodily lifted into the air. I was in a temple of sound, vibration and bliss. Gathered around me were giants in ornate costumes of gold and multi-coloured feathers blowing smoke and fanning me, these were the spirits of ayahuasca, and then this soft gentle and exquisitely soft and sensual voice spoke to me of creation and the universal mind.

To reinforce this poetic insight, the words appeared before me in bold neon-like script. When I related this after the session to the maestro (Javier Arevalo), he said, *"Ayahuasca wanted you to understand."* He continued, *"Ayahuasca opens doors to different dimensions. Often the mind can be obstructed from accessing inner knowledge. Ayahuasca can open up the mind to abstract things that cannot be seen in the material world. If I hadn't had the experience, I would not be able to believe that a tree could have its own world or have a spirit. But when you begin to discover these dimensions personally, little by little you begin to recognise and accept the mystery of it."*

I discovered that ayahuasca is a medicine so unlike the Western understanding of the word – a medicine which works on every level, on our physical and non-physical beings, our consciousness, our emotions, and our spirit. It is as if you are drinking not just a liquid brew but imbibing an 'other' intelligence which knows exactly what is needed to help you. This is a communion in the true sense of the word, an intense experience of euphoria and ecstasy. A journey of deep and profoundly meaningful personal and trans-personal insights, a searchlight on the hidden thoughts and feelings in the sub-conscious mind, an erasing of the ego boundaries and a merging with the greater field of consciousness of creation.

There was more to experience with other 'teacher plants' such as *ajo sacha* and *guyasa*. I feel my senses being altered and expanded in some ineffable way. I become aware of the song, the very rhythm of the rainforest. The sounds, smells, and sights around me I had not been aware of in my normal everyday waking state, and I zoom-in on these smells and sounds. I realize that the rainforest is one entity – the insects, birds, and animals being part of the totality of the rainforest. I am in paradise when lying in my hammock; it is like floating within a living three-dimensional sensorial experience of sound, color, smell, movement, and vibration all in harmony and great beauty.

My work with visionary plants not only provides a philosophical frame of reference for my life, so to speak, but is also a path for deep soul healing, and generates a desire to engage fully and with enthusiasm in the world. Celestial visions are always very nice and pleasing, but they must never cloud, disguise, or distract our real purpose to live in the full embodiment of being a human on this beautiful planet and striving to enrich that special and unique experience – our 'earth walk'. I recall some years ago when I led a group to the Amazon Rainforest, the initial gathering with our shaman Javier Arevalo to introduce ourselves… Javier was very curious about Westerners, and was interested in knowing what we were searching for with the visionary plants. One participant stood up and said she wanted a clear and definitive understanding of the male and female principles of the universe, the cosmic "ying and yang" as she put it. Well, Javier was totally mystified by this question, as when I have attended his sessions with local people who visit him for a consultation or session they ask about everyday problems and concerns such as "Is my boyfriend / husband / girlfriend cheating on me?", "Why am I unlucky in finding a job?", or "I need help to overcome this disease". We worked with our participant to explore what the *real* question was behind her initial enquiry, and finally she admitted that she was really looking for love in her life. Of course, Javier could understand this deep desire completely, and was subsequently able to help her discover and reconcile the inner obstacles, which had been preventing this.

In this context, the teacher plants can provide a doorway to great and meaningful insights in the adventure of personal growth and healing. The growth and healing has therefore to also be in the physical world, thereby offering the opportunity to reveal our emotions, traumatic and turbulent experiences, hidden or otherwise, so that these can be released and ourselves restored. This access to our soul companion (our greater selves), this flowing omni-present force guiding our lives, which presents us with what are often described euphemistically as 'growth opportunities' for us to overcome. The plant teachers can show us these. We can transcend linear time itself, and journey within this eternal *now* at the very place in time where we experienced such a difficult event or suffered a troubled pervasive period in our life. We can re-experience this albeit from a different perspective – learn what happened, the reasons why it occurred, the subsequent impact and consequences on our life, and then release any pain and trauma locked within our being. This release within the ayahuasca experience is called *'la purga'* – the purge. When we literally purge this pain from our being, it is not only the contents of our stomach that are being released, but also the deeply stored bile and sourness in our bodies generated from these difficult events. The plants offer us the potential for deep soul healing so we can become stronger and more able to engage fully in the precious gift of life.

Developing a personal relationship with ayahuasca is within a background of an ancient body of practices. For example, there is a dietary regimen, and prohibitions regarding libidinous thoughts and activity. These considerations need to be respected and can not be ignored if one embarks on a path of communion with the plant. On observation and study (also called trial and error), this regime helps us to become more 'plant-like', therefore increasing our receptivity to the plant-spirit-mind.

Many of my visionary experiences with ayahuasca have led to a deeper understanding of my life and the role that various people had played in it. Sometimes I *became* those people, lived their lives, and came to understand why they did what they did, what decisions they had to make in their lives. These revelatory experiences invariably led to some form of closure with that person, like completing an open chapter, or a profound healing of my relationship with that person.

An example of this pertained to my mother. We had a difficult relationship, a part of me never fully trusting her. During one ayahuasca session, I experienced a deep visionary communion with the Earth Mother. I understood the love that the spirit of our planet has for all who live within her. This visionary and kinesthetic experience was like floating within an exquisite and sublime loving womb-like embrace. Then the vision of the Earth Mother metamorphosed and became my own mother, and I re-lived her life, her childhood, the things that had happened to her, and the decisions that she faced so she could have a child. Then I realised that I had judged her, and it was her misfortunes that had led to this lack of trust. I was able to see my mother in a very different light.

I was joyful and filled with ecstasy following this experience. The gulf between us had been bridged, and ever since then the affection between us has flowed freely. That wonderful insight and transformative experience I owe completely to ayahuasca, the exquisite gift of the plant-consciousness.

The ayahuasca has revealed to me more of the great dream of the Earth, and how disconnected we have become from our relationship with the living planet. I experienced the evolutionary process of DNA. I was shown that many of the problems that we experience as a species are because we are primates, and even though humankind has done everything possible to dissociate ourselves from our animal origins, we remain driven by our animal glands and hormonal systems. Yet at the same time, we are in harmony with our higher state of consciousness, which approaches that of dolphins, who are aware, and in conscious communion as part of a soul mind.

This great question, the mystery of the communion of mind, soul, and body is a search that we humans have been on since we first raised our eyes to the night sky in wonder. Some of the ancient myths of the jungle from the Ashuar people of the Upper Amazon tell us of this separation, the myth of the 'Moon Man' as collected by Alonso Del Rio from Peru is such a one;

'In the time of the ancestors there was a ladder, like a rope which connected the world of the Ashuar with the upper world. Here lived other beings just like the Ashuar but they were spirits. These beings were very powerful and could transform themselves into anything they wanted. One

day Moon-man cut this ladder so that the people could no longer communicate with their spirits above, and thus they lost their power.'

In the Ashuar tradition the Moon Man is associated with the analytical mind and it is rational thinking, therefore, which has severed our sacred connection to the cosmic mind. This legend therefore speaks of humanity's need to re-unite with the consciousness of the universe, using the rope (ayahuasca) to climb our way back to the oneness we once knew. Only then can we re-enchant the world through imagination and inspiration. If we look deeply into our hearts, can we say that we are any different from the indigenous peoples of the rainforest? The reflections of Carl Jung in his book, *'Modern Man in Search of a Soul'* point to the very same dilemma as the peoples of the Amazon;

"If we are still caught by the old idea of an antithesis between mind and matter, the present state of affairs means an unbearable contradiction; it may even divide us against ourselves. But if we can reconcile ourselves with the mysterious truth that spirit is the living body seen from within, and the body the outer manifestation of the living spirit – the two really being one – then we can understand why it is that the attempt to transcend the present level of consciousness must give its due to the body. We shall also see that belief in the body cannot tolerate an outlook that denies the body in the name of the spirit."

The visionary plants and ancient traditions of the plant shamans reveal a hidden universe, in which the separation between the physical and the unseen universe is an illusion caused by our limited sensory perception. The body and soul permeates and infuses each other. The plant teachers show us a path to an expanded consciousness and communion with our sacred source, our soul companion.

So much has happened since my 'entry' into the world of shamanism, nearly 25 years ago following a serious accident (an elevator crash), which resulted in severe injuries and a near-death experience. I feel greatly privileged to do this work. I am fortunate to be able to encounter, work with, and bring groups to meet some extraordinary shamans and healers in the Andes, the Amazon Rainforest, and the Philippines. It gives me enormous pleasure to witness people become more empowered and engaging in life with more creativity, energy, and happiness through the shamanic body of practices.

photo credit: Megan Moore

NATURE'S SONG

Rabbi Gershon Winkler

Gershon Winkler is both a renowned scholar as well as a rabbinic trickster. He has authored fourteen books, including seven works on Jewish mysticism, philosophy, and folklore, and was initiated in 1978 by the late Kabbalist Rabbi Eliezer Benseon of Jerusalem. For the past 25 years, he has lived very close to the earth in remote wilderness regions. His personal draw to wilderness-living has brought him to a fresh gleaning of rich Hebraic teachings about the attributes and powers of fauna and flora. Rabbi Winkler flavors his teaching-style with hefty doses of humor, storytelling, ceremonies, and chanting. The Jerusalem Post recently described him as, "a blend of Robin Williams and the Baal Shem Tov." He is also co-founder and Executive Director of the Walking Stick Foundation – a non-profit organization devoted to the recovery of aboriginal Jewish spirituality, located at the base of the Santa Monica Mountains in Southern California.

My first memory of communication with nature was at the age of five or six. I was in rural Denmark. My mom was picking strawberries nearby and I felt a huge old tree tugging at me psychically. I sat down and leaned against it and I felt that an elder grandfatherly spirit was embracing me. The tree 'spoke' to me, saying something like, "Deepen your roots and you will soar." This came as no surprise to me – it was very much a part of my mindset growing up in an Orthodox rabbinic household where I was exposed all the time to songs about animals and trees and mountains singing to God. My father, a rabbi, would often take me to the forest and speak of the wonders of Creation. He would sometimes stop at a blossoming flower and say, "Look, God is saying hello," or, "Look, that beautiful tree is waving at you!" I would then remind him it was windy, and he would say, "If it is from the wind, then why aren't the other trees waving?" and, sure enough, in those moments it was just that one tree.

To this day, I am often drawn by trees and stones, which call me and communicate their desire for me to sit by them. I learn a lot from them. My ability to listen to nature is something that has developed and deepened over the years… this is why I cannot live anywhere else but in the wilds.

Nature speaks to me through resonance – it doesn't speak to me in English or Aramaic! This resonance is a vibration that translates itself into my human language. Sometimes it becomes a song in my head, a melody… sometimes an aphorism of wisdom.

I am most drawn to the huge ancient oaks that are rare in the Galilean mountains of Israel, more than to any other tree species. These huge and ancient trees are extensions of the ancient masters whose teachings have guided me throughout my life and which I share with others all the time. See, the tradition was to bury the teacher with a seed in his or her mouth. These trees grow out of the teachers. They are living manifestations of the ancestors. When I sit underneath their mammoth branches, leaning against their ancient trunks, I sink back into the arms and embrace of the ancient ones. I *feel* them. I have visions of these elders and they speak to me or look at me or sit with me in ways that fill me with inspiration and learning. Often at a lecture or seminar someone will come up to me afterward and ask, "Wow, where is that teaching from that you gave us?" I would remind them of the name of the rabbi I quoted with the teaching during the talk, and they would say "But where can I find that teaching? What folio in the Talmud, what tractate? I want to look it up." I say, "Actually, it isn't written anywhere. He told it to me personally when I was in Israel." I get these strange looks, but that is how it is.

Trees speak to each other and to all creatures. This is an ancient Jewish teaching. They move with the wind, and are central gathering venues for spirits of animals and of earth. Their voices are heard in the rustling of wind, their song in the gentle dance of breeze. They groan when one of them is cut down, and they rejoice when we appreciate them, when squirrels scamper across them or birds build their nests on their branches.

In the Hebrew language, they are given many names, each a lesson in itself – *Ey'lo'nah* or Goddess, *Ey'lon* or God, *Eytz* or Counsel, and *See'ach* or Speaking. Trees and plants teach us that the farther you bury your roots in earthiness, the higher you soar in spirit, the closer to the heavens you reach, and the more expansive your branching and fruition will be. They are us, and we are them.

Their song is clear and enriching, if we only listen and hear it. Yes, the grasses sing, they sing all the time. *All the time*. The shepherds of ancient Israel knew the song of the grasses well, without which they would have no foliage with which to nurture their flocks. The earth – every space of her – has a unique song known only to those who live in those spaces, but who live there in respectful relationship with the land, for the earth yields little or no gift if there is discontentment and conflict.

My teachers of long ago taught that the spirit of an animal communicates in its chirp or growl or bark, or the sound of wings beating through the air when a bird is in flight overhead. I hear the animal or stone or tree itself in the silence. I hear their spirits in the sounds of wind, of stone, of animals, and of trees. Rabbi Eliezer of Worms (11th century) put it this way, "When God spoke and 'said', 'Let there be...' this or that, the intention in the word manifested as a living being, such as tree or stone or animal. And the breath of God that carried that utterance became the spirit of that being."

I am particularly drawn to ravens. Ravens in my tradition represent the Contrary. So much of my life and teachings is about that, about the paradox and contrariness of this life realm. One of my people's chieftains, Sh'lo'mo (tenth century, B.C.E.) put it this way, "This, too, opposite the other, did Many Powers create."

The raven comes to me often. When I hike, they seem to shoot out of nowhere and begin to flock near me, fly around me. They feel to me like wise elders who are well-seasoned and well-versed in the ways of this world. I do use raven feathers sometimes. Or I call to them when I do a ceremony for someone… I ask them to help me turn situations around, and to heal.

The Trickster in our tradition is the Snake, na'chash in Hebrew, which translates literally as To Trick, or To Fool, or Cunning. I have been dubbed as a Rabbinic Trickster and do live up to the snake attribute of that, as well as the raven attribute. I do both when I teach.

The earth is replete with remedies for ailments of all sorts – physical, emotional and spiritual. All grasses and all plants are healers. "There is not a single blade of grass," taught the second-century Rabbi Shim'on bar Yo'chai, "which does not have a spirit who empowers it, and which does not have great wisdom and great power."

"Ask of the earth", the ancient Hebrews admonished, "and she shall teach you. Speak to the animals and they shall guide you. Inquire of the birds, of the sky, the fish of the seas, and they shall inform you." The planet is brimming with Creator's passion, taught Rabbi Shim'on bar Yo'chai – the trees, the rocks, the plants, the animals, are all imbued with

God's passion. But are we?

References:

Trees talk to one another (*Midrash B'reisheet Rabbah* 13:2)

Trees have feelings, too (Babylonian Talmud, *Er'chin* 2:6)

Plants have healing powers (*Likuttei HaMaHaRaN*, No.277, para.2; ibid., *Tanina* 1:11)

Song of the grasses (*Likuttei HaMaHaRaN Tanina,* No.63)

Song of the land (*Likuttei HaMaHaRaN, Tanina,* No.63)

Earth gifts when there is no conflict (*Likuttei HaMaHaRaN*, No.277:2)

How animal spirits communicate (*Sefer Ru'ach Ha'Ko'desh, D'rush Gimmel*)

How spirits were created (*Sefer So'dei Ro'zi'a, beginning*)

"This, too, opposite the other..." (Hebrew Scriptures: Ecclesiastes 7:14)

Raven is the Contrary (Talmud, *Gittin* 54a)

Plants are empowered by spirits (Zohar, Vol.1, folio 251a; Vol.2. folio 80b)

Ask the earth, the animals... (Hebrew Scriptures: Book of Job 12:7-9)

Creator imbued trees and animals with passion (Zohar, Vol.1, folio 251a)

TREE GUIDANCE

by Thea Holly

Thea has lived in West Somerset in the UK for the past twenty years with an assortment of cats, dogs and pet pigs. She runs development workshops aimed at enabling seekers to fulfill their spiritual and psychic potential. Currently she is fortunate enough to be working with planetary beings in order to pass on simple but powerful healing tools.

I have always been able to sense Spirit in whatever form it takes – tree spirits, nature spirits, angelic beings, Other Worldly beings and of course, human spirits. It hasn't always been easy or acceptable being a sensitive or channeler. My family felt rather threatened by what I would come out with and so I learned to keep most of it to myself.

As a child, I had what my parents thought was an imaginary friend – a pretty girl called Katherine. I grew up with her and I always played with her if I wasn't playing with my sisters. I used to watch her climb up onto my mother's lap and rest her head against hers, but my mother would completely ignore her. One day, I asked if she could have a meal with us, and my mother asked, "Does this friend have a name?" When I said her name was Katherine, she dropped what she was carrying and I got sent to my room. My father came up and gave me a right telling-off. I was told never to mention her name.

It was years until they told me that, before I was born, my mother had a baby who only lived for two weeks and she was called Katherine. They somehow thought I'd found out and I was just being cruel. Some time later, I found a photograph in my grandfather's house of my father's brother when he was about nine – he had very curly blonde hair. I said, "That's what Katherine looks like." After that, they had to accept that there was something going on. But it took me years before my mother would accept that Katherine was around. I'm absolutely convinced that whether you miscarry or whether you touch the earth for a short period of time, if you don't choose to re-incarnate, then you continue to grow-up on the other side.

When I was in my teens I used to 'see' objectively – just like I see everything else in life. One day, I passed a nun on the stairs. I asked my mother where she was staying and she replied crossly, "What are you talking about?" I gathered by her reaction that we didn't have a nun staying with us. After that, I stopped seeing externally. Now I 'see' subjectively – as if there's a movie screen inside my third eye, like seeing on an inner screen.

However, as an adult I thankfully came into contact with more and more people who were not only more open-minded but who were also 'sensitives'. What a gift is was to start to meet more like-minded people.

Although I have known since childhood that none of us are ever alone – we are all surrounded by spirit helpers who endeavor to make themselves known to us in order to guide us and support us – I have learned that trees also have a role to play on our pathway through life.

I have always loved trees and couldn't imagine living in a world without their presence. I have, for a very long time, felt comfortable with my belief that there exists a parallel stream of evolution that encompasses a hierarchy of beings who attend to the needs of the Natural World. I now know that this commitment extends to the human race also.

A few years ago, while walking my dogs – Eva and Poppy – in the woods above my cottage, I came upon a rough stone that had a quartz-like substance threaded through it. It was beautiful and I stopped and picked it up. I wondered if it would be acceptable for me to take it home and instantly picked up a telepathic communication. I was unsure where the communication came from, but simply assumed it must be from a human spirit. It never crossed my mind that it might come from the spirits of trees that surrounded me.

My love of trees has grown with each passing season and eventually the desire to write about them began to take shape within my mind. I decided that I would investigate the significance placed upon them by different religions throughout history, but I found that several books had already been written around this theme. For a while, I felt that I had nothing new to offer to the subject, but all this was to change when, out walking with a friend, our dogs running ahead through the mixed woodland of ash, silver birch and other native species, I saw a tree spirit.

After this sighting, I felt that I might possibly find something to contribute to our knowledge of trees. I decided to take a pen and notebook on all my future walks in order to learn more about tree spirits.

After I'd written down the messages from three or four trees, I naively said to myself, 'Well, that's it. They've said it all – there can't possibly be any more spiritual guidance from more species.' After working with 19 different species, I was amazed to find that they *all* had something different to say…

The Sweet Chestnut

Here I sensed both a male and female presence and gradually was able to see two distinct forms not unlike human figures. I felt that I should ask permission to step within the tree's energy field and telepathically received the invitation to do so.

I was a little confused because by now I had become aware of more beings. They welcomed me and I asked, "How did you know I was coming?" To my amazement, it was explained to me that the other sweet chestnut trees that I had passed along the track had picked up my thoughts regarding the purpose for this walk.

This was my first lesson. I learned that all trees within one species are linked. The energy or vibration that they emit can be picked up on the air and transmitted from tree to tree as a means of communication. I, too, could somehow link in to this method of communication, which I equate with telepathy. I do not believe that trees communicate in words, but the energy or vibration that results from a human asking questions of them produces a response that is channeled by the tree spirits who enable us to receive it in the form of words.

I also learned from the sweet chestnut that their message is unique to their specific species and likewise all other tree species have a distinct message for humanity that differs not from tree to tree but from species to species. At last I asked this beautiful old tree about its message for humanity and this was its reply:

"We link in to the mystical questions. We try to settle the doubt and fear and self-denial. We teach of the link to all things, all life, all of time, now, before and the time to come."

The Ash

Ash trees are particularly beautiful, and I find that I am more at peace within their energy field than with any other species. It is hard to put into words what I am able to absorb from the ash trees, but it is almost like experiencing the most profound nurturing, the kind of nurturing that supports your own inner growth and yet encourages self-responsibility.

I sent out my request to approach and became aware of a sensitive, feminine energy that I immediately felt comfortable with. I took this opportunity to ask if, like the sweet chestnut, the ash had a message for humanity. Although I had already been informed during that first communication that all tree species carry a message, I still had my doubts as to what I had learned from the sweet chestnut and I suppose I was testing it. It was a matter of seconds before the words began to spill through my mind and onto my page:

"It is the duty of each soul to seek to live in harmony with itself as we do. Some (people) as you know are not evolved enough to tap the inner depths of their knowledge that link them to all things. We can teach the lesson of harmony, letting go, to live life as you are meant to live it, in trust that Life and all that links us will take care of you.

"Look at us, we send up our branches so that our leaves can live in the light. We strive for balance within ourselves, for harmony."

Then I knew that the spirit of the tree had become aware of my own negative state of mind. I was told to place my hands on the trunk of the tree and to breathe in deeply, and as I exhaled to let go of my negativity. Then, as I breathed in again the negativity would be replaced with the tree's own positive, healing energy. I asked how the tree would replace what I was absorbing and was told that it was all a part of a never-ending cycle. I decided to resume my walk and thanked the tree.

Soon the dogs appeared from the undergrowth and once more Eva dropped the ball at my feet. As I threw it back along the path I saw a tree spirit next to the ash – I again sensed a female energy. The features were so gentle but almost bland. The tree spirit seemed to be robed in a garment of brown and cream and as I gazed at this being I was filled with a surge of confidence.

Ever since I first worked with the energy of that first ash tree that stands by the woodland path above my cottage, I have often sought out the energy of these trees in order to link in and seek personal guidance. I have struggled for a long time to commit myself completely to trusting the guidance I get from Spirit Helpers and also from the trees themselves as regards my material life.

Although I am being presented with more and more opportunities to work as a medium and teacher within the field of spiritual and psychic development, I still find it difficult to let go of more conventional means of keeping the roof above my head. And yet, time and time again, when I approach the ash for guidance the same message is repeated, *"Let go of the past and trust that you will be taken care of."* I have been through many dark tunnels in my time and have allowed myself to almost expect another one just around the corner. But the wisdom of the trees speaks deeply to me and I am getting closer and closer to the point of letting go.

The Oak

I have to admit to having already thought about what an oak tree might have to convey, but was about to be taught not to have preconceived ideas about this amazing species:

"We can help the rigid and inflexible to bend a little in order to relax and explore their needs. We can support the timid and frail of heart to become more definite and purposeful."

This was not what I had expected. I have always associated the oak tree with strength and endurance, yet the message I was receiving was that, depending upon our needs, the oak would supply whatever was necessary for our individual growth and change. I wondered how this change could be brought about and was told that it is by absorbing some of the energy of the tree through breathing while standing within its aura.

Much later I learned that by standing quiet and still, a link would be formed between the energy of the tree and that of the 'seeker' and in that way any imbalance or negativity in our energy field could be rectified. I thanked the tree and turned to resume my walk back down the path to my cottage. But I felt drawn back within its aura and, once again, the words began to flow:

"You underestimate our teachings, our role within the lives of humans. We can open the door to hidden potential, we can teach you to tap in to all of Life and to link wholly with this Life force to truly enable the human soul to learn to express itself on all levels with confidence. Whatever you wish to be with your whole heart, you can be. We can instill in you the

confidence and the courage to achieve great things to fulfill your potential."

I found myself explaining that I didn't underestimate the teachings of this tree species and that I was merely in a hurry to get home after a long walk. I must admit to feeling a little self-conscious defending myself to a tree, and then I became aware of two people approaching with their dogs and decided that it was a good time to resume my walk back down to the cottage.

The Beech

Beech trees had always held a special place in my heart, with their serene beauty and air of peace and tranquility. Yet, when I approached and linked in to their energy, I felt negativity directed towards me. I was surprised and felt a little uncertain… I had not expected this. Then the words began to form in my mind:

"We can teach you to look at your life with honesty and clarity, only when you are ready to take stock of where you are and where you should be. We can help you to detach yourself from man's obsession with time and fear of trusting in something greater. Ours is a strong energy and you need courage to work with it as we show you where you are and your true path ahead. Sometimes this takes courage as you cannot hide from yourself."

I knew then why I had felt so uncomfortable. I knew that I needed to take stock of my life and to find the courage to commit to a path that I was only tentatively walking. I was afraid of placing my whole trust in an uncertain future and yet I had such support and encouragement from my Spirit Teachers – why was it so hard to let go and trust?

I walked away from the tree feeling a strange sense of rejection but now, looking back, I know that this wonderful tree was merely holding up a mirror for me, but I wasn't ready to gaze at the reflection.

The Douglas Fir

It was explained to me that in order to make the best use of the energy of this species, you need to clear your mind of any negativity, to let go of past problems and emotional trauma. The energy of this tree works best for those people wishing to completely change their lives. It helps you to tap into your inner courage in order to implement the necessary changes to promote a new direction in life, one of spiritual growth. Again, as with the beech, I am sure that I found this energy challenging simply because I had not yet reached my own necessary crossroads. The signs were all there but at that time I lacked the courage to read the message.

After a while, I began to sense the presence of the tree guardian and saw a being in white. I felt that I was being observed with tolerance and patience. If this gentle being could feel tolerant and patient towards me perhaps I should also be a little gentler towards myself.

The Rowan

I felt myself relax into the energy emanating from this tree and took up my pen and notebook. The energy was light and I sensed a feminine presence. After a while, I could see a form taking shape a little distance from the tree. Soft yellows swirled about as the form developed. The face that looked back at me expressed such gentle warmth and support and once more words started to fill my page as I tried to write down all that was being conveyed to me:

"We enable people to be lighter in spirit. We work well with those who take themselves and their problems too seriously. Linking in with our energy can help you to put all this into perspective, lifting your vibrations. We can help you to raise your awareness in order to link in more easily to the energy of other tree species that may at first seem a little difficult to sense."

The tree guardian moved closer and I felt her eyes look deep within mine, to the core of my being. I felt myself absorb a gentle warmth from this being and then it was gone.

The Scots Pine

I felt that I was being observed. I sensed a benign, masculine energy and then became aware of the presence of two other beings nearby, watching. I felt accepted here and soon the words began to form:

"We can teach Humankind to link in with its own species at the deepest level of recognition. We can stimulate your inner resources and illuminate the inner-flame, encouraging it to grow. We can help you to recognise those of your species who are on a similar path and enable you to clarify your vision of that pathway. We can encourage you to be steadfast in your purpose."

I asked what was meant by 'the inner-flame'. I believed it to be a reference to the spark of life within all things. This was acceptable to the guardian of the tree. It was then explained to me that the energy of this species is quite simple to access and I was told that my own energy levels were depleted. I had spent the last two days teaching at a school an hour-and-a-half away from my home. The daily journey always took a lot out of me. I was still recovering from major surgery several months earlier and my energy levels were easily drained. So, once more, I leaned into the trunk of the tree, and this time breathed in deeply and tried to imagine that as I breathed out, I was releasing all my fatigue. I left the little clearing feeling uplifted and revived.

The Sycamore

I love the energy of the sycamore. It is sensitive, yet strong. When I linked in to gain an understanding of their wisdom, I learned that they work well with people who have a particularly emotional nature:

"We can encourage greater stability in order to help the oversensitive of your species make sense of their world. Sometimes it is hard for those delicate souls to function in the material world in such a way as to protect themselves from those who are less sensitive.

"Learning to link in and absorb our healing energy can help these souls tap an inner strength that can help them to function without

absorbing too much hurt. We can enable them to retain their sensitivity and yet create a stronger core in order to survive your sometimes harsh world. We have a deep sympathy for these sensitive souls and can encourage them to take a step forward on their individual path without relinquishing their special gift of sensitivity."

I was aware of a very balanced energy emanating from these trees – sensitive but strong and supportive. I could see swirls of soft green and pale yellow forming around the trunk of the nearest tree, and soon I could pick out gentle features looking back at me.

The Hazel

I sensed the presence of the trees' guardian. I began to ask the role of this guardian and got the reply that it was one of many. I sensed a male energy, but became aware that there was also a female energy present. I was eventually able to see a seemingly young figure, quite human in features, swathed in greens and browns. I could not see a figure linked to the female energy. I am aware that the vibrations given off by the guardians of the trees form figures that my mind can accept. In the same way, the energy that the tree spirits channel from the trees form words that I can understand at my present level of development.

I was told that the energy of this tree species can help where people are faced with a number of choices, where there is a sense that they have arrived at a crossroads in their life:

"We can help you to clarify your needs to enable you to more easily identify your priorities. It takes inner strength to place your needs first, but how can you reach out to others if you are in the darkness yourself?"

I could feel the energy of the hazel working on my heart center and became aware of an inner voice telling me that I needed more laughter in my life. Then, again, the guardian was telling me that it was one among many. I asked what its role was with this tree and the reply came back:

"Just as you have Spirit Helpers to help guide you forward and to help you to make the best use of your life, so we are here for the benefit of the

tree in all things and also to create a bridge between the Natural World and that of the Human Species."

The Cypress

As the path neared the brow of the hill, I noticed five large oak trees that stand in a circle to the left of the track. Even before I approached them, I could see that the energy around them was charged. I knew that I had to go and stand within the center of that circle. I stood there with my eyes closed, absorbing the powerful energy from these great trees. I felt after a while that I was connected to all that was above and below the ground, and had a strange sensation of growth. I had to open my eyes and check the ground under my feet, for I felt that I must have chosen a small mound to stand upon. But there I stood on the flat earth. I felt so safe and secure. When I closed my eyes again I felt in that circle of oaks that this was the only place in all the world that was standing still and that everything else must be spinning, but when I opened my eyes again everything around me was still. I know that when the world gets too much for me to cope with, I can return here and let the world spin for a while without me.

As I lost myself in this wonderful experience, I became aware of a presence observing me. I saw a hermit-like figure robed in white and he asked me to follow him. I remained where I was, determined to enjoy this higher level of awareness. I was aware that he was a spirit helper rather than a tree guardian and he was very insistent that I follow him. I became aware of other visitors to the woodland and as I could see a small dog approaching, I decided it was a good time to leave the circle of oak trees. I followed the figure down a track that ran behind the oak trees. Either side of this track were evergreens of different kinds. After a short distance, he turned down a narrow track to the left that led downwards through Corsican pine. I was muttering to myself about not being too happy if I ended up getting lost and was advised to stand still and absorb the energy around me.

The peace that emanated from these trees became almost tangible, and

I felt a little guilty for having spent the last few minutes moaning. I then carried on down a track that was strewn with pine needles and, suddenly, the way forward was no longer clear. I started to moan again, and was told to look beyond the greenery that had suddenly seemed to spring up in front of me. Looking a little to the right, I could see a way through.

After a while, we came upon an even narrower track that ran left to right, and I was told to go to the left. The figure led the way and stopped in front of a beautiful evergreen. He told me it was a cypress and, looking around me, I noticed more of them together with pines and Douglas fir. I had seen some cypress alongside the main path and had noticed their beautiful bark, but had not been interested in working with this species. The figure in white had other ideas and told me that it was necessary to work with the energy of this tree.

Looking further on, I realised that this little track joined the main path that would take us back to the car. The figure disappeared and I took out my notebook and leaned my back against the tree.

I felt a delicate pressure at the top of my head and was told that this energy can help us link directly to the Universal Source that is within all things. I was told to strive for perfection in all that I do and to seek to make myself a channel for good. I began to feel a band of pressure around my head, but it was not uncomfortable. The conversation continued:

"Listen with compassion, seek and recognise justice in all you do, speak out the Truth, that all can work to release their demons of doubt and fear so that they can make progress forward on the path of Truth. The Truth is that we are all one."

After my book, *'Listening To Trees',* had been published, I had been with a friend and inadvertently absorbed some of the emotional pain she'd been through. Instead of standing by the window and working with the light to absorb it, I decided to take the dogs for a walk and work with the trees. I went on a familiar path that took me parallel to a beautiful stream and stood in front of this huge great ash tree. I explained my problem and asked for some healing, but, *"We cannot work with you – you need to go to the oak,"* came the reply. I thought, 'What a cheek!'– I felt really rejected. I went off in a huff down to the huge oak, but, before I'd even communicated my request, I could feel this black 'gunk', being drawn out of me – specifically from my heart to the sacral – into the trunk of the tree. I thanked the oak and then went on my way.

On the return journey, I was walking past the ash I had originally asked for help. *"We can work with you now,"* it said. The ash explained that different tree species work with different elements – the ash recognised that I needed to be cleared by the oak, because the oak links into earth energy and I needed to earth the negative energy I'd absorbed. Once I'd done that, then the ash could work on my mental and emotional state, because they work with the air element, which is better suited to emotional and mental clearing.

"Why didn't you tell me this when I was writing my book six years ago?" I queried.

"You never asked," the ash replied.

I do not claim that trees have a language that only I can receive. I believe that the lessons we can learn from each tree species can be absorbed by anyone willing to open themselves up to the energy of the trees in order to benefit from their ageless wisdom. You do not have to be psychic in order to benefit from the abundance that is present in Nature, you simply need to be willing to open up your mind to the infinite possibilities that exist all around us.

There is so much around us that can give us the nurturing that we need in order to take another step forward on our path. I don't think that I have met anyone who does not have some problem or other that is holding them back or clouding their vision. If only we could stand for a while and just look around at all that exists within nature that we sadly take for granted. If we could just take the time to look closely at the petals of a flower, or allow ourselves to really feel the breeze upon our face or lean our back against the trunk of an old oak tree in the hush of twilight. Make time for yourself, for your healing, for your growth. For as you clear your past of any pain or sorrow that has held you back, you will clear a path for healing to work through you to benefit others around you. Accept that you deserve to be made whole again and learn that there exists all around you in nature the healing energy to take you forward.

I realized that trees are more advanced than humans. They seem to be tapped-in directly to Source. They come out with the most beautiful eloquent guidance that I believe is the tree's own consciousness – the tree spirits watch over it and support what they communicate.

I feel that the tree spirit and the tree's consciousness are elements of the same thing… they're indivisible – just as humans have a physical vehicle with a spirit and this spirit is the vehicle for the soul.

Over the years, my guides have gradually changed the way I work with people and with animals. This has been a real education and I have often wondered how they put up with my doubts – they would teach me a particular way of working with Light or with crystals or with people and even though I would often say, "But that won't work!" – bless them, they have always been proved right. I think they see me as a wayward child, someone to tolerate with love and compassion. I am so grateful for that.

I am now working with energies I never knew existed and with the guides' support can trace back a sitter's past lives, purpose and origin. Sometimes I do feel that this is a bit strange, even for me. But if I can communicate what comes through for the sitter and they are able to recognise it, then I am doing what I am supposed to be doing. I just need to go on trusting in Spirit. It is a very interesting journey.

Includes excerpts from *'Listening To Trees'* by Thea Holly ISBN 186163 112X, published by Capall Bann Publishing, Tel: (UK) 01823 401528. www.capallbann.co.uk

RAHK DAHTSAHNI

Patrick Jasper Lee

Patrick Jasper lee is an indigenous Romani gypsy Chovihano (which means 'holy' or 'medicine man') and is author of 'We Borrow The Earth' and 'Beyond a Near Water' ('The Long Reflection' series of gypsy novels). As artistic director of Jal Folk Theatre, he has brought many aspects of Romani folklore and shamanic tradition into his performance, music and also his books.

Rahk Dahtsahni is a specific part of my culture, which not all Romani gypsies follow. It is very earthy and something that relates very much to earlier times. The principle idea behind Rahk Dahtsahni and its sacred-sexual teachings is that it is primarily related to the woodlands – that they are not only sacred but also very sexual by nature, which we often overlook. The connection between humans, the Otherworld and the woodland is an ancient one, and I think it's something that is missing from our understanding of sacred-sexuality today.

As a Chovihano, I help people learn about Rahk Dahtsahni in a respectful way, so that they can gain their own education and pleasures out of what it has to teach them about both spirituality and sexuality. It is very liberating and healing as a practice. Merging the spiritual with the sensual, it could be considered to be a tantric practice… although the woodlands element separates it from what is taught of tantra today.

I work with the gypsy woodland goddess, Leelis Raht Dai and a woodland faery teacher who I call Vohlo. An ancestor of mine, Puro, also talks to me a lot about sacred-sexual matters relating to the woodlands.

The Leelis Raht Dai, the ancient sacred-sensual deity who lives in the Dahtsahni realms, is a gypsy woodland goddess of extraordinary spiritual power and beauty. As well as being a very wise teacher, she is so gorgeously seductive, no one could ever resist her. Traditionally, she has black hair, dark eyes, and swishing classical gypsy clothes – full skirt and tight low-cut bodice. She dances and sings, luring both men and women into the wood, gifting them with a sense of animal sexuality – which we are wise not to lose. She is said to come to us on the breeze. And women who practice Dahtsahni aim to be like her, while men yearn for her.

I first encountered the Leelis Raht Dai, 'blossoming spirit blood mother', as a teenager. Most teenagers may encounter the woodland goddess when their sexuality starts to blossom. In our modern society we don't cater for the explosion of mental, emotional and sexual energy a youngster is introduced to in early adulthood, and the introduction of these sexual spirits at that time in my life was helpful rather than harmful, as it helped me give vent to stronger feelings and to express myself in a very natural and normal way.

As a teenager, I was also introduced to the Drahbo Saht. Much like the green man, he is a protector of the forest and all that is contained within nature. He is also a special protector of the sacred-sexual secrets of the forest. This woodland god is the 'medicine blood father' of the gypsy people. He is an intriguing, mysterious spirit who is able to merge into the woodland unseen, so he camouflages well with the trees and plants. He is also a great admirer of the Leelis Raht Dai, as most are.

As a Chovihano holy man, my job is to become a protector of all the spirits – a bridge between the two worlds. So when seekers go looking for both the Leelis Raht Dai and the Drahbo Saht, I act as a kind of agent or interpreter, speaking the languages of both… helping both mortals and immortals act out their roles to the best of their ability.

Vohlo

Vohlo is my personal guide, and he often appears when I'm lacking in energy, enthusiasm or courage. The closest image I can use to describe Vohlo is probably Puck from Midsummer Night's Dream – he is small, about four feet high, and very mischievous… sometimes seeming like a little boy, other times like a grand old man. But he is always wise. Sometimes he flies, sometimes he walks… and he seems to be able to shapeshift into different things I am working with, such as when I am playing music or writing. When he does this, I know he is involved with and concerned for what I'm doing. He is always present in the woodlands, especially when I am at Dahtsahni work and performing a ritual or just relaxing there.

He is what I would describe as a traditional magical creature – a fairy of the Old World, gnarled like tree bark and ugly in a beautiful sort of way. Old Romani fairy folk are very much like this, and less like the pretty fairies that were basically created in the 17th & 19th centuries. Some of the woodland fairy folk can be extremely ugly which wouldn't at all suit the new-agers of today! He makes me laugh and has a cackle of his own which I always love to hear. He is saucy and unafraid of being bawdy, but he also has a very kind heart and will do anything to help you learn a good lesson in the best possible way.

Many woodland fairy people will tease you if they want to encourage you. Tripping you up, removing something (so that you believe you've lost it), and basically championing your misfortune are all things that will help you learn a lesson. Usually it's all designed to toughen us up, because mortals are considered to be rather wimpy!

Sometimes things have gone wrong through the day for me… things not working out, something taking a turn for the worst and losing things, but that is when I know Vohlo is behind the scenes, smiling. It doesn't seem very supportive on the face of it, but when you really stop and think about it, we are often expecting everyone to do things for us, or circumstances to always work in our favor. But we don't learn if this happens repeatedly. We all need to have lessons that really teach us to make changes within ourselves and within our own behavior.

Although Vohlo comes only to me, we all have such guides if only we'll take notice of the lessons we're learning. This was more common in earlier times, and certainly common in my culture. The mischief, the playing-about with mortals, is very typical of old fairy folk long ago.

Vohlo is fun, and when you learn something from him he is very supportive, as all otherworldly beings are. But if you choose not to learn something, or repeatedly play silly-buggers, then woe betide you, because the fairy people will have a game with you, over and over and over again!

Puro

No one knows how far Puro goes back. His name means 'ancient one', and is used for 'grandfather' a lot of the time. I first encountered him as a small child when he communicated through Jack Lee, my great-grandfather, which he had typically done since the beginnings of time, or at the beginnings of the family line – whenever that might have been.

When Puro visits me it is usually through trance. I am aware of Puro when in trance, although I'm in a nice frame of mind and certainly a very open frame of mind because that's when I often receive messages and omens about things.

My own ancestors talked to the otherworldly really easily, just as my immediate family did when I was little… everyone sitting around drinking or having a cuppa and making contact. All very fun and simple. Puro is traditionally given offerings of whisky – a small glass of which he can partake whilst he is talking. There is otherwise no ceremony, nothing like a performance when he visits. No frills or ribbons, which have only developed in modern times because people have lost their links with simplicity and think everything has to be overly dramatic. He talks in a very casual but firm way, giving advice and answering people's questions, although he is well known for answering questions by asking more in return!

Puro also appears now and then as a hawk, which I often see flying around me. The hawk will appear at significant times in answer to my own questions, and I always feel safe when Puro, in whatever form he appears – either man or bird – is close to me. I would trust his advice and take my troubles to him without question.

The fact that this spirit – who isn't just a spirit in my eyes, but a dear and close friend and mentor – is with me, both amazes me and moves me. Having been in my family and communicating through Chovihanos going back through many generations is a rare phenomenon. But the accuracy of what he speaks and his care and wisdom makes my life and the lives of those who also know him, all the richer.

All this is really quite hard to describe in many ways. People who know me have often commented on how easily I communicate with other-worldly spirits. No drama, no frills, and no intensity – just plain communication, as I would do with anyone else. It's important, I think, to remember that communication isn't about putting on a show, whether you're communicating with humans or with spirits – it's about communicating in a straightforward and appropriate way. Why we believe spirits of the Otherworld need weird dramatic intensity, I can't understand.

We old Romanies consider that the Otherworld is the only place that can successfully teach us lessons in life. Its messages filter through to us in the mortal world or material world, and we either take the trouble to learn them, or continuously become tested by the 'unseen'. Forest spirits, fairies, angels & guardian spirits all have their place in Rahk Dahtsahni lore. Otherworldly lovers are also likely to become popular again, as they are an important part of Dahtsahni, helping an individual to heal from loneliness, widowhood, a broken heart and general sickness. If I can help people understand these things, then they will unite with Dahtsahni in a constructive way.

THE CYBERSPACE GENIE

by Christian Hummel

Christan Hummel is the author of the best-selling book, 'The Do-It-Yourself Space Clearing Kit'. She travels internationally lecturing and teaching people how to access nature in a co-creative spirit. Christan has been in communication with the devic realms of Nature since a teenager. Through this inner relationship, her Nature guides have helped her to recover ancient lost understandings of how to work with the earth to restore harmony and balance. A pioneer in earth energies exploration, Christan has taught thousands globally how to restore this lost relationship with Nature. In a grassroots network established throughout the world, groups have amazed government officials with results such as lower pollution levels, crime, earthquake activity, and restoration of weather patterns. Christan provides a unique synthesis of modern science and ancient wisdom in an easy and understandable manner accessible to us all.

Back in 1972, at the tender age of 14, my mother introduced me to my two spiritual teachers who first introduced me to the magical world of the devic realms. That event opened up to me the world of 'nature's unseen forces', as the devas have been called, and totally changed my life.

Communication with devas is more than just receiving pictures or words, but an interfacing of energies between the two kingdoms – devic and human. Our energy bodies need to be operating at a compatible vibratory frequency before effective communication can take place.

For many years, we just had what were private, personal relationships with these devas, who felt like friends and mentors to us. Their innocence, guilelessness and loving, supportive nature prompted us to often jest that our best friends were devas. It *was* true, though – after communicating and working with them for years, they were like 'invisible' friends.

The devic realm is a parallel kingdom to humanity, and their development ranges over a wide spectrum of consciousness, as does ours. Devas are hierarchical in nature and include elementals, fairies, gnomes, garden sprites and nature spirits among others. They are closely connected to the earth, and are very much bound to restricted territories. For instance, a tree spirit would not usually be able to venture out beyond the tree it embodies. It would be a 'master' of information about that tree, but may not have any wisdom or information about another kind of tree only two feet away. As devas progress in their own development, they assume larger areas of responsibility. So, while there is a deva for a particular tree, there would also be a more developed, mature deva for the whole forest of those trees, a more developed deva for the whole park the forest resides in, a deva for the city that the park is in, etc. If it has a name and it has a form, then it has a devic element that holds it together, whether it is a tree or a city. Seen in that light, one may wonder what was originally perceived when Los Angeles (the City of Angels) was given its name?

I have to confess that I'm a bit of a hypocrite when it comes to working with the devas. For a year now Ann Meril, my mother and partner in this work, and I have been helping people learn how to work with and communicate with devas in their own area, and in cities. It has been a productive partnership, as I could feel their presence and Ann could see them. So together, like the blind men and the elephant, we could put together a more complete 'picture' of their world.

Over the years, they have guided us in unexpected ways, helping us to learn how their world works, and how we can work together as a team to bring about a better future for both kingdoms. The results have been astounding, and the devas have been overwhelmingly happy to see humanity come to them in a spirit of co-operation after all these years. However, when it came to technology, I would freeze up. In my personal life, it seems that everything technological that either Ann or I owned would go on the blink regularly and we would become disabled by it, being somewhat technologically inept.

Well, one wonderful thing about doing workshops is that you are put to the challenge of walking your talk. This is what happened one day while doing a workshop in Sao Paulo, Brazil. I was staying with a woman who had an electric garage door opener. We had the car parked inside the garage and the door wouldn't open, and we needed to leave to get to the workshop. We tried everything we knew. We put a Caduceus ring (a Tesla-type tool that I talk about in the workshop) around it, we pushed all sorts of buttons, but nothing would happen. We were trapped. Finally, the woman I was staying with, Magali, asked, "Don't garage door-openers have devas too?" Well, I suppose they do, yes – though I had never thought of it like that before. And then she asked the next logical question, "Can't you speak with them like you do the other devas?" Well, again, theoretically, yes – but I'd never done anything like that before…

I looked for what might be the central command unit and began to 'tune' my consciousness to the garage door-opening unit. I tried to put myself on its wavelength, so to speak. When I felt that I was there, I introduced myself and asked, "What's the problem?" To my surprise, I received an answer back immediately: *"I'm stuck!"* It sounded like a little girl in my mind, and all she kept saying was, *"I'm stuck, I'm stuck!"* Well, my heart melted when I heard her. When I asked what to do, all I kept hearing was the same, *"I'm stuck."* Yes, yes, we got that part… what do we *do?* Then I got a vision of going over to the bottom corner of the garage door and pushing it while Magali pushed the switch again. This time it opened right away!

That was my first 'contact' with the devic life of a mechanical device. I know auto repair people who just seem to know where to look for problems and what to do, even before they put the car on the monitors. They intuit or get a gut feeling about what to do. I've seen computer troubleshooters do the same thing. Could it be that they are in 'communication' with the deva of the thing they are working on and receive that communication in the form of hunches and pictures or impressions? What I had been teaching people in the workshops we give, is that often devas communicate that way, and very seldom do they use words directly.

Recently, I was confronted by what seemed like insurmountable printer problems. I was getting ready to move all my things into storage, preparing for a long trip on the road, and was trying to print out all the business items I would need before I left – but the printer wouldn't work. I tried calling the computer tech person who usually helps us out of such jams, but he was laid up with health problems and couldn't come over. I also attempted to transfer the items onto a disk to print elsewhere, but I kept running into disk errors.

So there I was. The words *'I'm stuck'* kept ringing in my mind. Yes, I was stuck. But what to do? I shared the garage door opener story with Ann while commiserating with her, when she suggested that we contact the deva of the printer. Yet again I was on unfamiliar turf… but what did I have to lose? I'd tried everything else I knew to do and I was still stuck.

We tuned into the deva and immediately there was a response. I actually saw her (which is rare for me) looking like the traditional genie in a bottle, with blue complexion and all. She was *not* very happy, though.

Ann pointed out that I didn't have a very loving relationship with either my computer or printer, as they frequently didn't work even though almost new. So, the first thing that we did was to invoke the violet flame to purify all the past thought forms around the printer – mine and those of anyone else, since devas are required to carry out the thought forms imposed upon them by humanity. This was a technique we had been shown to help release devas of the land from past traumas they were still holding onto energetically. So we released the deva from the previous thought forms about the printer. Then we invoked a thought form called a *'Buddhic column'*, which connects it with the Will of the Mother and with the Heavenly Realms directly. After that, we asked, "What do you need?" All I heard was, *"Loose cable"*, so I jiggled it. Upon doing that, I realized that she was upset or saddened about not being included and acknowledged. Especially because she knew that we worked with devas! She felt neglected and unappreciated. She was aware of all the deva articles and emails and reports that went through her, and yet we didn't acknowledge *her* as a deva. We felt awful. We immediately apologized and began to acknowledge her as a being.

"Is there anything we can do for you?" we asked,

"I want a ring!" she pouted. Evidently she was jealous that all the other devas got one of the Caduceus rings I teach about in the workshops, as we use them a lot in our work, but she hadn't – so we put a ring around her base. Then she shared that she wasn't happy sitting on the CPU… that she wanted her own space – so we moved her, and visualized a globe of energy around her to represent her own space. I was guided to jiggle some paper in her paper cartridge – I heard her say, *"I'm happy now"*, and suddenly she started printing the backlog of printed articles that had been jammed for a day!

We had been taught an important lesson. She began to converse with us inwardly saying that she was 'nature' too. She said that technology is what man has done with nature, but it is *still* nature and has a devic consciousness. *Of course!* Everything has life and a consciousness.

Before anything exists on the physical plane, it must first be created as a thought. This happens whether we are conscious of it or not. The clearly formulated thought, energized by desire is picked up by the devas and is then materialized into form. Anything that we can see on this physical plane is a result of a thought (humanity's element) energized by desire, which the devas manifest and hold in form. So everything, without exception, contains devic life. They are, in fact, the life within the form, like the soul of a thing. But, just as with humans, there are varying levels of consciousness within that form.

Well, both Ann and I were sitting there in amazement at this newfound discovery and relationship with my printer when she began to speak to us again, stating that she didn't want to be kept in a storage locker while I was gone – she wanted to go to Ann's house instead, and said that she could help Ann with her internet problems. She showed us that the computer devas are interlinked, or networked, in a kind of collective consciousness – something like the Borg in *Star Trek.* She knew how to help us with fax, internet and computer devas, and *wanted* to help us learn how to work with these devas.

She then proceeded to show us how we had put a barrier between us and what we call 'technology' – we thought of the devas we worked with as being a part of nature, and thought of technology as alien to nature. She showed us that they are the same, and that our attitude that we held towards technology caused the devic life within those forms to respond to our alien and hostile manner in dysfunctional ways. Our own attitude towards these technology devas created many of the problems we were experiencing with their functions.

We marveled at her language capacities and had never encountered that before in a 'machine' deva. She pointed out that she held within her consciousness many language facilities because of her nature and function and because of her constant exposure to words. She also revealed that she had a microprocessor unit (I don't know if that's technically correct, but it's what it looked like when she showed me the picture) inside of her that was analogous to the human brain, making communication in words easy for her as it was something she was familiar with. She was very interested in helping us learn to work with the technology devas in our environment – the internet, modem, fax and computer. She showed us that they were networked together in consciousness and understood something of each other's function and nature. She was willing to act as something of a translator to help interface between us and the other technology devas.

Within about 30 minutes of communicating with her and interacting with her, Ann began to perceive her inwardly as being 10 times her original size, and looked like a moving mandala. As we focused our attention on the deva, she began developing in consciousness and organization of her energy patterns, right in front of us.

The technology devas are very interested in working co-creatively with humanity to come up with solutions by recognizing and co operating with the devic life of technology. Connecting with one deva of technology puts us into contact with the collective consciousness of all of cyberspace. Humanity has a responsibility of how we use the internet as we come into relationship with this interfacing kingdom called cyberspace. It is a bridging kingdom composed of silicon (crystal), with devic life and man-made technology. Silicon, deva, human – the three come together in computer technology… a meeting of the minds, so to speak. We believe it is possible to have an interactive relationship with technology that recognizes and co-operates with the life force within it.

AT THE CROSSROADS OF SPIRIT

R. J Stewart

R.J Stewart is a Scottish author, musician and composer of international acclaim. He has worked, researched and written extensively on the spiritual and magical core of the Western Tradition. R.J. currently has 40 books in publication, translated into many languages worldwide. He works with myth, imagination, music, and the primal magical arts of inner change and vision. For the last ten years he has concentrated mainly on writing and working with small groups in Europe and the USA, specifically working towards regenerating ancient traditions of inner transformation for practical modern use.

As a teenager in the 1960's, I discovered meditation when it became popular in Britain. To my surprise, I contacted a spirit teacher, who appeared to me every day at the same time, and taught me meditational techniques. This was the first clear contact that I could definitely affirm as something outside myself. Not long after this, I moved to a remote part of North Devon, living in a small caravan at a crossroads.

At this time, I encountered many spirit beings of the land and of ancient priest and priestesshoods. These early encounters formed the basis for much of my writing and teaching in my Inner Temple Traditions work, which has been ongoing from the 1980's to the present day.

I usually contact my guides not only during deep meditation, but also in my dreams. In recent years, I have much more direct contact during waking consciousness, often while walking. Much of the material in my books comes to me in an altered state of consciousness as I write. Some of their deepest intimations and hints come in highly illuminated dreams. And sometimes things just hit me over the head!

Many spirit guides are trivial. The spirit world is like a huge market square or meeting place, with many people milling around bumping into one another. We have to find the quiet corners or the less overt groups, where the deeper contacts are ready to commune with us. There is no need to blindly accept the first few guides or contacts that come along, any more than must accept all overtures in the outer life. We must have discretion, judgment, and common sense.

Why do we have them? For the same reasons that we have friends and family... consciousness is a commune, not an isolated individual. Yet within that commune, we can remain individual and choose our relationships. If we make mistakes, well fine – we learn from them and make better choices later. This is why many spirit guides are trivial... when we outgrow them we can reach into deeper contacts.

The Western esoteric tradition is a very ancient tradition reaching back to Greece and Egypt – also in Britain, to druidic sources. So my 'guides' are usually in two broad categories. The first are spirit beings that are not human, such as nature spirits, faery beings and angelic contacts. One set are a Working Team of faery beings, usually around seven in number. These are large powerful beings, not little 'cartoony' figures from fantasy. They are concerned with healing energies, communion with Nature, and aspects of seership and the Second Sight. They only work with me when

I undertake the faery work, including as the workshops and classes that I teach with material from my books such as *'Earth Light'*, *'Power Within the Land'*, and *'The Well of Light'*. All the methods in those books were given to me by the Team, but based on ancient tradition.

The second are ancestors and evolved trans-human beings, often appearing as priests or priestesses of Inner Temples in spirit places. This set of contacts come through very strongly in my classes and workshops on Inner Temples and the Inner Convocation. These are powerful, highly evolved trans-human mentors. They tend to work with Overworld spiritual themes, angelic and archangelic forces, and the cosmic powers of the Seven Directions.

Another significant contact, who I introduce to students, is a Go-Between. These are human beings in the faery realm... in other words they are discarnate, but once were humans who worked deeply with the natural magic of the faery and land-based traditions. They should not be confused with 'spirit guides' in the popular sense, as they are highly specialized mentors of deep consciousness working uniquely within the faery and Underworld sacro-magical traditions.

My inner contacts (guides) tend to expect me to do things for myself... they are more concerned with results and good quality work than with my 'self-development'. However, they do point me in certain directions, and if I follow the intimations and hints, I often find that new abilities will begin to open out, especially in spiritual magic and subtle perception of the spirit worlds.

As most of my inner contacts are task-orientated, they are concerned with our service to spiritual transformation, and not especially concerned with our individual lives or personalities. If I had not taken up the spiritual work, I would have continued as a composer and musician, working in the film industry and in theatre. In fact, I gave up most of that work to undertake the spiritual tasks that were given to me. In that sense, following the spiritual path that my inner contacts required, has substantially changed my direction in life.

CHAPTER 8

THE ANGELIC REALMS

Angels are intelligent reflections of light,
that original light which has no beginning.
They can illuminate. They do not need tongues or ears,
for they can communicate without speech, in thought.
~ John of Damascus

Angels are the collective name for all celestial guardians of the universe. Of all spirit beings, angels are perhaps the most widely recorded throughout history – in religious texts, adorning the walls of temples and churches, in paintings, songs, poetry and prose. In modern times, angel imagery is just as popular, if not more so… continuing to inspire creativity.

Organized religions have 'adopted' these vast spiritual beings of immense power as their holy icons and the messengers of 'the Word of God'. Human 'saints' are even portrayed as having achieved angelic status in the afterlife. Angels, however, are *not* human beings with wings, although they may choose to disguise themselves in human form now and then in order to be of assistance. Angels have no physical form per se, as they are beings of Light and Divine love – the essence of unconditional love, rather than 'love' in the emotional sense.

The notion of an angelic hierarchy largely originates from an anonymous Greek theologian and philosopher of the 5th Century, Pseudo-Dionysius the Areopagite. He believed that the closer a hierarchy is to the source of Divine light, the greater the degree of purity and resemblance to Source.

In his work, *'Celestial Hierarchies',* he presents an angelic order divided into three groups of three hierarchies each – the first, or most exalted, being the Seraphim, Cherubim and Thrones; the second the Dominions, Virtues and Powers; and the third the Principalities, Archangels and Angels. Pseudo-Dionysius wrote that these hierarchies are a co-equal unity, emanating 'from the most spiritual origins down to the most material planes', and that, 'to undertake the divine ascension, there are intermediaries for every level of reality like the steps on a ladder. The higher hierarchies, receiving a more direct illumination, can transmit that light to the lower hierarchies at the level they are able to perceive it, and the higher hierarchies also serve as an accessible image of the transcendent – an example for the hierarchy immediately below, whose members can contemplate in order to rise to a higher level'. All, he said, 'can rightly be called Angels in respect of their participation in the Divine likeness and illumination, both in the higher and lower ranks'.

The notion that angels have a ranking order is a human concept – one that I do not feel is accurate, as it implies that it is an authoritarian force comprised of angelic leaders and subordinates. I do not feel that the angels themselves would define themselves in this way – in fact, I believe they are beyond definition, and that they have been (and continue to be) misrepresented. Angels are so often portrayed as the 'spiritually advanced elite', yet angels will be the first to tell you that they are no closer to God than we are – they just walk a different path.

It is often said that at birth every soul is assigned a guardian angel that holds the blueprint of your true nature. This angel could be described as the guardian of your soul, whose purpose is to protect, heal, guide and inspire you throughout life, and at the death of your body accompany your spirit as you cross over to the 'other side'.

Additional angels can also be called upon to help you with particular tasks and group projects as and when needed – they are especially drawn to activities that will be of benefit to others, or will serve others in some way. There are also angels whose purpose is to oversee the spiritual evolvement of life on a larger scale… from all earth's oceans, wooded valleys and towns and cities, to whole countries. Others are immense, ineffable beings beyond our comprehension, charged with the macro-cosmic guardianship of planets and the entire universe.

It is believed that angels have a big part to play in the evolution of humankind during these times – to remind us of, and help us awaken to, our own Divinity.

NATURAL EMPATHY

by William Bloom

William Bloom is one of the U.K's leading spiritual educators and authors. He is the Director of the Foundation for Holistic Spirituality, the Spiritual Companions Project and the Open Mystery School. He is a meditation master and his books include the seminal 'The Endorphin Effect', 'Feeling Safe' and 'Psychic Protection' – and most recently 'Soulution: The Holistic Manifesto'.

Born in 1948, William Bloom grew up in central London. His mainstream career includes a doctorate in psychology from the London School of Economics (LSE) where he lectured in Psychological Problems in International Politics, ten years working with adults and adolescents with special needs, and delivering hundreds of trainings, many within the National Health Service (NHS).

Since the late 1970's, William's writing and teaching have reflected his interest in new approaches to exploring consciousness and spirituality. In 1988, with his wife Sabrina Dearborn and friend Malcolm Stern, he co-founded and directed the popular Alternatives Program at

St. James's Church, Piccadilly. He is a Fellow of the Findhorn Foundation. He teaches and runs workshops internationally and is well known for his clear, practical and friendly style of teaching.

By instinct I am a communard and celebrate the unity of all life. I feel rooted in the Middle Eastern religions and am happy sometimes to be called a mystic Christian with strong Taoist tendencies. The essence of my Christianity is an experience of a cosmic force that redeems everything with unconditional love. Sometimes I call this force the Cosmic Christ. It is also, I believe, true Buddha Consciousness. But I am not attached to labels. I prefer to call my beliefs 'Holistic'.

Academically, I can be located in the school known as 'critical theory'. In essence, this means I believe that all our opinions and beliefs require careful self-reflection so that we can understand how our social, cultural and psychological backgrounds determine how we think.

But at root, if everything is stripped away, I believe in love. Not sentimental romantic love, but that compassionate and engaged consciousness that cares for and gives importance to every tiny detail of the whole fabric of life.

The first event that opened my heart was not a dramatic experience of a psychic or clairvoyant nature. It happened when I was about four years old… I was in a nursery school playground and I saw a little girl with red frizzy hair and very thick spectacles, crying because she'd just been bullied and ostracized. Something happened in that moment and my heart exploded with anger and a knowing that this wasn't fair.

At the same time, as a child, I had a very powerful sense of the beauty and wonder of life. Just looking at the blue sky was enough to make me experience and know that there was a power and goodness behind everything. I experienced nature and the universe as being alive and benevolent, but I also had no trouble in recognizing that within this beautiful and radiant cosmos there is also pain, cruelty and suffering.

I also kept noticing that there was more to me than just the child, the personality I presented to the world. Within me there was another identity that was watchful, strong and loving.

Like many people, I was born with a nervous system and esoteric anatomy that made me naturally empathic and psychic. From a very early age, I could feel what was going on with people and in certain situations and places, a bit like Commander Troy in *'Star Trek'* – she's the one who knows what others are actually feeling, regardless of what they're saying. I don't think this was unusual. I think many children have this ability… it's just that I didn't close down. I could feel what kind of spirits were in a tree and what somebody was carrying in their aura, but I didn't have a language for it – I was just simply a child feeling all that stuff.

The problem was that I was brought up in a very cultured, educated family. My parents were atheists who thought all this kind of stuff was rubbish. I was having my experience of this inner world and at the same time couldn't talk about it with anyone, so I grew up very cautious about how I communicated my experiences and always wanted to explain it in a way that could be accepted.

Growing up in an intellectual environment also had its advantages. My father was a Freudian psychiatrist and, during my early twenties, I underwent psychoanalysis with Dr Edward Glover – one of the founders of psychoanalysis – for three years. This helped build that most important of spiritual tools – the ability to self-reflect and self-manage one's own development.

At about this time, I was working as an editor in a publishing house and I received a book about angels. I read it and part of me was saying, *"What a load of rubbish"*, while another part of me was shouting, *"Yes!"* The 'Yes' won. I began to read about three spiritual books a week after that, especially following the different exercises and strategies – such as meditation, ceremony and visualization. One day, I came across a book called *'The Sacred Magic of Abramelin the Mage'*, which was about a six-month ceremony to purify and meet your guardian angel.

I decided I had to experience the things I was reading about for myself. I went to Southern Morocco and retreated to a wooden hunting lodge in the High Atlas Mountains for two years to undertake this ceremony. This was a spiritual quest that changed my life (you can read more about this in my book *'The Sacred Magician'*). For six months, I meditated and prayed for at least five hours every day, and finally met my guardian angel.

The experience is still difficult for me to put into words. If my angel were a colour, it would be gold and silver combined. But it wasn't a colour or a winged being or any of those things – it was an intense feeling of love, comfort, power, expansion and connection. It was also a specific identity. Since this retreat in the mountains I have had continuous perception of the angelic and deva world. 'Deva' is a Hindu term that includes angels and nature spirits. I learned that their realm is not separate from ours – it is interwoven with it. For me, this world of spirits is half of reality. There is the solid human world and there is also this interwoven spirit cosmos.

I understand that many people may think that this is delusion and imagination. Of course I disagree with them, but am also sympathetic because so many people who are into angels and spirits have not necessarily learned the skills of discernment – how to distinguish between imagination and spiritual reality. Personally, when dealing with spiritual matters I find it useful to imagine a radar dish on either side of my head. I call them my 'bullshit detectors', scanning for bullshit inside me and outside.

Another important lesson here is to try and catch the *essence* of an experience. When people come to me, telling me about a wonderful experience they've had with a guide or angel, they describe it in colours and images, but I always ask, "How did you *feel?*" Just because something looks beautiful, it doesn't mean that it is benevolent. How it makes you feel is crucial. Good or bad? Creative or destructive? These are simple but important questions.

Most people can be aware of what has come into their energy field and will 'feel' it as it affects their nervous system and chemistry. This is no different from walking into a house or a bar and immediately catching the atmosphere. Or a close friend or relative may come to see you and you immediately feel what kind of mood they are in.

This same sense is used to know what is happening in the spirit world. Spirits, though, usually have a more subtle energy than people, so if we are going to be connected to angels we need to have a more refined and sensitive awareness. This just means that we need to get used to being silent, receptive and very aware.

Nowadays, I am conscious of the presence of many guardian angels around me. I don't do ceremony nowadays to contact my guardian angels. The interaction is there all the time. When you've had a bad day and you go to bed feeling frustrated or miserable and as you drop off to sleep, you feel a warm comforting feeling – what is that? Your guardian angel is always with you. They carry our life contracts. When we're on the right path, they'll help and assist, but if we go off track they'll send us lessons. Almost like a parent, they assist, support and encourage. They always love us, forgive us and see our full potential.

Angels can help you to develop your talents and abilities. There are angels of horticulture, angels of healing, of business, of the arts and so on. Whatever you want to do in life, if you call on a specific angel they will help take things in the right direction.

ACUSHLA

Anne Hassett

Anne has been psychic since childhood. Although she comes from Ireland, she has been based in the West of England in Bath for the past twenty-five years. Anne is also known as Acushla – she chose the name to honour her Celtic origins and to have a name in keeping with her mission in life, which is to heal emotional, spiritual, psychological and life issues through insight and inspiration. The word 'Acushla' is Gaelic and means pulse (of the heart) or love in the sense of compassion.

Anne has worked in Europe, America, Australia, New Zealand, the Middle East and Far East. Anne also works several times a year in Hong Kong, where she has a huge and loyal following. She has featured on T.V, radio and in many international newspapers and magazines. Anne is also author of 'Reading your Child's Hand', which has been of immense help to parents, and she has three more books in the pipeline.

Anyone who tells me faeries don't exist… well, they do! As an only child living in the Irish countryside, I was thrown on my own resources. I spent a lot of my time in the woods and I saw nature spirits that were about three or four feet high and a brownish colour. They were my little friends. I didn't have names for them… I just saw them and they were there. I feel now they came from another dimension. All around you and I in this very moment in this so-called 'space' (because there isn't any space, really, it's a creation of our minds) there are a multitude of other beings living lives. They may not even be in human form – they could be something entirely different! And they're all living here, now, but on another frequency… that's why we don't see them. Of course, the Irish were particularly very aware of this.

I thought everybody saw them until I went to school and the other kids made fun of me! It was a terrible shock for me to discover that other people couldn't see things, and so I clammed up. I developed a terrible stammer that I didn't get rid of until I was about 21. My mother, being a very staunch Catholic, discouraged it as well. She used to beat me – she said she was beating the 'devil' out of me. So my ability to perceive the spirit world got pushed away for a long time.

About 30 years ago, I went through a huge personal trauma – what I call the 'dark night of the soul'. I was in a bad way… I was suicidal. I called out for help and I think that's when I began to open up again. I heard voices. You could say I was going mad, but I don't think so.

One evening, I'd just finished meditating when an immense being of light appeared in front of me. I feel it was an archangel. It didn't seem to be male or female… just a being of light. It was about 20 feet tall and continued on up through the ceiling. I felt an immense love radiating from it. I tried to re-create that situation again and never could. It was a gift.

Soon after that, I became aware of my guardian angel, who has a name I could never have made up – Agnemantha. It's an androgynous being with a female vibration. I also started to see angels around people a lot. Sometimes I'd see them as human-shaped beings, and sometimes just as a ball of light or a wisp of something that I couldn't put a name on. I realised that other people were having really bad times in life and that maybe I could help them.

Soon after I chose the name 'Acushla', my first spirit guide appeared. He was an Irish monk called Malachy. He had bright red hair and he was dirty – all the food he'd been eating dribbled down the front of his vestments and he was a real character. I sometimes saw him with my physical eyes, but mostly with my 'inner eyes'. I worked with him for a long time and then he suddenly disappeared. I thought I'd done something to upset him, but in a short space of time a Chinese guide called Master Ho appeared. I've been with him ever since – for about 19 years. He helps me and I work with him a lot. He's quite stern, though. With all due respect, he hasn't got a great sense of humour! He's very good with medical things, if my clients have a medical problem. Somebody told me, later on, that there *was* a Chinese physician called Master Ho who invented the first anesthetic. Now, I didn't know that...

My Chinese guide has a form that represents his vibration but I don't need to see it anymore. I did when I first got to know him because I had to know who he was. He's more of a presence now than form. I still know when he's around. I think that the high vibrational spirit guides are beyond ego. Only ego needs form, a body and clothes. They don't need that because they are formless and egoless, but they are very obliging, so they'll put on a form… a costume to make themselves acceptable to us humans.

I feel I've had many past lives in China and I connect very much with Chinese culture, which is very strange for an Irish woman. I feel very at home when I spend time there. I also work with Kwan Yin – the Chinese goddess of compassion. She's one of the ascended masters. I sometimes see her with my clients. I think that Kwan Yin was somebody I was 'devoted' to in my past life as a Buddhist nun in China.

I once had an interesting experience in Hong Kong where I work in a shop giving readings. A Chinese guy came in – he paid for a reading and he sat down in front of me … told me all about myself, about my past life as a Chinese nun (which I already knew, but he confirmed it), and then he said, "And you have a Chinese guide called Master Ho". He told me some other things about the future, stood up, shook hands with me and walked out – never had a reading *and* paid for it! I wonder did he exist at all? His money was very real, though!

I think that so many people have this idea that the 'New Age' is all pink clouds and everything's lovely and there's no bad, but of course there is. There's hot and cold, so there's got to be good and bad. On a path of development, I think that all of us sometime along the way have a choice to go to the light or away from it. I've had experiences with other kinds of beings that aren't so nice. I was in bed one night and I could feel something behind me. I could 'see' that it was black and it was like a ball with arms. It wanted to stroke me and cuddle me. It was really very seductive. I found myself praying and asking it to go, and it actually screeched and left.

The negative forces also want the power we have. They want to use it for their own agenda. And of course they're not going to present themselves in a nasty way, as a demon with horns! They're going to be as seductive as they can.

I think there is some vested interest that doesn't want us to progress. There are fourth-dimensional beings operating through certain people who live on the planet. These people are being used. You can see it in their eyes… the eyes are a window to the soul, so they say.

Not all spirit beings are well-intentioned – just because they're dead doesn't necessarily mean they're wise. There are people stuck in spaces very close to ours, almost on the astral level, and of course they're going to know everything about us and 'guide' us, but it may not be for our own good if they have their own manipulative ends. I don't mean to be disparaging, but I think that even when so-called 'dead relatives' appear to mediums, one has to be discriminating because anything could pose as a loved one. Not all things are benevolent.

I trust my Chinese guide implicitly. I always go through him to check that the spirits are not imposters and to give me the go-ahead that they're okay. I think the negative ones have given up on me now, but I must be on guard. I test everything. Always be discriminating – don't live in fear of anything, but just be discriminating.

I believe that we are raising our vibration. It's actually been measured by scientists who study calibrations, that the frequency of mankind as a species is rising. I think this will make it easier to perceive angels and other beings, but I also feel that the angels are here with great interest to observe this wonderful shift that's happening. I'm not at all pessimistic by what I see on the news or anything. I don't watch the news anyway because I don't want that energy in my consciousness. If you don't watch or read the news, the *real* news is so fantastic – there's so much good happening all over the planet everywhere. I'm very positive that these are changes for the better.

I believe that angels are at work all the time around us. I am guided by angels a lot – they put things my way. They help me with the big, profound questions as well as the little things. When I'm driving my car, I ask them to ride shotgun – to sit on the roof and take care of me! I ask them for parking spaces and to help me with my computer. Not only that, but I've got five sons and I take the liberty every night of asking their guardian angels to take care of them. I think as a mother, I can do that… and it seems to work. The angels will help us with anything, but one has to ask, because they won't interfere with our own free will. It's getting into the habit of asking. It's judgmental to say that one thing is trivial and another is important… you can ask them for *anything* and it will come.

Many years ago, I was travelling in America and I was on a budget. I arrived in Flagstaff and I was hoping to go to the Grand Canyon. I got there at dusk and there was an air of menace about the place, so I asked for help. A man appeared in front of me who told me his name was Jim, saying, "Can I help you, ma'am?" Normally I wouldn't trust a total stranger, but for some reason I did. I needed to get some food and go to my motel, so he took me to a supermarket, waited at the checkout till I'd paid and walked me back to the motel. As I turned around to thank him, he disappeared into thin air. I think he was an angel.

Angels have never been incarnate, but they can take on physical form temporarily. They can manipulate molecules and matter. It's easy for them, I should think. In our arrogance, we think an angel should look like a human being, but I think they could appear as a dog or a horse should they choose to do so!

I think the angels 'job', if you like, is to help mankind. There are different angels – there are the angels that are closest to us, which is why we see them, then there are the archangels who are on a higher vibration again – they are more concerned with groups rather than individuals. Above them there are the 'powers' and so it goes on, and on. There are immense angels – angels that look after galaxies – that we would never see in a million years because they are way beyond our understanding. Angels we call 'principalities' oversee towns and cities. When I go to Hong Kong, as the plane is landing, I will tune in to the overlighting angel of Hong Kong and ask to be taken care of while I'm there. And when I leave, I always say thank you. It makes a huge difference. Try that the next time you're travelling…

Reality and life have fascinated me since I was a child. I always think of the mind as a computer that's programmed to calculate and understand the reality we happen to be living in, but it's too limited in its perception to be able to understand it all. The mind doesn't have the answers. But the higher-self knows, because it isn't operating through mind. Through meditation, we can access the higher-self and get the answers.

It's important to remember who one truly is because we're so caught up in the identity, with the part we're playing in this life, but that's not *really* who we are. It's just a role we're playing. The *real* us is beyond all that. Once you get on this path of enquiry, the vista opens up and the questions get more fascinating. It's the most exciting journey we will ever make.

We have an aspect of ourselves that is beyond the physical. That part of us that is all-knowing and all-powerful is also your guide. And, maybe, I just wonder, is Master Ho an aspect of me? Is he another part of my soul? I don't know!

I think our soul puts down many projections of itself. It hasn't just got one body that it's operating though – it has several. When I was a little girl growing up in Ireland, I was very conscious and aware of also being a Nazi in Germany. I was a young man in my late 30's, early 40's. I could see my boots, I could see my great coat, I could see the whole thing. But I was a little girl living in Ireland… how could I be there?

Because of our Western culture, we're taught to think linearly. The past is back there, the present is now and the future is over there. I *know* that we can live lifetimes simultaneously rather than linearly. As an individual, one could have other possible selves living simultaneously in this time frame, as well as being in the past and the future. Maybe you and I are working somewhere on another level helping someone right now? The soul has many facets. It's not as simple as one thinks and it could drive one mad thinking about it!

I believe that at one time there was only one of us – there was just Source. The Source split into trillions of fragments… some became human and some became angels. But we got lost. We came into physicality and we forgot who we were, but the angels never did. Out of their love for us, they are there to help us… to remind us who we are. I think that they're also here to help and oversee the growth and evolution of everything on the planet.

In reality, there's only one of us – there isn't a 'you' and a 'me' and a guide and an angel… we're all part of the One. Eventually, we must all return to the One and merge, but I'm not sure quite how that's going to work to be perfectly honest. It's beyond my comprehension. Do we lose our individuality? The ego has a great fear of being lost, of losing its identity, so we don't like to think about that, do we? But there is a school of thought that says we won't lose our individuality, whatever that might be.

Guides are wonderful, they're all around us, but as mankind evolves as a species, we're beginning to remember who we are. I have a great belief in the Divinity of Mankind – that we are all Divine beings who've forgotten who we are. I think the highest form of healing we can do is to remind each other of that, when it's appropriate.

A MESSAGE FROM THE ANGELS:

Dearly beloved ones, you will all be aware that now is a time of great change. We are here to help and guide you; just call on us. It gives us great joy to be of help. This is the time we have waited for, to be able to assist you to wake from your long sleep. At long last you are beginning to remember the true nature of your being. You are all Divine beings, only you have forgotten. You have thought that you were small and limited. You are not. Step into your magnificence. Embrace the glory of your Spiritual selves. We will assist you all the way; we are here to help remind you of who you truly are. Despite the apparent negativity you see all around you, there is a groundswell of light and goodness rising up. Rejoice.

THE MIDWAYERS

by George Mathieu Barnard

George Mathieu Barnard is Dutch by birth, French by descent, and Australian by choice. Since childhood, he has been aware of Spirit Guardians who often guided and protected him. In his career as an industrialist, and later a therapist, these Spirit Friends assisted him in emergencies – from saving lives to rescuing companies from disaster. They seek to make us aware that this unique human-celestial liaison is available to all who seek it and wish to serve.

Now that I am in my sixties, I can look back over a lifetime of frequent verbal and visual contact with celestial beings. Even from my early childhood, I could see these spirit visitors, whom I simply thought of as my family's 'spirit friends', who regularly visited my home, mostly at mealtimes. But it was obvious to me that our visitors would go to their own homes to eat dinner, since there was no more room at our table. They just seemed to hang around, patiently waiting for the meal to end, as if they wanted to draw my parents aside for casual conversation.

I had no inkling that, of the eight other members in my family, not one was aware of these celestial arrivals, though it did seem strange that no one ever talked with them. And it was hardly my place to address them, for small children were meant to be seen, not heard, at the table.

I had long assumed there was a simple genetic reason for my extended family's closeness with these Spirit Guides. My mother often conversed with unseen celestial beings and her father was widely respected for his having been 'a great dowser' in his younger years.

All throughout my teenage years, I received countless prompts from these beings and, because of the positive advice these prompts contained, I renamed my friends the Spirit Guides. Although I saw them less often, their valuable guidance had a highly positive impact on my life – in my studies for business management and industrial psychology, in my work and even in my decision to leave Europe to settle in Australia as a lone migrant at age eighteen. They especially helped me in new business ventures.

From the time I was twenty until I turned thirty-two, as I cared for my young family, my contact with these spirit friends was sporadic. I seldom heard their voices and yet their subliminal input about the future was an almost daily event. I understood their input to be pure intuition on my part and all who knew me well pictured me as a talented psychic, capable of hitting the nail on the head when it came to predicting future events. That conception was about to change-drastically…

For every meal in the Barnard homestead, over a period of more than four years, an extra place was set at the dining room table. This place, directly to George's right, was for Simone. George never saw Simone eat anything. In fact, he never saw Simone. She was invisible… but not to his eldest daughter.

To the six-and-a-half-year-old, Danielle, Simone was very real. On a few occasions, the advice that was supposed to have come from Danielle's 'invisible sister' made excellent sense.

"Simone suggests you eat at least half of your green beans," the father jokingly told Danielle at their Saturday evening meal.

The youngster gave him a troubled, sullen look. Then she pounded her little fork down hard on one of the offending beans.

"That one is quite dead now," George informed her. "You killed it. I think you can safely put it in your mouth now. It won't be able to get away."

Her shoulders hunched, her lips pressed tight, Danielle kept glaring at the annoying little green trespassers on her plate. She wasn't going to show him she enjoyed the humor. She simply hated those dreadful beans too much.

The father carried on softly, "When I was little – and I was always very, very little – your grandmother cooked us only one meal per week, on Sundays. And so, on all the other days we had to eat grass, like your pony does. Green beans are ever so much nicer than grass."

The child turned on him in anger and proclaimed loudly, "When you were little – and you were always very, very little – Grandpa forgot to teach you how to walk. And so you skipped around on one leg for the rest of your life. We know that story already, too!"

She was clearly advising her father on behalf of her siblings, and perhaps on behalf of the invisible little Simone, that none of them would believe he was ever forced to eat grass.

"You ask Simone about it," George suggested. "See what she's got to say. She'll soon give you the score."

"She says the tree is going to fall on the house, Daddy," came the immediate but utterly inappropriate reply. It was the second time George had heard that comment. It was no longer a joke. He was beginning to feel uneasy.

From his place at the table, he glanced at the big White Eucalypt. It stood fully forty meters from the homestead, right on their boundary fence. There was no chance of it falling on their home. It was old, big, wide, but not very tall. It did, however, carry some large dead branches.

Perhaps they should be taken down? Be made safe? he mused.

Danielle's remark still bothered him that evening, but even trying hard as he did, he could extract no further information from his Spirit Friends. And to this day, he has no idea why they either did not know, would not tell him, or could not tell him, what he wanted to know about the potential danger with that tree.

"What does Simone say about going to the beach on Sunday?" George asked at the evening meal.

"She says she will come, too," Danielle answered, "but the tree is going to fall on the house." Her last remark was so unemotional, so unreservedly casual.

I live in a different time slot, the father thought. I go and whiz around this universe, looking at the future, and I do a second-rate job in coming back. I'm getting the same dumb, unbecoming answer to the question I asked last weekend. Either that or I'm hearing a strange, long-distance echo. I may be a week out of sync with the rest of the world.

"Leave your dinner, young lady," he told her. "You, and I, and that big tree over there, are going to have a lengthy discussion."

As he stood and headed for the door, Danielle slipped down from her chair and followed him. Through the door and down the steps, across the driveway and up the garden steps, then across the expanse of their finely mown lawn, they finally reached the Eucalypt. There, father and daughter faced each other beneath its wide crown. The child was wearing a most thoughtful but somewhat distrustful look.

"This here tree is a White Eucalypt," George told her as he tapped the bark. "It has been standing right here for a long time, even before you were born. It told me just recently that it likes this particular spot and it does not want to leave us. It's happy to be part of our family and it grows thousands of leaves out of sheer delight. It's a clever tree. When there is a drought, it will let some branches die. And when the rains come, it grows new branches. This tree can actually prune itself. Smart, eh? See those dead branches up there? The tree let them die, years ago, when there was no rain."

The youngster stood staring at the foliage, spotted some dead branches, and nodded energetically.

"So, Danielle Yvette Barnard, you tell me why this blissfully contented, psychologically well-adjusted, emotionally stable tree of highly superior intelligence, standing here, holding its breath, waiting to see if you might perhaps acquire a liking for green beans, should hop all the way across the lawn to jump on your house."

Always ready to enjoy yet another of her father's impossible stories, Danielle had listened attentively and not missed a beat. She spared him a genuine smile for his effort, but she seemed hardly impressed. Pointing at the White Eucalypt, she said,

"It's not this tree, Daddy." She turned on her heels and pointed to another tree. "It's that tree," she said. "Simone said so."

She was keeping her little finger pointed at a towering Gray Eucalypt that leaned slightly over the homestead. Its massive crown provided shade from the hot summer sun for all the bedrooms, as well as the living areas, of the Barnards' sizable home. Around twenty tons of potential calamity stood poised, ready to crush all occupants, should a north-westerly squall decide to write their death warrants. Only George's clinic would remain untouched, but the family might all be dead.

She looked up at her father, to see if he was paying attention, but George was stunned into silence. It felt as if a cold hand had reached into his chest and was squeezing his heart to stop it from beating. That little finger was still pointing at the Gray Eucalypt. She was waiting for an acknowledgment from the man.

But George was listening to a loud inner voice, telling him, ordering him, "You have less than a week to down that giant, George Barnard, and you are going to contact a tree doctor now." The hair on the back of his head and neck was bristling up with the knowledge that this was a deadly serious matter.

"You go and finish your dinner, young lady," he told Danielle. "Tell

Mom your father is going to have a talk with a tree doctor." He made his way to the clinic, shaken, but determined to make his call in private and to smartly get someone's attention. That big tree had to go…

By some form of coincidence, the Yellow Pages fell open to the right page. For some reason, George unwittingly picked the first name his eyes fell upon. And by some stroke of luck, the telephone was almost immediately answered by a real person, not some dumb answering machine, even though it was after five-thirty in the afternoon – and on a Friday!

In the rush to get the attention of someone – anyone – who could take that Gray Eucalypt down, the father feverishly moved like a machine, a robot, a servomechanism, programmed to protect his family. Surely, nothing else could have existed in his mind.

Not until many weeks after the event did he begin to realize what had happened. And he needed to sit down and think about it all. "My God!" he heard himself say. "George Mathieu Barnard, what a stupid clod of a slow learner you are! The Spirit Guardians have worked ever so hard to make you take notice."

Douglas Shannon, tree surgeon, sounded tired but was friendly enough. He would be around forty years of age, perhaps a little younger. His deep voice sounded like that of a confident man, a decision maker.

"You caught me in the nick of time, Mr. Barnard," he informed George. "I was about to close up shop for the day. Two minutes from now, and the gate would have been locked, and I would have been contemplating a large, cold beer."

Shannon listened to George's directions, then he cut him short. "I know exactly where your hobby-farm thing is," he commented, "because I grew up around there when it was practically all still bush. I probably know that very tree. My whole crew will be working most of the weekend, and we will be less than three miles down the road from your place. We are snowed under with work, and the electricity people are pushing us to complete the job so they can hook up another farm." He paused. "Does your farm carry livestock?" he asked.

"Two cats, one dog, a duck, two geese, three goldfish, and a pony," George told him. "Then there is this huge herd of freeloading kangaroos."

"Bloody city farmers," Shannon laughed. "Are you growing anything, harvesting anything from the place?" he wanted to know.

"Oxygen," George told him, "Lots of it. Ten hectares were cleared when we got here. The rest is covered with trees, all individually adopted by us, and they can stay. We love trees. But one of them is no longer welcome in this family. We're divorcing that one."

"Those bloody city farmers," Shannon repeated. He was enjoying himself. Serious broad-acre farming might well be in his background, George thought.

"I'll tell you what I can do," Shannon said. "I will come and look at your tree first thing in the morning, but it will take us a fair while to drop her, if she needs taking out. I will see you around six-thirty. Now, you had better get yourself ready, Mr. Barnard," he told George in a most solemn tone of voice. "Start thinking about herding up, and fencing out, your extensive numbers of livestock." He laughed. "Those city farmers…" He rang off.

The converted army "Blitzwagen" had bumped its way into the home yard.

"Thanks for coming," George told the two men in the cabin.

The driver was obviously the boss, and he appeared to have no intention of either switching off the noisy engine or hopping down to terra firma. He seemed somewhat rushed and preoccupied. His voice was terse as he said, "Was it you I talked to last night?"

"Yeah, sure was, Doug!" George shouted to make himself heard.

"Which tree, mate?" Shannon wanted to know.

"That Gray Eucalypt, next to the house," Barnard answered loudly. Shannon casually glanced at it.

"Nothing wrong with that!" he barked. "I'm busy! We're going. I'll see you later!" He moved to put his stubborn old vehicle into reverse gear, but the gears just wouldn't engage.

"Doug! Eh, Doug!" George was shouting as hard as he could to make himself heard over the clamor of grating gears. "You've come all this way! Can't you at least take a good close look at it? Just to make sure?"

From his perch up in the cabin, Douglas Shannon looked down on him as if his patience were being sorely tried. His expression seemed to be saying something quite familiar to George's ears – something about city farmers, and hobby-farm things.

Getting out of bed so early in the morning, George mused, has got to be unhealthy after all. I knew it! What happened to the congenial Douglas Shannon I spoke to last night? He left his sense of humor under his pillow in the rush to get away.

Finally, Shannon stalled his engine, grabbed up a large screwdriver, and came down to earth. His young friend stayed in the cabin, grinning from ear to ear. His staying there was a statement: "Hobby farmers know nothing."

Talking to no one in particular, the tree doctor moved all around the tree, prodding it with the screwdriver, and with great force. He was saying, "Nothing wrong. . . Nothing wrong here. . . That's okay. . . Bloody nothing wrong. . ." He levered up a large section of bark and made a great show of straightening his back. "There's nothing bloody well wrong with your tree, Mr. Barnard!"

George took his time to answer him. "Doug, my little girl tells me this tree is going to fall on the house. And when she says this tree is going to fall on the house, then that is what it will do. It will fall. And it will land on the house."

Shannon was losing his cool. "We're all bloody experts!" he cried out. "What a load of bullshit!" The angry, frustrated tree surgeon grabbed hold of the loose bark and ripped off a strip to well above their heads.

"Ker . . . rist!" he shouted. As a shower of little white insects landed on their heads, the two men jumped out of the line of fire. Urgently, they brushed the tenacious, biting little pests from their bodies and clothes.

“Shees . . . sus!” said Shannon. Then he stood there in a long, purposeless silence, watching a stream of tiny “timber workers” as they continued to fall in their thousands from a gaping big hole in the monster Gray Eucalypt. Finally, he rediscovered his tongue. His humor as well, so it seemed. “You told me your name was George?” he asked.

“George Mathieu Barnard. That’s what my momma always called me, Doug.”

“Well . . . George Mathieu Barnard. . .” he drawled. “I think this tree is going to fall on your house.”

“It kind of . . . looks like it,” George suggested. He could do that drawl just as well as Shannon could. “What are you . . . uh . . . going to do about it?”

“We can’t fix her. It’s a shame. She still looks good, but she’s too far-gone. There are millions and millions and millions of them up there. She’s had it. We’ll have to cut her down.”

He stepped back some more from the trunk and looked up at the foliage, still shaking his head in disbelief. “You would never know. They have done all that in the space of a year, I tell you, and she’s only months away from dropping all her leaves. You know, you could have built a whole house out of what these little blighters have chewed up. What a shame. . .” He paused. “I could have never picked it,” he admitted. “And your wife knew?”

“No, my little girl knew,” George corrected him. “My daughter, Doug. That’s her, way over there in the sandbox, in her red jumpsuit. She’s probably fabricating some breakfast for me right now. The child simply looks at what will happen tomorrow when it is still yesterday. It’s a bit spooky, but it’s handy to have her around. She has the Gifts of the Ancients. That’s what we sometimes call it.”

Shannon had once again lost his tongue. He was looking at Barnard in disbelief, but since George would only smile and nod his head, the tree doctor must have finally understood it had truly been petite Danielle who had sounded the alarm.

"Feed her regularly," Shannon suggested, "and when she gets to be twice that size, send her around. I'll give her a job." He turned to the young man in the Blitzwagen. "Rodney! Get your lazy butt out here! Something worth looking at!" He turned back to George. "That's my son and heir. I'll trade him with you for your little girl." Then he smiled. "I'm joking, mate. He's a good one, our Rod."

"When can you cut her down?" George asked.

"In a week. When we're finished down the road," the tree doctor answered.

"No way, Doug. I want her down today. I'd like you to do it, but I will get someone else if I must. I can't ask my family to keep living under that booby trap."

"You're right, I wouldn't either. Tell you what, we can knock her down now, but we won't cart her away for at least a week. There's still more than twenty tons up there. Is that okay with you?"

"Suits me fine, Doug. Just do it," Barnard suggested. "Rodney," Douglas Shannon addressed his son, "Get the gear out pronto, or I will ask Mr. Barnard's little girl tomorrow to do it for me yesterday and in half the time."

Expertly, the two men attached a heavy steel cable around the trunk at about three and a half to four meters up from the ground. The other end of the cable was hooked onto the winch cable of their ancient Blitzwagen.

Way out in the field, well beyond danger, Rodney Shannon skillfully made the winch increase the tension on the cable. Time and again, Douglas eased the chainsaw into the massive trunk. Slowly, the insect-laden Eucalypt gained the upright position.

Holding on to their cats, dog, and goldfish, the Barnards watched from a safe distance. Their pet duck, geese, and pony were nowhere to be found. Somehow they all knew what was going to happen.

Finally, the tree leaned over the other way, bit by bit, more and more. Then she dropped, flattening the fences and shattering into dozens of huge chunks. The echoes of its eardrum-splitting impact roared and bounced around all through the valley below.

"You're just about bankrupt, George," Jodi told him with a devious smile on her face. "You've got no money and no real estate. You're out of business. And it just goes to show you that what I've been telling you all these years is right on the button: You are totally irresponsible with your money."

"It's only a monopoly game, Daddy," Danielle tried to console him. "But Mum and I are winning and . . . we like that!"

"That's making me feel so much better," he told her. "Your concern for my welfare has made my day. It touches my heart."

Moments later, a powerful gust of wind was unleashed on the homestead. Doors and windows shook and rattled violently. Then the storm carried on as it had been blowing all evening.

"That was it, you guys," George casually noted. "That big blast of fresh air just then, that was the moment our Gray Eucalypt would have flattened us all."

Morning light revealed twenty-two smashed roof tiles strewn across the home yard by the previous evening's savage gust.

"That was it, Jodi. It came precisely from the northwest."

"I've got the feeling 'They' like us up there, George."

A whole trainload of Spirit Guides had worked their ethereal butts off to make this turn out right. George was sure of it now. Douglas Shannon's home base was right at the opposite end of town. There was no logic in his picking one of the most distant firms to do the urgent job. Someone knew Douglas's crew was working nearby.

Shortly after the Gray Eucalypt episode, the Simone phenomenon simply evaporated into thin air. There were now only five places set at the Barnards' dinner table. With the arrival at Danielle's school of a new classmate, Simone – a flesh and blood version to be sure – there no longer seemed to be room for the invisible Simone, who for more than four years chose to share a meal with the Barnards, and was reported to "really,

really, really and truly" enjoy, as well as need, their company.

Nevertheless, it took our daughter's ability to pick up the message of her unseen playmate for me to realize that I had lost contact with something that was precious to me and that I wanted back. The urgency I felt to rediscover my spirit friends prompted an intensive search to find out where these childhood acquaintances could possibly be in time and space.

When I finally faced the Spirit Guides myself and looked them in the eyes for the first time, a powerful bond was established and a remarkable Celestial-Mortal Alliance evolved. I began to count on them for assistance more often, and they more frequently depended on my doing their bidding. As they led me out of danger on a number of occasions using time-prompts, 11:11 and other double-digit time-prompts on clocks, VCRs, microwave ovens, etc. I renamed them the 11:11 Spirit Guardians.

These new spirit friends guarded me closely, and we soon became much more involved with the welfare of those around us. We were, and still are, a Celestial-Mortal Alliance for Progress simply called the Unit, or the Emergency Platoon. But they were still just my old childhood friends-revisited.

As my contact with the 11:11 Spirit Guardians grew closer, my business ventures picked up even more, and on occasion we boldly took on the task of troubleshooting and breathing new life into near-bankrupt companies. My celestial friends regularly advised me about my personal life and assisted me in countless emergencies that involved many of my patients. They even helped me to design specific therapies for clients in great need.

In 1992, I promised the celestials I would begin the big task of documenting our nearly countless combined endeavors, in order to reveal to others the exciting opportunities for cooperating with these hard-working planetary helpers. They wanted as many people as possible to read about the successes that can be achieved, the wondrous healings that take place with their aid, and the fascinating revelations about our planet and life in the greater cosmos – as well as about the spiritual advancement an association with them has to offer.

Unlike us 'temporary' mortals, who live on Earth for such a short span, the 11:11 Spirit Guardians are the permanent citizens of this planet. They are capable of causing, through you and me, many small and grand events for the benefit of all – today and into the planet's distant future. The brilliantly minded 11:11 Spirit Guardians are seeking worldwide human involvement for their task of promoting planetary progress and greater spiritual awareness.

STARCHILD

by Celia Fenn

Celia is an international spiritual facilitator and Channel. An Indigo/Crystal adult, she works primarily with the Archangel Michael energy to bring information about the transformation and ascension of the planet.

Celia holds MA and PhD degrees in English Literature, and has also studied Art and Music. She worked for 12 years as a University academic before switching to a career in Healing and Therapy. For the past ten years, she has helped many people to find their own personal healing path to wholeness and inner peace.

Celia has worked intensively with Indigo adults, teenagers and children, and has developed specific programs to assist these special beings to find their path in life in peace and balance. Celia is the author of 'A Guide to Complementary Therapies in South Africa' and 'The Indigo Crystal Adventure'.

In the course of her work, she has appeared on radio and television. Her current projects acknowledge the Indigenous people of the planet

and their wisdom as a necessary part of creating balance and ha ***on the Earth. She lives in Cape Town, South Africa.***

I have been aware of working with Spirit guidance all my life. I am primarily an Empath, but I am also clairaudient and clairvoyant. When I was about five years old, an angel appeared to me in my garden – the huge, fiery angelic figure of Archangel Michael. Even though I was only a child, I wasn't afraid of this huge apparition. I ran inside to tell my mother because I was so excited, but she wasn't too impressed… I was always seeing things, and her response was always, "Yes, dear".

I spent ten years as a healer before becoming a channel. I was put into training for this with the Elohim angels – who are in charge of the evolution of humanity and the planet – through the Ra material. I was able to rent a small cottage in the countryside where I would go once a month. They taught me how to still my mind and how to 'hear' the material that was being given to me. It was very slow at first… it took me a whole year of weekends once a month to channel one article, even though it was quite long. Now I am able to work very quickly, because I can hear so clearly.

In 2002, I was 'assigned' to Archangel Michael, who works with the Indigo beings and with the greater plan of Spiritual evolution. In hindsight, I think that the visitation I had of Michael as a child was to remind me that I was being guided and that I had work to do with him in later life.

I work with a local community to put into practice the concepts and ideas that are given in the channels about creating communities that honor the Earth and support human life, which is the 'plan' that Michael reveals in his channels. My website, *'Starchild Global'*, allows me to reach people all over the planet, as this material is translated into several languages. We have several sub sites and communities attached to the site... so we have created what we call a 'community of light' in an online way.

I also work as a shaman. As a shaman you also learn how to feel the presence of spirit guides. When I work with shamanic techniques I tend to work with the ancestral Spirit Keepers, as shamanism is an Earth technique and is more grounded in Earth reality. I work in Africa, so the Spirit Keepers are the *Khoi San*, who are an indigenous race and not at all related to me as a white person of European descent. They hold the sacred Earth energy and protect access to the grids. Spirit Keepers, as I understand them, are those who watch over the Earth. We can also call them the Ancestors.

My work as a shaman and with Michael are just layers of the same work. It is all One – there is no separation. They are just different ways of working with the energies of the Spirit World, so they may be combined. The indigenous peoples of the Earth have always been happy to assimilate different spiritual traditions. My latest channel from Michael, entitled *'Walking in the Dreamtime'*, brings together shamanic techniques with spiritual knowledge.

We are all from the Stars. We are all ancient souls derived from the One Source energy who have spent millions of years journeying through the Cosmos in many forms of light. This is just one incarnation. We are right now engaged in one of the most wonderful adventures of transformation and light on this planet. The Indigo and Crystal children and adults are part of this adventure – a grand adventure of Becoming.

MESSAGE FROM ARCHANGEL MICHAEL

The Earth is once again experiencing an acceleration in her energy field on her path of personal Ascension and Evolution. For us, as humans on Earth, this provides another opportunity to accelerate our own personal growth. Archangel Michael brings us this information about the opening of our heartspace and emerging into authenticity to assist us at this time. We are preparing to enter into full alignment with our new energy-bodies and become heart-centered beings.

In order to allow the emergence of your true essence and authentic nature as a being of love and creativity, you need to release what works against this realization – that part of you that believes in fear and scarcity and lack, and in abandonment, rejection and pain. This part of you is the rational mind and its associated personality complex, the ego. Your rational mind needs to be busy, and will keep repeating to you the fear stories of all the other minds around you, on television, radio and in newspapers, until you switch it off and start to listen to the broadcast of your heart. Your heart will send you feelings of love, peace, serenity, compassion and acceptance. Now is the time to align with this message. Tell your mind that it was designed to assist your unfolding on earth, not to dominate it. Your mind is a fearful child – your heart is a wise and loving elder. Your heart speaks the truth of your soul. Far better to follow the voice of your soul/heart that speaks with Spirit and is guided in Love.

When you make this switch, you will begin to *feel* more than you *think*. You may imagine that this will be wonderful – and well it should be. But most of you have repressed your feelings since you were children. Your parents, teachers and the culture in general told you what to think and feel, and so you switched off your authentic feeling voice – your heart – and repressed and denied your true feelings. They somehow were not 'right' or 'accepted' by those around you.

As adults, many of you are subject to addictions: to drugs, alcohol, nicotine, food, television, work, sex or even religion. All ways of avoiding feelings and authenticity in favor of escapism and other people's ready-made solutions to your life.

As you once again 'switch on' your heart voice, you may have to face many painful feelings that have been repressed for many years. Many of you may feel lingering depression and sadness as you struggle to understand why you feel this way. These are authentic feelings, so not reject them or judge yourself. Rather understand that your soul is asking you to recognise these very old feelings relating to inauthenticity – and to clear them.

The process of clearance is through forgiveness and allowing the emergence of vulnerability and tenderness in your life. Forgiveness will happen as you emerge into compassion, for you will understand how we have all been taught to switch off the heart and follow the mind as a survival technique. Those who taught us to do this thought they were doing the best thing to help us to be ‘real’ and ‘rational’. So we will not need to hold onto angers and resentments about the past as we move into this new and empowered space of freedom to be who we authentically are.

We were brought up to believe that we need to be strong in order to survive and gain love and acceptance, and so we learn to repress any feelings that might represent ‘weakness’ as we understand it. We are taught through movies and television soap operas that ‘love’ involves heartbreak, rejection and abandonment, and as we experience these things, or imagine we do, we close our hearts and nurse our angers and hurts.

But the true voice of unconditional love and acceptance says that these things are mind-created illusions, and that we only have to enter into our authentic being to experience the supportive and all-embracing love that surrounds us. But to enter this heart-space we must be willing to be vulnerable – to show others who we truly are and to trust that they will accept us. Even if this acceptance is not forthcoming, being authentic and acting in integrity will release immense power in your psyche. It will allow you to truly feel your reality and act from a place of power rather then victimhood.

Emerging from vulnerability is tenderness – a deep feeling of compassion and acceptance… an understanding of your own vulnerability and that of others, producing gentleness and kindness and caring, no matter what the circumstances. And in this tenderness will arise a true understanding of the experience of love at the center of all things, and that every experience is a gift of love and can be lived as such, without anger or hurt. Tenderness and vulnerability provide the bridges from one heart to another and create a space for sharing and growth.

Once you have learned to master your own feelings through authenticity and acceptance, you will be asked to move to the next level. This is where you will experience the repressed feelings and sadness of the Planetary Collective Consciousness. Many Lightworkers and Crystal beings are today channelling the sadness of the collective through their bodies in order to assist the planet to release these emotions. And as each Lightworker enters into their own Heartspace and begins to act from authentic soul-motivated feelings, then humanity will once again remember how to love.

You will cease to live your lives as you do now, in a mad scramble for money, recognition and possessions. You will once again learn the value of human life, of people and animals, and plants – of the planet itself. You will understand once again how valuable these things are because you will see once again how valuable you are.

When you cease to measure your worth through your achievements and what you consume or acquire, then you will understand that you are a vehicle for the loving, creative and sharing energies of your Soul and Spirit. You will once again begin to love, to dance, to sing – to truly be ALIVE. Then you will fully enter into your inheritance as a Human Angel – Spirit in a Human Body.

photo credit: Eli Lund

BROTHERHOOD OF LIGHT

Desy 'Blue Arrow Rainbow' Roodnat

Blue Arrow Rainbow (formerly known as DesyRainbow) is a channel for Universal healing energies and an artist through whom Spirit creates special paintings based upon a person's energy. She is the mother of two wonderful children and guardian of over 30 contemporary crystal heads.

Together with Joshua Shapiro she has authored a book, entitled 'Journeys of the Crystal Skull Explorers', and they organize international crystal head conferences. Over the years they have 'met' many crystal heads, and believe they hold a vital key for the future of humanity.

I have had asthma and bronchitis for as long as I can remember. Due to this so-called 'weakness' of my physical lungs, I had several lung inflammations. About 17 years ago, I became very ill from double pneumonia in both my lungs, and then got the flu on top of that. My condition deteriorated to the point that my physician told the father of my children (then first husband) that she could not do anything for me. The light in the room became very dark and shady for me, even though the sun's rays shone brightly though the windows.

I remember lying in my bed feeling so desperately ill, when suddenly a very golden bright light appeared in the room and I saw Master Jesus with Archangel Michael and my 'personal' guide (who, years later, I found out is called 'White Feather') and he said, "It is time to come with us my Child of Light, as we would like to show you some places."

They took me up through different levels or states of frequencies. It happened so quickly that I didn't notice much – only that we 'flew' instead of walked to our destination. When we arrived, Michael left our group and Jesus said (telepathically) that they were needed elsewhere and that they would both join us later. Another angel, female in energy, joined White Feather and I.

What I was shown was how a person who passed over was brought to a 'room' to recover from their trip to the heavens after leaving their physical body. A well-loved person would guide the person so they would not be too confused, frightened or disorientated at suddenly finding themselves on another plane of existence. After they were given time to recover from the life they had just left behind, they would review the major events during that life (like a movie). White Feather said that people would get another opportunity to view the other details of their lives, later on.

I wanted to know what happened to children when they 'die', as I have lost some of my children during this lifetime due to spontaneous abortions in the early months of pregnancy. I had hardly thought or felt this 'desire to know' inside me when we were already on our way to a different part of the heavens.

I was brought to the entrance of a wonderful but huge garden filled with light, love, compassion, kindness and 'Oneness'. Here, White Feather told me he would be waiting for me to return, and the angel who was with us took me into the garden.

I saw children and angels playing, and women taking care of the children with so much compassion and love that tears came to my eyes. I saw and heard the singing of many birds, and the children were playing with them as the birds perched on their arms and sang to them. It looked like the children understood their language, as they were talking back to them.

I wondered why I saw no men or children older than 12 or 15 years or so, but before I could voice this question, the angel explained that children are considered to be 'spiritually grown' by the age of 14, and the older children's souls would go to different level of light than this one. They would go to that place according to the inner light they were emanating in their soul at the moment they left the physical plane, as they have the vibration needed for that particular state of existence. The angel also explained that the ladies I saw were granted to take care of these small children as in their physical lives they desired to become a mother, but it was not 'written in their contract' during that particular lifetime… due to whatever reason, their souls needed that experience. But when these ladies crossed over, they were allowed to experience a similar kind of motherhood with these beautiful children who had already crossed over and looked like angels to me.

As we left this beautiful peaceful garden, White Feather walked towards us with master Jesus and Archangel Michael, and I noticed that the wonderful angel from the garden had disappeared. What happened next was a very profound experience, as I was brought to a realm in which the energy was still very beautiful and also of high frequency, and yet very different than the garden I had just visited – perhaps somewhat denser in its quality of vibration. Although nobody asked me to make a decision, I felt a little sad as, deep down, I *knew* I had to choose whether to remain in this unbelievably beautiful, peaceful and loving light world or return to the earth plane. I cried and sank to the ground and begged at the feet of Jesus to let me stay in this world where I felt I belonged.

I was then shown a glimpse of my future in this current lifetime, as I stood between these beautiful Light Beings. I could see thousands of people waiting for something, and I asked, "What are so many people waiting for?" He replied, "My beloved. *Whom* are these beautiful people waiting for, is the question."

"Please tell me whom – he must be special as so many are waiting."

Then Jesus looked me deeply in the eyes and answered, "They are all waiting for a lady… they are waiting for YOU."

"For me?" I asked unbelievably.

"Remember your birth name. Remember the name you chose before you were born."

I tried to remember but couldn't. I felt so much compassion and love inside me welling up to the surface for all those who were apparently waiting for me. I felt that I had to go back, I just *had* to…

And with that thought, I re-entered my physical body. White Feather was with me when I opened my eyes. I could see his smile and he was so content that I made this decision, which was of my own free will. And my name was running through my mind… Desirée, Desirée. My birth-name Desirée means 'the one who is waited or desired for'.

Although I had felt that I was 'away' for more than a day, all this had taken place during 30 earth minutes or so. It took me a long period of time to recover from this near-death experience (NDE). I was never the same again. It took me years to fully remember and recall all that had happened, if I ever will remember it all? After remembering the universal truth of free will, I believe that one of my tasks is to help, along with many others, to bring heaven back to earth.

Because of this experience, I know how much help and support we all receive from our Light Friends from other dimensions, who are always near – they are with us every single step we take, helping us through difficult situations by holding us in their loving energy, celebrating with us on happy occasions, comforting us when we feel ourselves in pain and sorrow, supporting us through deep transformations, and so much more.

They are the ones who give us inspiration and connect us with other people, sometimes for reasons beyond our comprehension.

In 1996, I was a singer in an operetta group in Holland. I had gone away with the group for a weekend filled with singing, dancing and rehearsals. All 20 girls were deeply asleep after a hard day's work, but not me… my mind was spinning around and reviewing all that happened that day.

I was lying in my bed but totally awake, when suddenly I heard a voice… a male voice, calling "Witte Veder, Witte Veder", which means 'White Feather'. I looked around, but didn't see anyone.

At first I thought that I was imagining things. I scratched my ear, thinking this would stop the voice in my head, but the voice seemed to come from outside myself and it was loud and went on and on… it was so loud that I was afraid that it would wake up some of the girls!

Because I was very tired and wanted to get some sleep before it was time to start the next day, I said out loud to this voice, "Yes, yes I hear you saying 'White Feather', but what does this mean?" But the voice stayed silent after that. This was the first time that I heard my guide, White Feather, speak to me. Later, he told me he had been with me since I was two years old.

A year later, in honor of my guide, I bought a ring made from white shell that was carved in the form of a white feather and wore it on one finger. White Feather told me he was so happy I did this, as now he could share with me that I was once his bride in a previous lifetime.

We had a very close connection from that moment on. He 'showed' me that he came to visit me when I was a small girl and that, because he wears a Native American outfit with headdress, he had appeared to me then wearing a long khaki rain-coat, so that this would be less surprising to me as a Westerner. And, yes, I do remember that many times a person dressed like that visited me in the night. He just stood there and looked at me, yet I was never frightened.

Over a year ago, we had a visit with a very special friend who is a medium. During this session I talked to White Feather. I missed him around me, as for several months I had felt that his energy was not as present as usual and was unable to hear or see him. It was as if his energy had changed frequency, making contact between us more difficult. White Feather acknowledged this feeling and told me that he had raised his vibration – but he re-assured me that he is still close by… only it is more difficult for me to feel this. As I raise my own vibration in the physical world, our energies will be on a par and strongly connected with each other.

White Feather always stands on my right, in front of me. He protects me very strongly – he once said to a clairvoyant man, “Nobody comes between NaNehNa (this is my Lakota name and means ‘blue arrow’) and myself… I will always protect her.” This man told me that he had never felt such a strong connection between a guide and earthly person. White Feather once said to me that he is, in this current lifetime, what I was once for him… a personal Light-guide.

In 1999, I received from a friend a picture of a ‘new’ guide called White Bull. I saw him for the first time during a Wolf Song Gathering in 1998 in Holland. A Native American Elder was talking to the audience about his guide named White Bull – at that moment I saw a white bull floating above the Elder’s right shoulder. Many months later, I understood that this was my first encounter with my new guide.

The following year, I sought the help of a shaman – to journey to make a conscious connection with my guide. White Bull told me he was once my physical father on the earth plane and that now he would be my spiritual father, helper and guide. White Bull took my hand and led me on a bridge made of rainbow rays. I don’t know how to explain this, but it was as if we were walking or floating on a real rainbow! Then he showed me the other side of the rainbow or what we call the New Earth. All people lived in peace and harmony - they had open and compassionate hearts filled with love. All people had a natural connection with all our relations, with all beings, all spirits. They talked telepathically with each other – no wars, no more poverty, all were equal… all were One.

White Bull revealed that a huge number of people will remember how to lead the way towards this New World he just showed me, and that I could be among them who signed up for this task. I didn't know what he was talking about, but what I saw during my vision was so powerful and wonderful… so much beauty, compassion, harmony and love. So much light emanated from these human beings. Before I said goodbye to my 'father' I told him I like to carry the name Rainbow. He nodded and smiled… he said I was always a Rainbow child, so I did not surprise him with this request. And he granted it.

The first time White Eagle came to me as a Spirit, it was during the special ceremony our friend Moonhawk was performing with for us in Colorado Springs with the Crystal Heads and to initiate Joshua and myself through this ceremony, using smoke blown through an Eagle bone. This was for receiving permission to work through 'our' crystal skulls – 'Mozes', 'Unity' and 'Portal' – in order to initiate other Crystal Heads with a Crystal Head light grid.

The energy of White Eagle can be present whenever I am a channel for healing using the Crystal Heads, and sometimes when we give talks about the adventures we have encountered with our wonderful crystalline friends. He is there when I participate in sacred ceremonies. It was White Eagle who asked me to work with two circles of twelve quartz crystal heads and one central head, to achieve the effect of a circle within a circle – a powerful energy, creating a vortex of Light that remains at the place where it is created. This is part of the work we do at spiritual centers and sacred places.

White Eagle, White Bull, and White Feather are all connected – they are part of a collective 'higher' consciousness… a 'Brotherhood of Light'. White Feather has been granted a place within this group of evolved souls.

I can imagine that those reading my story might feel that these words are the product of an oversized ego. Yet I feel humble and filled with respect and gratitude for everything that happens to me – every day life amazes me, how much truth can be found in the little things that occur, when we are open to the signs from the Universe to help us.

I believe that every person has his or her own Truth. In Holland – as I am Dutch – we would say, "nothing more, nothing less". What I experienced is no better or worse than any other person's experience.

If we humans only knew and understood how much love and compassion these Light Guides have for us, how 'proud' and joyful they are when we progress, and how intensely they work to help us, we would live our daily lives with deep gratitude and humbleness to have such wonderful, loving friends.

A MESSAGE FROM WHITE FEATHER

AHO (to you All),

When a person feels the connection with a spirit, whether they hear, see, sense or even smell the fragrance he or she brings forth, makes no difference. It is all the same energy. Please do not feel it is different or better to see or to hear – you all have the beautiful ability to sense your guide in a unique way, as this spirit is connected to you and is part of your energy.

All are equal. Only people from Earth (living in a 3-dimensional reality) put a label on it… a name to the way. WE ARE ONE and we will always be ONE. A so-called 'spirit guide' is here to help you with little loving pushes for you to keep on the right path – the Red Road, as we call it – as this journey is not easy for a human being on the Earth. We are so happy when a person succeeds their task… our hearts are then filled with joy. Lessons to remember can be very deep and difficult – but it is your choice, and yours only, how to experience this lesson. Pain and sorrow does not have to be involved in situations that need to be remembered and to be acknowledged. But people choose to relive this experience through pain and agony.

Sometimes, as guides, we need to step back when an old lesson repeats itself and you are not ready to release or look at this situation in a different light or way. Your own choice will be respected by all of us, as it is your birthright to make your own decisions. We step back but stay connected, as we never leave you when you are in doubt. After some time, when the Light comes back into your consciousness and you have chosen a path, we are able to guide with loving suggestion again.

Sometimes people want to experience exactly how a situation had happened before (in a former lifetime, as you call it). This can be deep and tough and is difficult on a person's emotional body or state of consciousness, as to re-live the experience is to relive it all. But this time you may now choose a smoother transformation to acknowledge the energies involved.

Remembering is forgiving. To forgive, first forgive yourself and from this place of peace you will be able to forgive the other friend or party in the play, as you both chose this roll to play in a special circumstance – your individual setting of your play. Forgive each other and remember to love again.

As for love… it heals all. Love opens all doors. With love, we heal others and we heal ourselves. Each of you is part of the Oneness of Love. When you feel separation by pain, it is because you are doing this yourself to remember important lessons, which you might have forgotten in eons of time. We say now – WE ARE ONE. We are one energy… we are all one light of the All That Is. May your path be smooth and full of joy, filled with light and peace within. Be the example of the New World of Light & Peace in the higher frequency of Joy and Purity and Love. Play well, Children of Light… do not be afraid. All is in Divine time. We will be with you when you ask us to join your travels back to the Light, as we are all awaiting you in the place you will be soon, in the Light of Oneness. We greet you all.

CHAPTER 9

THE ANCESTORS

To forget one's ancestors is to be a brook without a source, a tree without root.

~ Chinese proverb

Respect for the wisdom of the elders is innate in every indigenous community worldwide. Honoring the ancestors is a natural progression and continuity of this relationship beyond death.

Over the years within Western society, there has been a growing disregard, particularly among the younger generation, for the elders (and thus the ancestors). The elders among us today, whether they are our family members, schoolteachers, priests or politicians, often do not behave with integrity and are rarely wise. We sense that they do not respect us and, therefore, we do not respect them. This chicken-and-egg situation can be resolved and healed with the compassion and understanding that, in actual fact, they do not respect *themselves*. It is being aware of and respecting the spirit that resides in all living things that makes you a spiritual person… one who is truly wise. By respecting ourselves, we may one day become ancestors worthy of honoring.

It is only natural that one would feel a strong connectedness and love toward elderly family members as a result of actual physical experience and interaction. With the breakdown of communities in modern times, family groups have become 'diluted' and contact with relatives is too often lost. Our elders are placed in nursing homes. Many people these days know little about their elders, let alone their ancestors… nevertheless, we all have them! We are a living physical continuation of them. Part of them is genetically contained within the DNA in our bodies.

Within us, they live on. Without them, we wouldn't be here.

Your ancestors are always with you and, if you ask them, will send you a sign to let you know. Sometimes, they may make their presence known when you least expect it...

When my dad was offered early retirement from his job of 38 years in the Civil Service, he took the opportunity to enrol at college to learn something new. He'd always been inspired by a Celtic knot stone carving he'd inherited from my great-great uncle Albert – a stonemason who died in 1959. Working with stone runs in the family... my great-grandfather, Frank Sawyer, was a builder who ran a family business – *F.Sawyer & Sons* – from the village of Box in Wiltshire during the Victorian era. So, following in the footsteps of our ancestors, Dad decided to study the traditional skill of stonemasonry. On his first day at college, as his chisel struck the block of stone he'd been given, a tiny fragment of stone flew up his left nostril. On the next strike of the chisel, a stone-chip flew up his *right* nostril! My dad reckons that the ancestors were having a laugh at his expense... but I feel that this was their way of 'initiating' him into the craft, and a clear sign that he was on the right path.

It is not essential to know who your ancestors are in order to acknowledge and honour them, but it helps! Interestingly, genealogy has become popular in recent years – more and more people are becoming curious about where they come from and feel compelled to trace their ancestral roots. Although a family tree is fascinating to look at on paper, I feel it is even more exciting to physically travel to and experience firsthand those places where our ancestors lived their lives...

A few years ago, I traveled to North Wales on a quest to find the small-holding where my great-great grandparents had lived – now a complete ruin atop a mountain in Snowdonia with the most breathtaking views. Much of my journey had to be undertaken on foot and it was difficult to find, but, suddenly there it was – the place that my grandmother had so often described to me. Evidently, they had lived a self-sufficient and simple life at one with nature and at the mercy of the elements, with no telephones, no electricity – just a few animals, eight children and their house (which was very basic with just one storey and two rooms). I clambered over the ruins and sat where the living room would have been. The crumbling stone walls held the memory of their lives. It was a very poignant moment for me. I felt their love, sitting in that place… their love of the land, of nature and of the wild mountain breeze.

Although I was born in England, I have Welsh ancestors on both sides of my family. As a child, we would go camping in Wales and, over the years, the feeling of returning 'home' whenever I crossed the Severn Bridge from England into Wales grew stronger. Eventually, I moved to Wales – I have been living here now for the past seven years, and feel very much at home.

There is a strong link between the land and our ancestors. Geographical locations carry the ancestral memory of those who lived there before us. The land and the ancestors become one. This is beautifully depicted in the Welsh National Anthem, *'Mae Hen Wlad Fy Nhadau'*, which roughly translates as 'The Land of my Fathers';

The Land of my Fathers

The land of my fathers is dear unto me,
Old land where the minstrels are honored and free;
Its warring defenders so gallant and brave,
For freedom their life's blood they gave.
Home, home, true am I to home,
While seas secure the land so pure,
O may the old language endure.
Old land of the mountains, the Eden of bards,
Each gorge and each valley a loveliness guards;
Through love of my country, charmed voices will be
Its streams, and its rivers, to me.
Though foemen have trampled my land 'neath their feet,
The language of Cambria still knows no retreat;

The muse is not vanquished by traitor's fell hand,
Nor silenced the harp of my land.

In addition to our genetic ancestry, we also have a *past life* ancestry. The places to which we are drawn are places that we hold an energetic connection with. I believe that we are also drawn to periods in history and certain people in our lives for the same reasons. We hold the memory of and attunement to a particular location or person both genetically (via our DNA) *and* at a deeper, soul level. Some places and people are definitely more compatible than others, and I feel this may well have something to do with it – that the feeling of déjà vu, of familiarity and 'belonging' that we experience with certain places, cultures and individuals is because we've experienced them before, even though we're not consciously aware of it.

And if we have ancestors from other incarnations we have lived in the past, then we must also acknowledge our *future life* ancestry. As I am writing this, the penny finally drops… that we ourselves are also our own ancestors.

SACRED SONGS

by Jonas Trinkūnas

After studying Lithuanian philology at Vilnius University, Jonas became involved in the ethnical movement 'Romuva' in 1967, in order to revive the authentic traditions of Lithuania – a country at that time under Soviet rule. The Romuva movement is an integral part of the revival and recovery of Europe's ancient religions. The name 'Romuva' was chosen in honour of the famous Baltic Prussian sanctuary, which was destroyed by Christians. It means 'temple' or 'sanctuary' as well as 'abode of inner peace'.

The movement became popular and, in 1971, was prohibited by the KGB. Jonas was expelled from University when he was discovered working on a PhD thesis exploring ancient Baltic religion.

After Lithuania restored its independence in 1990, the majority of previously suppressed organizations were re-established. Romuva established connections with other similar movements aiming at preserving cultural diversity and traditional religions. Lithuania Romuva currently embraces 10 communities and has several thousand

members.

In 1997, Jonas received a National J. Basanavicius Award for his contribution to the ethnic culture of Lithuania. He works at the Lithuanian Institute for Social Sciences, and is a member of the Council for the Preservation of Ethnic Culture to the Lithuanian Parliament. Jonas is chairman of the World Congress of Ethnic religions (WCER). He continues to work towards a sustainable future, fusing ancient and modern values in Lithuania.

Jonas was officially inaugurated as Krivis (highest priest) of Romuva in 2002. He is the author and editor of the book 'Of Gods and Holidays: The Baltic Heritage', (Vilnius, 1999).

Around 30 years ago, I participated in ethnological expeditions throughout the Lithuanian countryside, exploring and recording the local culture and traditions of the ancient Baltic religion. I heard songs and stories that had been passed down orally from generation to generation and learned many traditional folk songs from the elder locals. These sacred songs, or hymns, are called *dainos*.

Romuva embodies the oldest religion in the Baltic region (Lithuania, Latvia, Prussia, etc.), which has no beginning, predates recorded history, and extends its spirit indefinitely in the Baltic culture. This religion has no human founder and no major scriptures. The central focus is the sacredness of Nature, based on Baltic beliefs and ethnic folkloric tradition. The *Romuva* emblem depicts a holy oak with an eternal flame. Such an oak tree is typical of Baltic Lithuanian folk art. The three levels symbolize the three spheres of existence – the world of the dead (the past), the world of the living (the present), and the divine heights (the future) – all three in unity. A runic inscription shows that *Romuva* is part of the Baltic region and its cultural traditions.

Romuva worships one supreme reality, which encompasses the worlds of the living and of the dead, the family and tribe, including all ancestors, all of nature, and the universe. It proclaims no eternal hell, no damnation, nor eternal salvation – only the continuity of life in the presence of divinity. It accepts all genuine spiritual paths. Each soŭl is free to find its own way, whether by devotion, meditation or service to society. Festivals, pilgrimage, the chanting of holy hymns (*dainos*) and home worship are our most valued dynamic practices.

I became involved with the Lithuanian Baltic Religion from this time, which is the Lithuanian branch of *Romuva*. Lithuanian folklore, especially the mythological *dainos*, legends and the traditional way of life, is the basis of this religion. These traditional attitudes and beliefs correspond with other contemporal ecological and spiritual ideas of other cultures – love, kindness, inspiration, positive action and conduct in accordance to the universal law of *Darna* (harmony).

Darna – the rule of harmony, has always been of significance in the ancient faith. Man lives and the world exists due to harmonious interactions rudimentary to life and through man's own correct and moral behavior. Such differing pairs like light/darkness, fire/water, man/woman, etc., do not necessarily imply a good/evil relationship. These opposite pairs are not static. They not only interact but also change and grow. From the human standpoint, there are neither absolutely good nor absolutely evil Gods or Goddesses. Goodness is born from interaction of differing but not of hostile forces, with man's interactive participation. *Blogis* (evil) is harmony's downfall – the absence or inability to restore harmony. This is most evident in nature's devastation, man's activity against nature and her order. The communities of man and nature and of family and community bear the fruit or create *dora* (morality) and *darna* (harmony). *Darna* is the most important ideal of both man and nature, attained and maintained with constant work and toil. *Darna* is not a steady and unchanging happiness and good fortune. It depends heavily on the efforts and concerns of man and his Gods. The Baltic word '*Darna*' is very close to the Hindu '*Dharma*' – the principle moral order of the world.

The primary goal of *Romuva* is to create a true nobility of spirit through proper education of tradition and experience in both meditation and action within family, society and nature. Old tales are studied and songs are sung to discover these ancient virtues. Such experience creates unity with one's ancestors. Respecting the ancestors is an essential part of Baltic religion. It is expressed in a multitude of ways. In Lithuania it is said that, "The souls of the dead are the guardians of their living relatives, or their close ones – especially parents, who become the guardians of their orphan children".

In the rituals practiced by *Romuva*, folk songs *(dainos)* play an important role and, like other traditional customs and symbols, become imbued by special power and meaning. Singing these ancient songs creates harmony in my body and soul.

Myself and Inia Trinkunas founded the ritual folk group, '*Kulgrinda'* (whose name means a secret or sacral path of initiation) in 1990, in order to perform Lithuanian folk songs at rituals and ceremonies according to Lithuanian tradition. We wear clothes from 10th–12th Century Lithuania, as reconstructed from archeological finds. Most of the members of the group are young people between 17 and 25 years of age. We have participated in many festivals and state events, including the consecration of the Lithuanian President's flag in 1993. Our repertoire consists mostly of *sutartines* – songs characteristic of round polyphony – with singing, dancing and instrumental accompaniment of the zither, drums, panpipes and violin.

Through the chanting of the *dainos* the soul is cleansed and the wandering mind is stilled. When I sing these ritual songs, I feel at peace and the deeper meaning of life is revealed to me. These songs connect me with the ancestors, who are my guides and the source of my spirituality. Within the songs, I hear the voices of the ancestors. They speak to me of eternal ideas – the Sun, the Moon and the Stars… They are connected with the Earth, which is the Mother of all beings. The Earth embraces all beings, together with all ancestors.

One of the main hymns of *Romuva* describes the mythological 'world tree' (its emblem) that is symbolic of the three levels of the world…

A poplar stood by the roadside,
Oh glorious plant of rye,
From below the roots, the ringing kankles,
In the middle, the buzzing bees,
At the summit, the falcon's children,
A group of brothers rides by.
Please stop, young brothers,
Behold the falcon's children,
Listen to the buzzing bees,
Listen to the ringing kankles.
The kankles ring for our dear father,
The bees they buzz for our dear mother,
The falcon's children – for our brother.

The roots of the tree are underground and represent the past, water and death, as well as the beginning and spring of life. The ringing of kankles at the roots is symbolic of the world of the old, the wise, and the dead. The buzzing bees in the middle represents the world of working, toiling people. The falcon's children at the summit symbolizes the heavens, the world of warriors and heroes. Death and life – an uninterrupted linking of evolution. A tree, even though it drops its leaves in the autumn, goes to sleep in winter, but its life goes on and its soul remains alive… such is man's path – through birth, death and rebirth.

Looking into our folk traditions and art we can see the true essence of the *Zemyna* – the Goddess of the Holy Earth. The return of the ancient Goddess is unavoidable… it is demanded by nature and peoples' conscious disposition. We begin to understand that we – people, animals, trees and plants – are the children of one Mother, and that the Mother lives here, within us. I receive messages from *Zemyna* in dreams, rituals and especially in singing the ritual songs.

The voice of the ancestors clearly stated the need to revive our traditional Baltic religion. How? The answer came from the common people of our country – villagers, farmers… the keepers and protectors of our folk culture. The moral code of our ancient faith, the stories of Gods and Goddesses, relics, rituals and chants – the wisdom itself was handed down to us by respectable village elders. We live in the 21st century, the century of modernization, having maintained the cultural heritage of our ancestors. We still live with our Baltic Gods and Goddesses – we believe in their power and the omnipotence of our Earth-Zemyna.

Romuva teaches great reverence for all forms of life. It is a religion of human nature and human life with nature. I receive messages from the ancestors when I am in quiet meditation in nature. About 3,000 sacred sites of the old pagan tradition still exist in Lithuania. I live 100km to the north of Vilnius, where hundreds of pagan burial grounds are located in the forest around my countryside home. It is believed that man is put on the earth to affirm and approve the world, not to deny it or to escape from it – thus fulfillment is sought and found in nature and the active spiritual participation therein.

Historical documents indicate that at the end of the 19th and beginning of the 20th centuries, people had been continuously worshipping and making offerings to the Gods – *Perkunas* (Thunder), *Zemyna* (Goddess of the Earth), *Laima* (the Goddess of Fate), and *Gabija* (Goddess of Fire) – at the ancient sacred sites. These shrine-mounds, sacred springs, oaks, and stones are still celebrated by local people.

The festivals and rituals of the old Religion of the Lithuanians take place within Nature. The central focus of the rituals is the *Aukuras* – the altar for the Sacred Fire. Contact with the ancestors is sought through the fire. Fire is the most important symbol of Lithuanian traditions. In ancient times, the Baltic people were known as fire worshipers. The Eternal Flame burned at Sventaragis Valley at the very center of Vilnius. Every household had a hearth, which was particularly respected by each member of the family, but cared for and safeguarded by the mother. The fire had greater meaning than merely a source of light and warmth – it symbolized the unbroken lifeline of the family and its ancestry. The Eternal Flame of the community served to unify not only its immediate members, but was also the unifying link with ancestors who had long since died and were now with the Gods. It was believed that numerous generations of the dead continued to live on at the hearth of the fire.

Our folk group, *Kulgrinda*, perform the Rite of Fire, where the sacred fire is lit and honored with songs and dances. Many of these are a special type of song called a *sutartine*. This is a uniquely Baltic type of polyphonic canon, which produces unusual harmonies and is a genre of ritualistic chants that often combines mystical texts with archaic symbolism. Sometimes they include strange words of incantation – the meaning of which is not always known.

All cultures as well as Native religions and faiths should be equally valued and respected. Each region and each people have their distinctive local traditions (native faith, world outlook, mythology, folklore, etc.), which articulate their love of their land and history, and cultivate a regard for the sacredness of all life and the divinity of Nature. Just as Nature survives through a wide variety of species, so should humanity be free to develop without interference along a wide variety of cultural expressions.

According to our ancient traditional ethics, the Earth and all creation must be valued and protected. We as human beings must find our place within the web of all life, not outside or separate from the whole of creation.

We believe that the dawn of a new era of individual and intellectual freedom and global exchange of views and information gives us an opportunity to start afresh – to return to our native spiritual roots in order to reclaim our religious heritage. We are worshippers of Nature just as most of mankind has been for the greater part of human history.

Ethnic and/or 'Pagan' religions have suffered great injury and destruction in the past from religions claming they possess the only truth.

It is our sincere wish to live in peace and harmony, and to strive for co-operation with the followers of all other religions, faiths and beliefs.

I believe in the principal of ethnicity, and that respect for different traditions and religions is a way to an harmonious and peaceful World.

HONORING OUR PAST

Elliott Rivera

Elliott was born in New York and raised in Puerto Rico until the age of five. He has been working as a medium for more than 30 years and* was *initiated as a priest of Santeria in September of 1988. He is also a massage therapist and a drug and alcohol counselor with over 25 years experience in teaching, counseling and bodywork. Elliott has designed and presented workshops to non-profit organizations locally, nationally and internationally. He has also made featured presentations at national and international conferences.

Elliott has a private practice in The Netherlands, where he facilitates workshops and retreats for people seeking skills in taking care of themselves and others through awareness of touch, mindfulness and regenerative therapies. Presently, Elliott is providing private classes in Santeria and conducts regular experiential teaching, healing and initiation trips to Cuba.

I was made aware of my guides early in life, at around five or six years old. You see, during my early years, in the 1950's and 60's, I was raised by my grandmothers, who were both Spiritualists and mediums. The Catholic Church's influence was very strong – we were all very Catholic – but we also had the old traditions.

One of my Grandmothers, although she was a church-going woman also visited Spiritualists, and was very good at reading cards and 'seeing' things. From what I can remember, although she never manifested or channeled any spirits, she always said things that were very poignant that nobody else could know, so she did have the gift of Spirit speaking through her. That's basically what she tried to instill and teach in me – how to listen to Spirit.

My other Grandmother, although she was Spiritualist and a medium, used to work with the 'dark side'. I have learned a lot from her – both in life and as an ancestor-guide. She taught me how to protect myself against negative influences. The medicines she taught me helped me counteract negative energies that other people might be working with.

I was initiated into *Palo Mayombe* over 25 years ago – a tradition that originated in the Congo in Africa. Palo is a very 'earthy' tradition, where one works closely with the ancestors and spirits of the dead. We make our medicines – our magic, if you will – from the earth.

When the slaves were brought to the 'new world', different African tribes had different practices. What has happened in South America as well as in the Caribbean is that people just integrated. So you will find people from the Yoruba tradition that are also practitioners of *Palo*, such as myself.

In the Yoruba tradition, we have Deities and we have spirit guides. They're not the same. Deities are just that – they're Gods and Goddesses. We are expected to live within the tradition of the Deities. We *live* the tradition. In the Afro-Cuban tradition of Santeria, we are told that a Deity is given to us at birth – you can say that it is a 'birth-rite'.

I was initiated as a priest of Santeria into the rites of Yemaya in 1988. Yemaya is considered to be Mother Nature, and is the mother of all

Orishas, or Deities, of the Yoruba Tradition. Yemaya is the guardian of all waters – sweet waters as well as salt waters – and is often depicted as a mermaid. However, she allows Oshun, which is one of the other Deities, to inhabit the sweet waters. There's also an aspect of Yemaya that lives on land, where she takes the form of a female machete-wielding warrior.

The aspect of Yemaya that I work with is called *Assessu*. She lives in the swamps and the marshland, and is the owner of all witchcraft, all medicines – both good and bad. In my case, it would be all healing medicines – not so much 'medicinal', but anything that heals the soul.

I have so many different levels of work, but, in general, as a teacher and as a healer, she helps me when I am working with people to see what has happened to them in their life. A person may change because of an incident that leaves an imprint on them, and they go throughout their lives carrying that, or living from that incident, blocking them in their everyday lives. You can't fix something that's already been broken, but you can help someone heal so that they can move on with their lives. The past is in the past. What I do is to help them to accept what has happened, and help them work through the pain so that they can leave it behind.

I attended a Catholic school in New York City. When I was about 9 years old, I got into a fight with another boy, Kevin Driskel (funny I still remember his name). During the fight I pushed him, and he fell and cut his ear. It started to bleed quite badly, and so I knelt down next to him and placed my hands over the area. I felt a presence of energy come over me and I started saying some words and the bleeding stopped. Of course, I got into a lot of trouble because of the fight, but probably more because I did this 'strange healing work' – remember it was Catholic school, and it was considered wrong to speak in tongues. That was the first time that I felt such a strong power that came from outside of myself.

At the time, I was unaware of the names of my guides. My father, being a non-believer, would not allow my mother or grandmothers to have me initiated at an early age. In our tradition, when you are evolving on a spiritual path, there's a ritual that you undertake to identify your spirit guide in order of their importance to you. The first spirit guide that manifests is your principal guide – they direct any other spirit guides that you have. When I did this particular ritual, the first spirit that came through was called Tomasa. She is an Afro-Caribbean healer who, in her time, was the wife of a village Shaman and she his assistant. Along with her, I have an African guide known as *Siete Rayos* (Seven Thunderbolts), whose origin is from the Congo.

Sometimes, Tomasa may direct another spirit to work with me for a specific purpose. For example, when I am channeling, I always call Tomasa. I go into a trance state and she speaks through me. Tomasa only speaks Spanish, which is my Mother tongue. I was recently channeling to a group of English-speaking people, so she sent one of my English-speaking guides (a minister from the American South who speaks with a heavy Southern drawl) to speak for her.

What I teach people when I'm doing my workshops is that, first and foremost, we need to identify who our guides are. Once I became aware of my guides and was shown how I could communicate with them, and vice versa, they taught me how to work with them to help myself and others. I learned to meditate and was able to listen to what I was being told. Sometimes, I would question myself because I was unsure of what I was hearing, but, following instinct, I always did what was needed to be done.

I studied psychology and sociology at university in New York, which helped me to understand other people and cultures much better. During my studies, I found I was able to call upon a friend of mine who had died a while ago – how this happened, I still do not know. Be that as it may, it was as if this friend guided me through the course – not giving me answers, but as if he were a tutor. I did well in the course.

Nowadays, I have the ability of being in contact with my guides 24 hours a day. Messages come to me in many ways – sometimes I may meditate on a specific situation, sometimes I may hear a clear voice, but many times they come to me in my dreams.

Recently, I gave a workshop in Munich, Germany. I had lived there during the late 70's to early 80's with my partner. During the workshop, I circled the room asking people to share their experience of a particular exercise we had completed. As my workshops are conducted in either English or Spanish, I had a translator with me. On this particular occasion, after the first few people had spoken, I told the translator to stop. I was able to understand 100% of what the participants were saying because another voice in spirit was translating for me. This was a powerful and very emotional experience for me, because the voice I was hearing was that of my partner and 'soul mate' who had died 15 years before. This was the first contact we'd had since then. Needless to say, I was overwhelmed after this experience. I was amazed as to the power of this contact – it was as if they were in the room with me. After the workshop, I was informed by the guide to walk in the area where we had lived in order to have closure for myself. I did and, again, it was overwhelming. I hope that the next time I give a workshop in Germany they will assist me again.

Spirit guides come from many places and lives, both from this lifetime as well as from our past lives. We all have them – the difference is that many people choose not to believe in them, or have been brought up without any real spirituality. Please understand that there is a major difference between 'spirituality' and 'religion'. Santeria is more than a religion – it is a way of life.

My guides help me to help others in their spiritual development. How it works is pretty simple… I sit with a client and begin to talk to them and they to me and, at some point during the conversation, I begin to pick up bits and pieces of that person's life. I attribute this to *my* spirit guides communicating with *their* spirit guides. I sometimes make slight of it by telling the person that my people are talking to their people, but it is really true – my guides allow conversations with other people's guides, whether they think they have them or not. This can sometimes mean connecting with the ancestors of the person in front of me.

The ancestors are very important in our tradition because we believe that without the ancestors we cannot develop in a spiritual way. In my tradition, we venerate the ancestors in a very strong way. Honoring our past makes our tomorrows stronger and brighter, because it gives us direction. All rituals begin and end with the honoring of the ancestors, no matter how wise or foolish our ancestors may have been when they were alive. I always encourage people who have children to talk to them about their grandparents or, if the grandparents are still alive, to encourage them to ask them questions and find out as much about their ancestors as they can.

Once you start to venerate your ancestors, you bring them closer to you. What I teach people first is to open up to the messages from their ancestors. It's all about *listening*.

My grandmothers still communicate with me in my dreams and sometimes in my waking moments when I am working with clients for healing. In particular, they are the ones that guide with some of the medicines I need to make. When I say 'medicines', I am not only talking of medicines taken like a prescription, but anything that makes people feel better about themselves in all aspects of their life.

Working with ancestral spirit guides is just as effective if a person is adopted. The people who adopted them become their family – it may not be their bloodline ancestry, but they will be able to connect with the spirits of that particular upbringing. Later on, maybe in their dreams and in the course of finding their roots, they will make another connection with their bloodline ancestors.

Our ancestors can also be our past life ancestors. I help others with past life regression work, and I strongly believe that the ancestors from our previous lives become spirit guides. That's why I say to people, "You don't *know* how many ancestors you have."

For example, eight years ago, I was working in South Africa for a period of time as a treatment specialist for AIDS. One day, I was approached by one of the Chiefs of a village that I was visiting. He saw that in a previous life I was a *Sangoma* – which is the South African term for a healer, medicine man or shaman – and he invited me to be initiated in order to be 'complete'. Initially, I was a little skeptical of this, being a Westerner and having been brought up in New York most of my life – not to mention feeling a little scared. I meditated and called my spirit guides to ask them if this was the right thing for me to do, and they were jumping for joy – it was like they were saying, *"Well, it's about time!"*

In being initiated as a Sangoma, I also learned new medicines and new healing techniques – but not so new, really because, going back to the ancestors of this life and previous lives, a lot of what I learned was second nature to me... it felt 'right'. The initiation is a rite of passage that I consider myself very fortunate to be able to have had. It changed my life in knowing that I can help people in almost any situation in their lives. It also made me very grateful to be alive.

If it were not for my guides, I do not think I would be the person I am today. They have taken me through both good and bad times. Sometimes they test me and sometimes I fail those tests... However, they always bring me back to the reality and to the good in my life.

People sometimes ask me why, if I have such a good connection with my guides, am I not rich? I reply that I *am* rich, as I have something that money can't buy... the ability to connect with my ancestors and the ability to guide others in their spiritual growth.

THE SHINING ONES

by Faery Shaman Tira Brandon-Evans

Tira is the founder and moderator of the Society of Celtic Shamans and the author of many books and articles on Celtic tradition. She is an historian and scholar who has spent twenty years researching Celtic history, folklore, and mythology as well as studying the shamanic and healing traditions of many other cultures. She is the editor-in-chief of "Earthsongs: Journal of the Society of Celtic Shamans".

Tira is also a Reiki teacher and Master Herbalist and holds a Chartered Herbalist designation from Dominion Herbal College. In addition to her scholarly accomplishments and degrees, Tira is a practicing Faery Shaman who has journeyed in the Shining Realms since she was a young girl.

She currently lives in the Fraser Valley in southern British Columbia, Canada – surrounded by the natural beauty of the Cascade Mountains. She spends her days teaching and corresponding with her students and apprentices.

The Shining Country knows no stain or sorrow. It is a land of light. Each blade of grass glows with life. Light fills each rock, tree, stream, and hill. There dwell the Shining People – tall, stately, graceful folk clothed in light and adorned with wisdom. This is the home of the ancestors. This is the land I first visited many, many years ago as a little child. In fifty-five years it has not changed. The Shining Country knows no stain or sorrow.

I found my way into the Shining Country when I was a girl of five. My mother remarried earlier that year and took me from our home – my grandmother's house, a house of women – into a dark, narrow house where I found myself alone with only mother and her new husband. I was not familiar with men, with their loud voices and their rough ways. Until we moved, my life was filled with kind voices, gentle hands, and smiling faces.

All my familiar haunts were gone. The swing beside the kitchen window where I learned to fly was far away from the narrow house. The perfectly clipped lawn, the flower garden, the sandbox… gone. The mysterious wood beside the house filled with ancient trees growing down to the small stream… gone. All the familiar faces gone, too.

The separation from my great-grandmother was very hard. She was the world to me. She taught me my letters in a wonderful alphabet book. She told me of the queen and how I must learn to be a lady like Elizabeth. She took me for long, slow walks and was always patient when I stopped to examine every leaf and bug. In the narrow house no one had time or patience for me.

It is little wonder I fell ill with one childhood complaint after another until the German measles finally brought me to the point of death. It was the sort of winter a Louisiana town seldom sees. There was snow on the ground, snow nearly a foot deep, for days and days. All commerce in the city ceased. The doctor had a hard time making his rounds and by the time he got around to seeing the little girl with measles my fever was raging and had been for hours.

There was little the doctor could do. He told mother how to bring the fever down – to make me drink water, to bathe me in cool water, to give me aspirin – but held out little hope that any good would come of treatment at that point. Even if I lived there was every chance I would be deaf, blind or mentally challenged.

I was not aware of the doctor's visit, of the fever, or even of mother hovering anxiously beside my narrow bed in that dark narrow room. As I lay on my narrow bed, burning in the oven of fever heat, I heard voices calling. Far-away voices called my name. Soft, musical voices called my name and there was a tiny sound of bells and a humming, buzzing sound as of gigantic bees at a distance flying nearer, closer, into the narrow room, into my burning head and then – away… away… away. And I, flying away with the bees – away… away… away. I found myself, standing on my feet, on the gently rolling shoulder of a green hill. Every blade of grass was perfect and each alive. Each blade brilliant, sparkling green, shone with its own life light. Light everywhere… golden light so sweet and solid I could almost taste it. Far and away the soft hills rolled to the far, far horizon and beyond. Between the hills, in the little valleys, sparkling bright green trees grew beside small streams I could not see but only hear.

It seemed I stood forever on that hill in that Shining Country but I was not tired. I was not lonely. I was not afraid. I was not waiting for something to change or something to happen. I simply *was* and being in that place was enough.

After an eternity of endless joy and peace I saw in the far, far distance a glittering cloud moving over the hills, swiftly flowing in my direction. In the blink of an eye the cloud was no longer a bedazzlement but a crowd of tall, stately, graceful, noble Shining People. Light shone from bright brows and clothed each form in brilliant gold.

In the second blink of an eye, the Shining People were all around me – greeting me, assuring me all was well and would be well, though I never doubted it. Their kindness was absolute and without any hint of pity. One of the Shining People took me by the hand and we were instantly flying over the hills. We were not flying as Superman flies, high in the air and prone. We flew upon our feet, upright, across the hills, down into the little valleys, across the chuckling, musical streams, away and away and away.

When we stopped we were in a wood of light. Tall trees circled us. Each leaf on each tree was perfect and shone with glittering brilliant green light. Golden light fell in long shafts among the trees. A pool rested in the center of the circle of trees. It brimmed with crystal clear water. Small pebbles of lapis, amethyst, clear quartz, white quartz, topaz, and many other crystals verged the pool and, looking into the water, I saw the floor of the pool was paved with these brilliant stones. A tiny stream flowed from the pool and, deep down near the outflow, a great fish flashed bright purple as it leapt from the stream into the pool.

The Shining One and I stood beside the pool forever, as I had stood forever on the hill. This is the Shining Country, the land without time. But even without time there is duration and within the duration there is choice and action.

The Shining One spoke in words and without words and I knew there was a choice for me to make. I had gone from this place into the land outside the Shining Country, the land that knows stain and sorrow that we call The World. I gone into the world to accomplish some tasks, there was work for me in the world.

Because those around me had made some decisions that were not good for me, I was given a choice. I could return to the body in the narrow bed in the narrow room in the narrow house or I could begin again in the world in a newborn body. It was up to me.

In that moment I saw the body I knew in the narrow bed. Beside the bed the woman who was that child's mother sat. She seemed sad. She was very worried. In that moment I wished I could make her smile again. I wished I could ease her heart. But I also wished, even more fiercely to remain in the Shining Country.

The Shining One spoke again in words without words. He showed me in a flash of light and color all that I had been and would be. He promised

I could return to the Shining Country whenever I wished and in times of trouble, when I was too confused by the world to wish, he would be at my side… my guide through all times and places.

I accepted his guidance. I accepted his gift. I made my choice.

In the blink of an eye I was back in my body in the narrow bed in the dark narrow room in the narrow house. I opened my eyes and mother's eyes widened in surprise. She placed her hand on my brow and smiled to find it no longer burned with fever. "Everything is going to be all right now, honey." She said. And she spoke more truly that she could even know for this was the beginning of my lifelong friendship with my ancestor guide whom I call Grandfather Merlin.

Now I leave to one side my first impressions of the Shining Country and the Shining Ones to explain as an adult what it is like to work with an ancestor guide.

I am a Celtic Faery Shaman. This describes who I am and the work I do to draw all worlds closer together in harmony.

As I have had said many times, in many places, and to many: *"This is the great work of the shaman; to make and mend, to help and heal, to dwell in the perfect shining moment in the heart of the mystic rose and be love in action."*

In order to do this work I need the help and the instruction of my ancestor guide. What is an ancestor guide? Here is the definition from the glossary of my book *'The Green & Burning Tree: A Faery Shaman's Handbook'*:

Ancestor Guide – a person who has lived in the Faerie Realms for many ages and who chooses to guide and guard persons living in the material world today. Most ancestor guides have not been incarnate in a fleshly body for many centuries. All shamans should work with at least one ancestor guide.

Ancestors – all of the human beings from whom you are descended by bloodlines or adoption.

Ancestral Totems – the animals and plants whose spirits guarded and guided your ancestors and their clans.

When I speak of my ancestor guide, I mean one particular person – Grandfather Merlin. Is he a 'real' person? Yes, to me he is. Is he the Merlin of Arthurian Legend? No, he is not.

He seems to be someone who lived long before stories were told of Arthur. Before the Romans came to Britain, before the Celtic tongues were spoken in Britain, even before the stones of the great henges were raised, Merlin was in Britain.

Sometimes I think he is the very spirit of the island itself. Sometimes I think he is both the spirit of Britain, the Green Man, the Wildman of the Forests, the Lord of the Beasts, and also the masculine progenitor of all my British and Welsh ancestors. Sometimes it seems that he never lived in any human body at all, was never born of woman, but instead his green-sage spirit enlivened that most distant British ancestor who stands at the beginning of my clan and tribe.

What do I mean when I say I am a Celtic Faery Shaman? I am directly descended from the Celtic speaking peoples of Britain, Scotland, Ireland, and Belgium; therefore, I work with my Celtic ancestor guide. I walk in the Faery Realm, which is the Shining Country I first visited as a little child. In those days I did not know where I was or understand that this is the land of the Faeries, the Land of the Sidhe, the Realm of the Fair Folk, the place where the Good Neighbours dwell.

A shaman is a person who travels in the Otherworlds and acts as mediator between the realms of spirit and the material world. They are priests and priestesses, healers, seers, herbalists, counsellors, and the spiritual leaders of their people.

The word 'shaman' is not native to Western and/or Insular Europe. This is what some of the native people of Siberia call their 'medicine men' and 'medicine women'. In Ireland and Scotland the medicine folk are called 'faerie doctors'. In other words, my ancestors never used the word 'shaman' at all. The terms 'Celtic Shaman' and 'Faery Shaman' are quite recent and first came into popular use in the 1980's.

What is it like to undertake the great work of the shaman under the direction of an ancestor guide? It is by turns amazing and ordinary. The first thing I need to make clear is that I work with and for Grandfather Merlin. I do not 'channel' Grandfather Merlin. I work with and for him in the same way one works with and for any employer. I run errands. I publish a magazine. I write and teach programs. I organize and run a non-profit society. I lead workshops. I help and heal. I make and mend. And I do all this under his direction.

Many times I don't even understand why I am doing some particular task he has set for me to do. Sometimes he will tell me why I am supposed to do this or that, other times he will not. One of his favorite stonewalling replies is, *"Information is given on a need to know basis only."* At times he will refuse to answer my questions on the grounds that if he tells me everything I want to know I will have no surprises to enjoy!

Everything I do for Grandfather Merlin is voluntary. I don't have to do anything at all. He has never and will never ask me to do anything that touches my life or my honor. In other words, he has never and will never ask me to anything illegal, immoral, unethical, or physically dangerous — although the physically dangerous part is sometimes a bit of a gray area because he is not completely aware of what living in the physical world means to a mere mortal. It is impossible to tell all the strange and wonderful things that have happened to me since I began to consciously and deliberately work with my ancestor guide, but I shall relate one of these experiences…

Being a shaman does not mean that everything in your life is forever perfect, that you are always completely aware of everything going on in this and Otherworlds or even that you are going to be healthy or spiritually aware all of the time.

There was a time when my life was in great confusion. I was in and out of a bad relationship. I was in financial difficulties and my energies were at very low ebb. It seemed there was no way out of my problems and so I endured misery from day to day with little hope of ever seeing a light at the end of a very long, dark tunnel.

One day I was waiting for a bus near the corner of a busy urban street, surrounded by concrete. Across the street a few stunted trees and pitiful weeds struggled to survive in a small patch of bare earth. I felt a great deal of empathy for those poor green folk. I was on my way to work and wishing I were a thousand miles away from the city.

An errant breeze touched the trees and me. The trees began to sway and dance. The weeds stirred in the wind. There was a sudden freshness in the air, from the west and I felt something – a presence that seemed very familiar – and a voice I knew but could not name spoke distinctly in my ear. *"Are you ready?"* The voice asked.

I replied, "Yes."

"Here it comes..."

And from the west it seemed a great wind and huge bright energy roared into and through me. The earth seemed to shake, the trees twisted wildly in the wind, dust devils rose around me – every hair on my body rose.

I was completely filled with energy. The wind cleared all the cobwebs and sad, defeatist thoughts from my mind. I saw clearly what I must do to improve my life and knew I had all the energy I needed to make those changes.

This story, as it stands, is wonderful and strange. As I worked to make my life better and to be free of the things that were holding me back and causing me pain I would sometimes remember that strange experience. As time went on and I moved farther away from the fey wind and the known but unnamed voice, the experience became more and more dreamlike – like something that happened to someone else or something I had seen in a movie or read in a book.

After a time, I seldom remembered that wild wind and had nearly forgotten that miraculous energizing moment. I had moved into another place in my life. A very good place. I was surrounded with love. I had an interesting, challenging and lucrative career and was in secure relationship with a wonderful and supportive man. We had a wonderful life.

One evening, I felt a bit tired and decided to go to bed early. As I lay in that state between waking and sleeping I saw myself from five years earlier. I saw my younger self, standing on that street corner, in a town that was east of the town where I lay. I saw my younger self, shoulders slumped, disheartened, waiting for the bus that would take me to work.

I felt infinite pity for that younger self and wished I could reach out to tell her all would be well, to encourage her and give her the energy she needed to reach this place where I presently lived.

In that instant, I knew that I *could* reach out to her. In my present life I had all the love and life and health and energy anyone could ever need. In fact, I had more of all these good things than anyone could ever need in a whole lifetime. I could gather up the extra and send it back to my younger self.

And so I did.

I gathered up all the extra love, good cheer, good health and energy I could spare and rolled it all up into a great big ball of light. As I did so I could feel someone else beside me, a presence I knew and loved. It was the same person who met me in the Shining Country when I was a very little girl. It was the same person who had walked beside me all those years in good times and bad. Now he showed me the nature of time and space and how both are related to the Shining Lands and how both are one together.

It seemed a sort of spirit wind was flowing from my present into my past. It was this wind that first stirred the trees and caught my past attention. And then I spoke to my past self. I said, "Are you ready?"

"*Yes*." Came my reply.

With all good will and intention I aimed my energy ball at my past self and released it. "Here it comes..."

And the rest is, of course, my history.

References: *The Green and Burning Tree: A Faery Shamans Handbook*, by Tira Brandon-Evans, Elder Grove Press, 2001, British Columbia, Canada.

MELTING THE ICE IN THE HEART OF MAN

Uncle Angaangaq

Angaangaq is an Eskimo-Kalaallit Elder whose family belongs to the Traditional Healers and Shamans of the Far North from Kalaallit Nunaat, Greenland. His name means 'the man who looks like his uncle'. Uncle, as he is frequently called, bridges the boundaries of cultures and faiths in people young and old. His work has taken him to five continents and over 40 countries around the world including South Africa, North America, South America, Asia, Arctic Europe, Russia, and Siberia.

As a Traditional Healer, storyteller and carrier of a Qilaut (drum), he conducts Healing Circles, Intensives and sweat lodges integrating the wisdom of traditional Inuit teachings from the unwritten healing traditions of the Eskimo-Kalaallit people.

He is internationally respected in native communities as an Elder of the Canadian-based Four Worlds International Institute for Human

and Community Development and with the World Council of Elders and is a keynote speaker at international conferences and symposia on environmental and indigenous issues. He participates in peace and spiritual vigils with the United Nations, speaking on panels for the United Nation Environmental Protection Agency, the Panel on Religion and Spirituality, the Permanent Forum on Indigenous Issues, as well as the Panel for UNESCO's Oceans, Fishers and Hunters. His work is acclaimed in promoting interracial and intercultural harmony.

Angaangaq is an Elder of the World Wisdom Council and Tribal Link Foundation, Inc. and is also a member of the World Commission on Global Consciousness and Spirituality acting as liaison to indigenous tribes. He is associated with the United Religions Initiative in alliance with the United Nations, the Club of Budapest International, The Masters Group, the Earth Restorations Corps., and the Jane Goodall Institute. He is an Elder in association with West Virginia University and speaks frequently at Universities and colleges in North America and Europe. Sharing healing circles with leaders of small villages and indigenous tribes from around the world is among his most rewarding work.

Most recently, he met with Tibetan Spiritual Leader, His Holiness the XIV Dalai Lama in Toronto, Canada where he performed a ceremony for the Kalachakra Initiation for World Peace.

My spirit guides were given to me by my grandmother. Many of my ancestors are my spirit guides. They know me inside out and it's really fascinating to be around them. They protect, guide and assist me. The next world after this physical life is no further away than a stretch of the arm – it's just that we have not yet learned to touch it. So spirit guides are closer to you than you think, which is a comforting thing to know. You can always call upon them.

There hadn't been a shaman amongst my people for almost 200 years. In 2006, I climbed a big mountain in Greenland to fulfill a wish and desire of the family to undergo a shamanic initiation ceremony – this had not been done since my great-great grandfather Angaakuq, who passed on in the 1840's, was called to the mountain in 1821. I went up there because I was asked. And I was asked to go alone without my spirit guides, without wearing my medicine around my neck. I'd never done that before and it was really fascinating.

I went there to tell the Creator about myself in 24 hours. It was incredibly difficult. I thought it would be a piece of cake but, once I started talking to Him, the man who made us, it was so incredibly difficult to do this without asking for something… for help and assistance.

It was snowing and raining – a storm the like of which I had never seen before. I was literally blown down by the wind. Luckily, I didn't hit my head, but I sure hurt my bum! I was lying there on the ground looking into the pitch-black darkness of the night. There were huge, palm-sized snowflakes falling down from the sky and exploding on my body. Finally, I got up – the snow stopped and was followed by huge sideways-falling raindrops. As I stood there against the wind, huge raindrops became visible half a meter away from me and exploded onto me. It was like fireworks in the reverse! The stars sent these fireworks to me and it was an incredible experience. I want to believe that I have become a much stronger person because of it.

I'm nearly 60 and I've done shamanic ceremonies all my life. I realised that doing ceremony is nothing compared to talking to Him, the man who made us, for 24 hours without ever asking for help or guidance. What I did was so incredibly difficult. I would never want anyone else to go through that if they were not prepared. I was under training for more than 57 years to do that and I still wasn't prepared.

I have kept so many secrets from God – things I didn't want Him or anyone else to know about myself. When I realised that I was avoiding issues, I thought, 'Holy shoot, I'd better talk… *really* talk'. I had kept many matters from my mind, my heart and my spirit away from Him. Of course, He already knows those things, but to say these things aloud was very hard. Even though, psychologically, there was nobody around – I was up a 2km tall mountain – it was such a painful thing, to reveal myself to Him. It was a fascinating experience.

When I was walking down the mountain I was tall – wow, I was tall. It took me about 4 hours to climb down that mountain. My mind was clear. My body was not. My body was stiff. I moved on from sheer will… at times I had to physically lift my pants up so my legs would move. But the adrenalin, knowing that I'd completed my task, my ceremony, was an incredible feeling.

One spirit guide – what we would call in the modern language an old man – has been coming to me for many years without ever speaking. He'd always look at me with piercing eyes. Now he spoke. He said, "Son, you are on the right path. You're doing good." It was so stunning to realise he was there even though I didn't ask for help.

Because of this experience, I have a better appreciation of my spirit guides because I realised they're really there for me. Now I make sure that when they come I am there for them.

When I was a little child, my grandmother started training me as a shaman. After my grandmother died, my mum carried on training me and before she died she gave me instructions to work. So I started *Sirmiq Aattuq* so that I could learn by teaching others – the more I teach, the more I learn. What an incredible gift I've been given. I really have to learn to say thank you to the Creator for all the privileges I have been given, for there's no-one to teach me to say thank you… all the old ones are gone. I'm the only one left. It's a very difficult path to walk having to find all your own answers. I can't say, "Hey, grandpa – tell me how you say that." Even though there were no elders left to teach me, I still had the stories. Before I was even born, my mother, Anna Annuq, started telling me the stories and chanting songs. I'm a very privileged man that I've been able to do ceremonies in the actual territories where all those ceremonies have been done. Most of them, not all of them, we know by story. I follow the story, so I've been able to do the ceremonies over and over.

Knowledge of the Eskimo-Kalaallit culture has been kept alive for thousands of years and generations through the art of storytelling. By telling stories with skill, detail and accuracy, the storyteller preserves the heritage that would otherwise be lost and forgotten, passing along spiritual beliefs and cultural traditions exactly the way they have been for generations.

We have a prophecy that when the once rock-hard glaciers become so soft that you could leave a handprint on them, this would be a sign that Mother Earth is in profound turmoil. I never thought I would witness the prophecy taking place in my lifetime…

About 15 years ago now, one of my people came back to our village and reported a strange phenomenon. *There is a trickle of water coming down from the ice cap*. Today that trickle is a river of water and the ocean is threatening to swallow not just your people, but all people.

I come far from my home to tell the people from the industrialized countries to wake up to the damage you are causing and change your ways. When will you change your ways? When the sea covers the first floor of your skyscrapers, the second floor… or the fifth? Because this is what is happening, yet you continue your ways. But this ice is easy to melt compared to the ice in the human heart.

In 1978, I spoke at the United Nations about the melting of the ice. I remember receiving a standing ovation for a long, long time, and my ego was huge! I went home and proudly told my mum and dad that I spoke at this big world government center. And my father said quietly, "But son, did they hear you?" I was very indignant and said, "Dad! They gave me standing ovation for ten minutes!" And he quietly asked, "But son, did they *hear* you?" I realised that, no, they didn't hear me. And no-one changed. So I went and asked my mum, "What can I do?"

She said, "You're going to have to learn to melt the ice in the heart of man."

"How do you do that?" I replied.

She looked at me for a long time. She just said, "You're going to have to learn to melt the ice in the heart of man. Only by melting the ice in the heart of man, man will have a chance to change and begin using his knowledge wisely." And then she walked away. So her wisdom is my guide. So that's what I do now.

Before my mom died, she asked me to change my ways. I would go home and complain to her, "Mum, nothing is working, nothing is changing." Because I've been talking of the melting of the ice for a long time. My mother used to say that the most beautiful smile is a smiling heart. When you think of it, it really is a beautiful thing to witness, when a person smiles – not with that thing on their face – but literally smiling with their entire being. When you see that veil being lifted of all depressions, you literally see the changes of the energy and the physical changes of that person being part of it and just watching it happen. I just love doing what I do. And that's what makes me go around. That's the intent of melting the ice in the heart of man.

When she died, she received so many letters from around the world, people we'd never heard of, who had changed their lives… and all she did was to give them an Eskimo kiss and touch their face. An Eskimo kiss is not rubbing noses – that's Hollywood. Hollywood is a powerful institution… it makes us believe anything. In the real Eskimo world, it is a kiss on the forehead with a sniff – like when animals sniff each other they get to know each other's scent. So do we.

That's why I wrote the song, 'Melting the Ice in the heart of Man'. I knew I had an incredible mother, but I didn't realise what an incredible privilege it had been to be her son.

We are told that (the way we call him in English) God is in our noble essence – that when you clean your mirror, dust it off, you see the image of the Creator, the one who made us. That's pretty scary isn't it? When I look at myself and say, "I am in the image of the Creator"… holy shoot! How can it be? But, nevertheless, that's the only way. The more I know myself, the closer I come to the creator. When you talk to Him, you're really talking to 'The Big Sky' – the world around you.

I grew up in a small village in Greenland. The villagers were, and still are, fishers and subsistence hunters. We lived very much like my grand-parents did – just living and surviving with the gifts of nature. Really there was nothing other than what Mother Nature brought us.

When you look at living things, everything has a spirit. That means you have a spirit, animals have a spirit, plants have a spirit, minerals have as spirit. Most people don't think of a mineral as having a spirit. Most people only think a few animals have a spirit. We smile a lot when we talk about dolphins. Everyone loves dolphins… certain animals have become very famous compared to others. But every one of them has a spirit and every plant has a spirit. When you look at them like that it changes your entire being and becomes the very medicine you need. Scientists have now figured out that when you say good things about the water, it lives. It is sad that we have to be convinced by the scientists before we really believe.

In Greenland, we have 'small people' that live there. All over the Native world we have the 'small people'. I think all of us have seen one, one time or another. If you haven't seen one you just haven't been paying attention to your surroundings. They can help you tremendously.

Plants are the most important medicines we have. Remember, those people in the Artic didn't have any doctors for centuries… for thousands of years. And they lived. My family became pretty old. My grandmother's older sister became 103 years old and just the other day one of my great uncles passed on at the young age of 81. And my last remaining auntie is now 84. All these people live for a long time and really live a good life – physically active, spiritually alive and really participating. And they did it with the medicine of the land and the medicine of the medicine man.

You know, everything else around us has not worked. Everything is failing. The time of challenge is coming to an end. Mother Earth is going to survive – she's okay. It's you and I, the human beings… we don't have much of a chance unless we change.

The biggest guide I have is to live a better life. To lift up my spirit and my depressions so I too can be given a chance to look with eyes of faith into the future – our future. Which we've been promised is pretty good if only we can understand it.

One of the most important teachings we have is that one day you and I will use our knowledge wisely. In 1980, I took my mum and dad to Chicago, to a big pow-wow. They don't speak English, so I had to be close to them. My dad was standing by the water of Lake Michigan, and I saw him pick some water up in his palm, smell it, and put his tongue to it. And he called to my mother and said, "Come over here!" (I was standing just two metres away from them and he hadn't seen me, or if he had seen me he didn't pay any attention to me at all.) And I could hear him saying to my mum, "Do not drink this water!" Many years later, she told me, "Remember what your father told us in Chicago? He told us that the water is not drinkable. If those people had used their knowledge wisely, they would have cleaned up their water right from the beginning." Here's a woman who'd never gone to school, who doesn't speak other languages, making a statement that if the people of Chicago really had used their knowledge wisely, the first thing they would have done is to clean up their water – that water is the most important essence.

We have a prophecy that tells us that one day the great sea-eagle will start descending from the mountains of ice, wafting with her a fresh scent of knowledge with wisdom. That means that one day, you and I, we will learn to use our vast knowledge wisely. How do we know we have not used it wisely? In Chicago you still cannot drink Lake Michigan… in London, England, you can't even bathe in the Thames! In Paris, you cannot even swim in the Seine. In Washington DC, you can't even see your nails when you put your hands into the Potomac River. This means we have not used our knowledge wisely.

In politics, nothing has worked. The philosophies of communism and capitalism, none of it worked. The economic development has made some people extremely wealthy and many more extremely poor. We are fighting and killing each other in wars. None of it has worked. We haven't used our education wisely. We have never had so many educated people, yet they can't even clean up the water! We're so 'educated' now that we have divided families completely. More and more children are alienated from their families. The old ones are more and more alone. One day, you and I will have to use our vast knowledge wisely.

Our guides can help us do this. We don't listen to them, we don't pay attention… most of us don't even know that we have them. Most of us are not in that sphere of reality. The reality of the world is so incredible – it's so powerfully beautiful. But we live just an inch in front of the nose. We are very shortsighted. We don't embrace the world as so powerfully beautiful… we don't take it in. Remember, more and more people live in big cities.

They say in the writings of the big religions that the city is the home of the body and the country is the home of the spirit… but more and more people are living in the home of the body. Have you ever flown over a big city at night? It's so incredibly beautiful, but when you land there, you get lost in the big lights. These lights are so deceivingly inviting, and the moment you enter them, it's like your spirit can no longer exist. All the needs of the body are there for you, and the body becomes the most important thing. But walk to the land and come to a small hill and watch the sunrise… sit there and then take in that incredible power and beauty. A whole different feel – your spirit can survive within it. It's important to care for ourselves.

Everything needs food – your body, your soul and your spirit. And when you do all that you eventually become calm and balanced. Talking to our food and thanking the food for having come to us will make our bodies strong. A 'thank you' for all the privileges, all the gifts you've been given… that's food for your soul. The food for your spirit is a song. We forget to sing songs. You and I, we should be singing to feed our spirit.

Each of our vibrations is important. I play the *Qilaut* – the Eskimo Wind Drum – a circle that has no beginning nor ending, in which we all belong. Only The Man Who Made Us – The Great Creator – holds the handle, and every time He touches upon the rim, He hears the heartbeat of mankind. The stronger the heartbeat the healthier mankind is.

There is an old prayer that goes: *My hope is that we will all have a strong heartbeat so we can be healthy together – and since it is your heartbeat, every time you talk to your heart she will always speak back.* So now, the lesson for you and I to learn is to listen to our hearts. Every time you talk to your heart, she will always speak back. Remember that.

photo copyright: GSM

THE HIDDEN PEOPLE

by Jörmundur Ingi

Jörmundur was born in Reykjavik, Iceland, in 1940 of Icelandic-Danish-German descent. He founded the Icelandic Pagan group, Asatru, in 1972. Jörmundur lived in Lithuania after the collapse of the Soviet Union, where he worked with the Lithuanian Pagans, Romuva.

Jörmundur was elected Allsherjargoði (supreme leader of Icelandic Pagans) between 1999-2003. He now holds the title of 'Goði of Reykjavik', one of two officially recognized Pagan associations in Iceland. In his position as Goði, he performs marriage and funeral services, and spreads the word of the naturalistic beliefs of ancient Iceland. He is currently retired and is studying the history and development of Germanic (including Anglo-Saxon) Paganism.

My great-grandmother would never have referred to herself as a Shaman, but she was, and so was her mother. She would have called herself an herbalist who interacted with the hidden people (elves). She was also a midwife. She would also have admitted to being able to travel in her mind over vast distances and witness things taking place on the other side of the country. But 'Shaman' was a term she would not have recognised. She would perhaps have accepted the Amerindian title of 'Medicine Woman'.

I never met my great-grandmother. She died just two years before I was born but all my life I heard stories about her, and I have read all that was written on her life. There is a written reference on her initiation to the control of her mother, who was a midwife and a fisherman's wife. I have also heard an oral account of this many times from my grandmother and her siblings. When I was a teenager, I read about Shamans and realised that my female ancestors had belonged to that group.

In the small grass field around the family farmhouse, there was a small knoll of big rocks partly covered with grass. In it was a square door-like alcove 3 or 4 feet high and wide. The children of the farm were afraid of the knoll – they believed that the hidden people lived there, but mainly they were afraid of the 'door'. One night, when she was six or seven years old, my great-grandmother 'dreamed' that two girls about her own age came to her and asked her to come with them. Reluctantly, she gave in and to the small knoll they went. There was a *real door* in the rock and the two girls told her to enter. After a slight hesitation, my great-grandmother agreed, but said, "Then I must remove one of my shoes, as my mother has told me that you should always leave something behind when you enter the Other World, in order to return." Then she unbound one of her sealskin shoes and pushed it into a crevice in the rock. Inside was a woman in labour and she encouraged the little girl to lay her hands on her in order to facilitate the birth. Her first instinct was to deny and refer them to her mother (who was a trained midwife), but the woman insisted. She did as she was asked and the child was born. The woman said, "Thank you very much. If you ever need me in your work as a midwife or a healer, I shall not fail you." Then she predicted that my great-grandmother would have great success as a midwife, as indeed she did. The next morning when she awoke, she remembered everything about her 'dream', *and* one of her shoes was missing! She was too afraid to go back to the knoll, but told her mother the story. Her mother scolded her for losing her shoe, and the matter was forgotten. The story of her trip to the knoll came up again, and then her mother went to the knoll and found her shoe in the crevice.

My great-great-great grandmother was the first in the family to be trained as a midwife, in the western medical tradition. We do not know how long the women in our family have been practicing the craft of ancient midwifery, but it is a tradition that goes back as long as a thousand years and more. The midwives in Iceland (as well as in other Protestant countries) were trained by priests, and the instructions consisted of learning which prayers to say in a given situation. The ancient midwives no doubt based their craft on the Old Religion, but it was also based on practical knowledge and experience. This knowledge must have gone underground with Catholicism or perhaps found refuge in the convents, and finally was judged heretical by the Lutherans. Some of the knowledge, however, survived in individuals and families such as ours.

Perhaps it would be a good idea at this point to present a summary of my view on the linage of the Icelandic/Nordic religion and, indeed, religion in general. I see the beginning of religions in the Shamans of the Ice-age who were in contact with the mother of the hunting animals – the staple prey of each tribe. In this way we have the mother of the seals among the Inuits. Among the ancestors of the Sami in northen Scandinavia and Siberia she would have been the mother of the migrating animals, such as the reindeer. As the Sami started to follow the herds all year around, she would have become the mother of the semi-domisticated herd (it is interesting to note that in Iceland as late as the middle of the twentieth century, this mother of the domisticated animals is still going strong and punishing those who mistreat her children). The Shaman dictates the method of hunting the pray, the method of killing and showing the proper respect to the Mother – he also predicts the future of the tribe, mostly fortelling the seasons and the migration of the beasts. He or she is also a herbalist well versed in the use of plants of all kinds. Amongst the plants they utilise is the *Amanita Muscaria* or the 'Berserker Mushroom', which induces a trance-like state, allowing the Shaman to travel to the netherworld where sickness and other unwholesome things swim in the dark waters under the earth. It is also here that the Mother is to be found.

Many Shamans had helpers or apprentices who helped keep the people at bay and preserve the image and power of the Shaman (see, for example *'The Masks of God'* by Joseph Campbell). I believe that these helpers later turned into the 12 Berserkers that appear to be the standard followers of Nordic kings until well into the Viking-age. Note that all the kings in Europe maintain large hunting grounds – people think that this is done for selfish reasions, but perhaps it is the lingering memory of the Mother of the Hunt that gave them their power in the beginning? At the time when the Nordic people turned to agriculture, the Mother of the Hunt was slowly perceived as the Mother of the Corn, preciding over the fertility of the land. She still lives in the subterranean waters and is venerated at springs, wells and in bogs – everywhere the worlds of the underground and the world of humans meet.

According to the Roman writers, the Germans worshipped the Mothers or *Matrones*. Most likely these were nine in number, as can be inferred from Snorri Sturlusson's *'Prose Edda'*. They may, therefore, be the nine mothers of Baldur the White of later Viking-age fame. This 'new' Mother seems to also have been a goddess of war, as massive offerings of Bronze-age weapons have been found in bogs and lakes, mainly in Denmark. In Viking-age Iceland, Freyja 'The Lady of Fertility and Love' was also a goddess of war, claiming that half those slain in battle were hers, with the other half belonging to Odin.

During the sixth century, people from the Far East came to Scandinavia and changed the culture and lives of people drastically. These were, in all probability, the Goths that had left Scandinavia 600 years earlier, having been in league with the Samarian nomads in the East

– but exactly where in the East it is difficult to say. In any case, not only the Samarian, but also Indians (Hindu) and Persian influences came back to Scandinavia with them. This probably also included Zoroastrianism, and many others. In any event, the decorative arts in Scandinavia, especially jewellery, changed almost overnight with the new style showing strong Samarian influences. There was also a drastic change and simplification of the language. The newcomers introduced their religious ideas and used their superior knowledge to take control of the Scandinavian lands (all this can be read in Snorri Sturlusons *'Edda'*).

Furthermore, the Danish Royal family discovered around this time that their divine ancestor was not Freyr, the god of fertility, but Odin – the newly introduced god of war and poetry. There was probably much conflict as the new ideas about the order of the Cosmos were gaining acceptance (Snorri refers to these events as the Vanic Wars).

The new class of gods did not seem to include any goddesses – rather, the new gods are seen to have *married* the local goddesses. In this way, the new religious order is a mixture of the old and new gods, as well as old and new ideas. The belief in the *Aesir*, or the heavenly gods, is known to us mostly from Viking sources in Iceland.

When Iceland was settled by Norsemen, mainly from the British Isles but also directly from Scandinavia and even further afield, these settlers must have had a variety of religious backgrounds if only to judge from the large area from which they came. One thing they must have had in common is a belief in the *Landwights* – the powerful female beings that protected the island and were not to be interfered with or disturbed in any way. Here we most likely have the goddesses of old Scandinavia – the ones that were venerated in the bogs and lakes. There are indications that people also brought with them local semi-divine beings from home and found new sacred places for them in their surroundings. When my great-grandmother and her family moved their household right across Iceland in the late 19th Century, her *Wight* (shamanic helper, elf or hidden woman) moved with her and settled in a small knoll remarkably similar to her former abode.

The Icelanders organized themselves into a democratic commonwealth in the year 930. This was a religious state ruled by the 36 *Goðar* or Lords. People had a wide range of religious beliefs – from classical Nordic Paganism to an ancient belief in the Vanir (or the Mothers) – and there were, in all probability, quite a number of Christian sects such as the Katars, Bogomils, Kelts and the followers of Arianus, all of whom we would find unfamiliar at best. When this was done, the necessity arose to have a uniform religious belief in order to hold meetings of the *Althing* (Parliament) with religious rituals accepted by everyone. The solution was to accept the religion favoured by the Nordic Kings as the official religion of the new Commonwealth. But there was also ambiguity here… the oath that everyone accepting an office or giving evidence in court had to take, mentions only the names of *two* of the Vanic Gods – Freyr and Njord – and then adds, like an afterthought, the almighty *As* (God). The first article of the law of the New State was that no one could sail warships (ship with a dragons head) in Icelandic waters – if they did, the dragonhead must be removed before they came in sight of land, in order not to scare off the *Landwights*. Even if the official religion was the classic Viking or Nordic Paganism, the old gods of the Vanir had a prominent place.

It is my firm belief that the old gods were venerated by a large part of the common people and this practise continued into Catholic times (from 1056) and further in Protestant times. By that time, all supernatural beings, including the Ancestors, were referred to as 'the hidden people'. These were the beings my grandmothers dealt with.

Helpers are entitles (spirits if you like) who appear to us as human beings or even animals, whose shape and personalities they assume. They also get a part of their persona and power from the Shaman and his cultural environment, consciously or unconsciously. A good friend of mine defines what he calls a Deva or nature spirit (that we in Iceland call a *Landwight*) as a being that uses land for a body. In view of the latest theories the whole thing could be explained by *Memes*, or memory genes, inherited over generations passing on knowledge. In actuality, some of the explanations from latter-day scientists on *Memes* sound almost exactly like medieval descriptions of genies, spirits or incubi. Have we come full-circle?

But back to my great grandmother. She was not only a midwife and herbal doctor in the ancient Icelandic tradition, she could also see things and events that were happening far away, and even appear at such far away places and be seen and recognised. I will render only one such story told to me by my grandmother when she was almost ninety years old…

One day, my great-grandmother was working outside and her children were nearby, including my grandmother who was approximately ten years old at the time. Suddenly, they noticed that their mother was standing upright and staring into the distance. "Mother is seeing something," one of the brothers said, and they all rushed to her side, but remained quiet. After a moment, the old woman says, "I am afraid that your brother has perished during the seal hunt. I have just seen him drown." At exactly the same time, her son saw his mother appear looking both sad and angry and he thought more of the distress that his death would cause her than of his own fate. Just at that moment, his fellow hunters found him seemingly lifeless and dragged him onto the warm sandy beach, where he recovered after a long while. This is only one of a multitude of such stories that have survived within the family and amongst their neighbors, many of them in print from the first quarter of the 20th Century.

My great-grandmother was a Shaman, as I think obvious from the above. She got her powers from her mother and grandmother; as such powers are difficult to come by on your own. My grandmother, who was a teenager at the turn of the century (1800-1900), felt that she should be a modern woman and not practise such old-fashioned things, so she didn't – but she preserved all the things her mother and grandmother had told her, and when my mother was born the whole circle seemed to start all over again, skipping one generation.

My mother played with children in the knoll, close to the farm where she lived as a young girl, and she could see clearly the animals (totems) accompanying people that came for a visit. My grandmother told me that she always knew when a certain man was coming well in advance, as my mother would climb onto the roof of the small farmhouse scared out of her wits because the totem animal of the man in question was a lion. This ability my mother had mostly disappeared when they moved into town when she was nine years old.

My great-aunt, my grandmother's sister, became a midwife in the family tradition, and there appeared to her a young woman claiming she was the daughter of her mother's helper and told her that she wanted to keep the tradition of both families going, and so they did.

When I was asked to write an account for this book of my experiences as a Shaman, I said, "Yes," without thinking about it. Then I realised that I was in no way a Shaman, and offered to write about my ancestors instead. But I found this difficult. When I sat down at the computer I had writer's block of the first magnitude! After a long telephone conversation with the editor, I realised what was stopping me… the old religion and things belonging to it, such as Shamanism, belong to the realm of circular thought, but writing about it brings you automatically into the Christian linear thought-process. As soon as I tried to write something down, it became linear and sidetracked me – so if this piece seems to jump between past and present, between my great-grandmother and religious commentary, indeed hither and thither, it is because I have been able to harness the computer to some extent into a verbal circular device.

After a few days of writing this, it no longer sounds so absurd that I myself process some Shamanistic trends – even powers – but that story would not nearly be as interesting as this one.

CHAPTER 10

STAR NATIONS

Man looks aloft; and with erected eyes
Beholds his own hereditary skies
~ Ovid (43 BC – AD 17) - 'Metamorphoses'

Who are these that fly as a cloud, and as the doves to their windows?
~ Isaiah 60:8

There are more stars in the universe than grains of sand on all the Earth's beaches and deserts. Using the most powerful telescopes in the world, a team led by astronomer Dr. Simon Driver of the Australian National University in 2003 estimated there to be 70 sextillion – that's seven followed by *22 zeroes* – and that's only the stars in the *visible* universe within range of our telescopes! The odds that life on earth is the only life in our universe, let alone other universes, are very slim indeed.

Many people believe that there exists not just one, but a multitude of life forms of different races from other planets and universes, yet scientists have been unable to find another planet similar to earth that would support life. While it is true that all life on earth depends on water and oxygen in order to survive, perhaps we are unique in this regard. Telescopes can only magnify the appearance of solid matter and will not register anything beyond our scope of vision. Other dimensional beings, including some 'extra-terrestrials', vibrate at a higher frequency than matter on earth – we have a denser form, hence they are largely invisible to us.

Star Visitors have been well documented by many indigenous cultures throughout history. Why would beings from other planets be interested in us? Perhaps humankind is descended from Star People, our ancestral home is in the stars, and we are, in effect, related. There are many indigenous cultures that indeed believe this to be the case, including a small tribe in Brazil, the *Ureu-eu Wau-Wau*, whose name literally translates as 'people from the stars'. The *Shuar* people of the Amazon believe that their starry ancestors appear to them as balls of light in the night skies, African lore tells of star people coming down from the heavens in 'magic sky boats', and there are artifacts from all over the ancient world resembling modern-day 'spaceships'. According to the author Jack Barranger in his book, *'Past Shock'*, 'More than 30,000 written documents from all over the world tell of advanced beings who either came to earth or who were already living on earth'. The historian and author Michael Tsarion believes that the true history of mankind stems from an alien visitation in pre-diluvian times (before the Great Flood), and has uncovered many covert references in the Bible alluding to this… the word 'Nephilim' was used to describe these beings, and means, 'those who were cast down'.

Despite the overwhelming evidence that supports our starry origins, most people disregard the existence of beings from other planets because they haven't shown up en-mass to introduce themselves on the nine o'clock news. But can you imagine what would happen if they *did?* (I can see the headlines now…) The very fact that they haven't shows that they have intelligence, compassion and benevolence towards the human race. Most people would feel threatened and afraid, for a start. Then, of course, the world's governments would step in and offer to 'interpret' their message for humanity, thus gaining power and control of possibly 90% of the human race in the process. Before long, we're being dictated to by the powers that be – on behalf of the 'extraterrestrials', of course. (Hmmm… this sounds familiar. Where have I heard this before? Ah, yes – *religion*. Just substitute the word 'extra-terrestrial' for 'God', and 'governments' for 'priests'.)

If, by any chance, by the time this book has been published this has indeed occurred and a starry fleet of UFOs have graced our skies and are currently in cahoots with the president, I would urge you, dear reader, to question its authenticity. (In April 2007, the BBC reported a UFO sighting by a commercial airline pilot and his passengers over Guernsey, so perhaps this is only a matter of time?)

I feel that the reason we can't see our starry friends is because, although they are more than capable of manifesting themselves into form, they *choose* not to show themselves to us. They are experts at travelling between dimensions and vibrate at a much higher frequency than we do, so, in order for us to perceive and interact with them, we need to refine our energy. This is a very clever and wise tactic they employ, because it encourages us to grow spiritually. Once we are aligned and compatible with their vibration, this communication is telepathically transmitted both ways – thus the energy of the message is personally experienced at the deepest level of our being and cannot be misunderstood or manipulated by a 'third party'. Everyone knows that direct contact with *anyone* is always preferable, whether this is with 'God', your higher self, Star Beings or a real person on the other end of the telephone instead of an automated service.

I have read that humans possess a natural telepathic ability, but that we closed off our ability to communicate telepathically because we don't want others to look into our minds and know what we are truly thinking and feeling. What have *you* got to hide? In order to be telepathic, we have to be willing to be open and honest, as we could no longer effectively hide our true feelings. This would, of course, make all lies futile, hence many businessmen/women and politicians redundant!

I once saw a Star Ship in a dream – it was transparent, like a jellyfish, with points of light on it. I intuitively knew that I could communicate with these beings. I was still contemplating the question I wanted to ask, when I received an answer telepathically. I thought a thought and they immediately responded. This wasn't the question of all questions that I would have chosen, but the experience taught me that to communicate effectively telepathically, it is necessary to 'think the right thoughts'.

Obviously, this would take some getting used to, as we are used to a process of communicating whereby we usually formulate what we want to say beforehand, and *then* communicate.

In recent years, the phenomena that have become known as 'crop circles' – the majority of which appear in the UK – have been attributed to the Star Nations. Since 1991, I have had the pleasure of visiting many of these firsthand. These complex and beautiful creations often incorporate sacred geometry within the designs, and are nothing short of inspirational. Rod Bearcloud Berry, a Native American artist of the *Niukonska* nation, believes that these sacred symbols – that he has come to call 'Star Glyphs' – are a gift from the Star Nation people. In 2005, I met him at Avebury to talk about his experiences, and he told me of seeing balls of light in the sky, and of other instances where he feels that the Star Nation people have telepathically communicated with him. Bearcloud interprets these messages with his intuitive *knowing* – for example, when and where a new formation will appear. This has motivated Bearcloud to travel to the West Country in the U.K every year, in order to research, talk about, and also paint these Star Glyphs. (See www.starnationgallery.com).

We are all One, thus the future of mankind affects the entire universe. The Star Nations – our multi-dimensional cousins – understand this, and draw close at this exciting time in earth's history in order to offer their help and assistance.

THE LAKOTA STAR NATION

Tiokasin Ghosthorse

Tiokasin is a member of the Cheyenne River Lakota Nation of South Dakota. He has a long career in indigenous rights activism and currently hosts a radio program on WBAI called First Voices Indigenous Radio in New York, NY.

We are often called American Indians, but we aren't Indians and we were never really American. We are Human Beings, which is what the word Lakota essentially means.

The way we, the Lakota people, speak about Spirit is not a rational process that can be measured. The Indigenous thinking process is relational and egalitarian, where everything is alive and everything is energy. We don't have a concept of time and have no word for, or concept of, death. We believe that everything changes shape and form into a different energy. You don't really die because everything is energy, everything is Spirit.

I was taught that we are one soul and that we are not separate from that soul. My body is in the soul, and everything else (including my body in the soul), is part of that one soul. When we go into the spiritual aspect of thinking about the whole, we have to realize that this is something that we cannot fully perceive because the body is limited by its senses. We all have the same truth, but many people are so far away from being Indigenous that they have forgotten, so they try to logically explain themselves into it. The rationale is usually explained through a hierarchical, patriarchal or matriarchal godhead, or for short, a religiosity.

The Lakota know that we live in at *least* seven dimensions, not just three. Spirit is the one who allows you to go back and forth between the dimensions. When the ceremonies happen in the Lakota way, these other dimensions open up. I have experienced this as a Sundancer. Sundancing is one of the seven rites of the Lakota – the others are the Keeping of the Soul, Throwing the Ball, the Rite of Purification, Crying for a Vision, the Making of Relatives, and Preparing a Girl for Womanhood. I simply cannot approach Sundancing in an explainable manner – to explain something that cannot be explained would only serve to quantify, measure and sensationalize.

I am not a 'medicine man' or some spiritual guru, nor do I hold a 'chief' status or anything equivalent. I am simply one who has Sundanced, and even say that with the utmost respect. I am an *ikce wicasa* – what we call a 'common man'. One has to experience or learn how to support Sundancing, and not just anyone can be a Sundancer. Although the language I just used seems 'exclusive', it is based on relational inclusivity – the rigorous attitude and spiritual preparedness one must have to endure and choose to suffer in light of all things. *Onsimalaye oyate wani wacin cu welo!* – I do this so that the people may live ('people' meaning not just the human species). It has everything in the universe to do with quantum thinking processes involving the evolving relationship we have to all of life.

I've had many visions – they are very precious and I've written them all down, from when I was a little boy to a few years ago. They don't happen all the time because I live in the city now. Both my father and my grandfather have come to me, in the sense of 'Letting me know things are okay'. All the visions, dreams and intuitions that I have I can't explain, but I know that they're *Wakan* (sacred).

We don't tend to objectify one single thing as a guiding force in our lives, as one thing has to be related to another in order to survive. Everything is life, and we have responsibility for that life.

As a Lakota people, we have different life *times* in each dimension and through those dimensions we have different guides at different times. Everything is alive, so the way the wind blows, the way the rain falls on you, the way an animal walks, the way a bird flies, the way the clouds float by or the position of the stars can all be guiding spirits. In a way, that may be too far-fetched for people to grasp… that absolutely everything is Spirit and can be a guiding force in our lives.

One of our Lakota ancestors (we say that we are all related in the Lakota country) is Crazy Horse. His real name was *not* 'Crazy Horse' – it was *'His Horse is Enchanted'*. When he travelled back and forth between the dimensions, he would say that we live in the shadow of the real world… that's why I say that dreams are the telling part of our spirituality, because they tell you how to live.

We are all born metaphysical thinkers and metaphorical thinkers – we are all born with dreams, visions and intuition that have been blocked from humans by teaching rational thought, objectifying things and denoting them as inanimate. This programming takes away our intuition, dreams and visions and gets in the way of Spirit so that we understand less and less about the spirit world, minimizing what Spirit really is and turning everything into religiosity.

When I go home to the reservation, the Native people there are losing our ability to tap into the metaphysical because Christianity runs abundant. Many have become patriarchal in how they present the way the Lakota religion or spirituality is. My viewpoint has not been Christianized as a lot of Lakota peoples' have been.

As Lakota people, we have a vast spiritual knowledge. That's why we think that those who manipulate the people here in America are very afraid of Indigenous people. We don't have total freedom of religion here in the United States, because we have to pay to visit our sacred sites to pray or hold ceremonies. It has taken its toll on our people. One reason why our spirituality was banned here in the United States is because they could not understand the concepts that we have. How can you explain what you don't own in a world where the English language is based on ownership and hierarchy? Around 20 to 25% of our language cannot be translated into other languages, because of their material foundation. I was taught that we, as Lakota, began with not having a word for 'I' or 'me', which is the start of war, selfishness and self-centeredness. We hardly spoke Lakota when I was a child, but I was lucky… I *listened.* I think in Lakota, so I have to turn my thoughts around and put them into English.

The English language, the way it's used, is very economical, it's very religious – but it's far from being spiritual. It specifies possessions and the material world, greed, patriarchy, war and domination. It doesn't describe feelings very well. This method of communication is given to those who speak English anywhere in the world as 'normal'.

I believe that the words we speak carry energy. There are so many words that throw us off track. For example, the word 'hope' – most people don't know that in the pre-biblical era it is the last evil out of Pandora's box! When you say this word, it takes power away from you and puts you in a wishful state of being. The original incantation of the sound of that word is using energy in an improper way, to take *away* something. We have to remember how to speak carefully.

Lakota is both an earth language and a star language. The Lakota Elders who have been in spiritual ceremony with what they call the Illuminated Ones speak the old Lakota language of the stars. It's almost like when people 'speak in tongues', but it's not that – it's a language of energy. I can't understand the old language that the Elders understand. We sing the songs that will invoke the attention of a particular dimension of spirit and spirit guides that *Wakantanka* understands. It's like a key opening up a dimension so, when we're conducting our ceremonies, certain songs invoke certain energies.

Energy is sound. Earth is singing a song to you of the star knowledge. Many Native people get their songs from watching the aurora borealis or northern lights. Likewise, when we hear a bird or an animal speak, we try to mimic them because they're speaking the language of the stars.

We have stories about how the earth came together, but the story that's not told about Lakota people is that we originated or came from the Pleiades – part of a constellation we have in the stars that we call *Tayamnipa.*

When the Europeans first came, they thought we were nomads because we were 'wandering around aimlessly'. But we moved with a purpose, because our spirituality was more or less with the stars – we knew we had to hold our ceremonies in specific places at certain times of the year, so we moved during those times.

Most of the creation stories that I know of are about coming from the Pleiades. There's the story about a woman who fell in love with a star and went to live with him and his people. She pulled a turnip because she missed her ancestors on Earth, which left a hole in the Star Nation and she fell to earth and gave birth to a baby who was half star, half human. A few years ago, they discovered a black hole in the center of the Big Dipper. I thought, "Wow! We have already had that in our stories!"

To my knowledge, no Native person in the United States has been abducted by extra-terrestrials! The Elders talk about us being visited, but we also go into ceremony with them because we remember that we are the people who 'fell from the sky' – that we are half Star Nation, half Star People.

We call ourselves 'The Children of the Sun'. Our babies are born with blue backs. When they were young they were taken away from us because the social workers and the American society thought the parents were beating and abusing their children. A lot of our children were taken away, and yet the Elders to this day continue to say that we are 'Children of the Sun' and that those blue backs indicate what people are now saying are the Indigo Nation. But we always have been here… My back is still blue.

If we only recognise that the Star People, who are here and who have always been here, are our cousins – that they are our relatives, then it doesn't become a big phenomenon. There are more sightings of UFOs on Indian reservations than anywhere else in the United States. These aren't reported. I think it may be a considered a threat or diminished by authorities, or that is it just tribal superstition. The other people, the non-Natives who report 'close encounter contacts' make a big sensationalism of it and yet it's in our everyday lives at home.

When I visit my mother on the reservation in a remote part of South Dakota, we talk normal chit-chat and then we'll go outside and face north in the evening and watch all the stars come up. One day, she said to me, "Oh, that star right there – watch it… it's going to go almost straight above our heads and then it's going to split in two." In a few minutes, it did exactly as she said it would… one light went one way and the other light the other way. "Yeah," she said casually, "It happens almost every night I come out here."

There is a being we call The Watcher who comes to the Lakota people to tell us to be careful, to take care of ourselves and to warn us when hard times are about to come. He is a tall, very light-skinned man – some say he's 10 ft tall – and he dresses mostly in black. Sometimes he wears some form of hat. He is seen on the reservations at different locations at the same time.

My mom described to me that tribal police were chasing a tall being and finally surrounded it with cars. They got out of their cars and they didn't know what to do – they were calling everybody else to get instructions, "What do we do – shoot it? What do we do?!" The Watcher, the tall being, standing with its back against the wall, slowly turned to face the police. Out of its back came these great wings and he went straight up and disappeared. There still are different descriptions and reports of the Watcher heard and seen everywhere.

In South Dakota when I was a child, about three years old, I was laying beside my father outside the house. (It is the first vivid memory I have of my father, who died when I was four.) I was resting my head on his chest listening to his heart beating and, at the same time, looking up and remembering the stars. When I looked up to the stars, I could see my home, in a sense – the home of our Ancestors, who are always here with us.

It is said we came along the Milky Way, down through the rings of the aurora borealis. We saw a heart-shaped landmass from above and we said, "Oh, we want to live there – right *there*" in the Black Hills. We have always called this place the heart of Mother Earth, the heart of everything that is… so how did we *know* it was heart-shaped if we didn't have flying machines? The Elders say that we came and landed there, saw that the earth was unfinished and went down into the Wind Cave – where the wind rushes in and out and you can hear Mother Earth breathing. We lived underneath the ground until the earth was created. The Wind Cave is one of our sacred sites – it goes on for miles and miles and miles. Currently over 123.52 miles (198.78 km) of passages have been mapped in Wind Cave. The Elders say that they discover at least 300ft more of it every day and that those caves and tunnels go all the way down to the Gulf of Mexico.

When we came out, we saw that the land was completed, but we didn't know how to live on Earth. So that's where you find the original 'spirit guides' – the 'animals', the brothers and sisters, the trees… they offered themselves and said, "We live here already… here's how *you* are going to do that, too." And so the trees offered us their food, they gave to us. And seeing that generosity of life here on Earth, we knew that the only way we could survive is to be generous like them and never 'take'.

In Lakota, we don't have a word for animal – in Latin, *ani* means 'soul' and *mal* means 'bad', so we can't call these creatures that we consider to be our brothers and sisters 'bad souls'. Each life form that we can name we call a 'Nation' – there's the Ant Nation, the Tree Nation, Air

Nation, the Water Nation… so when we look at those things in relationship, we know that one time the water will be a spirit guide, one time a tree will be a spirit guide, or maybe just a bird call will be a spirit guide, because they lead us into different dimensions all the time. The damage that we have done as Human Beings to the earth is because we have forgotten the many Nations of life that have given to us.

Our 'medicine' – our way to live amongst other life on earth – was gifted to us by these Nations. In fact, it was the White Buffalo Calf Woman who brought the pipe to us and went away as a buffalo. As a Lakota, I more or less adhere to how the buffalo taught us how to live in that location of the black hills and the surrounding northern plains area – they taught us about our medicines, so in that way the 'animals', our brothers and sisters, are considered spirit guides.

These days, everyone wants to have this magnificent animal as a spirit guide and yet there are people back home who say that that little bug down there, that little worm coming out of the earth or that little cockroach moving around there could be a spirit guide… it's not necessarily a bear or an eagle or a wolf! That just tells me that a person thinks less of themselves and they need a 'big' image to prop themselves up in an egotistical way.

We are realizing that, for us, it's the beginning rather than the end. We told the Americans when they came here more than 500 years ago that, if you continue to live this way, your generations are going to pay for it later. All these years they haven't listened to us… they continue to believe that 'their way' is the chosen way.

We have prophesized that all people would come to this country to this land called Turtle Island because they were running from something – war, disease or famine… for whatever reason, they were running to this land seeking something. The prophecy said that they would continue not to find what they came here for, and that is something we call *Wolakota*, which means peace. But the time is coming when the thing that they seek will eventually come to them.

You can't play with Spirit. Spirit is too big for that. You can play with religious and political concepts because you can manipulate that – it's all money-based. Our knowledge is Spirit-based, not based on man-made laws, books and money.

We may marvel at technology – the internet or the telephone – but we don't always use these tools in truth or appropriately. The secret is to not use things in excess and to always appreciate that we have them. If we don't use that energy in a bad way or improperly, then we'll be okay.

I live in an American society whose lifestyle is 90% possession, in contrast, coming from an Indigenous culture that is 90% generosity. The 10% of ownership that we *do* have is minimal. In our culture, the women *own* the property – they're the ones who are able to share because they see the babies grow up. These little children – the *Wakanheja* –are also spirit guides, in a sense, because they can be born Elders. As a child at three years old, I didn't feel young or old… I felt very present.

I have *so much* that other people don't have – not because I want it or hoard it – it's because I do two simple things… I pray for appreciation and I pray for the intelligence to *know* the appreciation. If you appreciate things, then the spirit of knowing what you need in order to teach other people to appreciate opens up to you and you're taking care of life in a spiritual way. I'm not going to just sit here and wish for things I haven't got, I'm going to recognize that what I *do* have is appreciated. I use the gifts I have to pass the message along.

Indigenous people have always given, no matter how much we have – we don't have much anymore… we have our Spirit and that's what keeps us alive. If we were not that way, we would risk all forms of knowledge that were given to us and if we continue to be generous then we preserve ourselves.

I came to New York to find voice on the radio for Indigenous people all over the world – not just for Native Americans. People all over the world are trying to find a way to live… trying to find *something*. I really believe that the Indigenous peoples have most of the answer to being able to survive here. This society is changing fast because the system, no matter who they put in place, no matter how much money they throw at it, how many bombs or technology or things they think they have, it's all for nothing because all they're doing is killing their own ability to live and get along with their own Mother Earth.

The system in place does not want Indigenous people worldwide, even those people who don't consider themselves Indigenous, to start getting along – to start 'getting it'… to start understanding the reality that it is an emergency *right now*. Our spirits need to come together. Our generation has to remember. Remember, real eyes realize real lies. If we paid more attention to our dreams, intuitions and visions, then I think we might just get somewhere.

We are trying to help other people recognise where they come from. We are of the Earth. We are not trying to get away from Mother Earth. Even though we originally came from the stars, our DNA is part of her now. Earth is a star too, you know? Indigenous people have always known that they belong to the land rather than the opposite, and that's the difference... peace *with* rather than peace *on* Earth.

photo credit: LJExposures

DANCING WITH THE STARS

by Llyn Roberts

Llyn Roberts was born and raised in a French Canadian Catholic community in southeastern New Hampshire in the US. She holds a masters degree in Tibetan Buddhist and Western Psychology from Naropa University and was a student of Chogyam Trungpa Rinpoche. Llyn has worked alongside indigenous shamanic peoples in remote parts of the world and runs the non-profit organization, Dream Change, dedicated to applying indigenous wisdom for personal and global transformation (founded by author and environmentalist John Perkins). Roberts has been initiated into Quechua and Siberian shamanic circles and teaches in Europe and the US. She is the author of 'The Good Remembering' and co-author of 'Shamanic Reiki', both published by O-Books.

God and Saints

Although both my Grandfathers trace to Welsh heritage, my

Grandmothers (Memères) were French Canadian. Most of my relatives and I lived in a small New Hampshire community predominantly consisting of working class Canadian Catholics. Though far from perfect, my Memères were nonetheless pious women – one raised by nuns from the age of three when her mother died and the other entering the convent at eighteen years old (she was later sent home and ended up giving birth to eight children!). My maternal Grandmother's devotional life greatly impacted me. A rosary string often wrapped around her palm, she rubbed the small wooden beads and muttered prayers throughout her day. Aside from praying, she called on the saints for common things like finding lost keys or to quell her terror during lightening storms. Memère also spoke to God and sought the comfort of, as well as sent prayers to, our dead relatives. Some of her children, who were my aunts and uncles, were also spiritual… one uncle later becoming a Mason and another prone to visions and spirit encounters.

Following Memère's example, I felt very close to God, the angels, saints, and my dead relatives. I felt them with and around me and spoke with them as I lay in bed at night. I questioned God on things the Catholic school taught me that didn't make sense to my young mind, like why the souls of children who died without being baptized were sent to a place called limbo. There was no room in Catechism class for questioning, only memorizing what was presented. I had a burning desire to know about the universe and concepts like infinity. I didn't experience God as a father figure in heaven but as a pervasive presence. My answers sometimes came in words, but mostly through palpable feelings and sensations. I often felt like my body and my whole being expanded way out to the universe when I spoke with God. I would know things at these times that couldn't be put into words. So strong was my personal connection to God that, never discussing it with anyone, at age eleven I stopped going to Confession. I saw no need for a middle man, as I spoke with God myself and I tired in making up sins to justify time in the Confessional booth. These weren't the ways of the God I experienced.

Growing up in a religious setting, I feel grateful to have been immersed from a young age in the icons and rituals of Roman Catholicism. I spent a lot of time in church and, although I never enjoyed being around that many people at once or the guilt trips parishioners endured regarding giving money to the church, I loved the environment and ritual. The Latin and High Masses, frankincense, Holy Communion and other Sacraments, the statues and stained glass depictions of the Virgin Mother, Jesus and of the saints, stories of healings and spiritual travails and miracles, fed my spirit. I traveled inward during these times, finding a deep, silent place where I connected with these people, energies and places. This carried into adulthood, as I am still awed by stories of St. Francis of Assisi, St. Teresa of Avila and others. I love High Masses and being in churches, especially when sitting quietly alone in a pew. Churches are sacred vessels, much like natural power spots on the earth, and the mystical legacies of saints and holy people proliferate in Catholicism. As a child, I believe I naturally tuned into the archetypal forces underlying the dogma of organized religion.

Light Beings

It was during my early childhood that I also spoke with spirit guides seemingly unrelated to my religious cosmology. These beings said they lived distantly in the universe, yet were always with me. I don't remember seeing them, but felt and heard them. It was similar in some ways to being with God, yet often with more energy in my body and, in addition to words, I could sometimes hear faint music or a tone inside my ears. Their words flowed into my mind as telepathy. When the beings spoke I listened attentively, understanding everything they said. Yet, as soon as I did, the words and meaning often evaporated like a mist from my mind, after which I couldn't recall anything. But I would feel intensely one with them during and after they spoke – as if I extended way out to their universe but remaining here and in my body at the same time. It was blissful.

I sense that these (which I now call) Star or Light Beings, have been with me all my life, though I don't remember being consciously aware of them before the age of five, except for one incident... In my thirties, through energy work I re-experienced everything I saw and felt when I was being born. Upon feeling the temperature of the room and being overwhelmed by the bright lights, a highly medicated mother, and people in white coats and masks, I wanted to go back. I saw above me the Light Beings in the spiritual realms that I had come from and determined not to leave them. I had similar experiences through my childhood as there was a lot of chaos and strife in my growing years. I would go out under the star-lit sky and ask the beings to take me back. I knew they were my true, spiritual, family and I was often devastated in feeling abandoned by them on this planet. The Star Beings were continuously with me yet as a backdrop to my life unless I became very relaxed or upset such as at these times. Then they would be at the forefront.

It's often much the same today. When I'm deeply relaxed, just rousing from sleep, or focus on them, I feel their presence and they may speak. The words carry a tangible vibration I feel in my body, which is expanded, loving, and makes me feel held by the universe. It is like a light trance-state and the words themselves carry vibration, often dissolving from my memory just as I grasp their meaning. Then, just the energy remains, mostly as an indescribable love that fills me, like my very soul has been touched. The words are always more than words and their concrete meaning – they are energy touching and awakening something deep inside me, my soul, and connection to God.

I was a quiet child, often teased for appearing spaced-out. Looking back, I understand this to be because I coexisted in another, more expansive reality at the same time as being in this one. When taunted for staring off into space, I'd explain that my mind needed a rest. I grew agitated in going too long without this 'rest', as I couldn't stand the disconnection I felt without it. Within it, I went to a place that was connected, expansive and in touch with the whole universe. Of course, I couldn't have articulated that as a child, yet I was conscious from a very young age that this everyday reality was an overlay reality to the real one. In the real one lived my Light Beings and the real, whole, me. It was as if who I really was extended from earth way out to the universe, to these beings. Their tones and vibrations and the expanded feelings in my body were different from anything I knew in regular reality. Regardless, it was intimately familiar – it was home. It was during this time that I began to feel that although I was reluctant to be here, I had come for a reason. That, and my profound relationship with nature, gave me solace.

I spent much of my childhood climbing trees, playing for hours in stream beds, collecting stones at the ocean, and lying on the grass gazing at the clear blue sky or watching the clouds endlessly morph new worlds. I was a dreamer, which kept my intuitive side open yet often made it hard for people to understand me, as well as for me to know how to fit in. From my youth I experienced intense awakenings, what I now call energy transmissions, within nature. I could cry at nature's beauty and how deeply she touched me. I would, and still do, sit by a stream bed or among a grove of trees or on a snow drift watching a darkening sky, resting my mind and quietly absorbing nature's qualities. Concerns, worries, limitations evaporate or shift into spaciousness, love and belonging.

I felt many of the same things in nature that I did with the Light Beings and now realize this is because the earth carries the universe within. Everything in our physical reality is made of the dust, energy and consciousness of the stars. Although not aware then of why I did it, I believe I learned at a young age to merge with the natural world in an attempt to find spirit here in the physical, on earth. It was a way for me to understand how I could stay here. I have the same feelings today. It can be hard for me to be true to my own rhythm which runs contrary to our frenetic modern world and by resting within nature's subtle rhythms I experience my total myself. I remember that I am one with the universe. As a child, I once merged so strongly with a grouping of trees that I cried in having to go back into the house when the sun went down. I wanted to *be* a tree and sleep with them in their dark night. This resonance has only deepened through the years.

In looking back, it's striking to see how intimately my childhood experiences with spirit guides and nature impacted me and my life's work. This is true, regardless of the fact that by around the ages of ten and eleven, I started to forget about the Light Beings altogether. Despite continued connection to nature and a growing interest in eastern philosophy, I went through my public school teenage years with no thought to them at all. I don't believe they ever left me but that I became distracted and unconsciously adopted more mainstream values. When in my early twenties the Light Beings came to mind, I was embarrassed in remembering my experiences with them. As an art student with a dual major in psychology, I reduced them to hallucination, disassociation or at best figured they were harmless 'imaginary friends'. I now see my long journey back to my Light Beings so clearly.

Transitions

After my hometown boyfriend of five years broke up with me early in my junior year, I dropped out of college to work at a deli counter at a local supermarket. I was depressed, directionless and cut off from friends. My parents supported this decision as their working class values told them I'd be better off making money than spending it. Over the months I grew very close to a girl named Kara who also worked at the deli. Kara was twenty-one, sweet, funny and very kind to me at a time when I was really suffering. She and her boyfriend, Danny, were planning their wedding and wanted to have children soon after they were married. Kara and I spent the days cutting cheesecake, scooping ham salad, wrapping bagels, laughing and talking. My heart began to slowly mend until one day Kara didn't show up for work. She'd had an asthma attack, slipped into a coma and died soon after. I became despondent, quit my job and moved out of town. More lost than before, I fell in with a fast crowd and spent the next two years living in a haze. Drugs were rampant and danger abounded. Nature and spirit guides were long gone, replaced by an unconscious death wish. Many young people I knew at that time never escaped this realm… A girl I shared a house with when first coming to town was strangled in her apartment a few years later, another man shot in the head while closing up a restaurant at two o'clock in the morning. He'd taken over my job when I decided I'd had enough.

I traveled throughout Europe and in the US for a while to get my head straight and was back in school within a couple of years. Traveling had sparked an interest in other cultures and my childhood love for nature resurfaced as a deep concern for the global environment. Studying World Issues at the School for International Training in Vermont fulfilled both passions, and I interned in India. The spiritual doorways started opening again. Living in India presented a haunting déjà vu as it was shockingly familiar, connecting me deeply again with spirit and nature. Each evening during my stay in a Christian Ashram in Poona I climbed with the nuns up the ladders to meditate on the flat-topped roof. These were esoteric Christian nuns, unlike the Sisters of the Holy Cross of my childhood. They moved and breathed with the spirit and history of the lands upon which they lived. As we sat in silence against the dusk sky, thousands of bats flew out of enormous tree boughs silhouetting the firmament. God was everywhere. Despite its magic, India was also tragic and overwhelming in terms of poverty and suffering. But viewing every phase of life right there on the streets, from birth to death, had its own truth, and so, power. In addition to my work with mentally handicapped Indian kids, I traveled extensively, and studied yoga and natural healing.

Upon my return, I was changed. India had evoked something intangible yet very real. In the months following, I had profound spiritual experiences. Once, upon waking up, a seven foot being made of swirling bands of light walked through my bedroom door. A blissful, humming energy pervaded the room and I fell into an altered state, unable to move. The being walked over to me, reached down, grasped my hand and began pulling me up out of the bed. But I soon realized that it was lifting me out of my physical body which still lay on the bed beneath me. The lightness and energy I felt in lifting out was at first ecstatic, yet when my spiritual body was out to my thighs I panicked. Suddenly I became very heavy and sleepy, the being released my hand, and I fell back into my body into a deep slumber. Another time, a friend and I were sitting in my room talking when a similar blissful, humming energy enveloped me. I watched as my friend's face and the room around me dissolved into a misty white light. All I remembered afterwards was being immersed in light. I came back to my body and into the room with a jolt to see my friend and I were still sitting together looking at each other, yet with mouths now agape! Fifteen clock minutes had passed during which we'd both been suspended in light with no other recollection. I never connected these incidents to my childhood Light Beings. I had too solidly relegated that experience to a mental health issue.

Buddhism and New Spirits

Over the next years, I became an avid student of Tibetan Buddhism under a Tibetan teacher in Colorado. As with India, Buddhism was another homecoming. It reverberated some of the power I had experienced in Catholicism, yet brought things to a deeper level. The rituals and iconography were vividly familiar, as if from another lifetime. A more systematized version of the *entering the silence* I had done as a child, the practices taught me to relax and work with my mind so it didn't shroud my natural essence. My graduate studies at Naropa University paralleled this journey, experientially applying it to therapeutic work with others. Staying with my cross-cultural focus, I interned with a Hispanic mental health facility whose tiny staff included a *currandera* – a traditional medicine-woman from Mexico. I had minor experiences with other realities during graduate school that increased when I attended a Tibetan Buddhist seminary in 1986 after completing my studies at Naropa.

Two months before the program, I began having lucid dreams. My teacher, Chogyam Trungpa Rinpoche, appeared to me in a cave with monks and in other locations set deep within the earth. He would whisper into my ear and blow energy into me that felt like a warm wind. In those moments, I felt something awaken in me beyond what I can explain.

More experiences came during seminary itself, held in a somewhat remote location in the Rocky Mountains. The land spoke to me. I attuned to weather patterns, winds, the skies and land. I felt as if the elements were communicating and dancing with me, and I had resonance with them beyond words. The land, practices and teachings evoked my inner vision. Sometimes I experienced ghosts, I saw phenomena in the clouds and beings with turquoise eyes, and many times before dawn I felt I was awakened by my teacher. When I shared the visions I was having with my meditation instructor I was told to, "Go back to your breath", which was good mind training – a helpful lesson in detachment, discernment and being grounded that served me well into the future. Yet it also frustrated me. I grew quiet about my experiences and years would pass before I would discover how to honor and integrate them. They didn't go away.

One day, a group of us participants hiked up at high noon to a point overlooking the rugged valley. We mediated while sitting directly on the earth, a welcomed relief after the hours spent practicing inside. Relaxing more deeply with each breath, time passed imperceptibly. Eventually, one person in our circle got up to wander silently over the land. After several more moments two others ventured off in separate directions, guided by their senses and intuition in an exercise called *aimless wandering*, a transition from intensive practices. Without realizing it I also stood up, ambling toward a thin grassy path leading up the side of the slope. Then it struck – it wasn't me who was walking.

Was I possessed? I breathed deeply to ease my growing panic, but the feeling was still with me – as if someone was directing my body's movement, another consciousness inhabiting me. Had I opened to confused, dead spirits, to ghosts on this land? There had been stories that summer… a distressed female spirit lived close to the old cabin by the stream and our Tibetan teacher ordered the structure to be burned. The tale circulated that he did so, and had performed a ceremony, to release her.

I tuned-in for several moments, instinctively knowing this energy wouldn't harm me. I thought to communicate telepathically. "Who are you, what is your story?" I sensed an adult male but nothing else. Then, warm, pleasurable sensations washed through me melting my resistance. My eyes became one with his eyes, my body becoming his body. As I let the feelings of him in, it was exquisite, familiar. Moving as one now we followed the grassy path to an open area, stopping to look out over the land. The scent of hot butterscotch flooded my nostrils from the sun-scorched pines. My eyes brimmed with tears. It was *his* emotion, now ours together, I expressed as I sensed him say, "How good it is to see this land again." After some time we followed the path to a rocky, dusty trail. Each step was ecstatic. Later, in spotting people from the group a short distance ahead of us, this spirit with whom I shared so intimately gently left. Had he been someone in the community who'd died, whose ashes had been buried on this land? I strolled toward the group. I told no-one of my experience.

Nine years following this encounter in the Rockies, this spirit would come into my life again.

Starry Brotherhood

The years since attending Buddhist seminary had proved spiritually quiet and it was during this time that I got married and had a child. The birth of my second child in 1991 was extremely difficult, initiating a lengthy period of illness during which my sensitivities grew acute. Other worldly phenomena now again surged. I'd had mystical experiences throughout my adult life but they'd mostly come sporadically, occasionally bleeding through the mundane fabric of my days but then receding into the background. Now the spiritual floodgates opened and mundane life was all but lost. The veils between this and other worlds had evaporated. Some of the stories of this period are told in my book, *The Good Remembering*. Others include time lapses, energy transmissions and wild synchronicities.

Once, when putting my toddlers down for a nap, I lay with them on a futon in between their warm little bodies. As soon as they fell asleep, I carefully hoisted myself up to lift quietly out of the bed without stirring them. I was halfway up and off the bed when a powerful force overtook me, freezing me in position. The world around me, including my body, children, and the room, dissolved. I saw nothing and had no physical sensations. Soon I heard a low, pervasive hum. I felt as if I were everywhere and nowhere at once, suspended in a vast, dark space. Within this space, a glowing symbol-inscripted disc appeared in front of me. Just as I saw the symbol clearly, I became aware of my spiritual body and the disc abruptly flew into my third eye, its energy instantaneously suffusing me. Another symbol encoded disc appeared and the same thing happened, then another, until *twelve* glowing discs penetrated and anchored their energy within me. I came to, still hovering, and now shaking, over my kids on the bed. The spirits had my attention again.

Such were some of the otherworldly events and extraordinary feelings coursing through my body-mind during the prolonged state of heightened spiritual awareness following my son's life-threatening birth. Overwhelmed, one day I prayed to God, the Buddhist lineage, spirit guides… whoever was out there who could tell me what was happening to me and why. I resolved that even two sentences could reassure me. Two sentences quickly turned into two pages and then several times a week for the next three months I was writing messages from *Star Beings*.

These beings telepathically communicated with me, explaining that they were inseparable from us, expanded aspects of our own consciousness. Some star guides had lived in the flesh on earth and others had never been incarnate. Some connected via individual human personalities, others through a collective voice. The most sublime conversed only through vibration. I experienced these as neither male nor female, transcending our ideas of gender. I was invited into this Starry Brotherhood and worked with a star-guide-in-training, the very being I had experienced at Buddhist seminary so many years back. What deep love I felt for and from this one, who had a distinctly human personality.

It was wrenching when the time came to let this one go, as releasing the spirit as a separate form was the only way to fully merge with it, its loving essence becoming one with my own. I also trained intimately with an Overcasting Soul who was different, closer to the God Source, and never spoke. Being in this presence was blissful, sacred, and purely energetic. Thoughts and emotions completely relaxed, all fixations dissolving within this space. I was one with everything and very present in my body and in this reality, at the same time expanding way out into the universe. I was one with God. These were so similar to the experiences of my childhood. This was the same Light Being, the same God.

It took me years to fully grasp the implications of all that was happening to me and the message itself. Though responding to my prayer the transmission was not personal to me, but a gift from the Light Beings to guide us all through changing times.

The Star Beings made clear that their purpose was to help us wake up. Trying to hold onto or solidify the spirits beyond this goal limited their expression. As we're one with these beings, the invitation is to embody their/our Light, love and wakefulness, allowing it to touch and transform every part of us and our world. They encourage us to shine our Light at a time when the world desperately needs it – we can manifest our God qualities here on earth and illumine all of existence simply by being fully who we are. This is what the star energies called AN. For those of us here on earth, the call is to open to a new way of being, a new consciousness which will heal our split from spirit. As we fulfill our human destiny here on this planet, guidance is ever available to us. In becoming one with our own Light we align with the deeper rhythms of change, the underlying intelligence of these times.

I had only shared about the Star Beings with my closest friend but, after six months, I finally told my husband of AN. Later that week, our three-year-old returned from a neighbor's holding a golf ball. Eben walked across the living room, stretched up his chubby arm and offered me the ball. I thanked him, but humored him to give it to his dad who was an avid golfer. Eben insisted on giving the ball to me. I took it, but when Michael and I glanced at the small sphere in my outstretched hand our mouths dropped open: "He's right Llyn, it's for you." Two large letters covered the golf ball's surface – AN. The universe is synchronistic and has a sense of humor.

Consciously reconnecting with the Light Beings of my childhood changed the course of my life. The extreme nature of my experiences caused me to look outside of my culture to seek a broader philosophical context that helped me to understand all that had happened to me. I found this within indigenous shamanism and worked for many years in remote parts of the world with peoples who revered the spirits, lands and elements that sustained and were one with them, as well as honored their ancestors from the stars. Just as India and Buddhism were a homecoming, indigenous shamanism embraced me as its child. With it has come a deep appreciation for my journey and greater clarity about what I came here to do. The soul calls us to shine the truth of who we are and each of our paths will be unique. My own journey was known to me as a young child but through many years it appeared that I had forgotten it. Yet the soul is persistent, especially in these times of change, and the starry energies *quicken* us to its voice.

Awakening to Star Energy

There are many ways to experience and activate our starry essence, yet among the most important is to connect through nature. Mainly hidden to ordinary perception, sublime forces, living cosmic intelligences, flow through the streams and oceans, lie concealed within trees, the earth, winds, stones, and radiate from the skies and celestial bodies. Our Earth Mother is alive and sentient and we cannot fully manifest our human potential until we forge a deeply conscious relationship with her. As do indigenous peoples all over the world, star wisdom urges us to look through the eyes of the heart to see our world as it truly is. In this way we become replenished and remember the magic and miracles of our birthright. A shift of perception is all that's needed. '*The Good Remembering'* includes guidance for attuning to the rhythms of these times, as well as powerful practices to reconnect with the Earth and manifest our Light qualities. Through our hearts and bodies we can attune to our larger, spiritual presence and that of the world around us. One way to do this is by *entering the silence* as I did as a child. We in modern cultures aren't so comfortable with stillness and space, yet allowing and going deeply into them awakens us to our soul's voice. It reconnects us to the larger reality with which we are one, yet have forgotten.

When in nature, try not having an agenda for an hour or two and take some time to sit by a swiftly moving stream. Relax your mind and open your senses. Notice what you see, hear, feel, smell, taste as well as what you sense beyond the physical. Don't think about it, *feel* it. As you do, feel your deep gratitude for what you look upon and invite the beauty all around you as a palpable experience. Don't try to communicate with your mind, telepathically get answers, or conceptualize what nature spirits are present with you. Simply appreciate and *be*. Invite the exquisite fullness of silence. When you notice your mind wandering or conjuring come back to your immediate experience, keep coming back to simply breathing and *being*. Venture more and more deeply into the sounds, sights, smells, and the natural physical phenomena all around you. As you rest more thoroughly and become simple in your presence, oneness envelopes you. This is elusive, as you may not recognize its power until later that day, or even the next. In simply being present and open in nature, we can mix with its subtle and cosmic qualities, which awaken our own.

Nature has great gifts to bestow, yet requires our relaxed attention. You can do the same thing next to a lapping lake, in a grove of trees, or if you can't go outside you can look out your window at the moon, or gaze through the glass at the sky or the sunlight dappling the trees. Gazing is an ancient shamanic, Buddhist and starry practice. It opens our eyes to see, enter, and become one with the sacredness all around us. Open the windows if you can in order to harmonize with nature's sounds. Open with the heart and mind of a child and push the boundaries of *boredom,* which is only a trick of ego. Surrender fully to the natural world with no expectation, inviting quiet and stillness as friends. A child's heart is trusting, present, and one with what is. As the universe is reflexive, sentient and inseparable from us, our very desire to open ignites the universe's longing to dance and to create with us. As we remember our connection with all things a new consciousness will arise. From this, we and our universe will dream the world freshly.

SOUND TRANSFORMATIONS

by Tom Kenyon

Tom Kenyon is a researcher, a therapist, a musician, sound healer and teacher. For over twenty years his research group, Acoustic Brain Research, has been a leader in the field of psychoacoustics and the use of sound and music to access the creative abilities of the brain and mind. The ABR Library has both science and a proven track record behind it and is in use by therapists, clinicians and by laypersons all over the world.

When I was around four years old, I would sit on the swing in the back yard and swing for hours, singing to the air. I was singing to angels and they sang back to me. My voice has always played an important part in my dealings with Spirit from day one.

As an undergraduate at University, I was on my way to a psychology class and I clairvoyantly saw two angels on either side of me. I'd become a rationalist by then, so I was very upset by the experience – I told them they had to leave… and they did. It was another ten years before I would become comfortable with that type of phenomena again.

I was still firmly anchored in the logical mind when the Hathors showed up on my doorstep. I was a practicing psychotherapist and I had a private practise working with Ericksonian hypnosis, which is used in altered states of consciousness to help a person move through issues. I was also working with a University laboratory and a team of independent researchers to document the effects of sound and music on the brain, so I was very much involved in a rational field, both in the research and in my private practice.

It all started about twenty years ago, when we moved from North Carolina to Washington State. The moving company had lost our furniture – they didn't know where it was, so we had a three-day delay before our things arrived. At night, I felt compelled to stand on our new deck that looked out over water and start tracing very strange geometric shapes in the air. It was like a Tai Chi movement, but instead I was tracing spheres and dodecahedrons. It was totally unlike me and I thought it was very odd at the time, but I was okay with it because it was dark and nobody could see me!

About three days into this, I was meditating and two beings showed up. I have meditated regularly since I was 18 and I wasn't trying to invoke this experience… it just happened spontaneously. One of these beings identified himself as a Hathor and proceeded to teach me about geometry and the structure of the nervous system.

I thought it was interesting until one of them said, "We entered your universe through the portal of Sirius and then we settled in your solar system on Venus." That was a total clash with my belief system about what was possible.

I wasn't afraid of channeling beings from other dimensions. Many years ago, I had a friend – a researcher at University – who was developing an automated anesthesia technology and was also interested in this type of phenomenon. I would go into a hypnotic trance and channel, and he would record and transcribe what the different beings that had come through had said. We did this for about two years as a scientific experiment. I had a logical foundation for my understanding of how channelling works as I was familiar with how it worked and what the neurology was. I wasn't upset by the experience of channelling… but I *was* upset by what they told me!

Nevertheless, the Hathor gave me a series of mental exercises that would make a person's brain consciousness operate much more efficiently and effectively. I tried them and they then quizzed me on what I had experienced. Afterwards he said, "We want you to present this to other people so that you know this is real, that it works for everyone."

I wasn't about to go into the world and claim that this had come from such a source, and so, having the researcher-based mind that I have, I decided to do some beta tests. I formed three groups in Washington State and presented this information and took people through the processes I had been taught.

As a result of these tests, people had amazing experiences and I had to acknowledge that whatever the source of this information was, whether it was real or an aspect of my own psyche, it had value because it helped other people. I began to work with it that way, as if it were an aspect of my own consciousness that had information that was valuable.

I carried on working with this technology with people for quite a few years, never saying anything about where the information had come from, until one day the Hathors came to me. They were growing in number – there were more than four at this point (I now have thirteen that work with me directly) and they said, "We want you to write a book."

"Yeah, right!" I replied, "I have no intention of writing a book! I have no intention of putting my credentials and my credibility on the line by saying that I work with beings from another world!"

"That's okay, it will be handled," they replied.

I didn't tell anyone about this except my wife at the time. I just dismissed it. Nine months later, I was running a workshop in California when a woman approached me and said, "Your Hathors have contacted me. I have a publishing company and I would like to publish your book. They said it was very important that this material get out into the world and I would like to help."

My mouth almost fell open because nobody knew about this! "I don't have time to write a book!" I protested.

"All you have to do," she replied, "is record tapes and we have people that will transcribe them and put them into a book format – it won't take any work on your part other than that."

Even though I am very deeply in the intuitive world, I still think that logic is an important piece of it all. I look for verifiable external things as significant information – and that was one of them. After a while, I came to realise that it is not just something of my own consciousness… there's something that's bigger than me involved in this, for sure.

I straddle both the esoteric and scientific worlds and for a certain number of people that's comforting. It helps to have a path that's based on logic even though ultimately at the end one has to give it all up. Logic is very good to have as one of our allies.

Being a logical-based person I'm still amazed at some of the things that get pulled off in their presence. About 10 years ago, they came to me and said, "We want you to establish a temple, a physical site."

"I'm not interested," I replied, "I don't have time… you go find the land."

"No problem!" was their reply.

I'd totally forgotten about this until, two or three years later, they came back and said,

"The land's been located." Several weeks went by and I had a telephone call. "A person in the Southwest would like to gift you with some land for you to do whatever you wish."

A non-profit organization was formed to receive it and, at the instruction of the Hathors, we built an initiatory temple called the Celestorium. It was essentially a portal where people could commune with the elements. This was created essentially through a technology that involved setting a 330-foot shaft of copper filled with programmed quartz crystal into the desert floor, covered, overlaid with a geometric grid and encased in stone. I occasionally take groups there for initiatory experiences. The energy is very clear – once you step foot into that area, it's like being in another world. It's very odd… you're obviously still in New Mexico, which is where it's located, but you're in many other worlds simultaneously. It is a fascinating experience. Whatever this technology is that involves the crystals and grid work, it unquestionably does something. It's fascinating to be standing physically in the desert but, within minutes, other realms are opening up to you, like you'd gone through days of ritual and mind-altering practices.

After 9/11, the Hathors shifted the emphasis of the temple towards earth healing and also asked that another one be established specifically for this purpose. Both sites operate as giant acupuncture needles in order to bring celestial energies to help earth as a living organism during this chaotic time.

For some time now, the Hathors have been saying that we are in the beginning of the earth changes. And the recent increases in the severity of storms and the changing weather patterns worldwide would seem to point to this. Since the Hathors first started giving me planetary information to be shared with others, they have always held the contention that human consciousness creatively interacts with the subtle energies of the planet, and that these interactions to some extent affect earthquake activity and even weather patterns. This concept is very outside the views of modern science, and yet something about it feels right to me.

I operate in my life as autonomously as I can. My guides come at critical moments when there is information they feel I need. I don't go to the Hathors and ask for things – they come to me when they feel it's important that I know. Usually it's around an area that I'm doing research in or exploring… then they sometimes come through. Quite a few people who work in this area, they talk to their guides constantly, but I really don't talk to mine that much. My attitude is very much: 'Don't bother me – if there's something important, you'll tell me ... otherwise I'm going to live my life the way that I feel that I want to live it'.

My guides have definite personalities – they even have differences of opinion! I have a very clear and strong visual impression of their appearance… but I rarely get that much detail unless it's really important. I lean more towards clairaudience and clairsentience.

I was answering questions toward the end of a Sound Healer's Training in Seattle, Washington in September 2005. A woman raised her hand and said that she worked with AIDS and HIV patients in Africa through a non-profit organization. She asked if I had any recordings or sound patterns that would help, as the situation was getting quite dire throughout that part of the world. I replied that I did not have anything substantive to offer, as my psycho-immunological work up to that time had been centered on general immunity and nothing that specific.

She then said that she had a request – a challenge actually. I recall the moment clearly as the room suddenly filled with a spiritual presence when she spoke. "I have a favor to ask of you. I know you are very busy, but North and South America, Europe and Africa are in distress and I know you can help."

The thought of adding one more thing to the list of growing projects I had committed myself to boggled my mind. I was about to stammer out something to this effect when I clairvoyantly noticed a being standing off to my right. He was an African shaman who was adding his weight to the request. And then all my guides came to me, and the stage was suddenly very full. I heard myself say, "I will find a way to create the time to do this."

Mind you, I had no idea how I would ever pull this off, given the fact that I was easily working fourteen to sixteen hours a day on other recording and writing projects. I was *running on empty* as the saying goes, plus Judi and I were in the midst of packing for another world teaching tour.

About four days after this encounter, I was awakened at three in the morning by my group of thirteen Hathors. They said that now was the time to begin working on the '*Immunity*' program. They said it would be pure vocal sound, without the use of any electronic frequencies, and would be channeled with the assistance of spiritual healers from many diverse realms of consciousness. They also informed me that most of the recording would usually take place around 3AM since this was the time of least interference from collective thought forms – including my own. They put me on notice, in other words, that I would not be getting much sleep for the next few weeks.

In fact, it took four weeks to record all thirty-two tracks, each of them consisting of a different being channeling his or her spiritual light into audible sound. It was an exhilarating and mind-expanding experience that kept pushing the edges of my own personal paradigms and beliefs.

The first two tracks were laid down by the Hathors. These tracks, I was told, would be of assistance with many types of cancer in addition to HIV/AIDS and other immunological problems. I was also told that the final recording would address immunity on many levels – not just physical, but emotional and spiritual as well. How it would accomplish this feat was not clear to me at the beginning, but as the recording process unfolded I began to see the larger picture. '*Immunity*' is not just the physical response of our immune systems to immunological threats. It is both the biological sense of self and the spiritual sense of self-identity.

After the first two tracks, the vibrational energy of the spirit healers changed considerably. An African shaman appeared to me clairvoyantly and indicated that he wished to offer the assistance of plant spirit medicine, meaning that he called upon the spirits of specific plants to help alleviate physical and spiritual illness. I knew about this type of healing and had experienced it myself on two separate occasions from two different practitioners. This way of working with plant spirits seems to have long traditions throughout much of North and South America, as well as Africa. This form of medicine may have traditions in other parts of the world as well – it's just that I am not familiar with them.

What struck me about this shaman/healer was that he had obviously not been in a body on Earth for a long time since many of the plants he used for healing were no longer physically present in Africa. They had long ago become extinct. For a moment he seemed to be in grief and disbelief. And then I watched him traverse the stars and the spirit worlds to find his spirit brothers and sisters (his plant medicine) in other realms of consciousness. He then called upon them and brought their spirit medicine back to Earth in the sounds that he sang through my voice. When I finished that sequence, I was sobbing from the power of the energies and from the pathos of what I had just witnessed. I stepped out of the recording booth to find a large African male standing etherically in the studio. I recognized him as a Masai warrior. He bowed and we communed for a few moments in silence – him thanking me for keeping my promise, and me thanking him for his visitation.

Over the years, I have become quite used to channeling many different types of spiritual energies and beings in the course of my work. But I had never channeled so many diverse types of energies in such a short space of time, and the experience was deeply altering to my perceptions of the spirit worlds.

Some of the beings who sang their healing from the realms of light into the world of sound were recognizable to me— lamas from Tibet, healers from ancient Egypt, India and Persia. Some of them were alchemists of the highest order, and some of them were creator gods and goddesses from ancient times and places we have no names for.

About a third of the way into the recording process a group of angels began to download their *healing codes*. Each of these codes had specific geometries of light associated with them, and as each angel sang through me, I was elevated to such heights that I would literally stagger out of the recording booth when I was done with his or her sequence. Some of these angelic beings I recognized from Christian and Islamic traditions. But some of them were unknown to me. My only sense of them, besides their majesty and power was that they had been sent forth from the heart of the Divine to aid in the immense task of planetary healing.

I will never forget one session, about half way through the recording, in which I witnessed the Tao sending forth a form of pure *chi* (or life force) from the Formless Heaven into a sound pattern. The sound seemed to be not of this world, but at the same time, deeply healing. Every cell in my body was both comforted and nourished by these primordial sounds. During one session, I watched as the Blue Medicine Buddha called forth an exquisite form of healing light from the Sambhogaya (the Tibetan realm of pure light and sound). I watched as he wove the light together and lowered its vibrational frequencies from that of spiritual light into spiritual sound.

In one session, a Mongolian shaman called upon the horseheaded god of healing known as Hevajra by Tibetans. As I saw Hevajra manifest within the realms of light, I saw thousands of wild horses running across the plains of Mongolia—a potent symbol of the primal healing power that was being released through these sounds.

In other sessions, Native American shamans and healers would sing and call forth healing powers through their intention. One in particular affected me deeply – Buffalo Calf Woman – a legendary figure of immense healing power. Her tones shook with a potency that left me in both amazement and appreciation of the feminine power to heal.

For twenty-eight days, in the early hours of the morning, these extraordinary and diverse beings joined together in one common purpose – to release to the world a form of healing and potential at a time of desperate need. Spiritual lineages that rarely meet and were often in conflict in this world were joining together to create a healing power that left me stunned and speechless.

Toward the end of the recording process, both Magdalen and Yeshua added their voices to the healing choir, and for me, this was both calming and integrative in its effects.

Throughout the recording, I would listen to each new voice as it was added to the previous ones. There were a few times when the sounds were too catalytic, too strong and volatile. They left me, and those listening shaking from the release of too much personal negativity. With the addition of Magdalen and Yeshua, the release of negativity was still present, but with a sense of comfort and stability. A fertile ground for healing was completed. All that was required were the seeds of intention that each listener will sow as he or she listens to the codes.

It is now quite clear to me that this unique psychoacoustic program is a co-creative matrix. It is an auditory trail of spiritual light whereby the healing intentions and energies of these spirit healers can be joined with the intentions of those listening.

My mother was a professional singer, so I inherited her vocal abilities. The Hathors work primarily through vibrational energies of emotion, especially ecstasy and love, and through sound. My voice was the perfect vehicle for them to express themselves – not so much the information that comes through language, but the transformation that comes through sound. Before I started working with the Hathors, I had a vocal range of slightly more than 3 octaves. As a result of working with them, my vocal range has expanded to almost 4 octaves. Because they work with sound so much and I have been in their field so much, when I merge with them I become like a tuning fork. I 'get out of the way', they come in and I resonate with their energy. Because it is such a high level vibration – the Hathors describe themselves as being from the 5th to the 9th and even to the 12th dimensions, depending on where they are individually – this has certainly stretched my mind and my understanding of different aspects of reality. It has definitely affected my work as a sound healer – I'm much more aware of how sound affects the subtle levels of consciousness and how a change in a sound can open up worlds in a person… lead them into a deeper contact with themselves.

I understand channeling simply being a receptive state of the brain and it has to do with shifting brain states and increasing alpha/theta activity so that a person can become more permeable, more open to different aspects of awareness than they're normally aware of or have access to.

I seem to be able to tune my brain to access any being or deity I choose. I think I was born with that ability. When I look back – at the time I didn't realise what I was doing, but I would interact with angels, devas, nature spirits… it's an ability I always had. As I began to understand it from a scientific and psychological standpoint, I knew what had to be done neurologically to support these states and I developed methods that I use now to do that. Essentially, I believe that anybody can develop this ability because it's inherent already in the human nervous system. It is simply making changes in the brain's activity so that you can have these experiences. There are ways to do that and it's available to anybody. Some people are born with that, some people have the ability more than others in this area, but it's something that can be developed by anyone.

INTERDIMENSIONAL CONSCIOUSNESS

by Lyssa Royal Holt

Since 1985, Lyssa has given seminars and sacred site tours for thousands around the world from the USA to Mexico, Japan, Europe, South America, Australia, South Africa and Russia. Her work is also featured in several books (in many languages) including 'Millennium: Tools for the Coming Changes', 'Preparing for Contact', 'Visitors from Within', and 'The Prism of Lyra'. Lyssa has appeared on numerous television and radio shows internationally, the most recent of which was a special produced by the Discovery Channel that is currently airing worldwide. Lyssa holds a B.A. in psychology. She is also a certified teacher of Taoist and Hatha yoga and continues to write and travel around the world. Though her teachings may range from ancient civilizations to yoga to inner spirituality to extraterrestrial consciousness, the practical applications of her work remain the utmost priority. She lives in Arizona, USA with her husband Ronald Holt.

As far back as I can remember, I have always been sensitive to spirit energy. I grew up in New England, USA, where there are many old houses that are haunted. When I was very young and didn't understand how to interpret the discomfort that I felt, I would just feel scared and think there were invisible beings in closets or dark hallways. But when I got older I realized that what I was sensing were spirits. There were a few times as a teenager where my parents had to take me away from an old house because of the uncomfortable sensations. I usually found out afterward that the place was haunted, or something traumatic had happened there.

As a child living in a very rural area, I would go outside to look for UFOs even at a young age. No-one influenced me to do this – I was the oddball of the family! I remember being very young and playing with my cousin. We would say that we were from the Pleiades, but we had lived in Orion, too. Now where would I come up with that? I look back at it now, and it makes sense, given the work that I've done as an adult. When I was very young, I wanted to be an astronaut and then an astronomer, until I realized you had to learn physics. Then I wanted to be a parapsychologist, in an age where no universities except for a few had a program to study such things! To me, beings in other realms (whether spirits or extraterrestrials) were simply a part of life and nothing strange.

In 1979, I had a UFO sighting with my family that was a turning point in my life. After that experience, I became very motivated to learn more about the spirit world and the reality of extraterrestrial life. I earned a B.A. in psychology, and during my studies I had to experiment with self-hypnosis. I learned that when I put myself in a hypnotic state that I could receive messages. Though vague at first, this ability grew as the years went by.

In the early 1980s, I had a very vivid dream in which a young Hindu boy appeared to me, touched my chakras (energy centers), and told me clearly, "You will be a channel." Understandably, this made me a little bit nervous, but my curiosity was stronger than my nerves. I somehow attracted a channeling teacher who was being studied by professors at

UCLA. I took her class and learned the 'ins' and 'outs' of channeling from a psychological perspective. The training wasn't simply new age 'fluff' – it was psychological in nature, which really appealed to me.

My natural ability to receive messages intensified and, in 1985, I began channeling for the public and have never stopped – not because of any ambition, but simply because it is what I am meant to do. When you know in your heart that you are meant to be a vehicle for a greater plan, there is nothing to do but to surrender to it.

The guides I work with primarily made their presence known in 1988 and I've been working with them since then. Numerous guides and helpers have come and gone (and still make appearances now and then), but these two have been very consistently there.

Germane

Neither male nor female, 'he' chose the name 'Germane' because, in English, it means 'coming from the same source'. He wanted to reinforce the idea that he comes from the same Source as we all do. Germane is a 'consciousness system' or group consciousness rather than an individual being. 'He' describes 'his' realm of consciousness as follows… If a bunch of planetary systems evolved themselves to the point where the barriers between them diminished, and the consciousness was non-physical in nature (not connected to physical bodies), then a consciousness system would be formed. He says that he is an amalgamation of the consciousness of our galactic family as it is integrated into one energy system. He has been a primary source of my channeling based on our galactic family.

Sasha

She says that she is a physical female from the Pleiades, existing in what she describes as the 'fourth density' – a consciousness state that still has physical bodies but whose consciousness is much more integrated than human consciousness. She also says that she is my reincarnational future self. She came to me after a series of UFO sightings while I was living in Los Angeles in the mid-1980s, but claims that she has been contacting me since childhood. While this information might sound a bit fantastic (and I was skeptical at first), Sasha has proven to me over and over again that she is who she says she is and I have come to trust her. The teachings and information that she shares always seeks to encourage spiritual growth, personal empowerment, and the evolution of human consciousness.

My allies are an interdimensional consciousness that serve as mentors and teachers for me. Sometimes, if I learn a new system of knowledge that was previously foreign to me (such as sacred geometry for example), they will 'translate' those teachings to me in a way that I can understand. Whether they are another part of my psyche or actual 'separate' beings, this has been remarkable to me. It is like having your own source of spiritual teaching without leaving your own backyard.

Generally, when there is a time set up for a formal channeling session, they are always there, ready to speak. There was only one time when this didn't happen… I went into trance and they didn't show up. I just sat there wondering what was going on, until someone outside started yelling, *"Fire! Fire!"* The apartment complex where I was channeling was burning down. Later, they said, "We knew the session wasn't going to happen because of the fire, so we didn't come. It was also a way to train you to trust us!" That was quite a humbling experience.

People often mistakenly assume that, because I am a channel, I always have the answers in every moment. But my guides say that I still need to live my life and learn and grow, and that being told what to do all the time serves no-one. Over the 20 years that I've been channeling, I have come to trust that the guides have a 'bird's eye view', so I can trust that if they have something to say to me, it is time to listen!

The messages that I receive fall into two categories: for myself, and for others. When I channel for others, the messages are spoken through me while I am in an altered state of consciousness. My brain is used like a translation device for the thoughts of the guides and the messages are spoken using my vocabulary. If I don't possess the vocabulary that they need, they will use metaphor instead. At other times in my own life, they will sometimes show up spontaneously to teach me something for a life lesson. However, when I am receiving messages for myself, they can come through dreams, synchronicities, or what I call 'downloads'. It is hard to describe, but I don't 'hear voices' per se – it is more of a telepathic download. They will 'download' a compressed batch of information that unfolds into understanding, unravels itself, in my consciousness as and when it is needed.

Because my guides started communicating to me through channeling when I was very young (age 24), they have been a part of almost half of my life. I cannot imagine not having them there. Sometimes people ask questions like, "Wow, it must be amazing to have that ability." But to me, it is normal and I do believe that it is a skill that can be learned, though some people might have a natural ability. I so enjoy teaching students to see their own potentials of channeling! I am very careful about never taking this ability for granted and always respecting it. One of the things my teachers had me learn early on in my development as a channel is that we channels always have to watch our ego – it will seek to filter what is received, which is natural for the ego to do. As you develop this ego-watching ability, you learn so much about yourself and channeling becomes not only a gift to give to others, but a tool for the growth of the channel as well. I am so grateful for this experience and opportunity in my life.

My experiences in communicating with dolphins began in 1988. I describe these in my book, *'Preparing for Contact'*. Myself and several friends went to the marine park Sea World in San Diego, California. Seven of us stood together at the dolphin petting pool. In the pool were pilot whales and several species of dolphins, all being fed and kept busy by many children and adults. Spontaneously, we began to emit a single vocal tone. As each person joined in, the sound reverberated around the tank. All dolphin petting stopped. Slowly, all the bottle nosed dolphins grouped together and came directly to us. As this happened, we began to feel an overwhelming sense of joy.

These bottle nosed dolphins then, in unison, bobbed their heads and chests out of the water right in front of us. We kept toning. The dolphins closed their eyes and, with a look of utter serenity, basked in the sounds we were making. The dolphins' bellies turned bright pink in their excitement. After the experience reached its peak, the toning stopped and the dolphins made eye contact with us. Then they returned to being fed fish by the tourists.

This experience changed us that day. In our exuberance, we proceeded to the huge orca tank that housed two orcas at the time. They were swimming around with disinterest, ignoring the few people who pounded on the tank. We stood in a secluded location at one of the tanks. Still buoyed by the excitement of the dolphin encounter, we began to emit a tone vocally directly to the Plexiglas of the orca tank. Several minutes later, we began to hear whale song. The urge was to stop toning in order to hear the beautiful music, but instead we kept toning.

To our amazement, we saw the massive body of an orca approach. He stopped directly in front of the group on the other side of the Plexiglas and began singing. The orca made direct eye contact with us as we sang together. The emotion was so overwhelming, that tears began flowing. We placed our hands upon the tank and the orca drew closer – still maintaining eye contact. His songs felt like piercing waves of ecstasy. Eventually, the singing and toning stopped. We returned to being human, and the orca returned to being an orca. But for those few brief minutes, we connected.

This began an interest in interspecies communication – not only with cetaceans but with extraterrestrial consciousness as well. Since 2000, we have had the good fortune of working closely with a dolphinarium in Mexico where we are given an opportunity to experiment and have further interspecies contact experiences. While the experiences are too numerous to name, here is a summary of one profound experience from 2001:

Mauricio (the owner of the dolphinarium) totally surprised us by inviting us for a private swim with the dolphins in the evening after the group left. We could wear snorkel gear and have private time in the water with the dolphins. Because I am such a poor swimmer, I had to put the wet suit on and then the life vest. This way, I could interact with the dolphins and not have to worry about keeping myself above water.

As soon as I got in the water, it was amazing. I moved away from the steps and five of the six dolphins immediately surrounded me in a tight circle, with just their melons and blowholes above the water, silently watching me. They closed the circle around me so tightly that I couldn't move. I just had to float with them while we had a silent communion. I could feel my heart open more widely than I've ever felt, and I had the interesting sensation of watching myself outside of myself and I noticed that there was no fear and I was totally in the moment. I was in the water with five 'alien' beings surrounding me and it was a moment of utter humility and communion. They were so close that they were almost touching me, silently floating in a circle around me with their heads pointed toward me. Honestly, it felt like the movie *'Close Encounters of the Third Kind'*, when the aliens came and took Richard Dreyfuss into the spaceship at the end.

For the first few minutes we stayed in that circle. One at a time they approached me and gently put their heads or noses under my hands, nuzzling my body, letting me pet their bellies and talking so I could feel their sound waves under my hands. They intuitively knew that I didn't swim well and they were so incredibly gentle.

Then Lluvia (the largest female, 600 pounds!) slowly raised herself out of the water and floated belly-to-belly with me. Her nose (rostrum) was about 4 inches away from my face and I just floated there enjoying the connection, but wondering what she wanted me to do. Then I telepathically heard her say, "Kiss me!" To my amazement and delight she bent her head and placed her rostrum on my lips. I leaned closer too and we had a long kiss that just melted my heart. [Note: In the trained dolphin swim, the dolphins understand that humans value a "kiss" - they are trained to kiss humans but rarely do it without prompting by the trainer.] Lluvia is quite an amazing being. In that moment I felt like I could see into her heart and further – to the depths of her cosmic consciousness.

About five minutes later, after Lluvia had swam around me for awhile, she popped up again and kissed me once more for an even longer time. It was both so natural and yet so surreal. I am totally in love with Lluvia. She has an amazing depth to her being.

A little bit later I was silently floating and I kept feeling someone under me, poking at my feet and making me laugh. As I looked down into the water, I saw Brisa looking up at me. Her head was at my stomach level, with her body parallel to mine. She was just gazing up at me under the water and I just gazed back at her and felt her enormous heart. We floated like that for a long time and I felt such a deep love and reverence. My heart was just exploding.

By this time, Mauricio saw how gentle we were with the dolphins and how happy they were, so instead of removing Ron and I from the pool, he invited the others to join us. That is when I realized that the dolphins were interacting with each of us individually according to the way each of us value contact. For me, I value silence, stillness, touch, and telepathic connection, and that is what I received.

We were in the water with them for about an hour. Later, I asked Ron if he felt there was a difference swimming like that with captive dolphins versus swimming with wild ones – I was wondering if captivity might have made connecting with them less profound. He said, "Absolutely not," and that these captive dolphins have just as much joy, despite their captivity. The biggest difference was that we knew these dolphins as individuals because we had spent two weeks with them. So it was even more personal and intimate and even more of a deep bonding experience.

In 2002, we started to notice strange bubbles of light appearing in photographs (from digital and non-digital cameras alike). It only appeared at workshops when groups went deeply into their hearts. At first it was a spontaneous phenomenon and we could not predict when the orbs would appear. We collected the photos and began to create a presentation. However, as the years went by we began to be able to predict when they would appear based on what was happening in the environment. We found that certain heart-opening exercises at workshops would create more orbs in photographs. They appeared in spiritual environments such as churches or temples. Then, around 2003, we started photographing them from different angles on different cameras simultaneously, and we came to see for certain that they were real, and not just dust or moisture as some people postulated. In 2004 we began to interact with them directly by asking them to "fly through my arms" as an example. Sure enough, they have done what we've asked and we photographed it. We've found that they have quite a sense of humor and love when we are laughing and having fun – they seem to appear more frequently in photos when there is an atmosphere of love and joyful connection between the people in the room.

This subject really excites me because it is so compatible with my research into extraterrestrial contact. The orbs are a form of interdimensional contact also, and they have definitely validated some of our working theories about contact through their actions in response to our requests.

When working with spirit energies – whether cetacean, extraterrestrial, or otherwise – one's emotional state is of utmost importance. You can consider, in some ways, the spirit realm to be like a mirror… it will reflect back to you what your own energies are. If you interact with spirits from a place of fear, you attract fearful encounters. If you center and balance yourself emotionally and interact from a place of unconditional love, your spirit experiences will reflect that balance and love. This may sound simple, but it is quite profound.

Their most frequent message at this point in time is that as the planet and human consciousness evolves, the 'veils' between realities are thinning. This means that we can expect more and more unexplained phenomena, spirit communication, orb appearances, etc. We should not be surprised by this or distracted by it. It is simply a natural part of evolution. As quantum physicists share their beliefs and findings even more openly now, we can help to bridge science and spirituality by keeping an open mind and recognizing that the language of science and the language of spirituality is ultimately saying the same thing – that we are all part of an interconnected universe in which there is no part that is insignificant.

CHAPTER 11

WORKING WITH YOUR SOUL COMPANIONS

As the experiences in this book so beautifully illustrate, working with guides is different for everyone. What works for one person may not work as well (if at all) for someone else. It is a personal relationship that will reveal itself in its own unique way. Try a few different techniques and trust your intuition on whatever feels right for you.

Throughout the individual stories in this book, you will find excellent advice on working with spirit companions. Here is an overview of some of the techniques previously mentioned, with further comments and suggestions…

Who are Your Soul Companions?

It is prudent to remember that Spirit is energy and this energy does not have a physical form unless it is incarnate. Because we have a body and an identity that goes with it, we assume that our guides and allies in spirit must 'be somebody', too. When you chose to be born, you took on a form – a bit like putting on a suit. Your body is the vehicle you use to physically engage and express yourself in the world of matter, like rummaging through a dressing-up box to play 'let's pretend'. When you've finished with the game, you put the outfit away.

We live in a world where physical appearance is important, as it is primarily how we identify others. We often initially gauge what a person is like *inside* by their *outer* appearance. It is a form of unspoken communication – the clothes we choose to wear tell the world something of who we are and what we believe ourselves to be… for example, "I'm sexy", "I'm rich", "I'm a rebel", "I'm cool", "I'm educated", "I'm different",

"I'm artistic", or "I'm important".

Just as we create an image to convey to the outside world what we are about, so can spirit beings choose to present themselves in a way that will best represent their essence and qualities. More often than not, they show themselves in human form. I suspect this is purely for our benefit, knowing this is something we can best relate to and interpret. If a loved one passes over and wants to let you know they're around, although they have left their body behind, it's highly likely that their spirit energy will show themselves as the person you knew in order to get the message across – they're not going to show up looking like somebody else.

It is worth bearing in mind the above when you're working with spirit helpers… that any mental picture you may receive merely *represents* the qualities and essence of a spirit. Even then, it's all down to your interpretation of the energy… what one person calls 'an Angel' another may call 'a Being of Light' or, perhaps, a 'Star Being'. A spade is a spade, but that doesn't (and shouldn't) stop someone else calling it a shovel, or describing it as 'a digging instrument' or 'an excavating tool' if they want to. You see, it's all down to terminology – you can call it what you want but, at the end of the day, the contents of the can remain the same regardless of the label you put on it.

Your guides and allies in spirit are an aspect of yourself. Conversely, you are an aspect of your guides. I am an aspect of you, as you are an aspect of me… *everything* is an aspect of itself in another reflection, as we all express part of the unified 'One that is'.

Getting to Know Your Soul Companions

It is not important to know 'who' your guides are in order to work with them. However, many of the stories throughout this book rightly caution you to trust your *feelings*, as this is a good indicator of the spirit energy you have encountered.

You might like to commission a painting of your spirit guide in order to help you connect with them, bearing in mind that the image is *repre-*

sentative of the energy of your guide. Try gazing at the picture and tune-in to how you feel – this is a helpful way to better understand the vibration of energy you are working with, as you will find that different guides have a different feel about them.

One of the first times I contacted my guides during a guided meditation, I was taken completely by surprise as I physically experienced tingles of energy flowing through me. I later learned that this is one way of recognizing when spirit beings are near. When I ask my spirit allies for assistance, I find it useful to have this physical confirmation as it signals they have heard my request.

Some guides have a strong definite presence, while others are more delicate. All spirit beings (including ourselves) have these 'energy signatures', which is how we sometimes know, without using our eyes, when someone has entered the room. Even though we didn't see or hear them we felt their presence. While interviewing people for this book, I would often pick up on the energy signatures of other people's guides – even over the internet!

One evening, I had a particularly intense reaction while interviewing someone over the telephone… I suddenly began to feel hot and cold, and my mouth began to water. I realized, to my embarrassment, that I was going to throw up. It all happened so quickly that I was still listening to this person talk as I ran upstairs to the bathroom! I was perplexed, as I had not been feeling unwell beforehand and I felt perfectly fine afterwards. As a synchronistic twist to this tale, an empathic friend of mine sent me a text message while this was going on, asking me if I was okay. Now, the person I was interviewing seemed nice enough, but I trusted my feelings and didn't include their story in this book.

As with anything else, the more time and energy you are willing to put into getting to know your soul companions, the quicker your friendship will likely blossom. Shamanic journeying, guided meditation and dreaming are wonderful ways to get to know your allies. Many people find it helpful to make a regular commitment when they know they won't be disturbed to work with their guides. Don't forget to let them know what your plans are too – voice your intent.

Tools of the Trade

Many people choose to create a sacred altar as a focus for their interactions with Spirit. On an altar, you can place objects of power that hold meaning for you – including crystals, stones, feathers, photographs of ancestors and images of totem animals. These items should represent the energies you are working with, or would like to connect to. To honour your spirit allies, you may choose to light a candle and burn incense as a daily ritual.

An altar can be inside or outdoors – I have visited many sacred sites on my travels in Ireland, where oftentimes there are candles burning beside images and statues of saints. Beside the 'Seven Blessed Wells of Killeigh' in Co. Offaly, there is a *'clootie'* tree, where people tie things (usually pieces of fabric) onto the branches that represent their wishes or prayers. These rag trees, as they are also known, can be found at sacred sites worldwide. People naturally sense that communing with nature *is* connecting with Spirit.

Creating a 'sacred space' outdoors – a place to commune with that Spirit – is very rewarding. When we bought our house, we purchased a small wooded piece of land at the rear of the property to dedicate to this purpose. Although my partner, Vince, had always wanted to build a stone circle, it became a reality largely with the help and advice of his spirit allies through a series of shamanic journeys, where he was transported into the sacred space and shown to make the stone circle/medicine wheel in alignment with the old oak tree in the north. He was told that this space could be used to develop contact with Spirit. In a subsequent journey, Vince was shown a place that he would later visit as a source of stones, which turned out to be very special. After two weeks of walking up and down the mountain, retrieving stones with help from friends, the circle was built. It is a very special place where most visitors can visibly perceive the energy as a 'heat-haze' above the stones.

Stone circles are powerful tools for ceremony and working with spirit and nature. Many other tools have been used throughout history by shaman and psychic alike to communicate with Spirit, including tarot (or other) cards, runes, dowsing rods and pendulums, bones, the I-Ching and yarrow sticks, tea-leaves, psychotropic plants, scrying bowls and crystals, pyramids and spirit boards (to name a few). More recently, the digital camera has become a valuable tool for communicating with spirit beings! Interestingly, we discovered that orbs were present in the flash photographs we took of the stone circle. A 'mist' also appears in some of the photographs. Neither of these were visible to the naked eye – however, others *were* physically able to see them. This rekindled my relationship with the orbs that I talk about in the introduction to this book.

Creating a space, wherever it is, is not necessary in order to communicate with your guides, but it certainly makes your purpose clear. The more love and attention you bestow upon it the better – as where attention goes, energy flows.

Communicating With Your Soul Companions

It is essential that you treat your spirit allies in a respectful and sacred manner. In fact, it's time we treated all life as sacred, including each other and ourselves. Make sure that your motives for wanting to work with spirit are clear. Every soul must work out its own destiny. You are here on the planet to live your life – not to have someone else live it for you! Spirit guidance should never be used as an excuse to avoid making your own decisions. Take responsibility for the thoughts you think, the choices you make, and the life you create. Although guides can help guide you back onto your path, ultimately this is your journey and you must learn your own lessons.

Your spirit allies will help you whether you are consciously aware of them or not. However, to have any sort of relationship, it is essential to communicate. Clear communication with your guides (or anyone else for that matter) takes your relationship to a new level of understanding. Basically, you can achieve a lot more together.

Although some people are initially shocked and surprised by the intensity of spirit contact, believing they are either 'making it all up' or are going insane, most of you will find that contact with your guides is not quite so dramatic. It's more likely to be a gentle process – one that will feel very natural. Each of us senses the information that our spirit guides convey to us in different ways.

When your guides 'speak' to you, it is often perceived as a 'gut feeling', 'intuitive knowing', or you may experience it as an *'aha!'* moment. As well as by an intuitive and empathic sense of feeling, we can also receive the information they transmit through our thoughts and imagination. We may translate these mental impressions into words or hearing an 'inner voice', or by 'seeing' images and pictures. People also report a particular scent when encountering a spirit presence – for example, a floral scent is often associated with angelic energies. It is said that we can commune with the angels from the heart level, rather than the mind, and perhaps this is true for most spirit contact, as true knowledge and understanding of anything or anyone cannot be processed solely by the mind.

Your soul companions like to be acknowledged (who doesn't?). They like to be spoken to. If you ask for help, they're only too willing to do their best. If you don't know who you're asking, that's okay… phrase your question something like, *"Spirit allies, please help me with ***, in the highest possible interests of all concerned."* Be as specific as possible about what it is you want – guidance, inspiration, advice, healing, or whatever it is. You only need ask once, so don't keep pestering with the same question. Give thanks, let it go, and be open and awake to the assistance offered. This applies to *all* your soul companions – your Self, faeries, Star Beings, ancestors, animal, vegetable or mineral.

Within the angelic realms, it is said that specific angels are said to specialize in certain areas, but I'm not going to list them here. You don't have to know the names of all the angels and their 'job descriptions' – simply ask for help from the celestial realms, specifying your requirements as clearly as possible, and the appropriate angel will come. After all, the angel that works best for you in that quarter will not necessarily work as well for someone else.

On the other hand, when working with your ancestors it is helpful to do some groundwork. Find out about them and visit the places they lived. Talk to an elderly family member if you can. If you have any old photographs of your ancestors, get some framed and put them up – on your altar, perhaps. All these things will help you form a stronger connection with your ancestral allies.

Cultivate the habit of talking aloud to your invisible friends (when appropriate!) as you would to anyone else, remembering that in order to have a working relationship with anyone it is equally important to be able to listen, and to be receptive and open to guidance. The answers may come in the following ways…

Synchronicities, Signs and Omens

Pay attention! Your guides are sending you signs and omens to help point you in the right direction. There are a myriad of signs everywhere for the observant eye to behold. How you interpret the meaning of the signs you are shown is a personal thing open to interpretation (and misinterpretation!). Use your intuition to understand the message and don't be afraid to ask them if you need further confirmation.

One of the most effective ways to 'tune-in' to your spirit allies is to connect with nature. If you live in a city, it is well worth the effort to visit the countryside as often as you can. I find that going for a walk is a very healthy way to receive help and guidance – if you live in a city, this is still effective. Walk with the intent to remain open and observant to the signs around you. Heed what you encounter on your journey and how you feel. Messages will come to you in a myriad of ways – for example, through a person, an animal, a tree, cloud formations, a river, a stone or a feather.

If you feel a certain lack of synchronicities and signs occurring in your present life, you can create opportunities for them… one of my favourite ways of doing this is to randomly open a book at page and read the first sentence I see. This works particularly well if I am in a relaxed, meditative state, and is especially effective if I choose a spiritual or inspiring one – try it for yourself using *'Soul Companions'*.

Searching for suitable contributors to this book appeared to be a random experience, yet I believe I was guided to each and every person I contacted. I did most of my research surfing the internet – which is a Zen artform in itself, and one that embraces synchronicity. My searches flowed easily to a person I felt drawn to contact, and often the timing was perfect. On the other hand, I spent hundreds of hours tapping key words into a search engine and getting nowhere, as well as sending e-mails that didn't arrive or to people that didn't reply, causing no end of frustration! My main challenge was in knowing when it was appropriate to be tenacious, and when to let go. The dilemma of perseverance versus surrender is very pertinent and is a common cause of why we seek guidance in the first place! Paradoxically, that decision can only ever be ours to make. Being led or guided by Spirit doesn't necessarily mean you'll be taken where you want to go, but will always take you where you need to be.

Your guides often like to leave a trail of very subtle clues that are not easy to decipher, being often metaphorical or symbolic in nature. Symbols speak to your subconscious mind, and hold great potency and power. They are metaphorical representations of the building blocks of the universe, which might explain why a Masonic symbol is the compass and square – the very tools needed to construct sacred geometry. Throughout history, many secret societies have used symbols in order to guard or hide esoteric knowledge… you only have to study the one dollar bill to realize how we are surrounded by signs everyday, yet are oblivious to the deeper meaning intended. It helps to learn about ancient symbols and their meaning – *'In These Signs Conquer: Revealing the Secret Signs an Age has Obscured'* by numerologist, clairvoyant and psychic Ellis Taylor is a fascinating study and well worth a read.

Signs and omens can also be a very personal thing, as what one person dismisses may mean everything to another. For example, whenever a friend of mine sees a specific courier van, this signals that an invitation is on its way. If a sign appears frequently for you, try playing the word association game – this will give you a good idea of how to interpret this particular sign and what it means to you. You may like to make your own personalized 'signs and omens' dictionary to refer to. This will also be a useful aid in helping you decode the messages in your dreams. Ask your guides for a specific sign that is significant to you and see what happens…

Generally speaking, the more that you acknowledge with thanks the meaningful co-incidences and signs in your life the more you will encounter them, and life becomes a naturally synchronistic flowing journey.

The Dreaming

Your guides will send you messages when you are most receptive, which, for most of us, is when we're asleep! I am fortunate enough to be able to remember my dreams and have kept a dream journal since I was in my teens, but for those of you who don't remember your dreams, it may help to try the following;

- **Always keep a pen and paper beside the bed.** Buy yourself a dream journal and a good pen specifically for this purpose – choose something special. On the first page, dedicate the book to your dreams.
- **State your intention.** Write down a specific request – you might ask for insight into a particular problem, guidance in an area of your life, healing for yourself or another, or a meeting with a particular person. Clearly ask yourself to remember your dreams when you awaken, then place the request under your pillow and literally sleep on it. As you drift off to sleep, pay attention to the images you see and sounds you hear…

• **"You don't need to go to sleep in order to dream,"** says Robert Moss, the pioneer of 'active dreaming' (a bridge between dreamwork and shamanism). You can consciously enter the same space by meditating, daydreaming, or via shamanic journeying. It is useful to purchase a guided meditation or shamanic drumming CD for this purpose.

I find that, however random my dreams appear to be, it helps to write them down and share them. Of course, people will interpret the same dream in a different way. It's valuable to get some feedback in order to gain a fresh insight into the meaning and message of a dream. If you use a 'dreamer's dictionary', use it for reference only. Ultimately, the dream is yours, so trust your own feelings about its message. You will *know* when something rings true for you. Sometimes, the meaning of a dream may not be immediately clear, which is why it helps to write them down... often, in hindsight a dream makes perfect sense. It's also worth bearing in mind that it may not make sense to you because the message is intended for someone else (as in my experience at the beginning of Chapter 2).

When you become proficient at recalling your dreams, you can try lucid dreaming – becoming conscious that you are dreaming. A simple and effective way to induce lucid dreams is based on a technique described in the book *'Journey To Ixtlan'* by Carlos Castaneda… before you go to sleep, focus on your hands and intend to look at your hands in the dream. (I tried this once… I looked at my hands in a dream and was surprised to find that *they weren't mine!*). On another occasion, while writing this book a friend of mine became seriously ill. He was in a coma in hospital, and I wondered where his spirit was and if I could find him. That night, I dreamed that I gave him a hug – it was so real, I could feel the bones on his back. As I held him, an intense healing energy like a white light blazed through me and into him. We both acknowledged the energy, and I told him that I was glad I saw him, as I had wanted to find him in a dream to give him a healing hug. Then it suddenly hit me… wait a minute, I *am* dreaming! After that, I knew he'd be okay (and he is).

Meditation and Journeying

The key to establishing contact with your guides is to be in a relaxed and receptive state – not an easy thing to achieve in the fast-paced, often stressful, lives we lead. Nevertheless, taking some 'time out' is essential if you want to tune-in to Spirit.

It is worth noting that nearly every person I interviewed for this book meditates as an effective way to developing the connection with their Higher Self and Spirit. As well as being an effective way to lower your blood pressure, relieve insomnia and relax your mind, emotions, and physical body, it is also a way to achieve an altered state of awareness. An altered state of consciousness is *not* a hallucinogenic state – it is a shift in perception in order to 'see' or contact what would ordinarily be an invisible world.

There are many different forms of meditation, the most commonly known being 'insight meditation' – a place of no-thought in order to become One with Spirit. Another form is often described as a 'visualization' or 'guided meditation', whereby you have a goal in mind – i.e. to connect with your soul companions! Yet another form of meditation is 'mantra meditation', where you use sound as a focus (often 'OM', which is the sound of the universe, or the vibration of all living things) in order to open the heart and mind. All meditation practices involve communing with Spirit. Personally, I find that guided meditation is a very effective way to contact your spirit allies.

Shamanic journeying is another effective way to enter an altered state of consciousness, involving the use of sound. This is often a drumbeat, but can also be a rattle, singing bowl, the didgeridoo, and the noises encountered in nature. These sounds are 'wing songs', in that they transport you to your destination. In this case, you journey to the inner-worlds – the lower, middle or upper worlds – in order to communicate with spirit helpers. See the contributor's pages for a list of shamanic journeying and meditation CDs available from the contributors to '*Soul Companions*.'

Journeying is achieved with the help of your Power Animal, who is your advisor, protector and guide on the journey. I attempted journeying three times intending to meet my Power Animal, but I was unsuccessful. I was trying too hard and was also concerned that I was 'making it up'. My partner, Vince, had recently discovered his Power Ally, so I asked him if he would journey for me, and I decided that I would simultaneously journey, too. When I reached the Lower World, I still couldn't find my Power Animal, so I decided that the best thing I could do would be to go to sleep… maybe I would have a dream on my journey? As I lay down, I felt a nudge on my leg and I looked up to see a stag. We had a little chat, and then Vince asked me if I could see an animal, as he could quite clearly see one. Suddenly unsure if the stag was my ally, I sent it away until Vince then confirmed it was! Thankfully, the stag came out of hiding and wasn't in the least offended by my faux pas… in fact, I think he was highly amused (I have since discovered he has a wicked sense of humor).

I now have no doubt in my mind that journeying is *real*. Journeying to meet your guides and allies is an enjoyable, magical experience, as well as being healing and informative.

Co-creating With Spirit

Spirit guides will work through an individual in whatever way they can – through relaxed or altered states of consciousness and *all* spontaneous creative expression, be it art, literature, music, dance or acting.

All artistic souls know that if you take yourself away from the hustle and bustle of life's routine, you plant a seed that, nurtured well, will emerge as creative expression. If it's inspiration you want, nature is the artist's finest muse…

Recently, I was taking the dog for a walk in the countryside around my home, when my youngest daughter asked me if we could visit the 'Giving Tree'. She pointed in the direction of a hollow beech tree by the river where we sometimes leave small 'presents' of acorns, leaves and crystals, whenever we pass by. On this occasion, I felt inspired to sing a little tune as my gift to the tree. I was alone the next time I passed by the old beech tree and, as I gently leaned my brow against its trunk, a tune I had never heard before flowed through me, complete with words. How apt it was that my daughter named this beautiful beech 'The Giving Tree', as the giving goes both ways – just as I had gifted the tree with a song, a song had been gifted to me by the tree.

Imagination is the tool you use to communicate with Spirit in order to utilize your creative talents and abilities. The messages that enter your imagination are very real and can strike you at any time – while driving the car, doing the washing up, or walking the dog, for instance. Your job as a spirit in a body is to interpret the message and *create* something in the physical world – whether it's a song, a painting, poem or prose, a joke that makes someone laugh aloud… whatever it is, spontaneously flow with it and let the inspiration guide you to express yourself in the most appropriate way. Allowing your creativity to flow *through* you rather than come *from* you will encourage your spirit allies to guide you to expand in new and exciting ways.

Imposters

Everything that exists in physical consciousness has a vibration that attracts both physical and invisible energies. It is inevitable that, from time to time, we experience events and situations that aren't so pleasant. During these times, the challenge is to keep our spirits high – not to descend into self-pity or other damaging emotional states of being. Everything happens for a reason, providing an opportunity for your soul to grow… it cannot be otherwise because *you are creating it all*. Although we all have our 'off days' it helps to bear in mind that everything is an illusion. As Shakespeare wrote, "All the world's a stage – the men and women in it merely players." And as was once said to a friend of mine, "Life's a game… you're supposed to enjoy it. If you're not having fun, then you're not playing the game properly."

Remember that your guides are your friends… perhaps the best friends you will ever have. If you find yourself saying, "My guide told me to", even though your inner-knowing screams otherwise, then it would be sensible to review the relationship you have with your 'friend'. In all spheres of life there can be a fine line between 'guidance' and 'manipulation'. If you ever feel that this relationship is detrimental to the well being of yourself and others, then it is wise to change the company you keep.

As there are certain unscrupulous human individuals who seem, by nature, to be deliberately manipulative and untrustworthy, so there are spirit 'impostors' who pretend to be what they are not in order to mislead and disrupt lives. An excellent book that illustrates this is *'The Siren Call of Hungry Ghosts'* by Joe Fisher. Not every spirit is benevolent, which is important to bear in mind. Do not be afraid to seek advice from a reputable shaman or medium if you are unsure of your guide's intentions.

Before opening up and inviting spirit energies into your life it is essential to protect yourself from any unwanted influences – there are some excellent books on the subject, including William Bloom's *'Psychic Protection'*. One thing that I personally find useful to have around the place is orgonite. In the 1930's and 40's, Dr. Wilhelm Reich studied etheric energy, which he called orgone. Orgonite was developed by other researchers based on the principles of Reich's discovery that stacking alternating layers of fiberglass (an organic substance) and steel wool (an inorganic substance) would attract and collect orgone energy – both positive ('POR') and 'dead' orgone ('DOR'). Orgonite is composed of metal shavings, copper, and crystals, among other things, that are compacted in epoxy resin. The result is a self-powered, perpetual, and efficient negative-to-positive energy transmutation machine, which can be placed on top of computers, televisions, or anywhere else that emits debilitating energy. Many people have found it to be a very effective aid in protecting themselves from harmful energies, as well as enhancing psychic ability.

If you do find yourself attracting negative energies or entities, remember to ask for help from your positive spirit allies. I was once given some excellent advice in a dream how to rid myself of 'monsters'… what you do is shine love and light onto them and they disappear. It's a simple technique and you have nothing to fear. In fact, if you feed the fear this will only attract more of them!

When you contact your spirit helpers, do question their integrity. Be sure they are who they say they are. Remember that we all have the ability to project ourselves in the form that is most acceptable to an individual… I see no harm with 'dressing up' as long as one is honest about it!

Remember, this is *your* life. You always have free will. You and you alone are responsible for your choices and actions, and the effect they have on others. You don't have to do what others suggest, whether that person has a body or not!

May you enjoy your journey.

AFTERWORD

This book has been gestated and nurtured for over two years, and is about to be birthed into the world. Suffice to say, I feel like an altogether different person than I was at its conception. I do not doubt that this particular book, which has opened me up to so many profound teachings and wisdom, has had a vital part to play in these changes.

When I started writing this book, I thought of myself as a conscientious observer – naturally slipping into 'journalist mode' when interviewing the contributors, I didn't much consider that I had anything of note to say regarding my own connection with spirit allies. I naively expected spirit contact to be all 'voices in the head', and seeing apparitions. Little did I know…

Before I wrote the introductions to each chapter, I would say to myself (rather like the character Manuel from *Fawlty Towers*), 'I know nothing!' but as I would start writing, I would amaze myself as I began to piece together the times in my life when I'd been so obviously guided in so many different ways. Memory after memory returned to me, and it has only really been in hindsight, by writing this book, that I have begun to fully acknowledge this guidance.

The big turning point for me came when it really dawned on me that *we're all spirit beings*. There's nothing 'mystical' about it in that sense, and this perspective has definitely grounded my ideas of what spirit allies are about. Michael Tsarion – an expert on the occult histories of Ireland and America – articulates how I feel about this so eloquently, *"The ancients couldn't understand the concept of spirit being 'trapped' in matter because they saw that matter is infused with spirit. There is no difference between spirit and matter – it's all one spiritual energy... one animistic living organism."* (Red Ice Creations Radio – **www.redicecreations.com**)

As our world rapidly moves towards ever-greater spiritual, environmental and political challenges there is an urgent need for us to listen to the voices of well-respected healers, seers, visionaries and shamans who can share their wisdom, insights and leadership to inspire and guide us to make our planet a healthier, more peaceful and equitable place to live.

If you have enjoyed reading this book, you might like to attend a Soul Companions event, which brings together the Wisdom-Keepers featured in these pages. Hear them speak, and participate in workshops and sacred rituals with some of these teachers. The calendar of events can be found on the website: **www.soulcompanions.org**. For those interested in meeting like-minded soul seekers, there is a forum for the Soul Companions online community, and anyone interested in organizing an event in their own area can contact the author through the website, or by email: **info@soulcompanions.org**.

ABOUT THE AUTHOR

Karen Sawyer is a writer, artist and musician. An established freelance journalist in the mind/body/spirit sector, Karen has written feature articles for many magazines on a wide range of topics. She sees herself as a bridge, offering access to resources and information to inspire others on their journey. By writing from fresh and esoteric perspectives, Karen's gift of seeing and articulating what's beneath the surface awakens others to the intrinsic magic of our world and what is truly possible. Karen lives on the southwestern coast of Wales in the UK. For information about Karen's work and forthcoming *Soul Companions* events, visit her websites: **www.impish.uwclub.net** and **www.soulcompanions.org**.

CONTRIBUTOR'S PAGES

Lyn Allen – To connect with your spirit guide through a painting, spiritual counseling, spirit healing and Australian bushflower essences, visit Lyn's Spirit Art website: www.lynallen.net or e-mail: lyn1art@bigpond.com or lyn@lynallen.net.

Uncle Angaangaq – To purchase Angaangaq's evocative double CD set *'Seasons'*, explore Angaangaq's in-depth teachings of the Far North through Intensives, through the Wisdomkeepers Program, and to learn more about melting the ice in the heart of man, visit: www.icewisdom.com or e-mail: info@icewisdom.com.

Alan Arcieri – A renowned spiritual medium, Alan does readings in person and worldwide over the phone. He also teaches psychic development and Kabbalah. For more information visit his website – www.alanarcieri.com. Contact tel: (001) - 239 772 5560 or e-mail: alanarcieri@aol.com.

Andras Corban Arthen – Andras offers lectures, workshops, performances and consultations throughout the U.S. and abroad. He can be reached at: andrasarthen@earthspirit.com. For further information about his work, and the work of the EarthSpirit Community and its internationally-acclaimed ritual performance group MotherTongue, contact EarthSpirit, P.O. Box 723, Williamsburg, MA, 01096 USA. Website: www.earthspirit.com. Contact: E-mail: earthspirit@earthspirit.com, or tel: (001) 413 238 4240. For more information on the Parliament of the World's Religions, visit: www.cpwr.org.

Elena Avila – For more information about Elena's work, workshops, and lectures visit her website: www.Elena-curandera.com. Contact e-mail: EAvila9234@aol.com. Elena is author of: *'Woman Who Glows in the Dark: A Curandera Reveals Traditional Aztec Secrets of Physical and Spiritual Health'*. (Tarcher/Penquin).

George Mathieu Barnard – For more information about the 11:11

Progress Group, please visit www.1111Angels.com or www.1111SpiritGuardians.com, and the message board http://board.1111angels.com. The group has published two books – 'The Search for 11:11' and 'In the Service of 11:11', as well as four pdf publications available from www.1111Angels.com. Its most important item is an affordable Meditation/Visualization CD, called *'The Akashic Construct'*, which is available at www.1111angels.com/Akashic.html. For further information, please e-mail book_sales@1111publishers.com.

William Bloom – For more information about William's work, trainings, school, project and books, visit www.williambloom.com and www.f4hs.org.

Tira Brandon-Evans – Tira is a Faery Shaman, Master Herbalist and founder and moderator of the Society of Celtic Shamans and the author of many books and articles on Celtic tradition, including *'The Green and Burning Tree: A Faery Shamans Handbook'*, *'The Labyrinthine Way: Walking Ancient Paths in a Modern World'*, and *'Through the Unremembered Gate: Journeys of Initiation'*. Tira is also the editor-in-chief and publisher of the quarterly journal *Earthsongs*. Through the Society of Celtic Shamans she offers several programs for those wishing to delve more deeply into Celtic traditions. These programs include: the Hazel Grove School of Bardic Wisdom, the Oak Grove Oghams Masters program, the Faery Shamans Apprenticeship Program, and the Twelve Journeys program. All these programs are available on-line at www.faeryshaman.org. Contact e-mail: info@faeryshaman.org

Simon Buxton – For further information, contact: Simon Buxton, The Sacred Trust, PO Box 7777, Wimborne, BH21 9JD, England. Website: www.sacredtrust.org.

Philip Carr-Gomm – In 1988, Philip was asked to lead The Order of Bards Ovates and Druids, and he combines his role as Chief of the Order with writing, and giving talks and workshops. His published works are *'Sacred Places'*, *'What do Druids Believe?'*, *'Druid Mysteries'*, *'The Druid Way'*, *'In the Grove of the Druids'*, *'Druidcraft –*

The Magic of Wicca and Druidry', '*The DruidCraft Tarot', 'The Druid Animal Oracle' and 'The Druid Plant Oracle' (with Stephanie Carr-Gomm).* Philip is also the editor of '*The Book of Druidry'*, and '*The Rebirth of Druidry'.* For information about Philip's books and workshops, please visit www.philipcarrgomm.druidry.org.
'*The Order of Bards Ovates & Druids'* offers an experience-based home-learning course in Druidry. In addition there are workshops, camps and celebrations in Britain and the USA and other parts of the world, and over eighty groves and seed-groups. The course is available in text and audio versions and in French, German & Dutch. Full details can be found at the website www.druidry.org or by mailing O.B.O.D, PO Box 1333, Lewes, East Sussex, BN7 1DX. Contact: Tel/fax: 0044 – (0)1273 470888 or e-mail office@druidry.org.
Howard G. Charing – Howard G. Charing, is an accomplished international workshop leader on shamanism. He has worked some of the most respected and extraordinary shamans & healers in the Andes, the Amazon Rainforest, and the Philippines. Howard organizes specialist retreats to the Amazon Rainforest at the dedicated center located in the Mishana nature reserve. He has co-authored the best selling book, Plant Spirit Shamanism (Destiny Books USA), and has published numerous articles about plant medicines. He was baptized into the Shipibo tribe of the Upper Amazon, and initiated into the lineage of the shamans of the Rio Napo. Howard is also an artist whose paintings have featured in major exhibitions in London and elsewhere. His artwork has also been featured on book covers. For details about his workshops and Amazonian Plant Spirit Medicine Retreats refer to his website www.shamanism.co.uk. Tel: 0044 – (0)1273 882027 or email: eagleswing@shamanism.co.uk.
Holly Davis – Holly runs the Nirvana Springs Healing Center in Pembrokeshire, Wales, in the U.K, where she gives workshops and seminars on animal facilitated 'Healing With Equus' that involves healing with the 'second heart' chakra, 'Animal Communication', 'Land

Energies', and 'Dowsing for Health'.

Holly offers the diploma course 'Energy Therapy for People and Animals', which covers animal facilitated healing, animal communication, energy therapy for animals and people, Bach Flower Remedies, Kinesiology and crystal therapy. These can be attended as workshops or as a course module towards the qualification.

For further information, including the 4-day healing retreat and self-catering holidays available, contact Waungron Barn, Velfrey Road, Whitland, Pembrokeshire. SA34 0QX, U.K. Tel: 044 – (0)1994 241255, Mon – Fri, 9.30 – 6.30pm. Website: www.hollydavis.co.uk. Contact e-mail: nirvanasprings@btopenworld.com.

Holly has also written the 'Animal Communication' and 'Dowsing For Health' courses for Stonebridge College – www.stonebridge.uk.com.

Her CD, 'Animal Healing Workshop' with Holly Davis (featuring music from Spa Gold by Aramara) is available from Paradise Music – www.paradisemusic.co.uk. Tel: 044 – (0)1296 668193.

Billie Dean – Billie has an animal sanctuary in NSW, Australia, teaches animal communication and traditional energy medicine for animals, and has founded the 'For Life' campaign to eradicate senseless euthanasia of healthy animals. She has produced a shamanic meditation CD, *'Time of the Drum'*, to help you reconnect with your telepathic nature and the world of animals. With her husband Andrew Einspruch, Billie writes and makes conscious films which entertain, uplift and inspire, including: *'Finding Joy'* and *'Seven Days with Seven Dogs'*. To purchase these and for more information about Billie and her other films and projects, visit www.billiedean.com and www.laughingowl.com.au or e-mail billie@laughingowl.com.au

The Barefoot Doctor – aka Stephen Russell, The Barefoot Doctor is a leading exponent of modern day spirituality who, with a keen desire to contribute a greater level of relaxation and peace to the world, has dedicated over 30 years to demystifying the ways of ancient Taoism and teaches it for everyday benefit via a variety of mediums: 12 books (to date), including *'Handbook For The Urban Warrior'*, audio CD's, T.V., music, seminars, shows and most importantly through his daily online busking platform: www.barefootdoctorglobal.com.

Michael Dunning – Originally from Scotland, Michael now lives in the Pioneer Valley in Western Massachusetts, USA. He practices and teaches a form of shamanism that evolved over a ten-year period under the sacred enclosure of a 2000-year-old yew tree in Scotland. Michael is also a qualified therapist specializing in Craniosacral Biodynamics. He offers training programs and workshops in shamanism and in Craniosacral Biodynamics in the USA. He teaches internationally by invitation. For more information on Yewshamanism, visit: www.yewshamanism.com. For Craniosacral Biodynamics, visit: www.craniosacralbiodynamicsusa.com. Contact e-mails: yewshaman@gmail.com and Michaelcranio@gmail.com.

For information about Chelynn Tetreault's photography, please visit: www.chelynn.com.

Celia Fenn – To purchase Celia's books, *'A Guide to Complementary Therapies in South Africa' and 'The Indigo Crystal Adventure'*, and to read more of Celia's work online, visit her website: www.starchild-global.com.

Patrick Gamble – As a psychic artist, Patrick is available for private sittings and workshops. He has developed a range of spiritually inspired paintings, which are available as prints, gift cards, and limited editions. To arrange a personal sitting or purchase some of his artwork, please see his website: www.patrickgamble.com. Contact address: Turtle's Rest, Cargentle, Langore, Launceston, Cornwall, PL16 8LN. Tel: 0044 – (0)7740949537. You can also join Patrick on a 'ghost watch' at various locations in the UK – for more information visit www.ghostwatch.tv. Patrick is also available for healing and is an active member of The Healers International Network (T.H.I.N), website: www.thin.org.uk.

Ailo Gaup – Ailo teaches shamanism based on Sami traditions and his own experiences. He is author of 7 books, including poetry, novels, and two shamanic books including *'The Shamanic Zone'*. For further information about Ailo and his work, visit his website: www.sjaman.com. Contact e-mail: ailo@sjaman.com.

Tiokasin Ghosthorse – Tiokasin hosts a radio program that gives voice to those remaining in the world who are Indigenous – with pure conviction that if Indigenous people are lost the rest of the human species will not survive, with confidence that many of those Indigenous peoples continue to speak the 'Star languages', and with prophecy that those Indigenous voices are the purest of the spiritual dimensions the human race seeks. Tune-into *First Voices Indigenous Radio* at 99.5 FM on Thursdays from 1Oam to11am – wake up call on Fridays from 6 am to 9am. Listen online at www.wbai.org. For archived programs please visit the website: http://archive.wbai.org. Tel: (001)212 209 2979 voice or (001) 212 209 2800 switchboard. Website: www.firstvoicesradio.org. Address: W.B.A.I, 120 Wall Street, 10th Floor, NY, NY 10005.

Anne Hassett (Acushla) – Ann offers workshops on a variety of psychic and personal development subjects, including Reiki and Angel workshops, which are very popular with her clients all over the world. Anne also clears homes and offices of 'stuck' or negative energy, and is available for psychic readings – either face to face or over the telephone, spiritual guidance and counseling, and palmistry readings for children and adults. These services are available by appointment, tel: 0044 – (0)1225 425117. For more information about Anne's book 'Reading Your Child's Hand', visit the website: www.readingyourchildshand.com. Other books and an Angel Meditation with Acushla CD can be purchased online via her website: www.acushlasangels.com.

Thea Holly – Thea's book *'Listening to Trees'* (published by Capall Bann) can be ordered from any bookshop or by visiting www.capallbannbooks.co.uk

Thea gives private sittings, telephone readings and postal readings – to empower positive changes in your life, to enable the full development of your potential, for working with your guides and higher beings, to clear past and present life blocks, to discover your purpose and spiritual origin and much more. For more information about these and Thea's workshops – Working with the Light, Working with Other Worldly Beings, Working with Atlantean Beings, and Teaching the Sekhem method of healing, visit her website: www.circlesoflight.co.uk.

Christan Hummel – Christan is author of the book DIY Space Clearing Kit, and teaches workshops internationally on how to connect with nature to reduce crime, balance weather patterns, and clear pollution. Her website, Earth Transitions, features quantum energy tools, and transformational CDs for personal and planetary use at: www.earthtransitions.com. Christan also does private space clearing sessions and is available for speaking engagements. For information, contact e-mail: earthheal99@cox.net.

Sandra Ingerman – For information on Sandra's work with reversing environmental pollution, workshops on the topic, on creating a worldwide human web of light, and workshops on shamanic journeying and healing, please write to Sandra at: P.O Box 4757, Santa Fe, New Mexico, 87502, U.S, or visit her website: www.shamanicvisions.com/ingerman.html.

Sandra has authored many books, including; 'Soul Retrieval: mending the Fragmented Self', 'Welcome Home: Following Your Soul's Journey Home', 'A Fall to Grace', 'Medicine For the Earth: How to Transform Personal and Environmental Toxins', and 'How to Heal Toxic Thoughts'. To order these books and to find a local shamanic practitioner or teacher, please visit www.shamanicteachers.com. Sandra has also produced a series of lecture, visualization and journeying CDs, which include; 'The beginner's Guide to Shamanic Journeying', 'The Soul Retrieval Journey', and 'Miracles For the Earth'. These can be ordered from Sounds True – website: www.soundstrue.com or Tel: (001) 800 333 9185 or (001) 303 665 3151. To read articles written by Sandra Ingerman please visit: www.sandraingerman.com.

Jörmundur Ingi – To contact Jörmundur, please e-mail:

jormundur@hotmail.com.

Patrick Jasper Lee – Jasper is the founder and artistic director of the Jal Folk Theatre Company. For information about current productions and available dates, folk theatre workshops, courses and life skills performance training for individuals, businesses, teams and children, please contact: Jal School of Arts & Life, PO Box 171, Hailsham, East Sussex, BN27 9AA, U.K. Tel: 044 – (0)1323 848923. Website: www.jal-arts.com or contact e-mail: info@jal-arts.com.

Jasper is author of *'We Borrow the Earth'* and the series of novels, 'The Long Reflection'. He is also a musician. For information about and to purchase Jasper's books and music, visit www.botkalo.co.uk.

For information about sacred-sexual teachings and the Leelis Raht Dai Gypsy Woodland Goddess Program, visit the website: www.dahtsahnigoddess.co.uk or contact: info@dahtsahnigoddess.co.uk.

Joel Kaplan – Joel has the gift of clairaudience and telepathy, which enables him to assist others all over the world. Joel can be contacted on: (001) 978 470 1489.

Tom Kenyon – For more information about Tom's work with the Hathors and Mary Magdalene, please visit his website: www.tomkenyon.com. Contact e-mail: office@tomkenyon.com.

Laurie Lacey – Laurie facilitates a wide range of plant medicine workshops, seminars, lectures and field walks. Please visit www.wildworldofplants.com for details. He is the author of *'Micmac Medicines: Remedies and Recollections'* (Nimbus Publishing, Halifax, Nova Scotia, 1993, ISBN# 1-55109-041-4), '*Black Spirit: The Way of The Crow'* (Nimbus Publishing, Halifax, Nova Scotia, 1996, ISBN# 1-55109-152-6), now available in ebook form as *'The Way of the Crow'* from www.thewayofthecrow.com, and '*Medicine Walk: Reconnecting with Mother Earth'*, (Nimbus Publishing, Halifax, Nova Scotia, 1999, ISBN# 1-55109-306-5). Laurie is also the editor of *Natural Healing Talk,* a bi-weekly newsletter on nature, healing, and wellness. To subscribe, visit the Natural Healing Talk website: www.naturalhealingtalk.com. Laurie can be contacted through any of his websites, including his art site at: www.laurielacey.com, or his blogs at: www.thenaturewriter.blogspot.com and http://olcoyoteschronicles.blogspot.com.

Denise Linn – Denise Linn is the founder of the International Institute of Soul Coaching – a professional certification course. She is also the best-selling author of 15 books including *'Sacred Space'*, *'Feng Shui for the Soul'*, *'The Soul Loves the Truth'*, *'Soul Coaching'* and *'Four Acts of Personal Power'*. In addition, she is a repeat guest on the Oprah Winfrey show and is a popular radio talk show host for Hay House Radio. Denise has taught in 23 countries and her books are available in 21 languages. For information about seminars, events, products, and newsletters, please visit her website: www.deniselinn.com.

Jessica Macbeth – Jessica is author of *'The Faeries' Oracle'*, *'Moon over Water'*, and *'Sun Over Mountain',* as well as numerous articles, essays, poems and short stories. For more information, see her websites: www.jesamac.com and www.FaeryWisdom.com. Blogs: http://360.yahoo.com/ceilear, http://sings-to-coyotes.blogspot.com, and http://faeriesoracle.blogspot.com. Though mostly retired from spiritual counselling, Jessica still does telephone readings as described on her jesamac.com web page.

Gary Mannion – In addition to his work as a psychic surgeon, Gary provides workshops on teaching people how to tap into and use their Psychic Abilities, Hypnotherapy and also runs courses teaching people how to work and care for Indigo and Crystal children. For more information, visit: www.garymannion.com and www.divinemessengers.com. Contact e-mails: divinemessengers@hotmail.co.uk or garymannion@123mail.org.

Robert Moss – Robert Moss is a world authority on dreams, a bestselling novelist and a former magazine editor and professor of ancient history at the Australian National University. His deep engagement with the Dreamtime springs from his early childhood in

Australia, where he survived a series of near-death experiences. He is a popular lecturer, creativity coach and radio talk show host. He teaches Active Dreaming – his pioneer synthesis of dreamwork and shamanism – all over the world and is the founder of the School of Active Dreaming, which trains teachers and facilitators. His many books include '*Conscious Dreaming', 'Dreamgates', 'Dreamways of the Iroquois', 'The Dreamer's Book of the Dead'* and *'The Three Only Things: Tapping the Power of Dreams, Coincidence and Imagination'*. He has also produced the DVD series *'The Way of the Dreamer'* and the popular Sounds True audio series *'Dream Gates: A Journey into Active Dreaming'*. Visit his website at www.mossdreams.com. Contact e-mail: mossdreams@gmail.com.

Master Ali Rafea – Ali has co-authored several books, including *'Islam from Adam to Muhammad and Beyond'* (also published under the title *'The Book Of Essential Islam'*) by Rafea, Ali, Aliaa, and Aisha, (published by The Book Foundation, Watsonville, California, Bath England, 2004). *'Beyond Diversities: Reflections on Revelations'* by Ali, Aliaa, and Aisha Rafea (published by Dar Sadek, Alexandria, Egypt, 2000 and Nahidt Misr Publication, 2005) is based on research into the major revelations of history – Ancient Egyptian beliefs, Taoism, Hinduism, Buddhism, Judaism, Christianity and Islam. To purchase these, and for further information about The Egyptian Society for Spiritual and Cultural Research (ESSCR), visit their websites www.esscr.org and www.aroadhome.org.

Elliott Rivera – Elliott offers many workshops and services, including: 'Introduction to Santeria' – a program with general information of the major deities in Santeria, including a short history of how Santeria became a major belief in the Western world. 'Ancestral Veneration Workshop' – a program on the importance of finding and connecting with our Ancestors, and building and maintaining an altar, and 'Finding the Healer Within – a program to help us look inside and heal ourselves.

Elliott is also available as a channel for Ancestor readings, for spiritual readings where he is used as a mouthpiece for the Orishas/Deities, and recreation therapy. For further information, visit: www.theansestors.com. Contact e-mail: lowerstress@msn.com. Tel: +31 – 20 615 6881 or +31 – (0)61 704 2835

Llyn Roberts – Lynn runs experiential workshops in Europe and in the US at the Omega Institute and other learning centers. She runs apprenticeship and other certification programs, spiritual expeditions, and facilitates individual, group and absentee healing work. For more information on Llyn Roberts and her work, please visit: www.thegoodremembering.com. To learn about Dream Change, visit: www.dreamchange.org.

Desy blue arrow Rainbow Roodnat – Blue arrow Rainbow is a caretaker of over 30 crystal heads and has been involved with crystal heads since 2001. She 'activates' crystal heads and has helped Joshua Shapiro with public presentations, workshops and private sessions working as a Universal Healing Light channel. She is co-author (with Joshua Shapiro) of "*Journeys of the Crystal Skull Explorers*".

Blue arrow Rainbow is also a channel for Energy Portraits created by Spirit through her. For more information, contact e-mail: DesyRainbow@hotmail.com.

Lyssa Royal Holt – Lyssa's books include *'The Prism of Lyra: An Exploration of Human Galactic Heritage', 'Visitors from Within: Extraterrestrial Encounters and Species Evolution', 'Preparing for Contact: A Metamorphosis of Consciousness', and 'Millennium: Tools for the Coming Changes'*. Lyssa teaches and channels a number of workshops on consciousness, yoga, the star connections of the human species, channeling, connecting with one's inner wisdom, and much more. She also offers sacred site tours around the world. For more information, contact Lyssa Royal Holt, c/o Royal Priest Research, PO Box 30973, Phoenix, Arizona 85046. Contact e-mail: royalpriestresearch@hotmail.com. Many free transcripts and articles are available on her website: www.lyssaroyal.com.

Leo Rutherford – For more information about workshops and events, contact: Eagle's Wing (Centre For Contemporary Shamanism), BCM Box 7475, London, WC1N 3XX, UK. Contact tel: 0044 – (0)1435 810233. Or visit the website – www.shamanism.co.uk, where you can also purchase *'The Shamanic Path Workbook'* (Originally published as *'Your Shamanic Path.'*) @ £10.99 + £1 P&P and *'Drumming For the Shamanic Journey'* by Leo Rutherford and Howard G. Charing – a CD with 2 twenty-minute journeys and 1 forty-minute journey @ £12 including P&P.

Joshua Shapiro – For information about Crystal Skull events, and to purchase the e-book 'Journeys of a Crystal Skull Explorer', visit: www.crystalskullexplorers.com and www.v-j-enterprises.com.

Julie Soskin – Julie Soskin is an Author, medium and lecturer. Julie has been working in the field of psycho-spiritual studies for twenty-five years (and has received a Master of Philosophy from Surrey University). Julie is author of seven books – 'Wind of Change', 'Alignment to Light', 'Cosmic Dance', 'Transformation', 'Insight and Intuition', 'Are you Psychic?', and 'Insight through Intuition: A guide to spiritual self development'. In 1996, she set up The School of Insight and Intuition to research and develop a full psycho-spiritual program. The ground-breaking four stage program is now university validated. For further information see the website: www.insightandintuition.com. Contact e-mail: insight.intuition@blueyonder.co.uk

David Spangler – David teaches courses on incarnational spirituality, which include classes on working with inner allies and spiritual forces. David's books: '*Alliances: Working with Spiritual Allies'* (published by Lorian books) and '*Apprenticed to Spirit'* (Riverhead Books), can be purchased online. For more information, please visit: www.lorian.org. Contact by e-mail: info@lorian.org, or telephone: (001) 425 374 7069.

R.J Stewart – You can find more about R.J's work, books, and a calendar of events and workshops at: www.rjstewart.org. A complete list of R J's many recordings, books, and productions can also be found at his website: www.dreampower.com.

Dr. Geo Athena Trevarthen – Geo works with individuals by phone, internet and in person. She teaches and has written mythic and shamanic stories for film and television, including Star Trek: Voyager. More information on Geo and her work can be found at www.celticshamanism.com. You can contact her by email at tuath@celticshamanism.com or by post at PO Box 14114, Selkirk, TD7 5YD, Scotland, UK. For information about her forthcoming book using Harry Potter's story as a guide for our own spiritual growth, visit www.o-books.com.

Jonas Trinkunas – With his ritual folk-group *Kulgrinda*, Jonas performs wedding and name giving ceremonies according to the Romuva tradition. More details can be found on the website: www.romuva.lt. For more information about *Kulgrinda* and to purchase their CDs, please contact: Jonas Trinkunas, A.Vivulskio 27 – 4, Vilnius LT – 03114, Lithuania. Tel: +370 5 2162966 or +370 6 7674057. Contact e-mails: trinkunas@romuva.lt or inija@romuva.lt. Jonas is also chairman of the WCER – World congress of the Ethnic religions – see the website: www.wcer.org.

Rabbi Gershon Winkler – Gershon is available for workshops or lectures on Aboriginal Judaism and Jewish Shamanism, and has several books, CD's and DVD's on these subjects. For information, visit his website at www.walkingstick.org. To contact him for a program in your community, e-mail: elkmesa@walkingstick.org.

SELECTED BIBLIOGRAPHY

Areopagite, Dionysius, The. *Celestial Hierarchy*. Montana: Kessinger Publishing, 2004.

Avila, Elena and Parker, Joy. *Woman Who Glows in the Dark: A Curandera Reveals Traditional Aztec Secrets of Physical and Spiritual Health.* New York: Tarcher/Penguin, 2000.

Backster, Cleve. *Primary Perception: Biocommunication With Plants, Living Foods, and Human Cells.* California: White Rose Millennium Press, 2003.

Ban Breathnach, Sarah. *Simple abundance: A Daybook of Comfort and Joy.* New York: Hachette Book Group USA, 1997.

Bloom, William. *The Sacred Magician: A Ceremonial Diary.* Glastonbury: Gothic Image Publications, 1992.

Bloom, William. *Psychic Protection: Creating Positive Energies for People and Places.* London: Piatkus Books Ltd, 1996.

Buxton, Simon. *The Shamanic Way of the Bee: Ancient Wisdom and Healing Practices of the Bee Masters.* Rochester, Vt.: Inner Traditions, 2006.

Calaprice, Alice. *The Expanded Quotable Einstein.* Princeton: Princeton University Press, 2000.

Campbell, Joseph. *The Masks of God: Occidental Mythology.* Souvenir Press Ltd, 2001.

Carr-Gomm, Philip. *The Rebirth of Druidry: Ancient Earth Wisdom for Today.* Shaftesbury: Element Books Ltd, 2003.

Castaneda, Carlos. *Journey To Ixtlan.* New York: Penguin Books, 1998.

Davies, Sioned. *The Mabanogion (Oxford Word's Classics).* Oxford University Press, 2007.

Eagle, White. *Walking with the Angels: A Path of Service.* Hampshire: The White Eagle Publishing Trust, 1998.

Emoto, Masaru. *The Hidden Messages in Water.* Oregon: Beyond Words Publishing, 2004.

Evans-Wentz, W.Y. *The Fairy-Faith in Celtic Countries: The Classic Study of Leprechauns, Pixies, and Other Fairy Spirits.* New Jersey: New Page Books, 2004.

Fisher, Joe. *The Siren Call of Hungry Ghosts: A Riveting Investigation into Channeling and Spirit Guides.* New York: Paraview Press, 2001.

George, Dan Chief. *The Best of Chief Dan George.* Washington: Hancock House Publishing, 2003.

Grof, Stanislav. *The Holotropic Mind: The Three Levels of Human Consciousness and How They Shape Our Lives.* New York: HarperCollins, 1993.

Guiley, Rosemary Ellen. *An Angel in Your Pocket.* London: Thorsons, 1999.

Guru, Heyeokah, The. *Adam and Evil: the God who hates sex, women and human bodies*. Oxford: Trafford Publishing, 2007.

Hay, Louise L. *Heal Your Body.* California: Hay House, 1984.

Holly, Thea. *Listening To Trees.* Taunton: Capall Bann Publishing, 2001.

Icke, David. *Infinite Love is the Only Truth – Everything Else is Illusion: Exposing the Dreamworld We Believe to be 'Real'.* Wildwood, Missouri: Bridge of Love Publications, 2005.

Ingerman, Sandra. *Medicine For the Earth: How to Transform Personal and Environmental Toxins.* New York: Three Rivers Press, 2000.

Jung, C.G. *Modern Man in Search of a Soul.* Oxford: Routledge, 2005.

King, Jani. *Act of Faith (Conversations With P'taah, Part 1).* California: Light Source Ptaah, 2001.

Linn, Denise. *How My Death Saved My Life: And Other Stories on my Journey to Wholeness.* California: Hay House, 2005.

Macbeth, Jessica. *Sun Over Mountain: A Course in Creative Imagination.* Lithia Springs, GA: New Leaf, 2004.

Moss, Robert. *The Dreamer's book of the Dead: A Soul Traveler's Guide to Death, Dying, and the Other Side.* Rochester, VT.: Inner Traditions, 2005.

Nichols, Ross. *The Book of Druidry.* Wellingborough: Thorsons Publishers, 1992.

Prechtel, Martin. *Secrets of the Talking Jaguar.* New York: Tarcher, 1999.

Roberts, Llyn. *The Good Remembering: A Message For Our Times.* Hampshire: O Books, 2007.

Russell, Stephen (The Barefoot Doctor). *Manifesto: The Internal Revolution – How to Get What You Want Without Trying.* Element Books, 2005.

Somé, Malidoma Patrice. *The Healing Wisdom of Africa: Finding Life Purpose Through Nature, Ritual, and Community.* New York: Jeremy P. Tarcher/Putnam, 1999.

Soskin, Julie. *The Wind of Change: A Record of Spiritual Dialogues.* London: Ashgrove Publishing, 1997.

Stewart, R.J. *The Well of Light: From Faery Healing to Earth Healing.* Roanoke, VA: R.J. Stewart Books, 2007.

Taylor, Ellis C. *In These Signs Conquer: Revealing the Secret Signs an Age Has Obscured.* Frankston, Texas: TGS Publishing, 2006.

Waite, Arthur Edward. *The Sacred Magic of Abramelin the Mage.* Montana: Kessinger Publishing, 2006.

Yeats, W.B. *The Celtic Twilight: Faerie and Folklore.* New York: Dover Publications, 2004.

BOOKS

O books

O is a symbol of the world, of oneness and unity. In different cultures it also means the "eye", symbolizing knowledge and insight, and in Old English it means "place of love or home". O books explores the many paths of understanding which different traditions have developed down the ages, particularly those today that express respect for the planet and all of life.

For more information on the full list of over 300 titles please visit our website **www.O-books.net**

SOME RECENT O BOOKS

Back to the Truth

5,000 years of Advaita

Dennis Waite

A wonderful book. Encyclopedic in nature, and destined to become a classic. **James Braha**

Absolutely brilliant...an ease of writing with a water-tight argument outlining the great universal truths. This book will become a modern classic. A milestone in the history of Advaita. **Paula Marvelly**

1905047614 500pp **£19.95 $29.95**

Beyond Photography

Encounters with orbs, angels and mysterious light forms

Katie Hall and John Pickering

The authors invite you to join them on a fascinating quest; a voyage of discovery into the nature of a phenomenon, manifestations of which are shown as being historical and global as well as contemporary and intently personal.

At journey's end you may find yourself a believer, a doubter or simply an intrigued wonderer... Whatever the outcome, the process of journeying is likely prove provocative and stimulating and - as with the mysterious images fleetingly captured by the authors' cameras - inspiring and potentially enlightening. **Brian Sibley**, author and broadcaster.

1905047908 272pp 50 b/w photos +8pp colour insert £12.99 $24.95

Don’t Get MAD Get Wise

Why no one ever makes you angry, ever!

Mike George

There is a journey we all need to make, from anger, to peace, to forgiveness. Anger always destroys, peace always restores, and forgiveness always heals. This explains the journey, the steps you can take to make it happen for you.

1905047827 160pp **£7.99 $14.95**

IF You Fall...

It's a new beginning

Karen Darke

Karen Darke's story is about the indomitability of spirit, from one of life's cruel vagaries of fortune to what is insight and inspiration. She has overcome the limitations of paralysis and discovered a life of challenge and adventure that many of us only dream about. It is all about the mind, the spirit and the desire that some of us find, but which all of us possess. **Joe Simpson**, mountaineer and author of *Touching the Void*

1905047886 240pp **£9.99 $19.95**

Love, Healing and Happiness

Spiritual wisdom for a post-secular era

Larry Culliford

This will become a classic book on spirituality. It is immensely practical and grounded. It mirrors the author's compassion and lays the foundation for a higher understanding of human suffering and hope. **Reinhard Kowalski** Consultant Clinical Psychologist

1905047916 304pp **£10.99 $19.95**

A Map to God

Awakening Spiritual Integrity

Susie Anthony

This describes an ancient hermetic pathway, representing a golden thread running through many traditions, which offers all we need to understand and do to actually become our best selves.

1846940443 260pp **£10.99 $21.95**

Punk Science

Inside the mind of God

Manjir Samanta-Laughton

Wow! Punk Science is an extraordinary journey from the microcosm of the atom to the macrocosm of the Universe and all stops in between. Manjir Samanta-Laughton's synthesis of cosmology and consciousness is sheer genius. It is elegant, simple and, as an added bonus, makes great reading. **Dr Bruce H. Lipton**, author of *The Biology of Belief*

1905047932 320pp £12.95 $22.95

Rosslyn Revealed

A secret library in stone

Alan Butler

Rosslyn Revealed gets to the bottom of the mystery of the chapel featured in the Da Vinci Code. The results of a lifetime of careful research and study demonstrate that truth really is stranger than fiction; a library of philosophical ideas and mystery rites, that were heresy in their time, have been disguised in the extraordinarily elaborate stone carvings.

1905047924 260pp b/w + colour illustrations **£19.95 $29.95** cl

The Way of Thomas

Nine Insights for Enlightened Living from the Secret Sayings of Jesus

John R. Mabry

What is the real story of early Christianity? Can we find a Jesus that is relevant as a spiritual guide for people today?

These and many other questions are addressed in this popular presentation of the teachings of this mystical Christian text. Includes a reader-friendly version of the gospel.

1846940303 196pp **£10.99 $19.95**

The Way Things Are

A Living Approach to Buddhism

Lama Ole Nydahl

An up-to-date and revised edition of a seminal work in the Diamond Way Buddhist tradition (three times the original length), that makes the timeless wisdom of Buddhism accessible to western audiences. Lama Ole has established more than 450 centres in 43 countries.

1846940427 240pp **£9.99 $19.95**

The 7 Ahas! of Highly Enlightened Souls

How to free yourself from ALL forms of stress

Mike George

7th printing

A very profound, self empowering book. Each page bursting with wisdom and insight. One you will need to read and reread over and over again! *Paradigm Shift. I totally love this book, a wonderful nugget of inspiration.* **PlanetStarz**

1903816319 128pp 190/135mm **£5.99 $11.95**

God Calling

A Devotional Diary

A. J. Russell

46th printing

"When supply seems to have failed, you must know that it has not done so. But you must look around to see what you can give away. Give away something." One of the best-selling devotional books of all time, with over 6 million copies sold.

1905047428 280pp 135/95mm **£7.99** cl.

US rights sold

The Goddess, the Grail and the Lodge

The Da Vinci code and the real origins of religion

Alan Butler

5th printing

This book rings through with the integrity of sharing time-honoured revelations. As a historical detective, following a golden thread from the great Megalithic cultures, Alan Butler vividly presents a compelling picture of the fight for life of a great secret and one that we simply can't afford to ignore. **Lynn Picknett & Clive Prince**

1903816696 360pp 230/152mm **£12.99 $19.95**

The Heart of Tantric Sex

A unique guide to love and sexual fulfilment

Diana Richardson

3rd printing

The art of keeping love fresh and new long after the honeymoon is over. Tantra for modern Western lovers adapted in a practical, refreshing and sympathetic way.

One of the most revolutionary books on sexuality ever written. **Ruth Ostrow**, News Ltd.

1903816378 256pp **£9.99 $14.95**

I Am With You

The best-selling modern inspirational classic

John Woolley

14th printing hardback

Will bring peace and consolation to all who read it. **Cardinal Cormac Murphy-O'Connor**

0853053413 280pp 150x100mm **£9.99** cl

4th printing paperback

1903816998 280pp 150/100mm **£6.99 $12.95**

In the Light of Meditation

The art and practice of meditation in 10 lessons

Mike George

2nd printing

A classy book. A gentle yet satisfying pace and is beautifully illustrated. Complete with a CD or guided meditation commentaries, this is a true gem among meditation guides. **Brainwave**

In-depth approach, accessible and clearly written, a convincing map of the overall territory and a practical path for the journey. **The Light**

1903816610 224pp 235/165mm full colour throughout +CD **£11.99 $19.95**

The Instant Astrologer

A revolutionary new book and software package for the astrological seeker

Lyn Birkbeck

2nd printing

The brilliant Lyn Birkbeck's new book and CD package, The Instant Astrologer, combines modern technology and the wisdom of the ancients, creating an invitation to enlightenment for the masses, just when we need it most! **Astrologer Jenny Lynch**, Host of NYC's StarPower Astrology Television Show

1903816491 628pp full colour throughout with CD ROM 240/180 **£39 $69** cl

Is There An Afterlife?

A comprehensive overview of the evidence, from east and west

David Fontana

2nd printing

An extensive, authoritative and detailed survey of the best of the evidence supporting survival after death. It will surely become a classic not only of parapsychology literature in general but also of survival literature in particular. **Universalist**

1903816904 496pp 230/153mm **£14.99 $24.95**

The Reiki Sourcebook

Bronwen and Frans Stiene

5th printing

It captures everything a Reiki practitioner will ever need to know about the ancient art. This book is hailed by most Reiki professionals as the best guide to Reiki. For an average reader, it's also highly enjoyable and a

good way to learn to understand Buddhism, therapy and healing. **Michelle Bakar**, Beauty magazine
1903816556 384pp £12.99 $19.95

Soul Power

The transformation that happens when you know

Nikki de Carteret

4th printing

One of the finest books in its genre today. Using scenes from her own life and growth, Nikki de Carteret weaves wisdom about soul growth and the power of love and transcendent wisdom gleaned from the writings of the mystics. This is a book that I will read gain and again as a reference for my own soul growth. **Barnes and Noble review**
190381636X 240pp **£9.99 $15.95**

Daughters of the Earth

Cheryl Straffon

Combines legend, landscape and women's ceremonies to create a wonderful mixture of Goddess experience in the present day. A feast of information, ideas, facts and visions. **Kathy Jones**, co-founder of the Glastonbury Goddess Conference
1846940168 240pp **£11.99 $21.95**

The Gods Within

An interactive guide to archetypal therapy

Peter Lemesurier

Whether you enjoy analyzing your family and friends or looking for ways to explain or excuse your own strengths and weaknesses, this book provides a whole new slant. It can be read just for fun, but there is an

uncanny ring of truth to it. Peter Lemesurier combines scholarship with wry humour, a compulsive mixture. **Anna Corser**, Physiotherapy Manager
1905047991 416pp **£14.99 $29.95**

Maiden, Mother, Crone

Voices of the Goddess

Claire Hamilton

This is a vividly written and evocative series of stories in which Celtic goddesses speak in the first person about their lives and experiences. It enables the reader to reconnect with a neglected but resurgent tradition that is a part of the advent of the feminine in our time. **Scientific and Medical Network Review**
1905047398 240pp **£12.99 $24.95**

The Sacred Wheel of the Year

Tess Ward

A spiritual handbook full of wisdom, grace and creativity. It dips into the deep wells of Celtic tradition and beyond to gather the clear water of life. This is a book of prayer to be treasured. **Mike Riddell**, author of *The Sacred Journey*
1905047959 260pp **£11.99 $24.95**

Savage Breast

One man's search for the goddess

Tim Ward

An epic, elegant, scholarly search for the goddess, weaving together travel, Greek mythology, and personal autobiographic relationships into a remarkable exploration of the Western World's culture and sexual history. It is also entertainingly human, as we listen and learn from this accomplished person and the challenging mate he wooed. If you ever travel to Greece, take Savage Breast along with you. **Harold Schulman**, Professor of Gynaecology at Winthrop University Hospital, and author of *An Intimate History of the Vagina.*

1905047584 400pp colour section +100 b/w photos **£12.99 $19.95**

Tales of the Celtic Bards

Claire Hamilton

An original and compelling retelling of some wonderful stories by an accomplished mistress of the bardic art. Unusual and refreshing, the book provides within its covers the variety and colour of a complete bardic festival. **Ronald Hutton**, Professor of History

Harp music perfectly complements the book in a most haunting way. A perfect way in to the tales of "the Strange Ones". **Wave**

1903816548 320pp with CD 230/152mm **£16.99 $24.95** cl.

The Virgin and the Pentacle

The Freemasonic plot to destroy the Church

Alan Butler

The author unfolds the history of the tensions between Freemasonry and the Catholic Church, which he sees as reflecting that between patriarchal and matriarchal views of the godhead. It is essentially a power struggle that continues to this day. He makes a valuable contribution to the relationship between inner and outer history. **Scientific and Medical Network Review**

1905047320 208pp 230/153mm **£12.99 $17.95** pb

The Art of Being Psychic

The power to free the artist within

June Elleni-Laine

A brilliant book for anyone wishing to develop their intuition, creativity and psychic ability. It is truly wonderful, one of the best books on psychic development that I have read. I have no hesitation in recommending this book, a must for every bookshelf. **Suzanna McInerney**, former President, College of Psychic Studies

1905047541 160pp **£12.99 $24.95**

Journey Home

A true story of time and inter-dimensional travel

Tonika Rinar

2nd printing

A lifeline that has been tossed out from the universe to help tether those lost in the wake of recent world events. If you are willing to open your mind, Tonika will take you on a journey home, to a place that shines bright within each of us...... all you have to do is reach for it. **Amazon**

1905047002 272pp **£11.99 $16.95**